Library of
Davidson College

CALIFORNIA'S TWENTY MILLION

FROM THE FIRST SYMPOSIUM ON CALIFORNIA'S POPULATION
PROBLEMS AND POLICIES, HELD IN 1971 UNDER THE AUSPICES OF THE
ASSEMBLY SCIENCE AND TECHNOLOGY ADVISORY COUNCIL

California's Twenty Million
RESEARCH CONTRIBUTIONS TO
POPULATION POLICY

KINGSLEY DAVIS and
FREDERICK G. STYLES, Editors

Institute of International Studies
University of California, Berkeley

Standard Book Number 87725-310-2
Library of Congress Card Number 72-184405
© 1971 by the Regents of the University of California

FOREWORD

Modern societies are losing faith in the basis of their survival. Having learned awhile ago to utilize science to meet their needs, they have come increasingly to depend on it for their existence. They have even learned how to create technology deliberately--that is, by organized research--thus speeding the pace of technical advance and facilitating fundamental changes in human existence within a few years. So much has been accomplished by this means that, until recently, strong faith in technological progress was widespread. If pursued diligently, people felt, it would lead perpetually toward utopian satisfaction. Yet, at the very moment of its major triumphs, when men had finally harnessed the atom and reached the moon, faith in technology began to wane. It did so because, as time went by, it became evident that technological solutions to human problems give rise to new and unforeseen problems, which in turn require more technology to solve, giving rise to still more difficulties. It became clear that the most advanced societies do not necessarily have the fewest problems or the least troublesome ones. Some skeptics began to say that the more advanced the society, the more problems it has.

The disillusionment with technology has occurred because the faith, like the skepticism that followed, was one-sided. That technology alone cannot lead straight to Utopia should be clear to anyone. By definition, technology is concerned with means, not with goals; yet many social problems arise specifically from conflict over goals--conflict between groups, classes, or parties, and even between the interests that individuals have for themselves and the goals they have for the community at large. The resolution of human conflict depends on authority and consensus rather than on the multiplication of means; in fact, since technology is neutral as to purpose, a conflict may be destructive in proportion to the means available. It is only natural, then, that an unqualified faith in technology leads eventually to disillusionment.

If any state in the United States epitomizes the dilemmas of advanced technology, it is California; and if any one of its problems embodies the dilemmas, it is rapid population growth. From its mechanized agriculture to its aerospace, electronic, and communications industries, the state utilizes scientific and engineering manpower and the latest productive techniques to an unsurpassed extent. The resulting productivity of its economy makes it a prime target for interstate and international migration,

FOREWORD

causing it to be, by now, the most populous state in the union, with an average density almost twice the national average. Although it has been subject to temporary lulls in growth--a phenomenon that appears to be occurring at the moment--its population increase has been remarkably persistent and, on the average, greater than that of any other state. Indeed, it has had the fastest long-run population growth of any advanced society in the world, not excepting Japan or Israel. The resulting environmental damage is greater than that found almost anywhere else in the United States. There is a higher degree of urbanization, a higher regional concentration of people, and a greater ethnic and racial diversity than in nearly any other state.

To solve the problem of rapid population growth is not a simple technological matter. The term "population" refers to people. Technology is ordinarily used _by_ and _for_ people--to increase their instrumentalities and maximize their satisfactions; to use it to limit or control people themselves goes against the grain. The population trend is not some phenomenon of external nature that requires physics and engineering to master; it is a product of human behavior and attitudes, and these are so well supported by tradition and sentiment that one risks resentment in even suggesting their modification. The woman who bears five children thinks of herself as making an honorable sacrifice, even though the state bears a heavy share of the costs of their upbringing. The man who brings his family to California for "a better way of life" feels he is doing the right thing, even when he is lowering the average level of living in the state. There is in this matter an inevitable conflict between the interests individuals have for themselves and their families and the interests they have for the community at large. No technological device will solve that conflict.

However, to say that a solution is difficult is not to say that it is impossible. If advanced societies are to solve their environmental problems, not to mention other questions concerned with the quality of life, they cannot indulge in continued rapid population growth. No sensible planning, no satisfactory management of land use, no long-run solution to urban problems is possible in the State of California if it continues to add half a million people to its population each year. To curb such growth before it is automatically stopped by the progressive deterioration that population increase brings will require a knowledge of what causes the growth as well as a willingness to exercise control over those causes that are found to be institutional and motivational.

In recognition of the crucial and yet problematic role of science and technology in the state, the Assembly of the California State Legislature created, in 1970, an Advisory Council on Science and Technology, consisting of 16 experts drawn from

FOREWORD

universities, research institutions, and private industry. Appreciating that this development represented an unusual effort to link scientific advice directly with the legislative process, the National Science Foundation, under its State and Local Intergovernmental Science Policy Program, gave a grant to the Assembly to further the work of the Council. With this added support, the Council set to work to investigate the technological aspects of some of the state's most critical questions of policy. It designated panels on solid waste management, future demands for energy and proliferation of power plants, unemployment among scientists and engineers, and massive population growth.

The present volume is an outgrowth of the panel on population. The Council began its work on this subject by sponsoring three seminars in which panels of experts from throughout California discussed a variety of potential state population policies. These seminars soon made it clear that the state is fortunate in having a large number of authorities on demographic and related topics, and yet unfortunate in that most of them have never turned their attention to California. Also, the discussions indicated that there is more public concern over the state's population growth, and more desire to stem that growth, than had been realized. Out of these seminars came the idea of holding a symposium on the state's population problems and policies. Such a symposium, it was felt, would encourage the state's experts to start focusing their attention on California rather than exclusively on somewhere else. It would also stimulate public discussion of population policies in California--discussion that must occur if fundamental changes are to be made; and it would start a process of interchange between legislators, public, and scientists that would, it was hoped, lead to action. The Council recognized that miracles could not be accomplished at one symposium, but it seemed a good way to start. A number of experts were invited to prepare analyses of the nature and consequences of population changes in the state, and to bring their findings to bear on potential population policies. The purpose was to promote basic knowledge considered relevant to policy--not to air opinions or express uninformed sentiments.

The symposium was held at the University of California at Davis with the cooperation of University Extension in March 1971. The results were gratifying. The present volume (which contains nearly all of the papers) shows that the contributions were both technically competent and presented in a manner that intelligent citizens and concerned legislators can follow. It constitutes, as a whole, the most comprehensive treatment of the state's population problems so far published, and the most thorough discussion of possible policies. A companion volume will soon be published giving an analysis of the state's demographic history and present situation with respect to population. It is the hope of the Science and Technology Advisory Council and

FOREWORD

the editors that this effort is the beginning of serious consideration of population policy for the State of California.

The Assembly of the State Legislature is to be congratulated for its courage and statesmanship in asking the Council to look into the population question. Our contributors deserve credit for the quality as well as the speed of their research. Special thanks are due to Mr. William O. Atherton, Analyst with the Advisory Council, for his able and amiable help in all phases of the work of the Population Panel, from the initial seminars to the present publication. The publication itself was entrusted to a superlative specialist, Mr. Paul M. Gilchrist, Editor for the Institute of International Studies at Berkeley, whose sense of style, format, and substance greatly improved the contributions.

Kingsley Davis
Frederick G. Styles

November 12, 1971

CONTENTS

FOREWORD v

NOTES ON CONTRIBUTORS xi

STATEMENT OF WELCOME xiii
The Honorable Bob Moretti, Speaker of the
California Assembly

PART I: INTRODUCTION

THE NATURE AND PURPOSE OF POPULATION POLICY 3
Kingsley Davis

PART II: THE SPECIAL PLACE OF MIGRATION

THE ROLE OF MIGRATION IN CALIFORNIA'S GROWTH 33
Peter A. Morrison

FOREIGN MIGRATION INTO CALIFORNIA 61
José Hernández

MINORITIES IN CALIFORNIA'S POPULATION 93
Peter Uhlenberg

PART III: WHAT CALIFORNIANS THINK

CALIFORNIANS' VIEWS ON POPULATION AND THE ENVIRONMENT:
RESULTS OF A SURVEY 109
Judith Blake

PART IV: REPRODUCTIVE PATTERNS, PROBLEMS, AND POLICIES

MARRIAGE REGULATION AND THE CALIFORNIA BIRTH RATE 165
June Sklar

ILLEGITIMATE FERTILITY IN CALIFORNIA'S POPULATION 207
Beth Berkov

CALIFORNIA'S ABORTION LEGISLATION AND ITS DEMOGRAPHIC
EFFECTS 228
Edwin W. Jackson

NUMBER OF CHILDREN AND FEMALE JOBS: SOME EVIDENCE FROM
CALIFORNIA 239
Samuel H. Preston

PART V: THE NATION'S MOST URBANIZED STATE

CALIFORNIA'S URBAN POPULATION: PATTERNS AND TRENDS   259
    Staff: Population Research Laboratory, USC

IMPACT OF STATE POLICY AND PROBLEMS ON CALIFORNIA'S
DEVELOPMENT   297
    Robert E. Grunwald

STATE POLICIES ON URBAN-METROPOLITAN RENEWAL   309
    William L. Pereira

URBAN GROWTH IN CALIFORNIA: NEW TOWNS AND OTHER POLICY
ALTERNATIVES   315
    William Alonso

PART VI: DEMOGRAPHIC RESEARCH AND INFORMATION
SYSTEMS IN STATE GOVERNMENT

DEMOGRAPHIC INFORMATION IN PUBLIC HEALTH DATA   329
    Yvonne Bristol, Harry Greenblatt, and Edwin W. Jackson

POPULATION RESEARCH IN THE DEPARTMENT OF FINANCE   336
    Walter P. Hollmann, Isabel Hambright, and W. Nelson
    Rasmussen

PROPOSAL FOR A CALIFORNIA POPULATION ADVISORY PANEL   346
    Kingsley Davis and Thomas J. Espenshade

NOTES ON CONTRIBUTORS

KINGSLEY DAVIS is Ford Professor of Sociology and Comparative Studies and Chairman, International Population and Urban Research, at the University of California, Berkeley.

FREDERICK G. STYLES is Executive Secretary of the Assembly Science and Technology Advisory Council of the California Legislature.

WILLIAM ALONSO is Professor of Regional Planning at the University of California, Berkeley.

BETH BERKOV is Associate Public Health Statistician in the Bureau of Maternal and Child Health, California State Department of Public Health.

JUDITH BLAKE is Professor of Demography and Chairman of the Department of Demography at the University of California, Berkeley.

YVONNE BRISTOL is Associate Public Health Statistician in the Demographic Analysis Section, California State Department of Public Health.

THOMAS J. ESPENSHADE is Assistant Specialist in Demography, International Population and Urban Research, at the University of California, Berkeley.

HARRY GREENBLATT is Associate Social Research Analyst in the Demographic Analysis Section, California State Department of Public Health.

ROBERT E. GRUNWALD is President of Grunwald, Crawford & Associates: City, Regional and State Planning Consultants (Hanford).

ISABEL HAMBRIGHT is Associate Demographic Analyst in the Population Research Unit, California State Department of Finance.

WALTER P. HOLLMANN is Chief of the Population Research Unit of the California State Department of Finance.

JOSÉ HERNÁNDEZ is Associate Professor of Sociology at the University of Arizona. He was formerly Associate Research Demographer at the University of California, Berkeley.

EDWIN W. JACKSON, M.D., is Chief of the Epidemiology Unit of the Bureau of Maternal and Child Health, California State Department of Public Health.

PETER A. MORRISON is Staff Member, Social Sciences Department, The Rand Corporation (Santa Monica).

WILLIAM L. PEREIRA is Chairman of William L. Pereira Associates (San Francisco) and a Fellow of the American Institute of Architects.

SAMUEL H. PRESTON is Assistant Professor of Demography at the University of California, Berkeley.

W. NELSON RASMUSSEN is Associate Demographic Analyst in the Population Research Unit, California State Department of Finance.

JUNE SKLAR is Assistant Research Demographer, International Population and Urban Research, at the University of California, Berkeley.

PETER UHLENBERG is Assistant Professor of Sociology at the University of North Carolina. He received his Ph.D. degree in Demography at the University of California, Berkeley.

STATEMENT OF WELCOME

The Honorable Bob Moretti, Speaker of the California Assembly

Ladies and Gentlemen:

It is encouraging that so large and distinguished a group has assembled here today at the invitation of our Assembly Science and Technology Advisory Council. The problem which you have come to discuss is immediate and complex. As a resident of Los Angeles for many years, I can personally testify to the damage large and concentrated numbers of people can do to our land and environment.

Certainly the situation is not getting any better. It is my understanding that within thirty years--most of our expected lifetimes--more than half the population of the United States will be packed onto less than one-twelfth of all available land in the country. According to these predictions, about 200 million people will occupy four great corridors of space--one stretching along the Atlantic seacoast from Maine to Virginia, another spanning the length of Florida, a third skirting the southern shores of the Great Lakes from Buffalo and Erie to Chicago, and a fourth--and of most concern to me--an area bordering the Pacific Ocean from the top to the bottom of California. As far as I'm concerned, this is at best a dreary prospect. Already the centers of these so-called megalopolises are heavily burdened with poverty, disease, hunger, crime, and filth. Stuffing more people into them can only deepen the misery. In the Legislature we see every day the result of these conditions in our central cities. The quality of life in many places in California deteriorates more and more each day.

Last February 8 President Nixon proposed consideration of state land-use plans which would include the following:

A method for state control over location of all focal points of growth, such as highway interchanges, major airports, and major recreational centers such as Disneyland;

A method for state control over all large-scale developments of property;

A method for state control over local attempts to block property developments of regional benefit. Such properties might be schools, hospitals, community centers or multi-dwelling residential settlements capable of providing good housing for the poor;

A method to ensure state protection of existing property identified as being of "critical environmental concern." This kind of property would include coastal zones, which is an area we are concentrating on this year as the top priority environmental problem.

The President's proposals are unquestionably bold and far-reaching, and all of you are probably acquainted with their details. A review of your program for the next two days indicates that you will be discussing many of the ideas and elements contained in the President's message. I would simply urge that in considering these questions and in making your recommendations you consider to what use they may be put. It has always seemed to me that seminars of this type can be productive if the participants are imaginative but realistic in their conclusions. Our purpose in the Assembly is to develop some approaches to legislation which will influence state population growth and distribution. Even though the personal decisions of individuals will always govern where they live, I do not agree that we are powerless to influence them through legislation. You will recall, for example, the people who argued that attitudes toward racial integration could not be changed through legislation. I don't think there is any question now that federal and state legislation in this field in the last ten years has contributed significantly to changed attitudes and population distribution.

We can no longer accept the proposition that all growth is good. In fact the quality of our life and our economic well-being may in the future depend to a great extent on more effective management of growth. What we need to seek is a balance between our resources of air, water, and open space and our population growth.

These are tough problems, and we're not so naive as to believe that there are any simple answers. I believe, however, that unless we deal with them, our efforts to control smog, clean up our waters, and provide open spaces will become mere stopgaps.

I want to assure you that we in the Legislature are sincere in seeking your help, and that the results of this meeting will receive thoughtful consideration. We have asked the Council to summarize the conclusions and recommendations of this meeting and to forward them to us at the earliest possible time. I am hopeful that they will result in specific proposals for new legislation directed to California's population problems.

Again, my appreciation to you for taking the time away from your other commitments to attend this meeting. I hope the program will be a productive and rewarding one ultimately for the people of California.

PART I

INTRODUCTION

THE NATURE AND PURPOSE OF POPULATION POLICY

Kingsley Davis

I. THE SOCIOLOGY OF POPULATION POLICY

The rationale for population control is simple: the number of people is too important to be left to chance. Population affects the level of living, the quality of life, and the worth of the environment. To ignore it in social and economic planning is foolish; for, if left uncontrolled, population change can upset any plan for human betterment. A plan that is ideal for a city of a million produces intolerable congestion when six million arrive. A plan to increase per capita electrical power by 6 percent per year for twenty years may seem ideal, but if the population is growing by 4 percent, generating capacity will have to be multiplied 6.7 times in 20 years!

If the human population were uncontrollable, as the sun and stars are, its trend would have to be accepted as a condition to which we must somehow adjust, but this is not the case. Population changes are products of human decisions, and these decisions, like others, can be influenced by altering the circumstances and incentives that govern them. Even with something as intractable as the weather, we make strenuous efforts at control--for example, by cloud seeding, fog dispersal, reforestation. Technically speaking, population is easier to control than many other things we control.

If, then, population control is both advisable and feasible, why does the idea seem unorthodox and difficult? The answer is that, in fact, human populations have always been controlled, but the type of control now being proposed is different.

Ambiguities of "Population Control"

If population control is both advisable and feasible, why does the idea seem unorthodox? Why is the task difficult? The answer is that the phrase "population control" is ambiguous. When used to describe the aim of contemporary population policies, it seems to imply that heretofore population has been uncontrolled.

KINGSLEY DAVIS

The less developed countries, in particular, are said to be experiencing "uncontrolled population growth." The population of the United States is said to be "out of control"; California is experiencing "runaway population growth."

Behind the implication of uncontrolled population is, frequently, the assumption that up to now population growth has been "natural," not determined by human decisions or social arrangements but by "nature"--like an avalanche or a flood that has come from external causes beyond our control and now has to be dealt with by human thought and effort. Nothing could be further from the truth. The human species has evolved for hundreds of millenia in societies based on culturally transmitted techniques and learned interactions. These societies have long since become necessary for survival. Without a sociocultural system no population could exist: its mortality would be complete, its fertility zero. With respect to human beings there is no such thing as a "state of nature" or a "natural" level of fertility or mortality. Demographic behavior, like other forms of human behavior, is made possible and determined by responses learned and motivated in social situations. It follows that the rate of fertility, mortality, and migration is a function of the character of the society. In this sense, human population has always been controlled.

Once the notion of a human "state of nature" is rejected, we become aware of another meaning of "uncontrolled population growth." People commonly use the phrase in such a way as to indicate a population growth that nobody <u>intended</u>. It was not the intent, and certainly not the desire, of the world's people in 1960 to increase their number by one-fifth in the next decade, although it was clearly they--their actions and their decisions-- that gave them that increase. It was hardly the goal of the 10.6 million Californians in 1950 to burden themselves with an extra 9.5 million in the state, but this is what their actions and inactions produced by 1970.

In other words, population growth has generally been an unintended, and in recent times an unwanted, <u>collective</u> consequence of individual behavior. Insofar as the individual's demographic behavior is motivated, population growth results from the goals that people have, but their goals in this respect are phrased in individual, familial, or religious terms, not in terms of the community as a whole. With respect to childbearing, for example, people have children because of the pleasure, group status, ego-satisfaction, and other advantages derived from children of their own, not because they want the total population to grow.

With this clarification, one can see that population policy seeks to achieve "population control" by making the

THE NATURE AND PURPOSE OF POPULATION POLICY

collective result an intended one. That is, it sets a population goal for the nation or state as a whole and then seeks means to achieve this goal. If the policy succeeds, the population is "controlled," i.e., intended.

In most of human history, population growth was considered desirable, because economic production and warfare were chiefly a function of manpower, and hence the strength of one's own group relative to other groups was increased if the population were growing. Yet there was traditionally little effort to ensure population growth by specific governmental effort. Instead, the very process of survival in a competitive world tended to select for continuation those folkways and mores, those beliefs and institutions, that led to favorable death rates and/or favorable birth rates. These forms of behavior were not followed, however, because people had in view their demographic effects; rather, they were followed because people wanted to stay alive, to marry, to have the advantages of children, to keep their children alive. Even when written laws and legislative enactments arose in complex societies, the tendency of the legal system to promote population growth was not the result of deliberate intention for that purpose. Rather, the laws were enacted or enforced because they seemed just, right, customary, or in the public interest, without reference to their demographic effects. For instance, the widespread legislation forbidding abortion had an obvious pronatalist effect, but this was not the purpose of the legislation. The purpose was religious and moral.

Insofar as population growth was considered by the public or by officials, it was thought to be a good thing but was regarded as difficult to achieve. The reason was that fluctuations in the rate of population growth were due overwhelmingly to fluctuations in the death rate, and these were virtually impossible to eliminate. It followed that population growth was associated in people's minds with good times--that is, times when there was no plague, famine, flood, war, or other man-killing disaster. The idea of deliberately generating population growth by governmental measures hardly arose. If it were ever considered, the population trend doubtless seemed plainly beyond deliberate control. Furthermore, aside from warfare and law enforcement, governments did little anyway. Above all, the main factor in population growth--the reduction of the death rate--was already motivated, since people wanted to stay alive if they could. One way of possibly beating the death rate was to have many children; the rewards built into the institutional structure were generally sufficient to induce a high rate of childbearing. In sum, in traditional society the desirable condition was thought to be population growth, and the technological and institutional aspects of the society were geared to supply such growth insofar as possible. These, however, were not deliberate measures thought up and instituted for the purpose of controlling population.

They were traditional customs that functioned in that way but which were justified, if thought of at all, in religious and moral terms. They were not population policies in our sense of the term.

What Is a Population Policy?

Strictly speaking, a population policy is a deliberate attempt, through governmental or quasi-governmental measures, to change or maintain the rate of population growth. If it is to change the rate, the aim may be to increase or decrease the growth in a nation or state as a whole. It may be to change the geographical distribution or to alter the ethnic composition from what it would otherwise be. Whatever the demographic goal, however, it is always viewed as instrumental to a non-demographic goal. The view may be (as often voiced in Latin America) that land and resources are abundant, awaiting only the manpower to put them to use. Population growth in that case is viewed as instrumental to prosperity. A growing population may be viewed as an asset in warfare, a guarantee of survival for a superior race, a political advantage for a minority group. The migration of rural people to cities may be regarded as a source of social decay, or the flight of city residents to the suburbs may be taken as a cause of city problems. Never, apparently, is a demographic goal sufficient by itself to justify a population policy. People judge a population trend to be good or bad only in the light of its presumed social and economic consequences.

It follows that a systematic classification of population policies, including potential as well as actual ones, must take into account their ultimate goal, as well as the demographic aims and measures considered necessary to reach that goal.

Once the question of the consequences of population change is seriously raised, a failure to take any action is itself a population policy. Such a position of deliberate inaction--which could be called a "maintenance" or a "standpat" policy--rests on an implicit decision by officials and leaders either that the desirable results of the current demographic trends outweigh its undesirable results or that the net undesirable effects are not worth the cost and effort it would take to change the trend. The latter judgment may be accompanied by an ameliorative policy-- that is, a program of effort in a non-demographic sphere designed to remove the undesired effects of the population trend without the necessity, at least temporarily, of altering that trend. Thus a country may decide it is better to make extreme efforts to clean up environmental pollution but do nothing about the population growth that is helping to cause the pollution.

Regardless of their particular type, all population policies have certain elements in common. First, by definition,

THE NATURE AND PURPOSE OF POPULATION POLICY

all population policies deal with a demographic trend or condition. If the policy is one of taking action to change things, it is not a population policy unless it undertakes to change the demographic situation from what it would otherwise be. Thus, the effort to "solve" the world's population problem by "growing more food" is not a population policy but rather an agricultural policy. In other words, a population policy is a policy that tries to eliminate the demographic causes of the problem to be solved. Instead of accepting the population trend as given, it seeks to alter that trend in order to avoid its undesired consequences or to retain it in order to keep its good results. Much futile argument occurs because people are unwilling to acknowledge that the same problem may have multiple causes. Additional argument arises because the effect of time on the causation of problems is not taken into account. A particular problem--say, urban congestion--may be solvable in the short run by working out a new traffic plan and doing nothing about the population trend per se, but as time goes by the population trend, if left unchanged, becomes a bigger and bigger factor in the creation of the problem, with the result that the original traffic plan becomes useless or perhaps worse than useless.

Second, population policies, including the standpat ones, rest on the assumption that it is known what the population trend actually is and what its future is likely to be. The trend may be a rate of population growth that is too slow, too fast, or just right; a geographical distribution that is highly concentrated or dispersed; or an age structure that is too old or too young--it makes no difference with respect to the essential point that the policy presumes the demographic trend or condition to be accurately known.

Third, population policies rest on a presumed knowledge of the social and economic effects of the population trend or condition, now and in the future. They rest on a theory of what is causing the population trend and a theory of how that trend is producing the consequences considered desirable or undesirable. "Interference" policies rest, in addition, on a judgment that the existing and probably future trend is producing unfortunate consequences for the nation or group, and that accordingly something must be done to change the trend and thus achieve more desirable consequences. Such policies rest on a theory of how the intervention will alter the causes of the trend and a theory of how the redirected demographic trend will improve the social and economic situation.

Finally, with reference to the presumed consequences of a population trend, population policies are seeking a collective goal. The goal refers to a future condition of the nation, state, or community. However, nations and communities have no "collective mind" that can formulate goals. It is only individuals

who have purposes and who make decisions to pursue those purposes.
To understand the nature of population policy, therefore, one must
distinguish between two types of goals--the type that refers to
the individual himself (such as a desire to get a better job or
marry a certain girl) and the type that refers to a group with
which the individual identifies himself (such as the desire of
a football fan to see his team win, or the wish of an American
of Muslim ancestry to see the Arabs defeat Israel). As the
examples illustrate, goals for the collectivity may be irrelevant
or even contrary to the individual's own career or physical
satisfactions; yet these are among the most powerful goals in
human existence, as shown by people's willingness to sacrifice
economic advantages and physical comforts for them. Without such
goals, social consensus and social existence would be impossible.
Accordingly, when we think of a population policy for California,
we are thinking of the entire citizenry as an entity. Without
such a goal there would be no reason to try to influence individual behavior, because there would be nothing to influence individual behavior **for**. Individual interests are served by a
population policy only indirectly, through the alleviation of
the societal condition, and particular individual interests may
have to be denied. The distinction is familiar; we frequently
sacrifice particular interests for public benefit--for instance,
by taxing people with no children to support public schools for
other people's children, or by preventing people with trash from
burning it in order to have cleaner air for everybody. But
population policy arouses such emotions that confusion of the
two sorts of goals is common.

A Peculiar Obstacle to Deliberate Population Policies

Talk of deliberate population policies arouses emotions
because it brings into the open conflicts over collective goals
and points to human behavior itself as the cause of the problem.
The demographic trend that a substantial body of opinion brands
as deleterious is a product of the society itself, a consequence
of cherished social norms, goals, and ingenuity. Whereas floods
or plant diseases can be dealt with in technological fashion,
because they are caused mainly by non-human forces and are
unanimously regarded as evils, human reproduction and migration
are activities pursued by human beings themselves. In the solution of the problem, people are therefore simultaneously the
guinea pigs and the experimenters--a situation conducive to
illogicality and frustration.

Illustrating the point is the frequent charge that some
particular population measure is, in the light of people's
feelings, "unacceptable." For instance, the idea that India
could lower its fertility if it quit allowing parents to marry
off their daughters at puberty is met with the argument that

THE NATURE AND PURPOSE OF POPULATION POLICY

Indian customs and "values" call for early marriage and that therefore this measure would not be acceptable. Obviously, Indian fertility is a product of the Indian institutional system; if the institutional system is not to be changed, then fertility will not be changed either. Any measure that is "acceptable" will therefore be useless. To demand that measures be acceptable is to demand that they be pointless.

What Makes a Population Policy Effective?

If what has just been said is true, it is not surprising that the scientific basis of population policies is usually deficient and that, accordingly, the policies are ineffective. The mere inauguration of a policy is no guarantee that it will succeed. Enthusiasm and vigorous support provide no substitute for a knowledge of demographic processes and of their causes and consequences. The same is true in other fields as well as in population. For examples of widely acclaimed policies that failed, one does not have to go back to the Prohibition era or to Diocletian Rome; one can take anti-inflation, crime-control, or medical-care measures in the contemporary world.

Population measures are frequently based on misinformation concerning the present and future course of population change and on erroneous theories of causation. The reason is that the existing society--elements of which an effective population policy must change--shapes every element in the proposed policy. It shapes the picture of the population trend, the interpretation of its causes, the evaluation of its consequences. The judgment that a given trend is desirable or undesirable depends not only on its actual consequences but also on what people think the consequences are. The notion of means of solving the problem is severely limited by the unwillingness to change the sentiments and institutions that cause the problem. Accordingly, a proposed population policy may be resisted, not because people want the harmful population trend, but because they do not want to sacrifice other things in order to change that trend. Seen in this light, erroneous theories of demographic change or of the social and economic consequences of such change are not the causes of ineffective policies but rather their rationalizations or excuses. The wrong theory is adopted out of a reflex fear that a correct theory would lead to conclusions or policies that would offend existing sentiments or interests. In other words, people hide the facts from themselves, not because they are blind but because they do not want to give up things they cherish. Even when there is general agreement that the population trend is yielding undesired results and that the trend should be altered by policy, the particular policy favored tends to be ineffective--its ineffectiveness hidden by leaving the underlying theory implicit, unexamined, and obscure.

If the notion of demographic processes and probabilities is itself elementary in the ideology of population policy, the conception of the social and economic consequences is especially primitive. In fact, there is hardly an area more fruitful of logical blundering. The effort to mobilize popular support for inaugurating or opposing a given population policy leads to gross exaggeration on both sides. Alleged ill effects of population change are accepted by assumption on one side, dismissed on the other side by denying their existence or attributing them to something else. Thus, in this field as in any other, there is a tragic conflict between science and action. Unless support is mobilized, a policy will have no chance of success regardless of its correctness; but if the theory on which it rests is invalid, it will have no chance of success regardless of its support.

Scientific inadequacy particularly characterizes population policies of inaction, because, by definition, they are adopted only after public concern over population change has grown sufficiently strong to demand some kind of official answer, and yet the only answer given is a standpat one. We tend to focus critical attention on the interference policies--that is, on deliberate efforts to change the population trend--but it should be recognized that these efforts, even when mistaken, show more consideration for collective goals than do policies of doing nothing about population. Since population change is an important variable in society, to ignore it is to invite defeat for whatever collective goals people may hold. A criticism of particular measures proposed or undertaken for population control is not, therefore, a criticism of the idea of population control in general. It is not an argument for no population policy at all. It is rather an argument for more effective policies. An action policy that is ineffective may be tantamount to no action at all--in fact, it may be adopted for that very reason; but this fact will not be known until the policy is subjected to careful scrutiny.

II. SOURCES OF WEAKNESS IN MODERN POPULATION POLICIES[1]

If our sociological analysis of the nature and problems of population policies is correct, it should fit the facts of particular examples in modern times, including those currently in vogue. I believe that the analysis does fit; in fact, it was

---

[1] This section is adapted from the author's paper "Sources of Weakness in Modern Population Policies," presented at the regional conference of the International Union for the Scientific Study of Population, Mexico City, August 17-22, 1970.

THE NATURE AND PURPOSE OF POPULATION POLICY

drawn from these cases. But let the reader see for himself, as we review some of the actual programs.

Population Policies and Demographic History

In the modern era it seems true to say that the history of population policies has been a history of failure. Even in the advanced countries, where intelligent population policies might have been expected as part of rising technology and science, an awareness of population did not produce enlightened policies. In these nations, the last part of the eighteenth century and the whole of the nineteenth century was a period of rapid population growth. Economic success went hand in hand with demographic expansion. Accordingly, the northwest Europeans multiplied faster than the rest of the world and colonized whole new continents. In 1750 they represented approximately a fifth of the world's population; in 1900, their descendants in Europe and overseas represented almost a third.

This population increase provoked much debate, but the debate was academic, because almost no collective policies designed to stop or direct the increase were put into effect.[2] On the contrary, population increase was generally regarded in official, religious, and business circles as a good thing. The policy adopted was therefore to allow the encouragements to population growth in law and custom to continue without interference. The effect was unfortunate for broad sections of the European population. It represented a tragic failure to seize an opportunity to balance people and resources in time to permit maximum benefit from the new technology. Europe became a continent so crowded that, despite the rapidly improving technology, tens of millions of migrants were forced or enticed to flee. In 1700 Europe was already as densely settled as Asia; by 1900 it was nearly twice as densely settled. And it was sending out migrants to new continents to use up virgin resources at a fantastic rate. Not only did migrant Europeans undertake the exploitation of these new areas, but they brought in slaves and indentured laborers to start reproducing and exploiting also.

It was in the eighteenth and nineteenth centuries that the stage was unthinkingly set for the population problems of

---

[2]In some of the German states during the period around the middle of the nineteenth century, attempts were made to curb population growth, particularly among the poor, by curbing marriages. See John Knodel, "Law, Marriage and Illegitimacy in Nineteenth-Century Germany," Population Studies, Vol. 20 (March 1967), pp. 279-294.

today. Instead of recognizing that rising natural increase was robbing the new technology of many of its potential human benefits, the authorities mistakenly assumed that it was "beneficial for progress." In addition to permitting an unprecedented human multiplication to occur, they allowed many of the old controls over family formation to be relaxed, with the result that a differential birth rate arose in which the lower classes, least educated and least equipped to transmit skills to their children, supplied far more than their share of each new generation.[3]

---

[3]The records show clearly that the long decline in fertility in the Western industrializing countries, first noticeable around 1870 and continuing to about 1932, began in the better-educated and better-off classes and spread downward. As a consequence, the paradoxical negative association between social status and reproduction became more pronounced as the nineteenth century wore on and reached its greatest point sometime between 1900 and World War I, after which the differentials began to recede somewhat. In general, the same negative association persists today, but to a lesser degree. In the Western region of the United States, for example, the number of children ever born to women who were 40 to 44 years old in 1960 was as follows:

School Years Completed		Children Ever Born Per Woman	
		White	Nonwhite
College:	5 years +	1.65	1.61
	4 years	2.10	1.91
	1-3 years	2.14	2.12
High School:	4 years	2.14	2.41
	1-3 years	2.53	2.57
Elementary:	8 years	2.75	3.02
	5-7 years	3.25	3.27
	1-4 years	3.98	3.08
	None	3.35	4.77

(Source: United States Census of Population, 1960, Women by Number of Children Ever Born [Final Report PC(2)-3A], p. 108.)

For an analysis of fertility differentials in the United States in 1950 and 1960, see Clyde V. Kiser, Wilson H. Grabill, and Arthur A. Campbell, Trends and Variations in Fertility in the United States (Cambridge: Harvard University Press, 1968), chs. 9-11. For historical trends, see Frank W. Notestein, "Class Differences in Fertility," Annals of the American Academy of Political and Social Science, Vol. 188 (Nov. 1936), pp. 26-36; and Gwendolyn Z. Johnson, "Differential Fertility in European

THE NATURE AND PURPOSE OF POPULATION POLICY

Although the industrial revolution was producing marvels in the speed of resource utilization, it was producing little understanding of human populations. The academic debate over population growth was mired in sterile ambiguity and confusion[4] and was having little or no effect on government policy.

The Rise of Pronatalist Policies in the Interwar Period

Ironically, the trend that eventually brought alarm and led to new policies was not rapid population growth but rather a slackening in the rate of growth. The decline of the birth rate in the industrial countries--a decline that resulted in net reproduction rates of .60 to .95 during the Depression--led governments to think that their populations were on the verge of imminent decline. In the 1930's deliberate policies designed to raise the birth rate were instituted in Germany, Italy, Japan, Sweden, France, and several other nations.

These policies all failed--not in the sense that the birth rate remained low, but in the sense that the subsequent rise was due to other factors. In not a single country can it be shown that the specific demographic measures had a significant positive effect.[5] Birth rates began to rise in the late 1930's,

---

Countries" in National Bureau of Economic Research, Demographic and Economic Change in Developed Countries (Princeton: Princeton University Press, 1960), pp. 36-72. For a discussion of the theory of class differences in fertility, see Judith Blake, "Are Babies Consumer Durables?" Population Studies, Vol. 22 (March 1968), pp. 5-25.

[4] See the writer's introduction to a Spanish translation of Malthus: "Appreciación crítica de Malthus" in Thos. R. Malthus, Ensayo sobre el principio de la población (Mexico y Buenos Aires: Fondo de Cultura Económica, 1951), pp. vii-xxxiv.

[5] The claim that Nazi population policies had brought a marked increase in the German birth rate was refuted by demographers. Dudley Kirk showed that the increase was mainly in first and second births, and that it was related to full employment rather than to the demographic policies themselves. See his article "The Relation of Employment Levels to Births in Germany," Milbank Memorial Fund Quarterly, Vol. 20 (April 1942), pp. 126-138. Five years later, John Hajnal--"The Analysis of Birth Statistics in the Light of Recent Recovery of the Birth-Rate," Population Studies, Vol. I (Sept. 1947)--demonstrated that the births by duration of marriage showed almost no rise under the Nazis. Theoretical reasons for predicting failure of the pronatalist

but they rose in countries with no special pronatalist measures as well as in those with them. As we know now, the leaders and politicians of the time were mistaken about the future course of population change. They predicted continued low fertility and declining populations unless government measures were adopted. This was due in part to a methodological error (the fallacy of misplaced concreteness in using a theoretical replacement measure, the Net Reproduction Rate, as a predicting instrument)[6] and in

---

policies were stated by the present writer in 1937--"Reproductive Institutions and the Pressure for Population," Sociological Review (British), Vol. 29 (July 1937), pp. 1-18.

[6]The Net Reproduction Rate (NRR) is a hybrid statistical device. A pure abstraction--because neither the assumption of constant age-specific fertility and mortality nor the assumption of a stable age distribution is ever true--it is nevertheless used as an index of actual trends. It is a period measure that is stated in terms of a generation, which makes it sound like a cohort measure. Although it refers to a generation, the data on which it is based normally relate to only a year or at most a few years. Actually, of course, it does not apply to any period except a theoretical one in the indefinite future. Only when the assumptions of the NRR are carefully remembered is it of any use; but its assumptions are so unrealistic, and its time-dimension so illogical in relation to its data, that even demographers have difficulty in interpreting it. In 1934 a British demographer, Enid Charles, said: "There seems to be no particular reason for assuming that the decline [of fertility] must stop at the point now reached. If the net reproduction rate were to fall further, say to 0.5, the population would be halving itself every 30 years, when a stable age distribution had been reached" (Twilight of Parenthood [London: Watts and Company, 1934], p. 76). In the same year, Frank Lorimer and Frederick Osborn in Dynamics of Population (New York: Macmillan, 1934), p. 6, said that "true rates [are] more useful than crude rates in studying long-time population trends." On p. 10 they say: "In California, we find a tendency to a reproductive loss of about 30 per cent per generation." Finally, on p. 19, they conclude, "Population growth in the United States is gradually slowing down. Population increase will presumably cease absolutely somewhere from twenty to forty years from now with a maximum population of some 150 millions or less." In reaching this conclusion (which was then considered alarming but would be considered comforting today), their crucial data were the statistics of 1930! In a similar vein, Gunnar Myrdal said in his Godkin Lectures of 1938, "Sweden fell below the line of 100 percent net reproduction in 1925, and is now down to a net reproduction figure under 75 percent. . . . Does this level represent a bottom or will the fall in fertility continue?

THE NATURE AND PURPOSE OF POPULATION POLICY

part to a substantive mistake--a failure to understand reproductive behavior and its determinants. The number of children that women wish to have, or will ultimately have, cannot be inferred from the number they are having during a short period. Surveys in the 1930's showed that the size of family women wanted was well above the replacement level. Given the professed aims, the governments thus had no need for the policies in the first place; but having decided to intervene, they adopted measures--economic incentives for marriage and childbearing and repression of birth control and abortion--that were ineffective. The birth rate revived when, and only when, general economic conditions and employment improved. It rose in Germany as the Third Reich ushered in full employment, but it kept on falling in Italy despite the Fascist pronatalist policies.

New Peaks in Population Growth and New Alarms

The postwar baby boom in most industrialized countries led to a rapid switch of public opinion. By 1947 the alarm over depopulation had been displaced by anxiety concerning overpopulation. This was an old worry, but it was now different from that of the nineteenth century. Instead of being mainly concerned with their own population growth, the industrial countries were worried about "world population" or about "population increase in the underdeveloped countries." The reason for this new twist was simple: the balance of population growth had shifted from the industrial to the non-industrial nations. It had shifted because of the rapid transfer of public health techniques--techniques that had been slowly invented in the industrial nations (the most effective ones invented late in the day, after the industrial nations had already achieved a low mortality) but which now could be transferred overnight to populations with high mortality. The result was an unprecedented decline of death rates. In Latin America, for example, the average life-time improved after 1930 at a rate that had never been even approximated by the industrial nations.[7]

... On the whole, the prospects are for a continued, and very considerable, fall in reproduction" (Population: A Problem for Democracy [Cambridge: Harvard University Press, 1940], p. 46). By the time his lectures were published, in 1940, the Swedish gross reproduction rate was already 13 percent higher than it had been in 1935, and by 1945 it was 36 percent higher!

[7]The acceleration in mortality improvement was a new phenomenon. For a hundred years in the industrial nations the improvement had been very steady. The contrast between the mortality patterns in the Latin American countries and the industrial

15

Antinatalist Policies in the 1950's and 1960's

After World War II the amazingly high rates of population growth in the poorer nations were increasingly regarded as a major obstacle to economic improvement. Cautiously at first, but with increasing vigor, world leaders began in the 1950's to advocate population control. The aim was to get governments to take three lines of action: first, to repeal laws banning contraceptive information and materials; second, to organize and finance programs to spread knowledge and use of advanced contraceptive techniques; third, to pour money into research to improve contraceptive methods. The first two lines of action were proposed mainly for governments in underdeveloped areas, but the second line was one in which the industrialized nations were ready to help with funds and personnel, and the third was one for which the advanced nations took the main responsibility. Foundations and international agencies were urged to assist birth control programs in underdeveloped regions and to subsidize research in reproductive physiology.

countries is shown by the following:

PERCENT CHANGE IN LIFE EXPECTANCY PER DECADE

	Latin American Countries	Three Industrial Countries
1860-1870	2.4	3.9
1870-1880	2.0	6.4
1880-1890	2.4	6.0
1890-1900	4.2	4.8
1900-1910	6.3	7.0
1910-1920	7.6	6.5
1920-1930	8.0	7.0
1930-1940	13.1	4.9
1940-1950	22.1	5.5
1950-1960	20.2	5.9

The three industrial countries are Sweden, United States, and England and Wales. (Source: Eduardo E. Arriaga and Kingsley Davis, "The Pattern of Mortality Change in Latin America," Demography, Vol. 6 [August 1969], p. 231.) Since the mortality drop was so swift, fertility could not change in relation to mortality as it had in the past history of the industrial countries. The natural increase therefore became much greater, regardless of whether the underdeveloped country in question was already crowded (as many countries in Asia were) or seemingly uncrowded (as some in South America and parts of Middle America were). The widening difference in rates of growth as between the two classes of country can be seen in the following:

THE NATURE AND PURPOSE OF POPULATION POLICY

Although Puerto Rico passed enabling legislation in 1937 and soon began installing contraceptive services in public health clinics, the effort was half-hearted and desultory. India was the first independent nation to start a national population control program. In December 1952, Prime Minister Nehru presented to Parliament the First Five-Year Plan, which called for $1,300,000 to establish family planning clinics throughout the country. Pakistan in 1957, South Korea in 1961, Egypt in 1966, and several other countries at recent dates have started similar programs. Sweden concluded a technical assistance agreement with Ceylon in 1958. American foundations started the Population Council in 1952 as a front organization for channeling funds into birth control.

For a long time, the United States government held back, despite pressure to "do something" about population. In response to a committee report recommending that the Agency for International Development include family planning in its work, President Eisenhower said in 1959 that birth control is not a proper concern of government. This remark, together with a statement by the Roman Catholic bishops of America opposing any use of public funds

CLASS*	POPULATION GROWTH PER DECADE (PERCENT)				
	1920-30	1930-40	1940-50	1950-60	1960-70
Underdeveloped	11.7	13.1	13.8	23.2	22.9
Developed	9.7	6.9	4.1	13.8	12.6

*(For each decade, the countries are the same at the beginning as the end, but from one decade to another some countries move from the underdeveloped to the developed category.)

Among the underdeveloped countries it is the Latin American ones that consistently show the highest rates of growth, although their saliency has slightly lessened over time. The rates of growth per decade are as follows:

	1920-30	1930-40	1940-50	1950-60	1960-70
Non-Industrial					
Latin America	19.8	20.2	23.1	33.9	34.4
Africa	10.7	11.0	21.7	30.0	30.0
Asia	11.0	13.1	13.7	21.9	20.9

Since Asia weighs so heavily in the totals for all underdeveloped countries, it tends to minimize the difference, on a country-by-country basis, between the developed and underdeveloped nations of the world.

for birth control, forced a showdown on the issue. A great debate ensued. The censuses taken in or near 1960 showed a marked acceleration in world population growth. The Kennedy administration joined Sweden in pressing the U.N. to discuss the question. Finally, on December 18, 1962, the U.N. General Assembly concluded its first debate entirely devoted to population, although it never mentioned birth control or population limitation. A year later the U.N. sponsored in Asia the first conference of governments ever held with a mandate to recommend population policies. In June 1965, President Johnson, in his United Nations anniversary speech, made his famous statement: "Let us act on the fact that less than five dollars invested in population control is worth a hundred dollars invested in economic growth." In February 1965, AID sent instructions to its missions abroad that it would provide assistance in family planning, excluding only the provision of contraceptive devices or equipment for their manufacture. In December of the same year, Secretary-General U Thant endorsed a declaration by twelve heads of state (later joined by 18 more) calling attention to the population danger and endorsing family planning.

In only six years officials of both the United States and the United Nations had reversed themselves, going from political fear of mentioning birth control to open advocacy of it. As governments began to organize family planning programs, the advocates of government population policy were achieving complete victory.

But success in inducing governments to enact population policies does not guarantee that the policies will prove effective. The preceding account demonstrates that the type of policy currently being adopted is exclusively limited to family planning. The question arises, then, whether family planning programs are adequate to control population growth.[8] The answer is that, by their very nature, they are not adequate for this purpose. Let us examine the family-planning approach in some detail.

---

[8] The question was raised by the present writer in 1967; see "Population Policy: Will Current Programs Succeed?" Science, Vol. 158 (Nov. 10, 1967), pp. 730-739. Spanish translation: "Política de población: Tendrán excito los programas actuales?" Demografía y Economía, Vol. 3, No. 3 (1969), pp. 201-229. In addition to references given in that article, see R.B. Tabbarah, "Birth Control and Population Policy," Population Studies, Vol. 18 (Nov. 1964), pp. 187-196; Judith Blake, "Population Policy for Americans: Is the Government Being Misled?" Science, Vol. 164 (May 2, 1969), pp. 522-529.

THE NATURE AND PURPOSE OF POPULATION POLICY

Family Planning as a Population Policy

In advanced circles it is now becoming recognized that family planning is not an adequate means of population control. In an article in Science in 1969, three prominent advisers to the federal government regarding population policy declared that "the federal program [of family planning] has been advanced, not for population control, but to improve health and reduce the impact of poverty and deprivation."[9] But, insofar as actual policies are being undertaken today, by national governments or by international or state agencies, they are still limited almost exclusively to family planning.

For instance, in January 1969, the United States pledged $7.5 million to the United Nations, on a basis of matching funds from other sources, to establish a United Nations Fund for Population Activities. The establishment of this Fund was widely heralded as bringing the United Nations into the field of action on the population problem. One of the first acts of the Fund was to grant Egypt $400,000 for "supplies of contraceptives" and "expert advisors on family planning services." Soon thereafter, on August 27, 1970, an agreement was signed with the government of Pakistan whereby the Fund would provide $1.7 million for the first twelve months "to render support to the Government of Pakistan in fulfilling the goals of its family planning programme, stipulated in the Fourth Five-Year Plan for the period 1970-1975. The Government's aim is to reduce the birth rate in Pakistan from 43 to 33.2 per 1,000 population. . . . It [the government] will designate the Central Family Planning Council as the 'co-operating agency' to represent [it]."[10] Similarly, a release from the United States Agency for International Development, recounting the agency's Population Program Assistance Activities for 1967, says: "Highest priority is being given to actions aimed at ensuring ready availability of acceptable and efficient means of contraception and family planning information throughout the developing countries."

On the domestic front, the three actions generally regarded as being the major ones recently undertaken by the United States federal government with respect to population are as follows: (1) the creation, in 1967, of a Center for Population Studies in the National Institute of Child Health and Human Development; (2) the appointment of, first, a President's Committee on

---

[9] Oscar Harkovy, Frederik S. Jaffe, and Samuel M. Wishik, "Family Planning and Public Policy: Who Is Misleading Whom?" Science, Vol. 165 (July 25, 1969), p. 368.

[10] United Nations, Population Division, Population Newsletter, No. 10 (Sept. 1970), pp. 3-4.

Population and Family Planning and then (March 1970) a Congress-enacted Commission on Population Growth and the American Future--both chaired by the same individual, John D. Rockefeller III, long prominent in family-planning circles; (3) the passage in January 1971 of the Family Planning Services and Population Research Act.

In all three of these actions, the emphasis is on family planning, as is evident in the names given the entities created and in the programs undertaken. In the advice he has received, President Nixon has been influenced by the representatives of family-planning organizations such as the Population Division of the Ford Foundation, the Population Council, International Planned Parenthood Federation, and the Population Crisis Committee. In his message to Congress on July 18, 1969, President Nixon said that "population growth is among the most important issues we face," that "it can be met only if there is a great deal of advance planning," and that "the time for such planning is growing very short." To meet this problem internationally he called on the United Nations, to which organization he promised American cooperation and assistance in "population and family planning." He praised the report, issued in May 1969, of a panel of the United Nations Association. That report recommended a strong family planning program as the overwhelming answer to the population problem, without reference to criticisms of this view. It said: "Today, unlike even the recent past, the means exist for achieving effective reductions in birth rates on a mass scale. . . . While nothing should detract from the urgency of developing, and properly testing, new methods of contraception, equally nothing should stand in the way of the fullest possible use of those we already have." It is worthy of note that the national Center for Population Studies was set up in a unit of the federal government which is concerned with child health, thus emphasizing the importance of children and the medical side of "population." So far the bulk of the expenditures by the Center have been for research in reproductive physiology and the search for a better contraceptive device. In the funding of the Family Planning Services and Population Research Act of 1971, the FY1972 budget request was overwhelmingly for the expansion of family-planning service programs. Eighty percent of the increase in expenditures over the previous year was for this purpose. There can be no doubt that family planning remains almost the exclusive approach to meeting the population problem, so far as official policies are concerned.

As a major policy statement addressed to the United Nations says, "The term 'family planning' is used to denote those programs which directly involve the provision of contraceptive information supplies and services."[11] The same document makes

---

[11] *World Population: A Challenge to the United Nations and Its System of Agencies*, Report of a National Policy Panel established

THE NATURE AND PURPOSE OF POPULATION POLICY

clear that this activity is the kind almost always undertaken or recommended "in the population field," regardless of whether it is governments, foundations, or international agencies that are involved.

An obvious defect of family planning as a population control measure is that it does not affect migration. It is a mistake to assume, for example, that population growth in the United States is purely a function of "family size." Since some 15.7 percent of the increase of the U.S. population between 1960 and 1969 was contributed directly by international migration, one can see the inadequacy of that assumption. It raises a question as to why Americans should be asked to restrict their family size in order to admit immigrants from other countries. When one adds that the immigrants, on the average, have much larger families than the native-born, and thus contribute disproportionately to the "family size" factor, the question becomes even more pertinent. In a state such as California, where the contribution of foreign immigration has regularly been above the average for the nation and where interstate migration has contributed anything from a third to two-thirds of the population growth, exclusive reliance on family planning would be futile as a population measure.

Even when family planning programs are used for limiting the birth rate (assuming something else is done about migration), they have the defect of providing control for couples but not for societies. The Declaration on Population, signed by 30 world leaders and endorsed by Secretary-General U Thant, says that "a great problem threatens the world . . . the problem of unplanned population growth." One then expects the Declaration to call for __population__ planning, but actually it calls only for __family__ planning. It says that "the opportunity [of parents] to decide the number and spacing of children is a basic human right."

The population problem is a national problem, not an individual predicament. The number of children couples want is not automatically the number they should have from a national point of view. To make individual decisions add up to a desirable population trend, a nation must find ways to influence the decisions in accord with an overall plan. Otherwise, individual planning will simply result in collective non-planning. To declare that couples have "a basic human right" to have as many children as they want is like trying to control firearms by telling people they have a right to own all the guns they want.

---

by the United Nations Association of the U.S.A. (New York: United Nations Association of the U.S.A., 1969), p. 57.

KINGSLEY DAVIS

The Family Planning Movement and Population

The fallacy of mistaking family planning for population planning is obvious. How then did it become the basis for action programs in which hundreds of millions of dollars are being spent? Why--even after the fallacy has been exposed--does family planning remain virtually the sole approach to population control?

Very briefly stated, there are three main reasons why family planning has been seized upon as *the* approach to population control. The first is historical. During the nineteenth and early twentieth centuries, the family-planning movement responded to genuine social needs. As a consequence, it became eminently respectable, well-organized, and powerful. When governments finally decided to take action in behalf of population control, the family-planning lobby was ready to move in, without competition. Second, the family-planning approach did not, and does not now, call for any drastic reorganization of society. By putting its emphasis on contraceptive services, it construes the population problem as a technological one. It leads people to think that the solution to the problem lies in finding a 100 percent effective contraceptive and distributing it to the people. It thus does not disturb the deep sentiments, family institutions, and social incentives that give society its powerful pronatalist character, and that are the cause of the high birth rates that are presumably to be overcome by "population control." The only "reform" proposed by the family planners is an extremely narrow one; the structure and conditions of the society remain undisturbed. Third, family planning requires no self-discipline or self-denial on the part of the individual. It gives him greater freedom: to enjoy sexual intercourse without fear of pregnancy, to have as many children as desired, to space children. It puts no restraint on him whatsoever; all he has to do is "use the method" for what he wants.

Although it is frequently assumed that the family-planning movement brought birth control to the people and thus sparked the decline of fertility in Western countries from around 1870 to 1933, it did nothing of the sort. The organized birth control movement was brought into being by popular interest in and use of birth control means, not vice versa. By the time of the Bradlaugh-Besant trial which led to the formation of the Malthusian League in 1878, the limitation of births had been widely practiced in certain classes for more than a century, and propaganda and instruction with respect to contraceptive methods had been around for half a century. The condom gained tremendous popularity after 1844 when the process of vulcanizing rubber was developed (a feat that made the pessary possible too). Coitus interruptus, an ever popular method, needed no materials at all; douches, sponges, astringent solutions, and the sterile period were abundantly recommended.

THE NATURE AND PURPOSE OF POPULATION POLICY

What then was the role of the organized birth control movement, which came so late in the day? It was to bring organized pressure to bear on the official forces in society--forces solidly arrayed against the changing practices of the people. Its role was to bring the laws, religious pronouncements, and administrative rulings into line with what people, faced with new conditions, were doing anyway in their reproductive behavior. The organized birth control movement became a lobby that gradually won over the control agencies of the society. First it won over the medical profession by stressing "medically approved" contraceptives, emphasizing the "health aspects" of family planning, and setting up "clinics" for birth control "patients." Then it won over the Protestant clergy, the judiciary, the politicians, and finally even a substantial section of the Roman Catholic clergy.

The movement was remarkably successful at just the time when governments began to seek measures for population control. In its ideological battles with the anti-contraception forces, the movement had claimed that nearly every evil facing mankind would be alleviated or eliminated by family planning. Among these evils was overpopulation, but this had been only an academic contention. During the Depression, when the advanced nations were worried about population decline, leaders of the movement disclaimed responsibility, saying that the birth rate is a function of other things than the use of contraceptives. As time wore on, however, the movement began to insist that governments not only tolerate the establishment of birth control clinics but _pay_ for them as well. When the question of government-sponsored population control arose in the early 1950's, the family-planning movement, organized around the world, assumed that it had the answer.

The movement's new respectability made its program acceptable. This respectability was enhanced by numerous organizational and propagandistic devices, such as defining family planning as a public health measure and contraceptives as medical instrumentalities, stressing family values (as seen in the euphemism "family planning" itself), dealing with problems of subfecundity as well as unwanted fertility, condemning abortion and painting contraception as the solution to "the abortion problem," and re-emphasizing the female's identity with the family and reproduction by making her, rather than the male, primarily responsible for contraception. Acceptability was also enhanced by an elaborate respect for religious taboos and superstitions. The movement stressed that "there shall be freedom of choice of method so that individuals can choose in accordance with the dictates of their conscience."[12] In other words, if religion dictated an

---

[12] John W. Gardner, then Secretary of Health, Education, and Welfare, U.S.A., "Memorandum to Heads of Operating Agencies" (Jan. 1966); reproduced in Congressional Hearings on S. 1676, p. 783.

inefficient method, the "patient" would be given that one. Finally, the attractiveness of "solving" the population problem without imposing any restraint whatever on the individual, but rather giving him what he wants, is too obvious to require comment.

But successful as the family planners have been in setting themselves up in the business of population control, they are now--as a result of that success--in the difficult position of having to make good on their claim. Unless they speedily get population control under way, they will lose support.

The inadequacy of family-planning programs as population control measures can be seen in the demographic facts. The industrial nations, although without any government birth control services, proved their skill in contraception during the Depression. As noted already, they lowered their birth rates to levels which, if continued, would have meant population decline. But in these same countries the birth rates after 1946 rose to levels that provided rapid population growth. Was this rise in the birth rate due to a deterioration of contraceptive technology? Was it due to a dwindling of contraceptive services? Was it due to enhanced taboos on the manufacture, dissemination, or use of contraceptives? On the contrary, it was an era of liberalization and improvement in contraceptive techniques and services. By no stretch of the imagination can the rise in birth rates be attributed to any attrition in contraceptive availability. The rise was due, instead, to the public feeling that jobs were secure and economic prospects good; therefore, they could get married and have nearly the number of children they desired. Polls in the industrial countries show that couples generally want more children than they actually have. When economic and political conditions are good, the birth rate will tend to rise. As a result of the postwar baby boom, the industrial countries, for the most part, have had a rapid growth of population during two and a half decades. Since the base is now larger, this means that in absolute terms the industrial countries have had the greatest population growth they ever had.

Alternative Policies

Unless policies in addition to family planning are adopted, there will be no national population control. Although the family planners frequently accuse those who mention additional policies of favoring "compulsion," the truth is that some of the measures now being proposed would free people from traditional pronatalist compulsions. Among the old compulsions is the ban on abortions, which forces pregnant women to bear children. Lifting the ban and subsidizing the costs of abortion would automatically provide a 100 percent effective birth control

THE NATURE AND PURPOSE OF POPULATION POLICY

method, regardless of the kind of contraceptive used, if any. Freeing women from the traditional discriminations in education and occupational spheres would enable them to develop the same career interests and outside contacts that men develop. Removing discriminatory military claims and taxes on single and childless persons, and improving the tax situation of families in which the wife works, would further weaken pronatalist compulsions. Further positive incentives proposed by advocates of effective population control include paying people to become sterilized (as in some states of India), giving couples a bond or a cash payment for each year that they refrain from childbearing, offering career fellowships to men and women who remain single, providing recreational facilities and social life around the place of work rather than the home, and giving housing advantages to childless people.

Since present rates of population growth cannot continue very long, it is obvious that something will stop them--if not fertility control, then a rise in mortality. If necessary to avoid that rise, many people think compulsory measures will be justified. If couples were required to furnish evidence of economic ability to support a family before being allowed to marry, many marriages would be postponed or avoided. If, in addition, illegitimate pregnancy were penalized--the women being required to secure an abortion and the fathers being punished-- the current high rates of illegitimate fertility and forced marriages would be avoided. Finally, if no woman were permitted to have more than four children, the birth rate could not be inflated, as it is now, by selfish couples who have five or more children. In the United States, during 1965-68, nearly 15 percent of the births were of fifth or higher order. If these had not occurred, the birth rate would have been 15.6 instead of the actual 18.3, and the NRR would have been only 8 percent instead of 27 percent above unity.

Mention of potentially effective population control policies seems immoral to many people, because traditional morality is highly pronatalist. It remains to be seen whether the revolutionary character of such policies will prevent their being adopted. Ironically, the fundamental amorality of pure voluntarism with respect to population is seldom understood, because the present system is one of built-in compulsions that are overlooked because they are taken for granted. A doctrine of purely voluntary action in all matters affecting population would be dangerous indeed, especially with respect to public health and migration. With respect to family size, an absence of any enforced responsibility whatever for the children people engender would be difficult to contemplate, much less to adopt as a national policy.

III. THE IDEA OF A STATE POPULATION POLICY

If the idea of deliberately curbing population increase is so unorthodox as to raise questions (particularly when effective measures are proposed), it is still more unorthodox to think of a mere part of a nation attempting such a feat. How much can California do on its own about rapid population increase? Is it dependent on what the federal government does? Let us consider the question.

Is the State Impotent with Respect to Migration?

One difference between a sovereign nation and a part of a nation is that the nation can regulate the flow of migration across its borders by direct legislation affecting that flow, whereas a constituent state or province cannot do so. Thus the immigration laws of the United States have always represented a deliberate population policy, for they governed the number of foreigners who could legally enter, work, or settle in the country each year. The movement of people within the country, however, cannot be directly controlled by law, except under very limited circumstances such as for purposes of public health or criminal justice. Furthermore, since the nation as a whole regulates foreign migration, a state cannot directly legislate with respect to the admission or non-admission of aliens.

These limitations, however, do not mean that a state is powerless to exercise an influence on the net flow of migrants into its territory. It simply has to use indirect measures, but in the last analysis these are probably more effective anyway. Many nations, including our own, have discovered that it is very difficult to keep out migrants by law, if they want to come; others have discovered that it is very difficult to attract migrants by law, if they do not want to come. So, if the object is to reduce population growth, it is necessary for a state to explore means for discouraging foreign and interstate in-migration, and for encouraging out-migration. This naturally raises the question of the causes of migration.

The motives for migration are as many as the situations affecting the lives of people. As the huge movement of escapees from Cuba, East Germany, and other satellite countries demonstrates, many people will do almost anything to escape a Communist totalitarian regime; others will move because their religious beliefs are not tolerated or made supreme; still others will move because they are retired and have nothing to worry about except cold weather and inflation. The main reason for the continued large volume of migration into the United States, in addition to less important political, religious, and ethnic reasons, is the economic opportunity provided by the world's highest level of living. Certainly, the main reason for interstate migration into California is the fact that wages are higher in California than in most of the nation.

If the chief reason is economic, it follows that an indirect method of limiting migration is to curtail economic expansion in the state. Here at once we encounter a profound conflict of goals. To the managers of business enterprises, to the elected and appointed officials of territorial districts, to the presidents of universities and heads of campuses, to the ministers of church groups and the representatives of ethnic majorities and minorities, there appears to be, and is, an advantage in sheer numbers. It is made a basis for budget allocations, political representation, welfare claims, ethnic demands. Furthermore, economic expansion (ever more land filled up, acres planted, lots sold, automobiles equipped, houses built) is confused with economic development (more goods and services per capita). Even when population growth in the abstract is viewed as unfortunate, no one is willing, when it gets down to cases, to sacrifice the growth of his enterprise, group, or district. There seems no escaping a certain amount of conflict, but the necessity of choosing between economic expansion in the state and continued rapid population growth seems clear. As the per capita advantage of the state declines, as it has been doing, then the migratory influx may subside; but the object of policy would presumably be to curb the influx before it brought the state's economic level down to that of the country as a whole. In this way, a high per capita income could be preserved.

If it wishes to use them, the state has the means to curb economic expansion. It has, within limits, control over land-use patterns; it has control over the licensing and siting of new business and industrial enterprises; it has control of the location and rates of public utilities which furnish most of the power that runs the industrial system; it has control over the construction of highways and harbors, the licensing of trucks, the taxing of gasoline. There is no denying the complexity of the problems that would ensue if the state undertook to use these means to halt expansion and thus cut down the flow of in-migrants and protect its level of living. Most of these problems arise, however, out of the fact that the institutional order has been adjusted in the past to maximizing, not minimizing, economic expansion. Once the necessity of reversing this mental set is clearly seen by the public and its officials, the ease of exercising the control may prove surprising.

The State and Marriage Control

Even if net migration into the state were reduced to zero, the state would still have a brisk rate of population growth due to the fact that its birth rate, though tending to be slightly lower than that of the nation as a whole, is still high enough to give considerable increase each year. For this reason, consideration has to be given to regulating fertility. Since in human societies the family is the institutional mechanism wherein reproduction is supposed to occur, so that two adults (the parents) can be held responsible for the care and upbringing of the children, there are two avenues to limiting fertility. One is to encourage the postponement or the abjuration of marriage, while keeping institutional controls over reproduction outside of marriage. The other is to induce the limitation of offspring within marriage.

Again, controls by the community at large can take the form of direct legislative enactment or indirect regulation of conditions that affect motivation and hence behavior. Since family law is reserved to the states, there is no constitutional difficulty even to direct legislation governing marriage and relationships within marriage, although which type of control (direct or indirect) is more effective is always an open question dependent on the particular aim in view.

It has to be recognized that a measure undertaken for the purpose of lowering fertility may have other benefits as well. For instance, the elimination of extremely young marriages in California would reduce the number of divorces, lower the number of neglected and abused children, and lessen the number of families headed by a female, as well as reduce the fertility. Reducing the number of illegitimate births in the state would lower the maternal and infant mortality rate, reduce the number of neglected children, and lower welfare costs. It has to be remembered that the tighter regulation of family relations in the society of the past tended to _lower_ fertility in some respects rather than raise it. However, it did not have this purpose for the society, the main purpose being to protect women and children from fraud and abuse.

There would be no advantage in attempting to encourage marital postponement or abjuration if illegitimate reproduction were to increase to a compensatory degree. Therefore, the first step in a program of controlling marriage as a means to lowered fertility would be to reduce or eliminate illegitimate reproduction. This can easily be done, for there are many societies in which illegitimate fertility is extremely low. It is particularly important in California, because here illegitimate births are a higher portion of all births (over 10 percent) than they are in the nation at large. The old system of holding the male economically and legally responsible for an illegitimate pregnancy is one device that worked fairly well in the past and could be made to work much better under modern conditions. Permitting or requiring women who are illicitly pregnant to abort would be an additional possibility. Most illegitimate pregnancies are not desired, most of the children born without a legal father are not kept by the mother. Quite apart from considerations of population growth, it seems preposterous that a society would permit new human beings to be brought into the world as a result of an unfortunate accident, by people so improvident or childish that they do not take the responsibility of preventing such accidents. I am not discussing sexual intercourse outside of marriage, but only reproduction--that is, the creation of new human beings.

As for marriage itself, the present situation is eminently pronatalist. There are virtually no requirements for marriage worthy of the name. One can get a marriage license easier than a driving license. The state might well consider requiring a demonstrated ability to support and care for children as a prerequisite to marriage. Indirect controls might also prove effective, such as more equal educational and career opportunities for women, easier divorce laws if there are no children, tax incentives for remaining single, elimination of family allowances in university fellowships and scholarships. The average age at which people marry in California is unusually low by civilized standards. If other societies have managed to achieve a higher average age at marriage, ours presumably could do so too.

Fertility within Marriage

Reducing the number of children within marriage is probably the hardest thing for official policy to accomplish. The reason is that the main purpose of getting married is to have children. The number of children couples want tends to be considerably higher than just enough to replace the population, particularly if nearly everybody gets married, as is the case in California. Since nearly all discussions of population policy are centered on fertility within marriage, I shall not review the well-known and varied proposals. It is simply worth noting that offering couples contraceptive means does not affect the number of children they desire. If parents are to be dissuaded from having a demographically unwise number of children it will have to be by offering opportunities and interests that successfully compete with those connected with children. This is easier to do prior to marriage than after.

P A R T I I

THE SPECIAL PLACE OF MIGRATION

THE ROLE OF MIGRATION IN CALIFORNIA'S GROWTH

Peter A. Morrison

The 1970 Census has indicated important distributional changes in the United States produced by the movement of population during the last decade. The long-term dispersion of the Black population persists undiminished, contrary to earlier indications. Whites, meanwhile, continue to move south and west. Overall, migration has siphoned population away from the heartland, focusing its impact on the coastal states, especially those along the Pacific. About half of the roughly 3,000 U.S. counties, rather than the projected one-third, lost population during the 1960's. Three out of four had more people moving out than moving in, serving in this way as net exporters. Preliminary figures suggest that California gained around 2.11 million migrants of all races (somewhat above an earlier estimate of 1.88 million). Migration's historical role in California's growth must be gauged within the broader context of these and other national population movements which have been under way for many decades.

Three major streams of migration, supporting an evolution of distribution patterns nationally, have contributed to California's growth. The first is the movement of rural population in all sections of the country to metropolitan areas. This rural-urban stream contributed a sizable fraction of the growth in urban population during prior decades; now, however, its effect has diminished as the number of rural inhabitants shrinks.

Second, there has been a substantial exodus from economically depressed regions in the United States of persons destined for areas of expanding employment and favorable opportunity. During the 1960's, population flowed out of a large crescent descending from the northern Middle West and curving east through parts of Texas, Louisiana, and Mississippi. The coastal states tended to receive the largest influx of new residents, and the most dramatic changes were seen in major metropolitan areas.

The views expressed in this paper are those of the author. They should not be interpreted as reflecting the views of The Rand Corporation or the official opinion or policy of any of its governmental or private research sponsors. . . . I am grateful to Judy Wheeler and Karen Eisenstadt for helpful comments on an earlier version of this paper.

Houston and Washington increased nearly 40 percent; the Anaheim-Santa Ana Standard Metropolitan Statistical Area (SMSA) ballooned from 700,000 to 1,400,000 residents.

Finally, a national system of migration--through which metropolitan areas trade population among one another--has directed a net influx of population to the Pacific states. A large share of this latter flow has been to California, the nation's most urbanized state.[1]

Within the larger context of these national trends, California's unmatched migration can be attributed to two reinforcing sets of conditions. On the supply side, these major geographic shifts in population, part of a broader process of urban structural change, have furnished large pools of people "on the move." On the demand side, the state's dominant coastal metropolitan areas have maintained a consistently favorable competitive position relative to other American cities. The product of these forces has siphoned large numbers of new residents into metropolitan California, accelerating the evolution of a highly differentiated urban system. As one authority has noted, California's growth "is not just the growth of one or two larger cities in the state, but the simultaneous expansion of its whole metropolitan structure, the nodes of which are linked with an interflow of people."[2]

This evolving system of cities has several distinctive features from a distributional standpoint. One is its domination by large concentrations of population in a few metropolitan areas. The other is the physical arrangement of people within these areas.[3] Characterized by extensive urban sprawl, they offer mute testimony to the overriding influence of transportation technology on physical patterns of settlement.

Projecting patterns of population far into the future is a necessarily contingent exercise. (As one of Damon Runyon's characters once put it, "Nothing what depends on humans is worth

---

[1] The 1970 Census showed 91 percent of California's population living in cities, towns, and suburbs.

[2] Donald L. Foley et al., Characteristics of Metropolitan Growth in California. Volume I: Report (Berkeley: Center for Planning and Development Research, Institute for Urban and Regional Development, 1965).

[3] Howard F. Gregor, "Spatial Disharmonies in California's Population Growth," Geographical Review, 53 (January 1963), pp. 100-122.

odds of better than 8 to 3.") Yet the outlines of California's future megalopolis already are clear. In all likelihood, the year 2000 will see a continuous coastal urban region, one of twelve national megalopolises shown in Figure 1. This urban region, already christened "San-San," would extend from the Mexican border to north of San Francisco, embracing nearly 50,000 square miles. With a population in the vicinity of 40 million, it would be surpassed by only two other megalopolises--the Atlantic Seaboard and the Lower Great Lakes urban regions (see Table 1).

About one-seventh of the entire population of the coterminous United States would reside in San-San, at an average density of 880 persons per square mile.[4] Projected magnitudes of energy consumption needed to support this population are staggering. By the year 2000, the level of waste thermal energy--heat given off to the environment as a by-product of all human activity--could pose fundamental problems of environmental disequilibrium. For the 4,000-square-mile Los Angeles basin, for example, waste heat may be in the vicinity of 15 to 20 percent of absorbed solar energy, whereas this quantity is now around 5 percent.[5] No one is willing to forecast the effects of this and other thermal anomalies centered over heavily populated regions. People who have been drawn to Los Angeles by its temperate climate may find it even a bit warmer 30 years from now.

The Historical Role of California's Migration

Population growth and redistribution are the joint product of two demographic factors: natural increase (the excess of births over deaths) and an elaborate migratory circulation of people among places. Both of these components vary from one locality to another. Migration is always the more volatile and changeable factor, being more responsive to spatial differentials in economic growth.

---

[4]Measures of density are quite crude and can be misleading. In particular, they are exceedingly limited in what they can reveal about micro-level conditions. It does not follow, for example, that people are necessarily "crowded" at a density of 880 per square mile--or less crowded at lower aggregate densities. As rough indices of regional environmental load, though, measures of population per square mile permit crude order-of-magnitude comparisons where levels of per capita consumption are similar. For further discussion, see O.D. Duncan, "The Measurement of Population Distribution," Population Studies, 11 (July 1957), pp. 27-45.

[5]See S.M. Greenfield, Projection and Distribution of Waste Thermal Energy, The Rand Corporation, P-4540, December 1970.

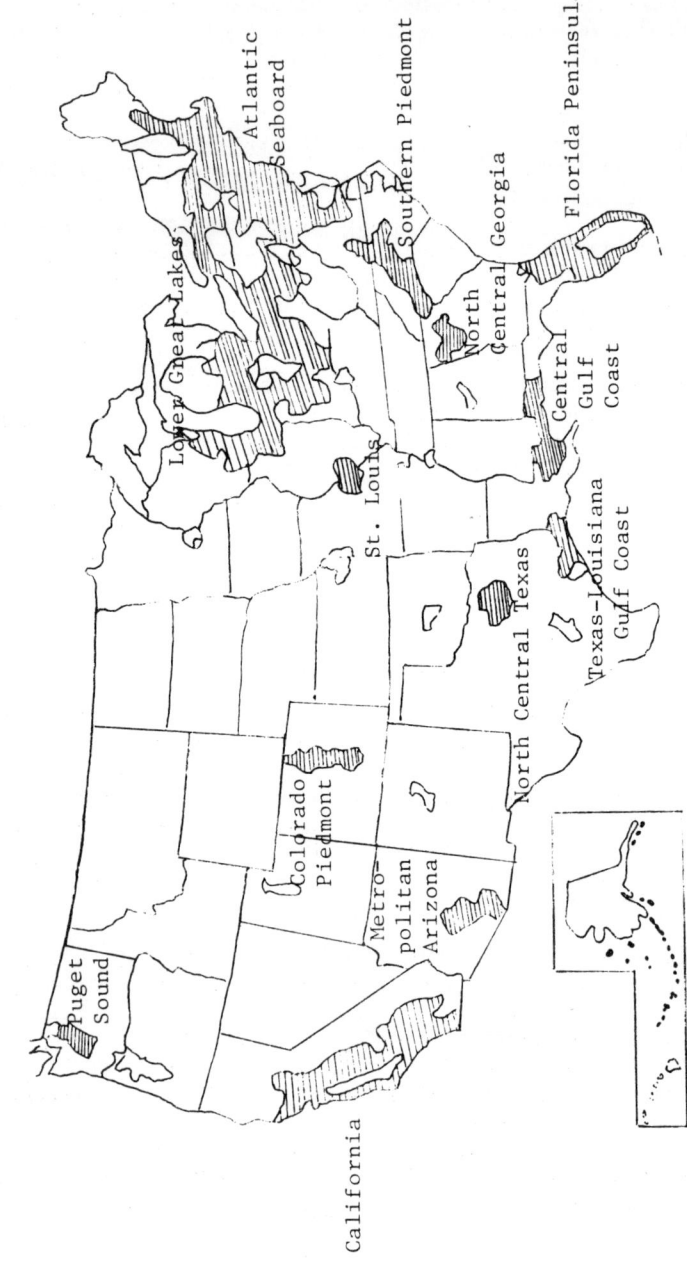

FIGURE 1. MAJOR URBAN REGIONS, YEAR 2000

Source: Jerome P. Pickard, Dimensions of Metropolitanism. (Copyright by the Urban Land Institute and used with its permission.)

THE ROLE OF MIGRATION IN CALIFORNIA'S GROWTH

Table 1

PROJECTED POPULATION OF LARGE URBAN REGIONS OF THE UNITED STATES, YEAR 2000, SHOWING LAND AREA AND POPULATION DENSITY

Urban Region	Land Area (Sq. mi.)	Population (000's)	Population Density
Metropolitan Belt	159,500	126,500	790
Atlantic Seaboard	65,000	67,400	1,040
Lower Great Lakes	94,500	59.100	625
California	48,000	42,500	880
Peninsular Florida	20,300	13,000	640
Southern Piedmont	14,500	5,200	360
Texas-Louisiana Gulf Coast	6,500	4,900	750
Central Gulf Coast	11,700	4,700	400
North Central Texas	7,000	4,200	600
Puget Sound	6,300	3,800	600
Metropolitan Arizona	14,200	3,550	250
St. Louis	4,700	3,500	745
Colorado Piedmont	6,700	3,200	480
North Central Georgia	5,000	3,100	620
12 Urban Regions, Total	304,400	218,100	715
Balance of Coterminous U.S.	2,655,600	86,500	33
Coterminous U.S., Total	2,960,000	304,600	103

Source: Jerome P. Pickard, "Trends and Projections of Future Population Growth in the United States, with Special Data on Large Urban Regions and Major Metropolitan Areas, for the Period 1970-2000," Technical Paper No. 4, Office of the Deputy Under-Secretary, U.S. Department of Housing and Urban Development, July 22, 1969.

Statewide Patterns

The state in general, and certain of its metropolitan areas in particular, have departed strikingly from the pattern of growth that has typified most of the nation. Unlike most states, where natural increase furnished the major share of net growth, California's increase was based more heavily on the migration component. Figure 2 shows that, for the civilian population, net migration far outweighed natural increase until the latter part of the 1960's. More recently, the importance of migration--both relative and absolute--has diminished as the state's base population has expanded. Natural increase has begun to dominate, conforming more nearly to the typical pattern prevailing elsewhere.

Where has California's migratory population come from? Unfortunately, the most recent data available at this time refer to migration between 1955 and 1960. Figure 3 indicates that during that period Illinois and New York were the leading sources of net in-migration, followed by Texas, Ohio, and Michigan. While there were substantial net gains from all these states, California was engaged in an active gross exchange of population with nearby states like Texas, Washington, Oregon, and Arizona.

Patterns of Urban Development[6]

Although migration to California has declined in the last few years, its impact throughout the state is far from even. Statewide figures do not differentiate among the several important processes of redistribution under way. These rearrangements of people are supporting an evolution of population settlement within California having important implications for future urban development.

California's urbanization reflects a structural differentiation of a statewide system of inter-metropolitan migration. A few dominant metropolitan areas exert a major magnetic effect, attracting out-of-state migrants from throughout the nation. The other metropolitan areas derive their migratory growth principally from streams of movement within the state. In the past, the development of this system has been sustained by a continual influx of new population into the state.

The magnetic influence of the dominant coastal urban centers can be gauged from Table 2. For the three largest metropolitan areas--Los Angeles-Long Beach, San Francisco-Oakland, and

---

[6] This section draws on an analysis originally carried out by Foley et al., pp. 34-48.

FIGURE 2. ESTIMATED COMPONENTS OF CHANGE IN
CALIFORNIA'S CIVILIAN POPULATION, 1945-1969

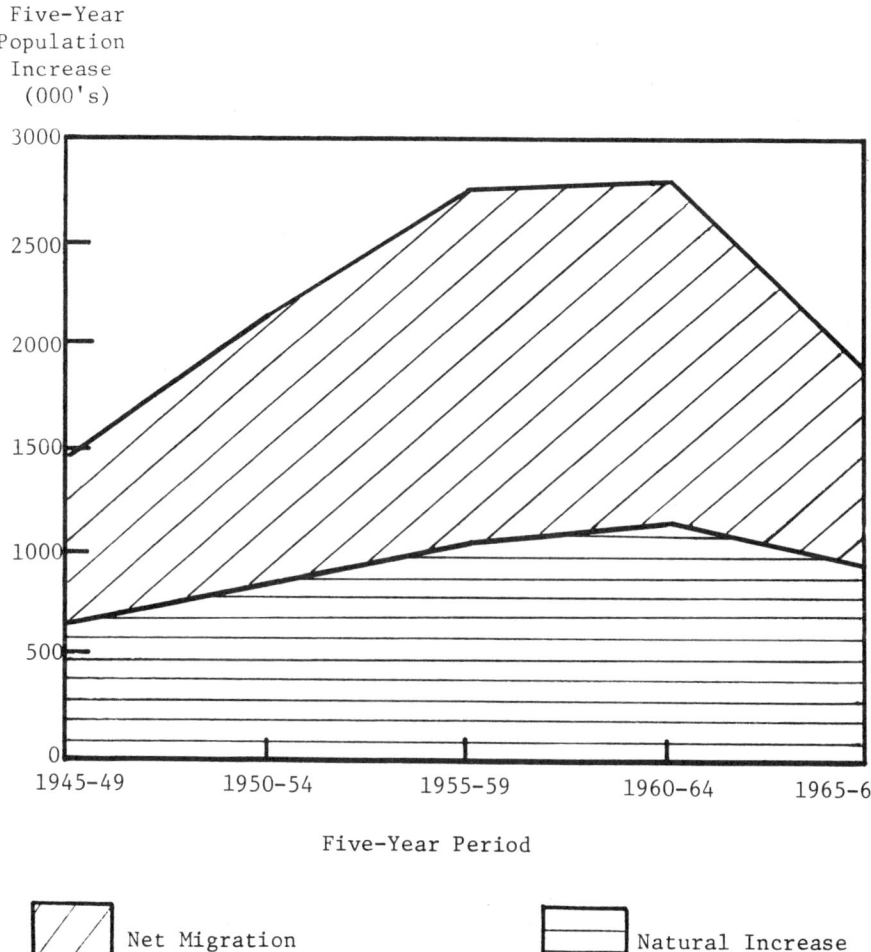

Source: Department of Finance, California Population, 1969 (Sacramento, 1969), Table 6 (Note: Loss to military has been excluded.)

FIGURE 3. GROSS IN AND OUT MIGRATION AND NET MIGRATION TO CALIFORNIA FROM SELECTED STATES, 1955-1960

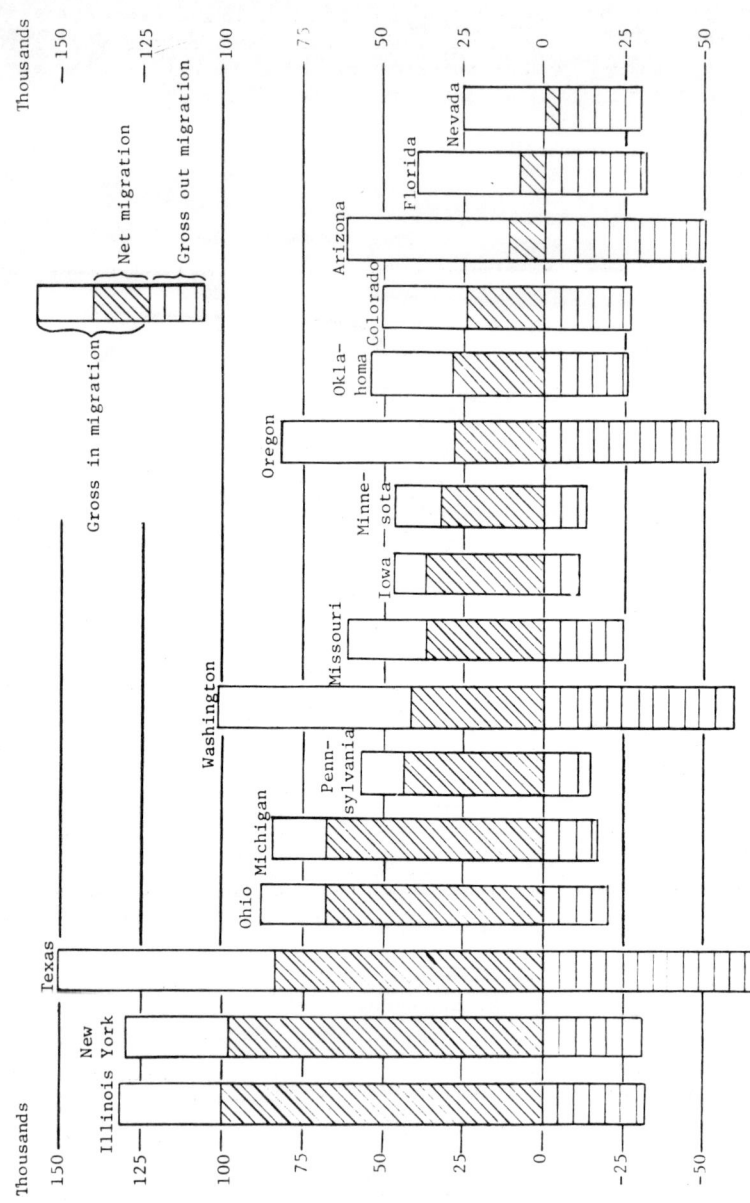

Source: Department of Finance, California Migration: 1955-1960 (Sacramento, 1964).

THE ROLE OF MIGRATION IN CALIFORNIA'S GROWTH

San Diego--the vast majority of in-migrants originated outside of California (81.4, 63.8, and 73.7 percent, respectively). For the period to which the data refer, these centers were acting as major importers of population from other states.[7] Migrants to San Jose, Sacramento, and Fresno, in contrast, tended to originate from within the state (56.1, 53.9, and 60.2 percent, respectively).

Table 2

PERCENTAGE DISTRIBUTION OF IN-MIGRATION STREAMS TO SELECTED SMSA'S FROM WITHIN AND OUTSIDE OF CALIFORNIA: 1955-1960

SMSA	Total Volume of In-migration	From Within California[a]	From Outside California[b]	Total
Los Angeles-Long Beach	1,048,175	18.6%	81.4%	100.0%
San Francisco-Oakland	416,747	36.3	63.8	100.1
San Diego	326,699	26.3	73.7	100.0
San Jose	203,066	56.1	43.9	100.0
Sacramento	138,697	53.9	46.2	100.1
Fresno	63,404	60.2	39.9	100.1

[a] But from outside the SMSA in question.

[b] Excludes foreign immigration.

Source: Donald L. Foley et al., Characteristics of Metropolitan Growth in California. Volume I: Report (Berkeley: Center for Planning and Development Research, Institute for Urban and Regional Development, (1965), Table 2-8).

---

[7] For nonwhites, this pattern was even more pronounced. Nonwhites from out of state showed an even greater tendency to enter California through its coastal urban centers.

Data on intrastate migration, shown in Table 3, reveal two processes under way. One is an exchange of population among California's metropolitan areas. On a relative basis, at least, these interchanges tend to favor the nongateway cities: whereas California's dominant SMSA's imported population from metropolitan areas outside the state, San Jose, Sacramento, and Fresno attracted their metropolitan population from other California cities. For example, 56.3 percent of migration into Los Angeles-Long Beach originated in non-California metropolitan areas; 45.1 percent of migration into San Jose, on the other hand, came from other California urban centers.

The second process is a movement of population out of agricultural counties into urban areas. For example, both Sacramento and Fresno drew comparatively large portions of their migration from nonmetropolitan parts of the state (18.8 and 27.3 percent, respectively).

Briefly, there appears to be a distinct functional differentiation among California's cities. The dominant coastal urban centers attracted a steady influx of new population from other states, while the smaller urban centers drew population from their surrounding agricultural hinterland and other centers within the state. In their net effect, these dynamics have created an exceptionally high level of urbanization. The vast majority of California's population now resides in the greater Los Angeles, San Francisco, and San Diego regions.

The combined impact of inter- and intra-state migration streams, however, is unevenly distributed over different SMSA's relative to their base population. Growth through migration is occurring disproportionately in some centers; others have gained comparatively little through migration, growing instead through natural increase. In several instances, natural increase is merely offsetting a net outflow of migrants.

Table 4 displays 1960-1970 estimated migration rates for California's 14 SMSA's shown in Figure 4. For all 14 centers combined, net migration had the effect of adding 110 persons for every 1000 residents at mid-decade. Four of these metropolitan areas--San Jose, Santa Barbara, Anaheim, and Oxnard--gained population through net migration at twice this rate or more. These centers of accelerated migratory growth show the uneven dynamics of California's urban growth. Although their mid-decade population totalled only 15 percent of California's metropolitan population, they accounted for 37 percent of the state's increase in metropolitan population (net migration plus natural increase), and around 56 percent of the total statewide metropolitan growth through net migration.

Table 3

PERCENTAGE DISTRIBUTION OF TOTAL IN-MIGRATION TO SELECTED SMSA'S BY METROPOLITAN OR NONMETROPOLITAN ORIGINS: 1955-1960[a]

SMSA	Total Inter- and Intra-State Origins			From Within the State			From Outside the State		
	Total	Metro-politan	Nonmetro-politan	Total	Metro-politan	Nonmetro-politan	Total	Metro-politan	Nonmetro-politan
Los Angeles-Long Beach	100%	70.8%	29.2%	18.6%	14.5%	4.1%	81.4%	56.3%	25.1%
San Francisco-Oakland	100	66.9	33.1	36.3	24.7	11.5	63.8	42.2	21.5
San Diego	100	68.5	31.5	26.3	22.3	4.0	73.7	46.2	27.5
San Jose	100	73.8	26.2	56.1	45.1	11.0	43.9	28.7	15.2
Sacramento	100	63.1	36.9	53.9	35.0	18.8	46.2	28.1	18.1
Fresno	100	51.7	48.3	60.2	32.9	27.3	39.9	18.8	21.0

[a]"Metropolitan" refers to the state's SMSA's defined as of 1960; "nonmetropolitan" is the remainder of the state.

Source: Foley et al., Table 2-9.

Table 4

ESTIMATED TEN-YEAR NET MIGRATION RATES FOR CALIFORNIA'S SMSA'S: 1960-1970

SMSA	Net Migration Rate per 1,000 Mid-Decade Population, 1960-1970
San Francisco-Oakland	50
San Jose	312
Sacramento	115
Stockton	31
Fresno	-28
Los Angeles-Long Beach	30
San Diego	127
San Bernardino-Riverside-Ontario	196
Bakersfield	-39
Santa Barbara	263
Anaheim	501
Vallejo-Napa	48
Oxnard	442
Salinas-Monterey	88
Subtotal: San Jose, Santa Barbara, Anaheim, Oxnard SMSA's	406
TOTAL, All SMSA's	110

Source: Computed from Population Research Unit, Department of Finance, "Population Estimates for California Counties: Advance Report," September 1, 1970.

These figures indicate that growth, particularly migratory growth, has become quite selectively allocated. As in other parts of the nation, a sizable fraction of metropolitan growth--and a far greater share of net in-migration to metropolitan areas--is flowing into only a few SMSA's. Viewed in historical perspective, moreover, rapidly growing centers as defined here have been capturing an expanding share of the total in-migration

FIGURE 4. CALIFORNIA STATE ECONOMIC AREAS

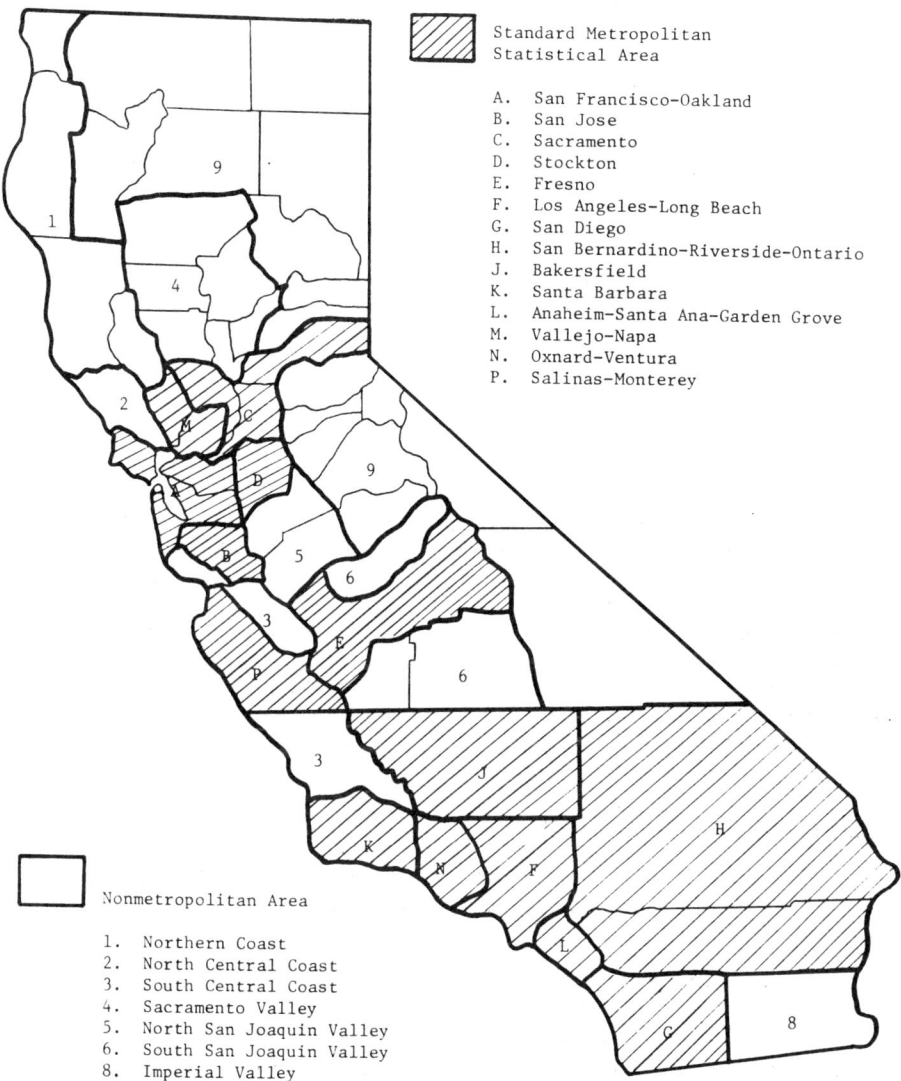

feeding metropolitan growth.[8] Migration today typically is inter-metropolitan; possibly as a consequence, it has become increasingly selective. "As the number of areas with substantial net inmigration has increased," Alonso and Medrich note, "so has the number of metropolises which are net exporters of people."

From the policymaker's standpoint, the demonstrable existence of spontaneous growth centers--places where the dynamics of the migration system come to a natural focus--warrants close attention. A clear understanding of the different types of growth taking place in various areas of the state is a necessary prerequisite to formulating an effective state population policy. Different kinds of growth call for different kinds of policies. For example, measures designed to reduce in-migration would be more appropriate for spontaneous growth centers than for areas expanding primarily through natural increase.

Factors Related to Interstate Migration

Overall generalization about geographic mobility is virtually impossible. Its complex determinants--which include a kaleidoscope of familial, occupational, and economic factors--are only partially understood. Long-distance migration tends to be dominated by economic motives, while local movement is typically a response to a family's neighborhood preference and its changing requirements for housing. Public policy measures could influence the flow of population, but to do so they would have to take maximum advantage of the natural forces that propel movement.[9]

Characteristics of Migrants

Three features of mobility deserve further discussion: pace, selectivity, and repetitive character.

---

[8] See William Alonso and Elliot Medrich, "Spontaneous Growth Centers in Twentieth Century American Urbanization," Working Paper No. 113 (Berkeley: Center for Planning and Development Research, University of California, 1970), p. 27.

[9] See Peter A. Morrison: The Rationale for a Policy on Population Distribution, The Rand Corporation, P-4374-1, July 1970; Urban Growth, New Cities, and "The Population Problem," The Rand Corporation, P-4515-1, December 1970; and Unresolved Questions about Population Distribution Policy: An Agenda for Further Research, The Rand Corporation, P-4630, April 1971.

THE ROLE OF MIGRATION IN CALIFORNIA'S GROWTH

Pace. Static features of population distribution, such as the relative balance between central cities and suburbs or between Northern and Southern California, disguise the continual flow of people under way. Every year the U.S. population undergoes a major rearrangement in space. Table 5 shows that about 18 in 100 Americans change residence annually; roughly one in fifteen--a total of 13 million people--migrates across a county line. These rates have remained remarkably constant over the years. To a considerable degree, they reflect movement to the suburbs. A little more than half of these 13 million, though, are interstate migrants, most of them undertaking a major move for economic reasons.

This stable annual level of geographic circulation is indicative of other healthy processes under way. A fluid population reflects the occupational and social mobility induced by demand for increasingly specialized manpower in changing locations. Individuals have access to, and avail themselves of, opportunities that may be locally nonexistent.

The spontaneous momentum of this migration is also a massive potential resource for shifting natural increase, enabling some localities to acquire the future fertility that others will avoid. Erected out of countless individual decisions, the flow of migration shifts more than mere numbers suggest. It

Table 5

ANNUAL MOBILITY OF THE POPULATION ONE-YEAR-OLD AND OVER: 1968-1969

Mobility Status	Number (000's)	Percent
Same House (Non-movers)	159,310	81.0%
Different House in U.S. (Movers)	35,933	18.3
Same County	22,993	11.7
Different County (Migrants)	12,940	6.6
Intrastate	6,316	3.2
Interstate	6,625	3.4
Abroad at Beginning of Period	1,399	0.7
TOTAL	196,642	100.0

Source: U.S. Bureau of the Census, *Current Population Reports*, Series P-20, No. 193, 1969.

represents a collective future investment, for it is composed disproportionately of young adults who have most of their economically productive lives ahead. Where migrants take their economic and reproductive capacity determines where future urban growth and economic expansion will take place. From the standpoint of policy, slight modifications in this ongoing circulation of human capital might have a considerable influence on future patterns of distribution.

Selectivity. Migration is a highly selective process, and the personal characteristics of migrants differ considerably from a typical cross section of the general population.[10] Of several dimensions of selectivity, age is the most pronounced in degree and of greatest practical significance. Table 6 shows the extent of age selectivity associated with migration. The degree of concentration among adults is particularly noteworthy. For example, people in their twenties account for nearly a third of all migrants (last column), far out of proportion to their overall representation (second column). These data reflect the high degree of residential and career experimentation typical of young adults before they experience the pressures for caution and stability that accompany an established home and family. Young migrants bring young children with them; one-tenth of all migrants are between the ages of one and four.

Table 6

AGE SELECTIVITY OF MIGRATION: 1968-1969

Age	Percentage Distribution of Population, 1968	Percent Who Migrated, 1968-1969	Percentage Distribution of Migrants, 1968-1969
Pre-Adults			
1-4	7.5%	9.3%	10.6%
5-17	26.8	5.7	23.0
Adults			
18-19	3.4	8.4	4.4
20-24	7.5	17.2	19.7
25-29	6.6	12.5	12.5
30-44	17.5	6.2	16.3
45 and Over	30.7	2.9	13.5
All Ages	100.0	6.6	100.0
	(196,642,000)		(12,940,000)

Source: U.S. Bureau of the Census, Current Population Reports, Series P-20, No. 193, December 1969.

---

[10] See Peter A. Morrison, The Propensity to Move: A Longitudinal Analysis, R-654-HUD, The Rand Corporation, January 1971.

THE ROLE OF MIGRATION IN CALIFORNIA'S GROWTH

The consequences of these differentials are not difficult to grasp. Figure 5 shows the age composition of net in-migration to California between 1955 and 1960. Areas receiving a heavy influx of new residents--such as Orange County, where the population has doubled in the past decade--are simultaneously undergoing a transformation in age composition. They can anticipate a relative as well as an absolute increase in educational demand as the ranks of the young are swollen by new arrivals. Conversely, sustained out-migration siphons off population with equal selectivity, reducing a population's capacity for natural increase and raising its dependency ratio. Migrants, in short, play a pivotal role in a complex redistribution of the "Gross National Product" of natural increase.

Repetitive Character. A third noteworthy feature of migration is its highly repetitive character. Individuals who move tend to do so repeatedly. This can be seen in Table 7. The column "Prospective Residential Departure Rate, 1966-1967" shows that movers and migrants in 1965 were three times as likely as their residentially stable counterparts to move again in 1966. Indeed, around 40 percent of all moves--whether local or long-distance--were made by a hypermobile fringe of about 18 percent of the population.[11]

In addition to being repetitive, moves are most likely to occur shortly after one another. Table 8 displays a pattern that has been labeled the "cumulative inertia" effect: the longer your duration of residence somewhere, the lower the prospects are that you will subsequently depart. Short-term residents (less than one year) are prime candidates for subsequent departure, with a 50-50 chance that they will change residence the next year.[12] Longer-term residents (five years or more) tend to be geographically inert.

These empirical regularities reveal little about the multiplicity of causal factors stimulating migration. They have practical implications for the policymaker, however, for they reflect the extensive self-selection involved. Migration tends to draw away those elements of a population who, for various social and personal reasons, are more responsive to incentives for movement and are the likely candidates for further movement in the future.

---

[11] For further details, see Morrison, The Propensity to Move.

[12] Most of these moves would be local; nevertheless, a significant fraction represent out-migration from the present county of residence. The "cumulative inertia" pattern appears for both.

FIGURE 5. AGE DISTRIBUTION OF "NET MIGRANTS" TO CALIFORNIA, 1955-1960

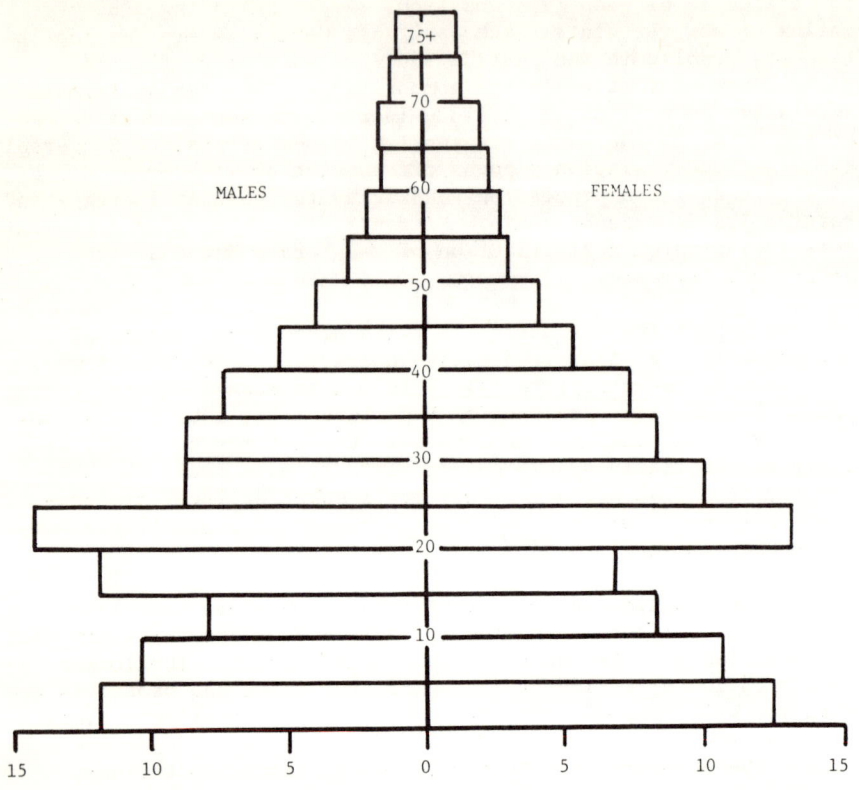

Source: California Migration: 1955-1960, Chart 3.

THE ROLE OF MIGRATION IN CALIFORNIA'S GROWTH

Table 7

DISTRIBUTION OF MIGRANTS AND INTRA-COUNTY MOVERS, 1966-1967, CLASSIFIED BY 1965 RESIDENCE

Previous Year's Residence (1965)	Percentage Distribution of Population 14+	Prospective Residential Departure Rate, 1966-1967	Percent of Total Moves
Same House	82.2%	.151	61.2%
Movers			
Same County, Different House	11.7	.419	24.2
Migrants			
Same State, Different County	2.8	.465	6.1
Different but Contiguous State	0.9	.532	2.3
Different and Non-Contiguous State	1.7	.532	4.5
Different Country	0.6	.584	1.7
All Residences	99.9	.203	100.0

Source: Peter A. Morrison, *The Propensity to Move: A Longitudinal Analysis*, R-654-HUD, The Rand Corporation, January 1971, Table 4.

Table 8

PROSPECTIVE RESIDENTIAL DEPARTURE RATE, BY DURATION OF PRIOR RESIDENCE IN PRESENT COUNTY

Duration of Residence in Present County				
Less than One Year	1-2 Years	3-4 Years	5 Years or More	All Durations
.51	.40	.29	.16	.20

Source: Morrison, *The Propensity to Move*, Table 3.

One consequence of this selectivity is that chronic movers probably are concentrated in certain regions and localities. Disproportionate numbers will have gravitated to areas that have been targets of a sustained and heavy influx of migrants in the past--states like California and Florida, and cities like Los Angeles, Houston, Dallas, and Atlanta. A second consequence is that an area's capacity to correct local manpower imbalances by exchanging human capital with other areas will vary with its relative abundance of hypermobile residents. A fluid population--heavily weighted with young adults, non-natives, and persons who have moved recently in the past--may well enhance an area's capacity to adjust to local employment change through a continual influx and outflow of occupational specialities.[13]

This "fluidity differential" can be identified indirectly in certain metropolitan areas. Table 9 shows the annual rate at which persons changed residence in twelve major SMSA's. (These rates comprise primarily local moves, but they also include some inter-county migration as well.) As can be seen, the highest rates are found in Houston, Los Angeles, San Francisco, and Washington. With the exception of Houston, these are precisely the cities in which higher fractions of the population are recent arrivals (duration of residence in present county under five years). Statistically, 48 percent of the variation in rates can be "explained" by this recency-of-arrival measure.

Characteristics of Origins and Destinations

From the standpoint of distribution, the factors that cause migrants to go where they do are critical. Once again, generalization is extremely difficult in view of the varied motives behind movement. Rural-to-urban flows, city-to-suburban movement, and inter-metropolitan moves are responses to fundamentally different situations. The last type is most relevant to the matter of California's future urban growth.

The majority of people moving to American cities today--especially long-distance migrants--come from other urban areas. Collectively, these flows erect an elaborate system in which metropolitan areas trade human capital. A metropolitan area

---

[13] It is interesting to note that in lagging regions we see the diametric opposite: most of the mobility-prone population has already departed and has never been replenished by a corresponding influx of human capital from the outside. In a relative sense, this population is frozen into immobility, and its stock of human capital is less able to adjust itself to slack economic conditions.

Table 9

METROPOLITAN MOBILITY RATES BY PREVALENCE
OF SHORT-DURATION RESIDENTS

SMSA	Residential Departure Rate, 1966-1967	Percentage of 1965 Population Residing in This County Less than Five Years
Baltimore	.171	14.7%
Chicago	.174	12.4
Cleveland	.164	11.0
Detroit	.166	13.2
Houston	.238	12.0
Los Angeles	.274	24.9
New York	.152	19.8
Philadelphia	.142	10.4
Pittsburgh	.166	8.6
St. Louis	.199	8.5
San Francisco	.237	23.9
Washington	.277	30.0
All SMSA's	.197	15.8

Source: Morrison, The Propensity to Move, Table 8.

that is exchanging manpower through a heavy influx and outflow (with a net positive advantage) remains economically vital and can adjust readily to shifting needs for manpower.

Research on inter-metropolitan migration shows that these flows are not responsive to local economic conditions in a symmetrical fashion, as a mechanical "push-pull" theory would suggest.[14] The pull of better economic conditions in a city is more

---

[14] Ira S. Lowry, Migration and Metropolitan Growth: Two Analytical Models (San Francisco: Chandler, 1966); John B. Lansing and Eva Mueller, The Geographic Mobility of Labor (Ann Arbor: Survey Research Center Institute for Social Research, 1967).

influential as a capturing mechanism than the push of poor opportunities at home is in encouraging departure. More specifically, the tide of in-migration to a receiving area varies closely with the attractiveness of its labor market to job seekers. Active labor demand, gauged by such aggregate indicators as wage rates and level of unemployment, attracts in-migrants from economically healthy localities as well as from less favorable labor market areas.

On the outflow side, however, migration from a metropolitan area appears to be largely spontaneous and insensitive to local labor market conditions. Contrary to intuition, people leave prosperous areas as readily as depressed ones. The rate of this spontaneous outflow seems to hinge on what kinds of people live in the area rather than on the prevailing economic climate. The reason for this is that different population segments vary enormously in their propensity to move, depending on their age, stage of their job career, and whether they have moved frequently before. A population heavily weighted with those who migrate readily--the young, short-term residents, the recently married, the highly educated, and other hypermobile groups--stands to lose many of its members. This loss by no means indicates a shrinkage of opportunities locally. Rather it reflects the normal geographic circulation of less inert segments of the population. To simplify a complex process: The prosperous area successfully replaces its spontaneous outflow by managing to attract an even heavier influx of migrants from elsewhere, but the depressed community typically is unable to replace its population loss. The weakness of its "pull," not the strength of its "push," is responsible for an area's overall net migratory loss (see Figure 6).

The result of all this is to create a complex system of self-replenishing regional and national migratory pools. There is, in effect, a virtually unlimited supply of "urbanization on the move" available to feed those areas in California that can continue to absorb new labor force at relatively high wages. Pools of migration-prone population from everywhere will flow selectively into a labor market so long as favorable conditions are sustained.[15]

An important consequence follows from the competitive nature of this process. While shrinkage of a local population is bounded ipso facto by the supply of migration-prone residents available to leave, growth is constrained only by competitive

---

[15] Harvey S. Perloff et al., Regions, Resources, and Economic Growth (Baltimore: Johns Hopkins University Press, 1960), pp. 590-92.

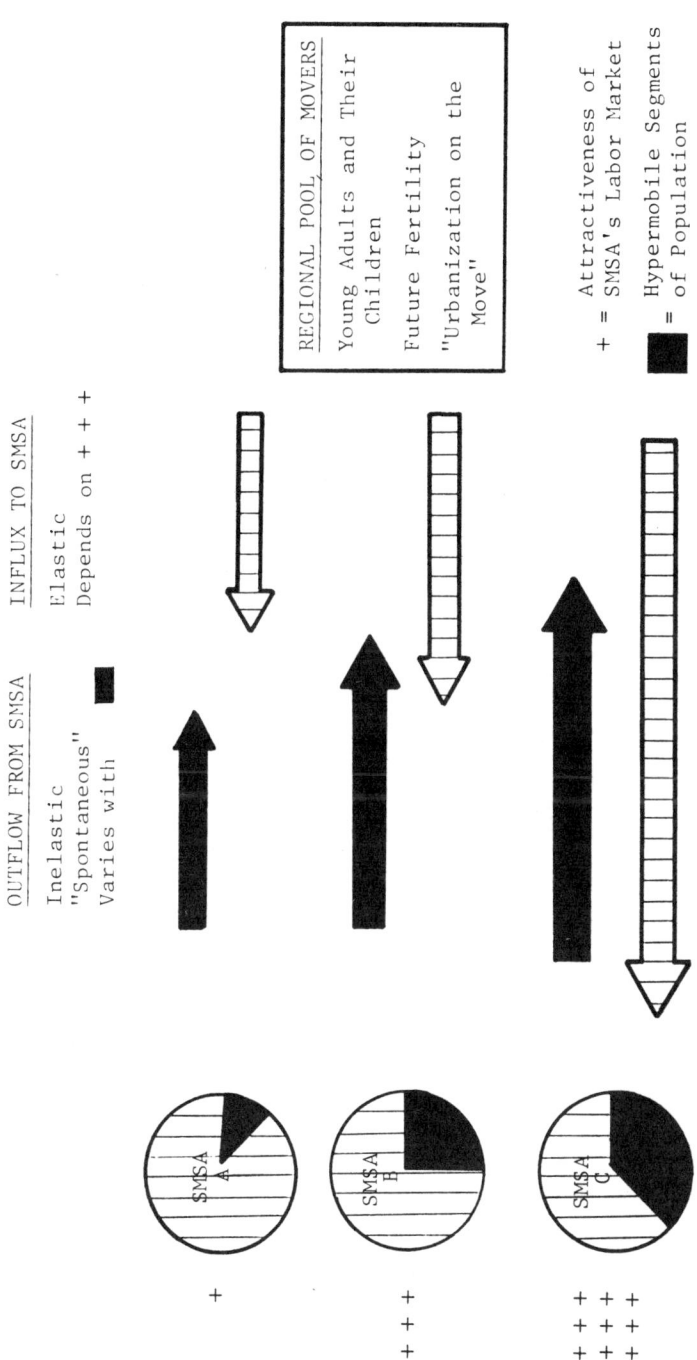

FIGURE 6. A PLUMBER'S DIAGRAM OF INTERMETROPOLITAN MIGRATION

disadvantage. With an unlimited source of potential growth available, the possibilities for increase are much greater than the capacity for decline. The effects of this imbalance show up clearly in the skewed pattern of variation in California's metropolitan migration rates. Table 4 shows that over a ten-year period, some metropolitan areas grew by as much as 50 percent through migration; none, though, lost more than 3.9 percent.

This interpretation of the migration process is consistent with research on how decisions to move are made. In choosing a destination, migrants consider only a narrow range of alternatives; they also rely heavily on friends and relatives for information on employment in a new locality and for help in adjusting. Nearly half choose destinations where one of their family already resides, and 7 out of 10 select destinations where there are friends or relatives.[16] This heavy reliance on familial and associational sources of information is especially characteristic of blue collar and Black segments of the population. Its effect is to circumscribe destination choices, limiting them to areas where friends and relatives have already settled. Thus, prior waves of in-migration to a city tend to be self-perpetuating, generating further population influx through a natural dissemination of information about employment opportunities and the availability of mechanisms for social support upon arrival.

Policy Implications

A Presidential message on population, several commission reports, and others have endorsed the concept of national and state urban growth policies.[17] Embodied in these proposals is a recognition that emerging settlement patterns and the complex systems of migration that support them need to be examined more critically and related to broader strategies for future urban growth. Distribution is only beginning to be envisioned as a proper domain of public policy. Political, ethical, and instrumental considerations have in the past discouraged serious exploration of practical alternatives that might exist. Our surprising

---

[16] Lansing and Mueller.

[17] See Advisory Commission on Intergovernmental Relations, Urban and Rural America: Policies for Future Growth (Washington: U.S. Government Printing Office, 1968); Daniel P. Moynihan, ed., Toward A National Urban Policy (New York: Basic Books, 1970); National Goals Research Staff, Toward Balanced Growth: Quantity with Quality (Washington: U.S. Government Printing Office, 1970); Lloyd Rodwin, Nations and Cities: A Comparison of Strategies for Urban Growth (Boston: Houghton Mifflin, 1970); Richard M. Nixon, "Presidential Message on Population," July 18, 1969.

THE ROLE OF MIGRATION IN CALIFORNIA'S GROWTH

indifference here stands in sharp contrast to the intensive efforts in many democratic Western European countries, where conscious distribution policies have been promulgated and acted upon with public support.[18]

A policy vacuum invites haphazard practices. Although the federal government is gradually evolving a more coherent policy to curb endless increase in numbers, it continues to implement other "hidden" policies having haphazard consequences for the migration and distribution of the population already alive. The building of highways, the guaranteeing of mortgages, the siting of federal installations, and the altering of zoning and tax laws are simultaneously redistributing employment opportunities, changing the racial and socioeconomic composition of cities and their suburbs, and altering the intricate system of incentives that attract the private sector. It is increasingly evident that the absence of a deliberate distribution policy cannot guard against other hidden ones. It merely facilitates passive acceptance of the consequences.

Migration and population redistribution unfortunately tend to be viewed as things that "just happen." The planner in Orange County prepares for the inevitable tide of new migrants; in St. Louis he is alerted to impending decline. Rather than be concerned with what may be impending, we ought to consider what we *want* to impend. Future programs for housing, mass transportation, new cities, and the development of energy and water resources will each pose alternatives for population settlement. Bringing these choices into synchronization necessitates formulating objectives and setting priorities.

A broader statement of objectives is essential. Sorely needed is a policy on population distribution--a clear and concise blueprint of what the State of California would hope to see develop during the remainder of this century. The California State Office of Planning correctly notes that government cannot and should not use its powers to affect population distribution without broad popular support. "To gain that support," it continues, "its rationale for action would have to be explicit, sensible, and fair."[19] This rationale is a critical element in the

---

[18] See H. ter Heide, "Population Redistribution Policies in Western European Countries," paper given at the International Union for the Scientific Study of Population, General Conference, London, 1969.

[19] California State Office of Planning, *California State Development Plan Program, Phase II Report* (1968), p. 66.

government's ability to carry out a coherent policy over a long time period.

To some, governmental policy in this area sounds unavoidably intrusive. Quite the contrary, a policy designed to foster a better pattern of settlement would not need to coerce movement directly or compel people to live where they did not choose to. The existing momentum of population flows is itself a massive potential resource for transferring and realigning population. The dynamics here--both economic and social-psychological--suggest several leverage points where policies might operate unobtrusively. Aggregate population influx (but not outflow) is elastic. Embedded within this relationship is a tendency for destination choices to hinge on the presence of relatives and/or friends. Both of these patterns suggest that policies should operate on the inflow side of migration, focusing effort on destinations as areas to be cultivated through an ensemble of indirect measures.

A policy promoting long-range distribution objectives need not sponsor movement directly. Rather, it should operate on the existing flow of spontaneous migration, steering it toward selected areas designated as preferred growth centers in accordance with an overall blueprint for future urban settlement. In providing services and making capital investments, government would ask not only "How much will it cost?" but also "Will it encourage more people to move there?"

Two general sets of policy measures for steering migratory inflow are needed. One set should promote active labor demand at selected growth centers. The other should intervene in the destination-choice process.

Measures for Promoting Active Labor Demand

Although California would be unlikely to succeed with a policy encouraging out-migration, it may well be able to regulate and steer the inflow of population by policies influencing new employment. Local concentrations of federal and state spending play a major role in stimulating labor demand. The placement of universities, defense installations, and NASA-type facilities, and the selective awarding of defense contracts have all proven to be accelerators of population growth in Southern California and along the Gulf Coast. Yet these investments rarely are made with any sense of potentially beneficial or adverse demographic consequences.

Financial incentives, such as tax, loan, or direct payment arrangements for business and industrial location, could also channel industrial growth and its derivative labor demand.[20] Location decisions might be influenced indirectly by routing highways and mass transportation to alter relative accessibility in favor of preferred configurations of industrial settlement. Deliberate investment in transportation should foster population distribution as well as merely service it.

Measures for Guiding Destination Choices

The promotion of labor demand could be augmented by programs to reinforce selection of preferred localities by migratory segments of the population. Resettlement allowances and on-the-job training programs, if tied to specific destinations, would be one strategy for steering spontaneous migratory flow to areas of the state in which new industries are locating.

Another mode of intervention is suggested by the "friends and relatives" linkage. Redirecting migration necessitates penetrating the highly personal information system of potential migrants. The case can be made for trying to capitalize on the strong influence of information links through family and friends on where migrants go. This might be done, for example, by setting up selective resettlement allowances and opportunities for on-the-job training. Offered to a calculated mix of migrants, these might enhance a designated growth area's power to draw others from the same place of origin.

Conclusion

James Sundquist recently suggested that population distribution policy may have to await a major shift in national psychology.[21] His contention that policies setting upper limits on local growth are unrealistic for the foreseeable future is undoubtedly valid. Yet policies on population distribution need not imply a frontal attack on the boosterism mentality favoring endless growth for growth's sake. Instruments like those just outlined are neither intrusive nor farfetched. Their efficacy in achieving distribution objectives, however, would depend on how well they can be orchestrated. Admittedly, some would take greater effort to implement than others.

---

[20] European countries rely heavily on such measures to implement distributional objectives (see H. ter Heide).

[21] James L. Sundquist, "Where Shall They Live?" The Public Interest, 18 (Winter 1970), pp. 88-100.

The perceived freedom of choice of those migrating would remain unaffected and hence should help deter objections. Measures designed to guide industrial location and public investment and spending, however, would be difficult to implement consistently. Public policy on private industrial location has had limited effect and proven difficult to sustain in the past. Localism is a formidable obstacle to making public investment a workable instrument of any policy. The research evidence indicates that, whether through inadvertence or design, future population and urban growth will continue to be distributed selectively and unevenly. Although a single "optimal" statewide distribution of population would be difficult to agree on, there are likely to be certain patterns of settlement that are more advantageous than others. To move in these directions requires three ingredients.

One, as noted before, is a state policy on population distribution--delineating the issues being addressed, stating the objectives to be promoted, and identifying appropriate strategies for influencing existing migratory trends. Second is a suitable institutional arrangement to separate the direction of long-term policy from the immediate crosscurrents of political bargaining. A permanent state-level organization--like the New York State Urban Development Corporation--would be required to maintain this independence. Finally, more frequent and current demographic information is needed between decennial censuses. Estimating population changes under existing arrangements, as John Lindsay has noted, is like chasing a black cat in a dark room. Parts of the analysis presented here refer of necessity back to the 1955-1960 period--it is the "latest news."[22] Specifically, policymakers need to know how the magnitude and composition of population flows are changing. Too often, information acquisition is geared to obtaining massive detail at one time point.

The above diagnoses may have the ring of truth, but the prescriptions for curing the malaise are admittedly vague. One is reminded of the story about the young man, just turned twenty-one, who came home to find that his wealthy father had bought him a hundred concubines for his birthday. The son reacted with a mixture of gratitude and dismay: "Dad, it's not that I don't know what to do--it's just that I don't know where to begin."

---

[22]To be sure, these data will be ten years more current within a matter of months.

FOREIGN MIGRATION INTO CALIFORNIA

José Hernández

Brief History of Immigration into California to 1950

Immigrants have always been an important component of California's population. However, from the time of statehood until the early 1950's, the percentage of foreign-born persons in the total population steadily declined, as the original settlers and early immigrants aged and died. There was a continual flow into California of immigrants who had first settled in other places (in particular, Europeans from the Northeastern and Middle Atlantic states) during the first half of the twentieth century, but this migration did not reach a level which would offset the increased mortality rate among the foreign-born, and was probably to be expected, given California's rapidly growing population and the westward movement which characterized the migratory patterns of Americans in general (Table 1).

Perhaps the most notable instance of the flow of foreigners into California before 1950 was that of Mexicans, most of whom came directly from the country of origin prior to 1930. In contrast to the pattern in other Southwestern states, during the 1930's and 1940's California did not have a decline in this nationality group. Return migration to Mexico, motivated by the Depression and World War II, was offset by a flow into the state from other places in the United States. California became a focus for resettlement, and was not affected by the general pattern of dispersal of Mexican immigrants during these decades. As a result, the Mexican nationality group remained a major component of the foreign population of the state.[1]

Recent Immigration into California, 1950-1970

The principal sources of information for the period 1950-1970 are the Immigration and Naturalization Service Reports, which provide annual figures for new immigrants according to the state of intended residence, and the results of the Annual Alien

---

[1] José Hernández, "A Demographic Profile of Mexican Immigration to the United States, 1910-1950," Journal of Inter-American Studies, VIII, No. 2 (July 1966), pp. 472-496.

Table 1

FOREIGN-BORN PERSONS AS A COMPONENT OF THE TOTAL POPULATION OF CALIFORNIA, 1860-1969

Date	Total Population	Foreign-Born[a]	Percent
1860	379,994	146,528	38.6
1870	560,247	209,831	37.5
1880	864,694	292,874	33.9
1890	1,213,398	366,309	30.2
1900	1,485,053	423,240	28.5
1910	2,377,549	594,387	25.0
1920	3,426,861	781,324	22.8
1930	5,677,251	1,118,418	19.7
1940	6,907,387	1,125,904	16.3
1950	10,586,223	1,132,726	10.7
1960	15,720,860	1,343,686	8.5
1969 (est.)	19,443,000	[1,650,000 - 2,065,000]	8.5-10.6

[a] Adjusted, 1900-1950, to include estimates of foreign-born Chinese and Japanese. The estimate for 1969 represents the calculated range of probable values for the total foreign-born population.

Sources: U.S. Bureau of the Census, Washington, D.C.: U.S. Census of Population: 1950, Vol. II, Characteristics of the Population, Part 5, California; 1960, California, Final Report PC(1)-6 A-D; Population Estimates and Projections, Series P-25, No. 436, January 1970. U.S. Immigration and Naturalization Service, Washington, D.C., Annual Reports, 1950-1969.

Address Program, which began requiring yearly registration of immigrants in 1952, by way of a mail-back form available at U.S. Post Office stations. Census data are available for 1950 and 1960 which provide information regarding foreign-born persons and the second generation of persons having foreign parentage. As yet, the published results of the 1970 Census do not include data related to the foreign population.

These sources clearly document a significant change from the downward trend of the 1860-1950 period. From 1950 on, the flow of immigrants into California and the percentage of foreigners in the population have increased. The percentage of immigrants specifying California as their intended state of residence has increased from about 8 percent to over 20, making California a close second in this regard to the State of New York. However, during the early 1960's California's share of new immigrants surpassed New York's by a sizable margin, reaching a total of approximately one quarter of the immigrants entering in 1962-1963 (Figure 1). The very recent dip can be attributed to new restrictive legislation, made effective in 1968, which limited the entry of certain nationality groups (principally Canadians, Mexicans, and Central Americans)--immigrants having a propensity for settlement in California.

In like manner, the percentage of aliens reporting residence in California has steadily increased from about 13 percent of the U.S. total in 1950 to approximately 25 percent in 1969. California has become the state with the largest proportion of the national total of aliens; New York, which occupies second place, has only 18 percent. Most other states have much smaller percentages, especially those surrounding California in the Pacific and Rocky Mountain regions.

As a result, the percentage of the state's population comprised of aliens has been steadily increasing, reaching a level of approximately 5 percent of the estimated total in 1969. This does not include aliens who have become naturalized United States citizens and are no longer obliged to report annually. On the basis of census figures for the entire foreign-born group in 1960 and records of naturalization, it seems reasonable to assume that the foreign-born naturalized segment comprises another 3.5 to 5.6 percent of the state's population. (This is the basis of the 1969 estimate presented in Table 1.) However, these figures are only partially representative of the impact of immigration on the social and economic life of the state, since they do not include persons born in the United States of foreign parentage, who have inevitably been influenced by the immigrant status of their parents. Rough estimates of this factor lead to a tentative conclusion that the total foreign "stock" (both first and second generations) is currently in the vicinity of 20 percent of the state's population, and may be as high as one quarter. Since

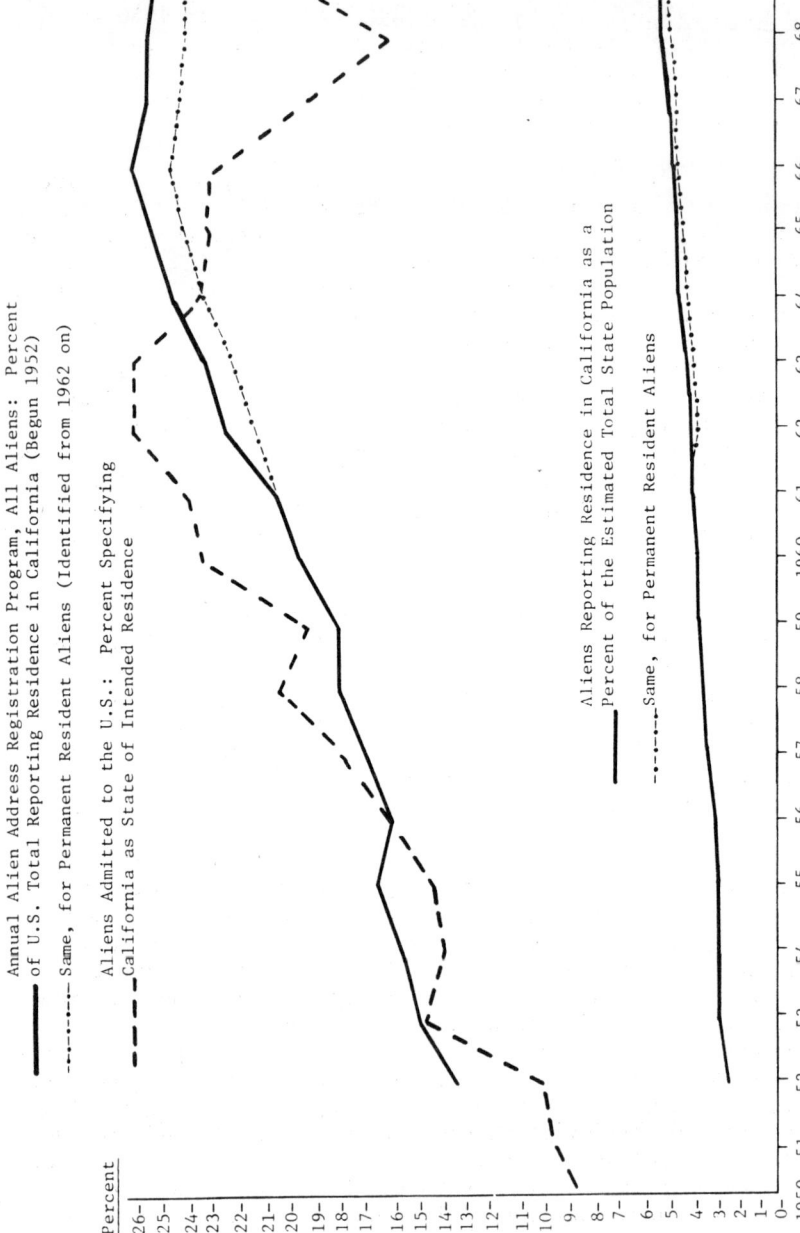

FIGURE 1. MEASURES OF ANNUAL GROWTH AND DISTRIBUTION, FOREIGN POPULATION OF CALIFORNIA, 1950-1969

recent information about the second generation is not available and the principal interest in studying foreigners in this paper relates to the immigration itself, the native ethnic groups will not be considered in detail.

Principal Nationality Groups

An important element for our understanding of the dynamics of the new immigration is a study of recent trends in the composition of California's foreign-born population, according to countries of origin. Data coming from the alien registration reports and the 1950 and 1960 Censuses suggest a four-fold classification of the principal nationality groups:

1. Declining Old Immigrant Groups (including those with few recent additions);

2. Replenished Old Immigrant Groups (having a moderate number of recent additions);

3. Old Immigrant Groups Showing a Renewed Wave of Immigration;

4. New Immigrant Groups with Sizable Recent Additions.

By way of introduction to these categories, it is important to note that in 1960 the median age of foreign-born persons in California was 51.1 years, more than 20 years higher than the median age figure of 27.9 for the native-born population.[2] This means that a rather large proportion were older persons who were likely to have come to the United States during the 1890-1930 period of heavy immigration, predominantly from Southern and Eastern Europe, and--of special importance for California--from Mexico, and to a lesser extent, from China and Japan. These groups, along with Northern and Western Europeans who came in moderate numbers during the same period, can be designated as "Old Immigrants," not only because of the greater likelihood of their having older persons, but also because of their long-term establishment as components of California's population.

The extent of recent immigration among these Old Immigrant Groups can be measured by three statistical indices:

(1) The percent increase or decrease from the 1950 to the 1960 Census count;

---

[2] U.S. Bureau of the Census, <u>U.S. Census of Population: 1960</u>, California, Final Report PC(1)-6 A-D.

(2) The ratio of native-born persons of foreign parentage to foreign-born persons, according to country of origin (based on 1960 Census data). Theoretically, the higher this measure, the closer the immigrants approach the final stages of the human life cycle;

(3) The number of aliens reporting residence in California in 1969 as compared with the number of foreign-born enumerated in the 1950 Census. This would detect increases and declines, either by way of death, naturalization, or migration out of California during the 19-year period. (Factors affecting this comparison are discussed on pp. 71-73 below.)

For the entire foreign population of California these measures were:

(1) +15.7 percent change, 1950-1960;

(2) 1.97 (or almost 2) persons of foreign parentage for every immigrant;

(3) 857,585 aliens reporting in 1969, as compared with 1,132,726 foreign-born persons enumerated in the 1950 Census.

As a first-order conclusion it may be said that, while a general increase is evident (reconfirming the recent upward trend in immigration), the effects of substantial aging, mortality, and naturalization are also clearly present, which is in accord with the high median age previously mentioned. This apparent contradiction can be understood in terms of the significant differences which result when these indices are calculated according to nationality groups.

The Declining Old Immigrant Groups show negative percentages or very slight positive gains for the 1950-1960 period, and in most cases, their generation ratios are above the state average for all nationality groups. Perhaps the most dramatic change is the sharp decline which appears in each case when the 1950 Census total is compared with the alien registration figure in 1969 (Table 2). It is clear that these nationality groups are representative of a rapidly diminishing segment of the state's population; it can also be inferred that most of the immigrants in these groups are relatively old persons, representative of the upper half of the median age figure of 51.1 years, and that many have become naturalized U.S. citizens.

Replenished Old Immigrant Groups show a moderate level of recent additions by way of immigration or movement to California from other states. (This category is made up of groups having

FOREIGN MIGRATION INTO CALIFORNIA

Table 2

OLD IMMIGRANT NATIONALITY GROUPS WITH FEW RECENT ADDITIONS: CALIFORNIA, 1950-1969[a]

Country of Origin	Number of Foreign-Born, 1950	Percent Change, 1950-1960	Generation Ratio, 1960[b]	Number of Aliens Reporting, 1969[c]
Italy	104,215	-1.8	2.40	13,933
U.S.S.R.	66,552	+3.2	2.27	3,214
Sweden	31,067	-14.5	3.55	4,913
Ireland	30,016	-4.7	3.90	5,346
Austria	20,818	+2.1	2.47	2,896
Denmark	18,053	-3.0	3.07	3,995
Norway	15,780	-0.4	3.55	2,863
Switzerland	15,143	0.0	1.90	3,727
Greece	14,330	+1.1	1.57	3,732
Spain	10,890	0.0	2.01	3,862

[a] Groups having 10,000 or more persons enumerated as foreign-born residents of California in the 1950 census.

[b] Number enumerated as born in U.S. of foreign parentage of a specific nationality/foreign-born of that nationality.

[c] As residents of California, under the Annual Alien Address Program, U.S. Immigration and Naturalization Service.

Sources: See Table 1.

a percentage increase from 1950 to 1960 of 10 to 50 percent--typically in the 30-40 percent range--or an annual rate of increase close to the average for the total population of California during the same period.) Thus, their continuity as significant elements of the state's population has been assured. In most cases, their generation ratios fall below the average for the foreign population in general, indicating an unusually large proportion of young persons in the early stages of the human life cycle. The numbers of aliens from Canada and the United Kingdom (which have many recent entries) reporting residence in California in 1969 approach the 1950 totals for immigrants from these two countries. This relationship does not hold in the case of aliens from Germany and the other nationality groups in this category, probably reflecting a decline in immigration during the 1960's and a differential in rates of naturalization. Undoubtedly many immigrants from Poland, Yugoslavia, and Hungary were refugees who entered during the post-World War II period, when special provisions allowed for greater numbers from these nations than the stipulated quotas; and it seems likely that refugees having no legal status of citizenship in other countries would have a greater tendency to obtain naturalized citizenship in the United States (Table 3).

The third category of Old Immigrant Groups, which by definition experienced much larger additions during the 1950-1970 period, shows ten-year gains of at least 50 percent, or an annual growth rate exceeding California's general population growth factor by a substantial margin. Generation ratios vary considerably, and reflect the individual characteristics of each nationality group, as well as the relative distance, in time, between the new wave of immigrants and those entering at earlier stages of the state's history.

Perhaps the most telling statistic is the number of aliens reporting California addresses in 1969, which is high in each case. For example, the generation ratio for Portuguese immigrants would, by itself, classify this group as Declining Old Immigrant, since on this basis alone one would expect the 1969 figure to be much lower than the 1950 enumeration. However, Portuguese aliens reporting in 1969 slightly exceeded the number of immigrants in 1950, which indicates continued growth despite the effects of mortality and naturalization. Immigration from the Netherlands, Japan, China (Taiwan),[3] and the Philippines seems to have been even more intense. California's geographic location was undoubtedly an important attractive feature for potential immigrants from these countries of origin. The Dutch immigration was an outcome of events surrounding strife between the Netherlands and Indonesia in the post-World War II period, and the eventual dissolution in 1954 of their Union; many Dutch nationals leaving the former colony in Southeast Asia emigrated to the United States and settled in California.

---

[3] During recent years, the Immigration and Naturalization Reports have listed immigrants coming from Hong Kong separately from those coming from China (Taiwan). Nationally, there were about three immigrants from China (Taiwan) for every one immigrant from Hong Kong during the 1960-1969 period, with a nine-year total from Hong Kong in the vicinity of 22,000. For purposes of the present report, only immigrants classified as coming from China (Taiwan) were included in the analysis.

Table 3

IMMIGRANT NATIONALITY GROUPS ACCORDING TO FORMER STATUS AND LEVEL OF RECENT ADDITIONS: CALIFORNIA, 1950-1969[a]

Country of Origin	Number of Foreign-Born, 1950	Percent Change, 1950-1960	Generation Ratio, 1960	Number of Aliens Reporting, 1969
A. Old Immigrant Groups with Moderate Recent Additions				
Canada	110,754	+34.8	1.63	86,667
United Kingdom	104,347	+13.3	1.79	63,914
Germany	70,791	+14.9	2.64	34,715
Poland	23,776	+34.1	2.45	2,745
France	18,447	+11.6	1.90	8,216
Yugoslavia	13,801	+31.9	1.55	3,834
Hungary	13,453	+47.2	1.55	3,211
B. Old Immigrant Groups with Renewed Wave of Immigration				
Mexico	162,309	+53.1	1.80	369,606
Portugal	15,134	+64.3	2.80	15,808
Netherlands	12,270	+91.6	1.24	18,710
Japan	--[b]	+50.0	1.09	22,837
China (Taiwan)	--	+50.0	0.80	29,205
Philippines	--	+50.0	1.91	27,010
C. New Immigrant Groups with Sizable Recent Additions				
Central America	--	+100.0	0.57	34,989
Cuba	--	+50.0	1.01	16,790

[a] Sources and annotations same as in Tables 1 and 2.

[b] Not available; minimum percent change, 1950-1960, was estimated on the basis of immigration and alien address report data.

It is difficult to judge the trends in migration from China, Japan, and the Philippines, since data published by the U.S. Bureau of the Census prior to 1960 provide country of origin information for the foreign white population only. Data available on racial types seem to indicate that the longest established of these nationality groups is the Chinese, followed by the Japanese, who began appearing in substantial numbers in 1910, 1920, and 1930, and by the Filipinos, who numbered only 2,674 in 1920, but increased to a total of 30,470 in 1930, and added about 10,000 more in the following decade.[4] This historical progression is reflected in the generation ratios, which document the extent of the gap dividing earlier settlers coming before the unsettled circumstances surrounding World War II from those entering after 1950, when entry regulations were somewhat more favorable. By then, most of the early Chinese immigrants had died and perhaps many of the second generation also; thus, the generation ratio in 1960 is primarily representative of the new wave of young immigrants and their children.

The new immigration from the Orient was particularly dramatic from 1950 to 1959, when the annual number of aliens admitted as immigrants to the United States increased from 76 to 5,851 Japanese, 1,494 to 5,722 Chinese, and 595 to 2,633 Filipinos. Thus, it is quite likely that a major portion of the foreign-born residents of California counted by the 1960 Census were very recent immigrants; on the strength of this evidence, it seems reasonable to estimate at least a 50 percent increase from 1950 to 1960, as shown in Table 3.

The most notable element of the new immigration, in terms of magnitude, was the rather large entry of immigrants from Mexico. As mentioned before, the net totals for legal entry of Mexican citizens into the United States in the 1930's and 1940's remained at a stable low level, or even declined as a result of return migration. However, due to the migration into California of Mexican immigrants from other states, this nationality group maintained its position as the largest among the foreign-born populations of the state. When immigration began again in the 1950's, the new arrivals showed a strong preference for settlement in California, thereby reinforcing the earlier internal movement. This trend was intensified during the 1960's, to the extent that at the present time there are probably twice as many foreign-born Mexicans in California as there were in 1959.

The Mexican generation ratio of 1.80 in 1960 reflects the situation before the upswing, and probably includes a fair

---

[4] U.S. Bureau of the Census, U.S. Census of Population: 1960, Vol. II, Characteristics of the Population, Part 5, California.

number of first- and second-generation persons who came to California during the 1930's and 1940's. It is quite likely that the current ratio is somewhat lower, a conjecture supported by our knowledge of the age-structure of the new Mexican immigrant group, which will be discussed below. In any case, this figure does not adequately indicate the longitudinal impact of the Mexican immigration into California, since it is limited to persons born in the United States of at least one parent born in Mexico and excludes the descendants of the state's population before acquisition by the United States, as well as the grandchildren of immigrants entering California during the period of heaviest immigration (1900-1930).

The fourth and final category of immigrant groups is comprised of two nationality or regional groups which were only residual elements of California's population before 1950, but which have recently entered the state in moderately substantial numbers: immigrants from the six Central American nations, which for purposes of convenience have been grouped together in this study, and aliens (mostly refugees) from Cuba. Both of these groups probably made up a rather small portion of the foreign-born residents of California, about 35,000 in number, who were classified as coming from "other America" in the 1950 Census-- that is, the entire Western Hemisphere except Mexico and Canada. In the 1960 Census, the foreign-born from Central America numbered 19,048, and since then this total has probably doubled. Similarly, there were only 3,108 Cuban foreign-born residents of California in the 1960 Census, which was taken only three months after the victory of the Castro revolution. By 1969, there were more than 16,000 Cuban aliens reporting residence in California in the Annual Address Program; thus, their rate of growth far exceeds that of the other nationality groups. Both collectively and individually, the Central American immigrant groups had generation ratios below 1.0 in 1960, indicating the relative absence of previous immigration and a preponderance of first-generation persons. The Cuban group had a slightly higher ratio, but still much lower than the level found among the Old Immigrant Groups.

General Consequences of Recent Immigration into California

The impact of the new immigration on the nationality composition of California's foreign population can be summarized by comparing the percentages of foreign-born enumerated by the 1950 Census and the corresponding measures among aliens reporting residence in the state in 1969 (Figure 2). This comparison only suggests general trends, since the data for 1969 refer to aliens reporting, and not to the entire foreign-born population. Excluded are about half of the foreign-born--principally those who are naturalized citizens, no longer obliged to report their addresses. It is quite likely that most of those excluded belong

FIGURE 2. COMPOSITION OF THE FOREIGN POPULATION OF CALIFORNIA, BY COUNTRY OR REGION OF ORIGIN, 1950 AND 1969

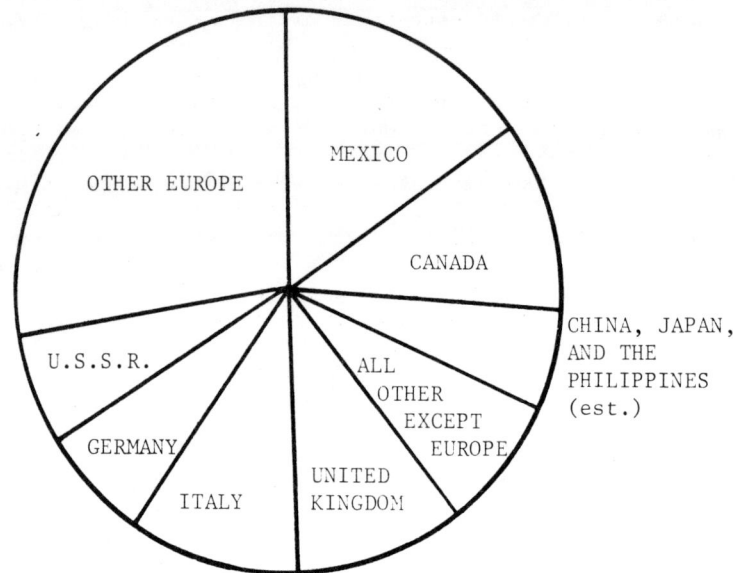

1950: PERSONS ENUMERATED AS FOREIGN-BORN IN THE CENSUS

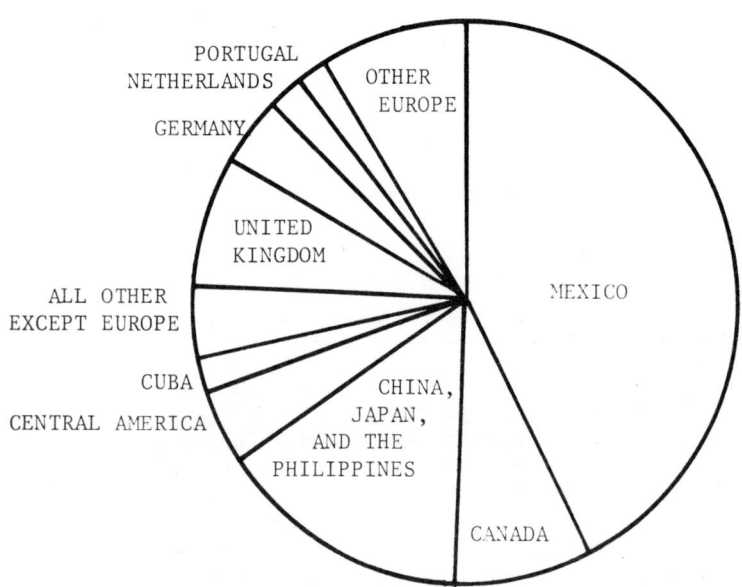

1969: PERSONS REPORTING UNDER THE ALIEN ADDRESS PROGRAM

Sources: As in Tables 1-4.

to the Declining Old Immigrant Groups; these groups generally have naturalization rates of at least 3 percent annually, out of the total reporting addresses during the previous year. At this rate, a major portion of a population of immigrants would become naturalized citizens during a twenty-year period, unless of course their numbers were replenished by new immigrants. These groups can also be expected to decline by an annual mortality rate of at least 2 percent--probably much higher--in view of their advanced age.

If naturalization and a few decades of residence in the United States are accepted as indicating integration into the social and economic life of the nation, the importance of Declining Old Immigrant Groups diminishes with respect to policy formation for the distinctively "foreign" element of the population. In other words, for purposes of reaching decisions regarding measures appropriate for individuals representing an unintegrated or partially integrated segment of California's population, it seems of greater relevance to focus attention on nationality groups having large numbers of recent additions. These are less likely to have many naturalized citizens, and more typically include immigrants in the early stages of life cycle development.

The relative sizes of these groups are shown in Figure 2. The proportion of immigrants from countries such as Italy, the U.S.S.R., Ireland, and the Scandinavian and Eastern European nations has declined substantially, while the proportion from the Latin American nations, Asia, Canada, and the four Western European nations having moderate additions during recent times has greatly increased. These groups having a recent wave of immigration are likely to add significant numbers to California's population through reproduction. For this reason we have selected them for special study.

The New Immigrant Groups

Data drawn from the statistics on aliens reporting residence in California from 1959 to 1969 are presented in Table 4. As already noted, the total of all aliens reporting showed a sizable increase, to the extent that at the present time California has one-quarter of the national aggregate. Within this population of foreign-born, the nationality groups we have selected for study generally have unusually high rates of increase. Mexico, Central America, China, and Cuba show the highest rates of increase. Canada, the United Kingdom, the Philippines, the Netherlands, and Portugal have moderate rates--higher than that for the "all other" category and somewhat lower than that for all aliens. In the case of Germany and Japan, a declining trend is discernible.

Table 4

MEASURES OF POPULATION GROWTH AND DISTRIBUTION AMONG PERMANENT
RESIDENT ALIENS REPORTING UNDER THE ALIEN ADDRESS PROGRAM
1959-1969 (INCLUDES NATIONALITY GROUPS WITH 15,000
OR MORE REPORTING CALIFORNIA RESIDENCE IN 1969)

Country of Origin	Percent Change, 1959-1969	California		Percent of U.S. Total Reporting Residence in California	
		Percent of All Aliens in State			
		1959	1969	1959	1969
Mexico	+93.2	36.2	42.4	38.0	52.7
Canada	+40.5	11.9	10.2	20.2	23.2
United Kingdom	+57.5	7.7	7.3	15.6	21.8
Central America	+149.1	2.7	4.0	42.7	45.0
Germany	+28.9	5.1	4.0	10.0	16.0
China	+99.2	2.8	3.4	34.5	39.7
Philippines	+52.9	3.4	3.1	29.1	35.8
Japan	-10.8	4.9	2.6	34.6	40.6
Netherlands	+59.7	2.2	2.2	25.2	42.5
Cuba	+842.7	0.3	1.9	2.9	6.3
Portugal	+53.6	1.9	1.8	32.4	22.8
All Others	+35.1	20.9	17.1	8.8	12.8
TOTAL	+65.0	100.0	100.0	17.9	24.9

Source: U.S. Immigration and Naturalization Service, Washington, D.C., Annual Reports, 1959-1969.

FOREIGN MIGRATION INTO CALIFORNIA

Recent differences in propensity to settle in California seem to account for the changes in the composition of the alien population of the state from 1959 to 1969: the percentage of aliens from Mexico, Central America, China, and Cuba increased, while the other nationality groups maintained approximately the same percent or declined. Currently, Mexicans comprise by far the largest group, followed by the Canadians and the British; these three make up 60 percent of the aliens reporting residence in California. The other nationalities selected for special study individually account for less than 5 percent; most of those included in the "all other" category have figures below 1 percent. Thus, although Central Americans, Chinese, and Cubans show high rates of increase, they as yet do not comprise a large proportion of the state's foreign population.

With regard to preference for residence in California, the data on intended state of settlement indicate that all of the selected nationalities (except Portugal) have an increased percentage choosing this state, from 1959 to 1969. California seems to be more attractive to immigrants from Mexico, Central America, China, the Philippines, Japan, and the Netherlands, as compared with other nationality groups and the "all other" category. This is in accord with the geographic proximity factor already mentioned, and may indicate a certain reluctance to move beyond California to other states of the Union. Immigrants from Canada, the United Kingdom, and Portugal currently have a somewhat less intense preference for California--about average for all aliens, but clearly higher than among immigrants from Germany and Cuba, whose degree of preference resembles that of immigrant groups not selected for special study (the "all other" category). For Germans and Cubans, the principal focus of attraction and settlement has been the East Coast of the United States.

In summary, it can be stated that the immigrant groups showing the greatest recent gains and greatest propensity for settlement in California are those from Mexico, Central America, China, the Philippines, and the Netherlands. Groups having a sustained, moderate level of growth and preference for California include those from Canada, the United Kingdom, and Portugal. The sharp increase of immigrants from Cuba seems to be primarily the outcome of the dispersal of the very large population of refugees admitted to the United States during the last decade. Compared with the situation in other states, the tendency among Cubans to select California for settlement is about average. In contrast, we find that the Japanese nationality group, declining during the last decade, continues to show a decided preference for California. Finally, German immigrants are typical of the "all other" nationality groups, having below average rates of growth in and preference for California.

Foreseeable Demographic Impact of Recent Immigration

At first glance, one would expect the greatest influence on future population trends in California to come from the nationality groups having the greatest recent gains and the strongest preference for residence in the state; an intermediate level of influence by groups showing a moderate degree of increase and preference; and so forth. While in general this line of reasoning is valid, the conclusions would have to be modified if a given nationality group (despite its size, propensity for entry and settlement) represented a population unlikely to contribute many additional members by way of reproduction. This would be the case if the immigrants were predominantly older persons in the post-reproductive stages of the life cycle, or if they included only a very small number of children, adolescents, and young adults. Conversely, a small group of immigrants might bring about a significant increase, over a period of time, if they were predominantly young adults, adolescents, and children, and if their country of origin had a pattern of high fertility rates and rapid population growth.

In order to explore these factors, age and sex data were gathered from the Immigration and Naturalization Report for aliens admitted to the United States in 1969; this information was supplemented by data on vital rates in the country of origin.[5] The age and sex indices for immigrants from the countries selected for study are presented in Figure 3. However, these refer to the immigrant populations in the United States as a whole, and to only one year; thus, there might be some variation in the case of California. Similarly, birth and death rates typical of the country of origin may not closely resemble the demographic condition of the immigrants, who represent only a small and selected fraction of the home country's population. Despite these limitations, some knowledge can be gained of use in policy formation, since the immigrant groups and their countries of origin show rather wide differences, allowing for moderate margins of error. The conclusions, therefore, should be interpreted as merely suggestive of trends, rather than as precise statements of probability.

The pyramids presented in the following pages (Figure 3) represent distributions based on the total number of immigrants admitted from a given nation; other derived statistics include the mean or "average" ages of males and females; the percent of each sex below 40 and below 20 years of age; the sex ratio, or the number of males per 100 females (of all ages); and the

---

[5] Nathan Keyfitz and Wilhelm Flieger, World Population: An Analysis of Vital Data (Chicago: University of Chicago Press, 1968).

dependency ratio, or the number of persons 60 years old and over, and those under 20 years of age, per 100 persons presumably in their economically productive years--from 20 to 59. The last measure is a particularly useful statistic from a policy viewpoint, since it is an approximate indicator of the economic burden which immigrants bring with them in terms of children, adolescents, and people approaching retirement and old age.

Concerning the age and sex composition of recent immigrants to the United States, we know in general that most are young adults between the ages of 20 and 39 and include a somewhat greater number of women than men; it is also known that a preferential scale is used in connection with admission, favoring the spouses, children, and parents of U.S. citizens, and that many of the immigrants selected on the basis of occupational skills are single. Thus, at the present time, immigrants do not typically comprise many integral family units, made up of parents and children, as was the case in earlier periods of U.S. history.[6]

In view of these general patterns, we have chosen to arrange the age and sex data for nine of the eleven immigrant groups along a continuum, ranging from the groups most indicative of a family-type migration to those showing the least evidence of such and the greatest likelihood of including many unrelated individuals. In the first few cases, as might be expected, the age-sex pyramids resemble the corresponding pyramids for the countries of origin. Those further away from the family type depart significantly from the home countries' profiles, revealing the direction taken by age and sex selection and providing a basis for characterizing the types of immigrants entering the United States as individuals.

The most typically "family-type" immigrant groups are those from Mexico and Portugal, since a large proportion of the immigrants from these countries are children and adolescents, and the percentages at each age level are approximately balanced between the sexes--in line with a general sex ratio approaching a one-to-one relationship. These two groups differ somewhat in that the Mexican immigrants are generally younger than the Portuguese and have a much larger base of children and adolescents. This is in accord with the demographic situations in the countries of origin, since Mexico is a typically high fertility/young age-structure nation. In contrast, Portugal has the typical European pattern of low fertility (with a birth rate about half of Mexico's) and a significantly older age-structure.

---

[6] For greater details regarding the general characteristics of recent immigrants, see "The New Immigration," The Annals of the American Academy of Political and Social Science, Vol. 367 (September 1966), pp. 1-149.

FIGURE 3. AGE-SEX PYRAMIDS OF IMMIGRANTS TO THE UNITED STATES, BY SELECTED COUNTRIES OF ORIGIN, 1969

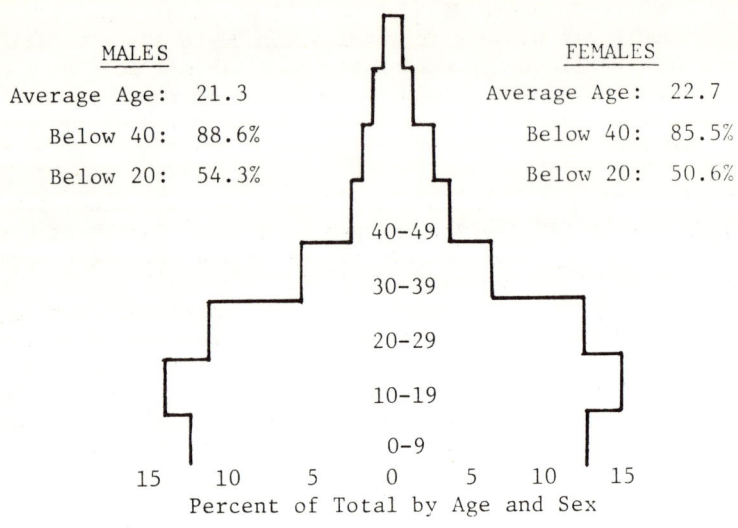

MEXICAN IMMIGRANTS TO THE UNITED STATES, 1969

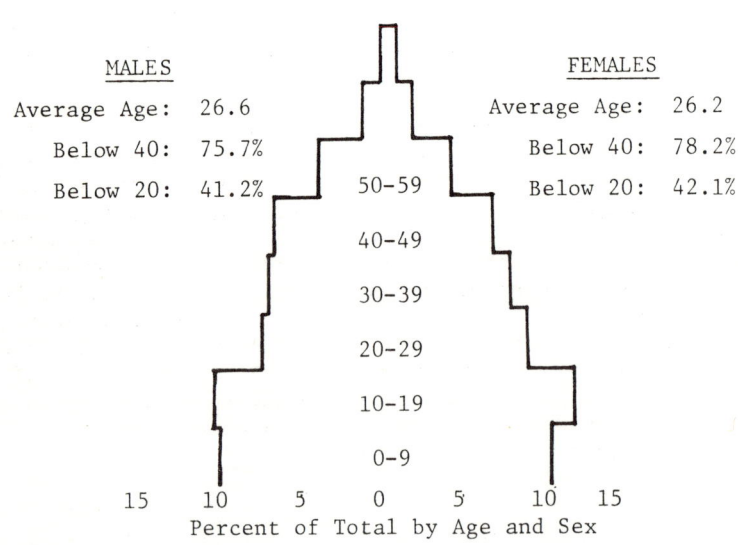

PORTUGUESE IMMIGRANTS TO THE UNITED STATES, 1969

The Canadian immigrants have an age-sex pyramid resembling that of the Mexicans, but revealing a decided tendency for family migration during the early stages of development (pre-school and pre-adolescent children) with a much smaller proportion of teenagers. Also different is the tendency for migration among young adult women, ages 20 to 29, many apparently single. As will be seen, this trend, which can be called the "young lady" pattern, becomes much more evident among nationality groups closer to the "individual" polarity of the continuum.

The age-sex composition of Central American immigrants suggests a balanced proportion of families in early and middle stages of development, with only a moderate number of children and adolescents. This departs notably from the profiles for the countries of origin, which are uniformly among nations having the highest fertility rates and the youngest age-structures in the world. Thus, immigration from Central America seems to be selective of young to middle-aged parents having a small number of children at the time of entry into the United States. It also seems selective of young women, which may be a response to the availability of employment in the United States as household service workers. Among both Canadians and Central Americans, the "young lady" pattern accounts for a lower sex ratio than in the case of Mexico and Portugal.

The Netherlands and the Philippines have very similar age and sex measures; in both cases, families with pre-school and pre-adolescent children seem to predominate, as in the case of Canada. However, in contrast, the children comprise only a moderate proportion of the total population; this suggests selection, as in the case of Central America, of families having a small number of offspring. It may also indicate a greater tendency for single young adults of both sexes to emigrate; certainly the "young lady" pattern is discernible, again accounting for a low sex ratio. As a result of these factors, the dependency ratio is about half of the measures found among Mexican, Portuguese, and Canadian immigrants, who appear to have the greatest economic burden.

A somewhat more pronounced version of the pattern just described is found in the case of immigrants from the United Kingdom and Germany; here, the proportion of pre-school and pre-adolescent children is slightly larger. However, the family component is overshadowed by the magnitude of the "young lady" group. In Germany's case, females between 20 and 29 years old make up more than 35 percent of all immigrants from the country of origin. Given the presence in Germany of many American military men, it seems reasonable to assume that this group includes a fairly large number of "war brides" who emigrate to the United States following the end of their husbands' overseas tour of duty.

FIGURE 3 (continued)

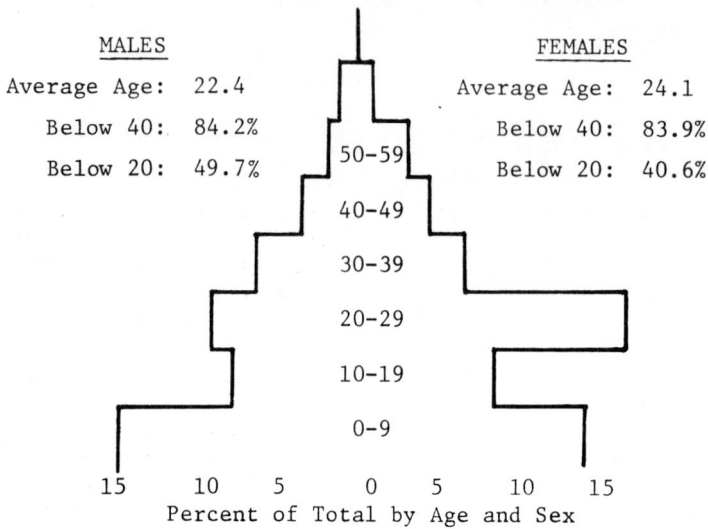

CANADIAN IMMIGRANTS TO THE UNITED STATES, 1969

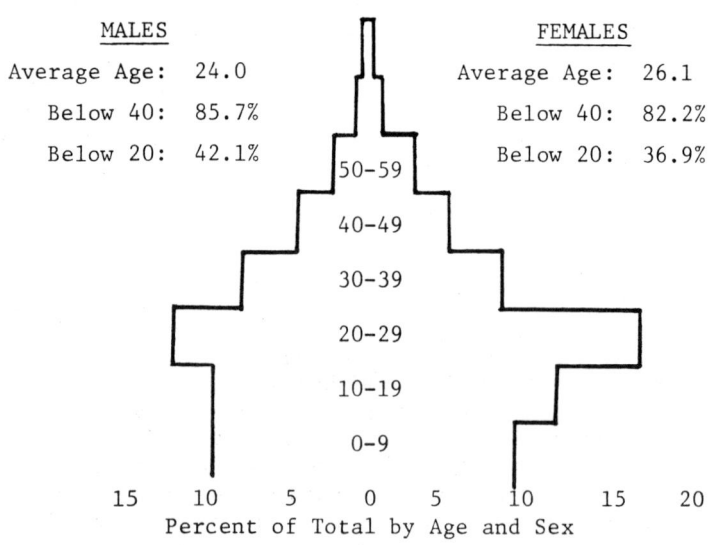

CENTRAL AMERICAN IMMIGRANTS TO THE UNITED STATES, 1969

FOREIGN MIGRATION INTO CALIFORNIA

Figure 3 (continued)

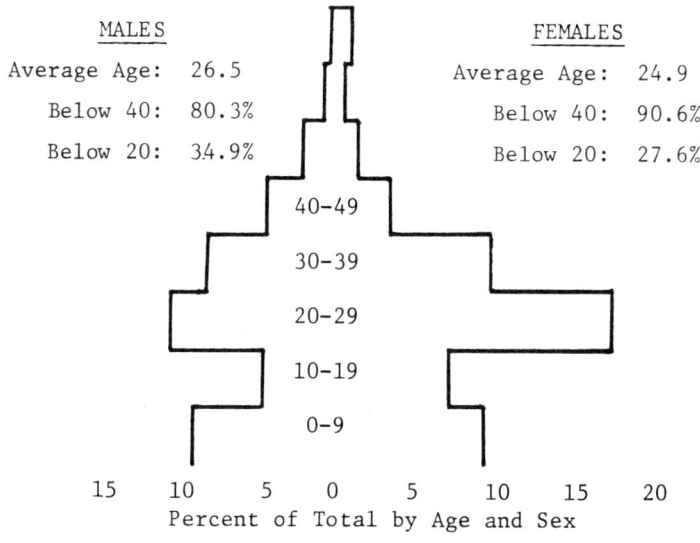

IMMIGRANTS FROM THE NETHERLANDS TO THE UNITED STATES, 1969

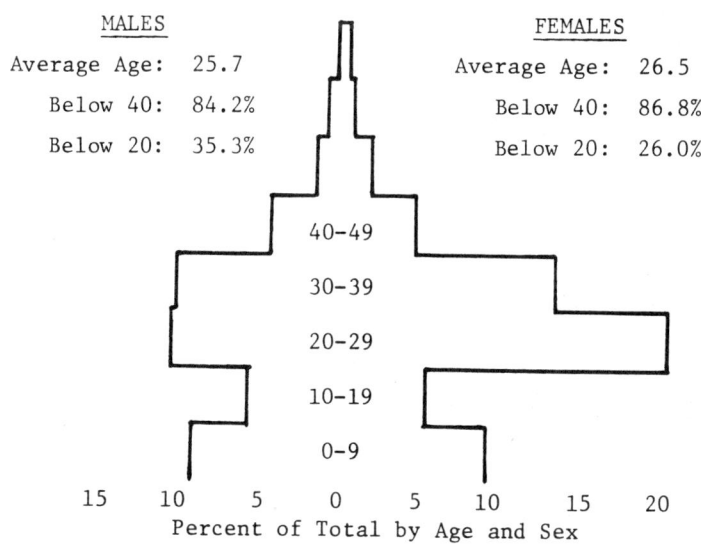

IMMIGRANTS FROM THE PHILIPPINES TO THE UNITED STATES, 1969

FIGURE 3 (continued)

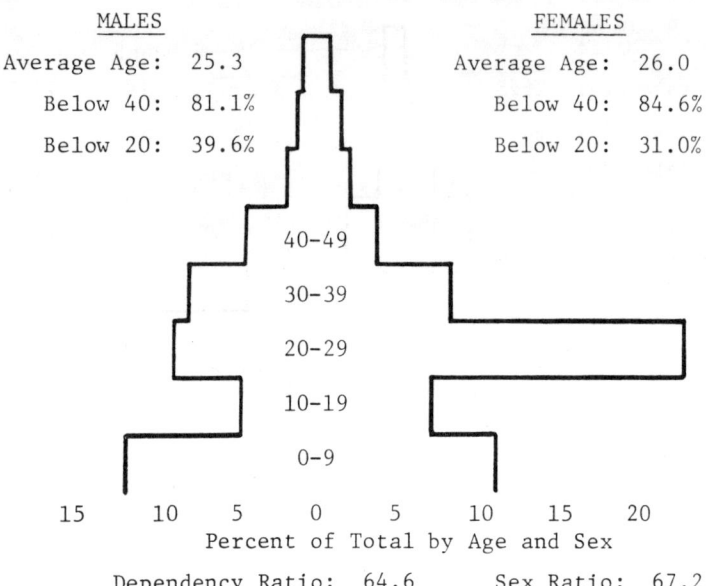

BRITISH IMMIGRANTS TO THE UNITED STATES, 1969

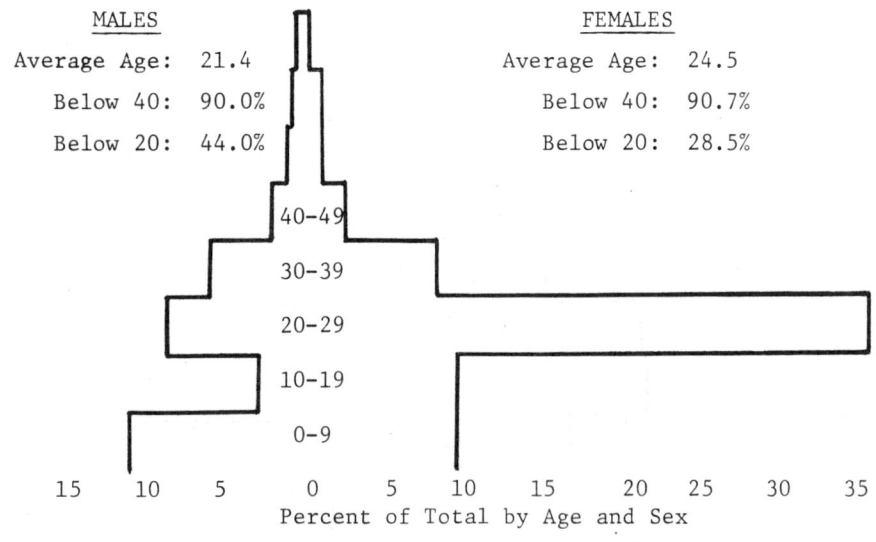

GERMAN IMMIGRANTS TO THE UNITED STATES, 1969

This "war bride" phenomenon may also help to explain the rather unique composition of the Japanese immigrant population, which is predominantly made up of young women; more than half of all the immigrants were females between the ages of 20 and 39, and there was only one male for every three females of all ages. This one-male element is of considerable importance, however, since it represents a significant flow of individuals who engage in professional and highly skilled technical occupations. As will be discussed in the following section, this "brain drain" or "brain flow" is also found in the other Oriental groups and among immigrants from some of the European nations.

A situation differing somewhat from that of the nationality groups represented in the continuum is suggested by the data for Chinese immigrants, who are from the island of Taiwan, and by those for Cuban immigrants, almost all of whom are refugees. Both of these groups have a much older age-structure than the other nationalities, including a notable proportion of persons 50 years old and over. They also have an overall balance between the sexes, approaching a one-to-one relationship. These factors suggest a certain degree of family-type immigration, mainly involving teenage families, and a selective movement of unrelated individuals, both male and female, mostly young and middle-aged adults, but also including a fair number of older persons.

In summary, the age-sex pyramids for Central American and Cuban immigrants are strikingly different from the usually broad-based configurations typical of high fertility/young age-structure countries; the same can be said of the Filipino and Chinese immigrants. In these instances, the immigrant group will probably have a much more attenuated effect on population growth in the United States than would be expected on the basis of the fertility and population growth patterns prevalent in the countries of origin. Perhaps the least likely to have a strong effect on future population growth in the United States are immigrants from the United Kingdom, the Netherlands, Germany, and Japan, who, in addition to the less familistic character of their migration, also come from countries of origin in which low fertility and a small family ideal are prevalent. Obviously, the "war brides," spouses of U.S. citizens, and young single women from these countries who may eventually marry Americans represent only a minor addition from outside in terms of reproduction.

Thus, in most cases, the probable future growth of population by way of immigrant fertility is somewhat less than would appear at first glance. The exceptions to this generalization are immigrant groups having a predominantly familistic age-sex structure, with large proportions of children and adolescents who will eventually reach marriageable age; principally, these are newcomers from Mexico, Portugal, and Canada. In this regard, Mexican immigrants have a special significance, since not only

FIGURE 3 (continued)

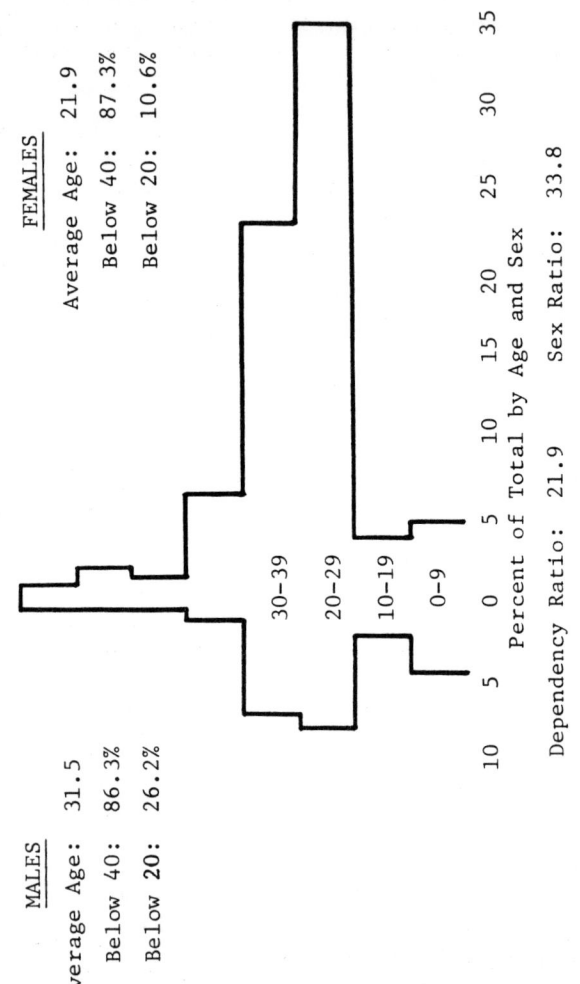

JAPANESE IMMIGRANTS TO THE UNITED STATES, 1969

FOREIGN MIGRATION INTO CALIFORNIA

FIGURE 3 (continued)

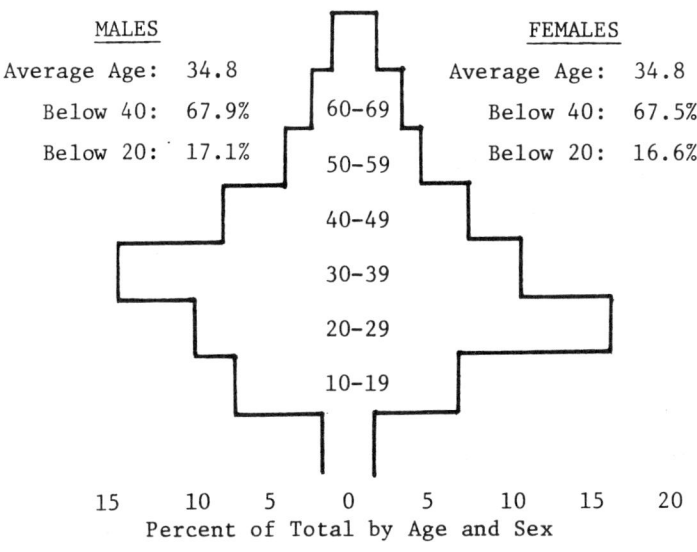

Dependency Ratio: 33.1   Sex Ratio: 89.2

CHINESE IMMIGRANTS TO THE UNITED STATES, 1969

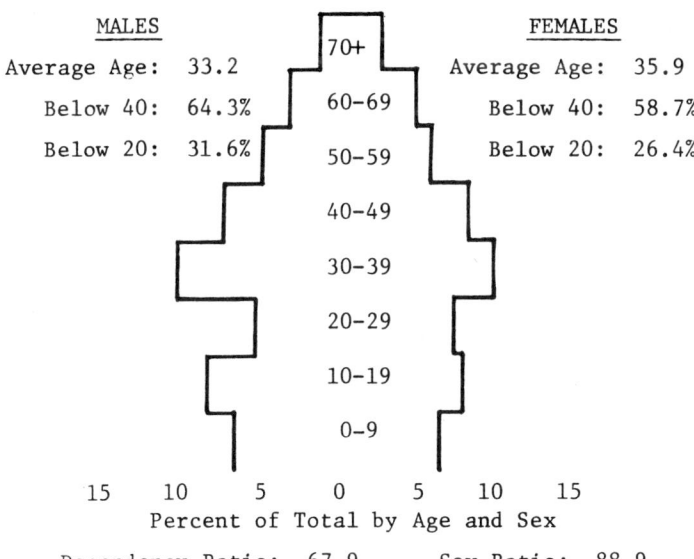

Dependency Ratio: 67.9   Sex Ratio: 88.9

CUBAN IMMIGRANTS TO THE UNITED STATES, 1969

do they come from a country of origin having high fertility and rapid population growth, but they also represent a much larger population than any other nationality group. This means that even a moderate or low rate of population growth will result in a rather numerous second generation.

Foreseeable Economic Impact of Recent Immigration

Another factor which might serve to qualify conclusions based on a simple comparison of rates of numerical increase and preference for California relates to the characteristics of the newcomers as human resources for economic activity. Most observers would agree that it is more beneficial for a modern industrial nation to take in highly skilled and professional workers than persons having a limited educational background or only a marginal potential for personal improvement and success in employment. Unfortunately, no information was found regarding the educational attainment of foreigners, since census and immigration statistics do not include such data by nationality group. As in the case of age and sex, cross-tabulations by country of origin are essential for an understanding of the differential impact of foreigners on the U.S. economy and for making predictions as to the likelihood of their eventual integration into the system of production.

Some idea of general trends can be gathered from the occupational distributions of immigrants entering the United States from 1960 to 1969. These data are presented in Table 5 for the eleven nationality groups selected for special study, listed horizontally according to the size of their total population at the end of this period. In addition to the percentages of immigrants reporting occupations by major work categories, this table provides a measure of the proportion of the total admitted comprising housewives, children, and persons not having an occupation. Along with the dependency ratio already presented, this statistic seems to be a valuable way of judging the extent of non-worker immigration--that is, the portion of the immigrant population representing an economic responsibility for those who can be gainfully employed.

Four principal clusters of nationality groups are discernible:

(1) Predominantly service, non-skilled manual and agricultural laborers, with few white-collar workers: Mexico and Portugal.

(2) Moderate proportions of white-collar workers, service, skilled and semi-skilled manual workers, with few laborers: Central America, Germany, and Cuba.

Table 5

IMMIGRANTS ADMITTED TO THE UNITED STATES 1960-1969, BY SELECTED COUNTRIES OR REGION OF BIRTH: PERCENT DISTRIBUTION BY MAJOR OCCUPATION GROUP

Occupation	Mexico	Canada	United Kingdom	Central America	Germany	China	Philippines	Japan	Netherlands	Cuba	Portugal
Total Reporting Occupation	100.0	100.0	100.0	100.0	100.0	100.0	100.0	100.0	100.0	100.0	100.0
Professional, Technical, and Kindred	3.9	28.1	29.6	14.1	18.0	33.2	62.2	44.5	29.0	20.5	2.2
Farmers and Farm Managers	1.4	0.6	0.2	0.3	0.2	0.4	2.0	2.4	1.0	0.5	9.6
Managers, Officials, and Proprietors, Except Farm	1.6	5.5	4.8	3.4	3.1	10.3	2.0	6.8	6.1	9.2	3.6
Clerical and Kindred	3.4	20.6	26.0	20.8	28.2	8.5	6.2	14.6	18.8	17.1	4.8
Sales Workers	1.4	5.3	4.6	2.2	5.7	2.3	1.2	3.0	5.2	5.1	1.2
Craftsmen, Foremen, and Kindred	8.9	12.9	11.8	14.0	15.8	4.0	3.8	3.6	15.5	10.2	13.2
Operatives and Kindred	4.8	8.0	9.5	11.2	9.1	13.7	2.9	3.4	8.4	21.5	9.0
Private Household	17.5	1.6	5.0	24.2	5.6	3.7	4.2	4.9	3.3	2.0	9.7
Service Workers, Except Private Household	3.4	7.0	6.4	7.3	9.9	21.5	5.9	9.3	8.2	8.2	10.6
Farm Laborers and Foremen	17.6	0.8	0.3	0.6	0.3	0.4	6.1	3.6	1.1	0.3	18.9
Laborers, Except Farm and Mine	36.1	9.6	1.8	1.9	4.1	2.0	3.4	3.9	3.4	5.4	17.1
Percent of Total Admitted Comprising Housewives, Children, and Others With No Occupation or Not Reporting	64.6	56.6	46.0	53.2	57.7	54.6	59.0	85.1	56.5	55.0	66.9

Source: U.S. Immigration and Naturalization Service, Washington, D.C., Annual Reports, 1960-1969.

(3) Predominantly white-collar workers, with a moderate proportion of skilled manual workers and small percentages of semi-skilled manual, service, and agricultural workers: Canada, the United Kingdom, and the Netherlands.

(4) Heavily represented by white-collar workers, principally professionals and managers, with varying smaller proportions of other occupations: Japan and the Philippines. China also follows this pattern, with the exception that it shows a secondary concentration of workers in the semi-skilled (operative) and service categories.

These clusters reflect degrees of educational and occupational selectivity among immigrants, resulting either from entry restrictions or from differentials in the propensity to immigrate among segments of the population in the country of origin. Where legislation is not permissive and severe competition surrounds the obtaining of entry (as in the case of the Asian countries), a large proportion of the workers admitted would tend to be highly educated persons, likely to engage in occupations having a favorable income and in demand by a modern, industrialized nation. Conversely, where admission regulations are permissive and immigration appeals to persons of lower social and economic status, an array of occupational commitments are likely to appear, weighted toward the bottom of the scale in terms of education and skills. Immigrants coming under these conditions might be subject to marginal employment and minimum levels of income, corresponding to a transitory demand for cheap labor. This seems to be the case among some of the Mexican immigrants, and is visible, in a more attenuated degree, among Cuban, Central American, and Canadian immigrants. However, the new restrictive legislation for Western Hemisphere countries, made effective in 1968, may eventually alter this pattern.

Obviously, the occupational distribution of immigrants will also reflect the prevailing manpower situation in the country of origin. Thus, it can be readily understood why certain nationality groups coming from nations having a large proportion of the labor force engaged in manual, service, and agricultural activities would tend to have few or only moderate proportions of white-collar workers. Portugal provides an interesting case study in this regard, being one of the relatively less developed nations of Europe, still dependent on manual labor for a major portion of the production of goods and services.

Finally, it seems significant that about half or more of the immigrants in each nationality group comprise non-workers--persons likely to depend on others for their livelihood in the United States. The highest percentage (85.1--Japan) is clearly out of line with the rest and reflects the predominance of young women, many of them wives of American citizens and housewives.

FOREIGN MIGRATION INTO CALIFORNIA

Among the other nationality groups a range of about 20 percentage points was found, from a low of 46 percent in the case of immigrants from the United Kingdom to a high of 65 percent among those coming from Mexico. Nationality groups having a high dependency ratio, as previously defined (Mexico, Portugal, and Canada), also scored high in terms of the percentage of non-workers, who in this instance would probably include many children. Following this line of reasoning, immigrants from Germany and China would approximate the Japanese pattern of mostly women non-workers, while the other nations (Central America, the Philippines, the Netherlands, and Cuba) would probably show an admixture of both housewives and children.

Conclusions and Additional Implications for Policy Formation

The first and perhaps most important conclusion which can be reached here is that California has recently experienced a new spurt of immigration, changing the long-term downward trend in the percentage of the state's population which is comprised of the foreign-born. Although new legislation, made effective in 1968, has meant a slight decline during very recent years, the ground swell of entry during the 1950's and 1960's has led California to assume first place among the states of the Union in the magnitude of its foreign-born population. Today, California has about one quarter of the foreign-born population of the United States, and about one fifth or more of the state's population is made up of first and second generation persons of foreign origin. Other than the obvious geographic factor of being located in the Pacific Southwest, and the general propensity in the United States for people to move in a westward direction, little is known about the reasons immigrants have for choosing to reside in the state. However, the preference seems to be increasing.

Immigration and naturalization statistics and the censuses provide information which indicates that certain old immigrant groups (principally from Italy, the U.S.S.R., Ireland, Austria, Greece, Spain, and the Scandinavian nations) are rapidly declining in importance, as a result of aging, mortality, and the absence of new immigration. Other European groups have had moderate numbers of new entries, assuring them of continuity as important elements of the state's foreign population: in the early 1950's, refugees from Poland, Yugoslavia, and Hungary entered the state, and during the entire 1950-1970 period, there have been numerous migrants from the United Kingdom and Germany. In the case of Portugal and the Netherlands, the 1950-1970 period has involved a level of entry into California which can be termed a new wave of immigration.

The non-European new immigrants comprise the largest and most rapidly growing portion of California's foreign population:

persons from Western Hemisphere countries and Asia. In particular, Canada, Mexico, and Central America--nations located in relatively close geographic proximity to California and having comparatively permissive entry regulations until 1968--now account for over half of the state's foreign population. Recently, a moderate number of Cuban refugees (having similar entry conditions) have settled in California, largely representing an overflow of migration to other states of the Union. In contrast to other groups from the Western Hemisphere, Mexican and Canadian immigrants represent long-established nationality groups in California, having had steady increases by way of immigration for several decades.

The 1950-1970 period also witnessed a renewal of immigration into California from China (Taiwan and Hong Kong), Japan, and the Philippines. Due to stringent entry restrictions, this movement has not been of great magnitude and represents a highly selective migration, mainly involving professionals and skilled workers.

Among the recent immigrant groups, only Germany and Japan show signs of a decline in the rate of entry during the last few years; they are also different from the rest, since their age and sex composition suggests an admixture of highly trained persons and a large proportion of young women, many of whom are wives of U.S. citizens. Thus, from a policy viewpoint, they represent a less important element than groups likely to add significant numbers to the population by way of reproduction, and those having a larger proportion of manual laborers and semi-skilled workers--occupational categories which have become problematic in our modern industrialized economy, as a result of displacement by mechanization and automation. These occupational categories are also indicative of rather low educational attainment, which suggests further difficulties surrounding employment and occupational rehabilitation.

If low levels of probable population growth by reproduction and avoidance of occupational displacement and unemployment are taken as the criteria for judging the impact of the new immigration into California, it would seem that the nationality groups selected for special study would fall into three major ranks, in terms of their likelihood of success:

1. Immigrants from the United Kingdom, the Netherlands and the Philippines: These immigrants generally have only moderate rates of entry and a mixed familistic/individual composition, with few adolescents and a moderate to low dependency burden and percentage of non-workers. They also have a rather large proportion of white-collar workers, especially professionals.

2. Immigrants from Canada, Central America, and China (also Cuba, if the migration continues): These immigrants

generally have high rates of entry, a largely familistic composition, with some adolescents and (except for China) a moderate number of pre-school and pre-adolescent children. They also have moderate to high dependency ratios and percentages of non-workers; however, a fair number of professionals and skilled workers are found among the immigrants, which may serve to offset a rather wide array of other occupational commitments, some of which might be subject to problems of employment.

3. Immigrants from Portugal and Mexico: These are, perhaps, the least likely to succeed, according to the criteria specified above. Their rates of entry are moderate and high, respectively, and their age-sex composition appears strongly familistic, with many adolescents and children, and high dependency ratios and percentages of non-workers, indicating a greater than average burden for gainfully employed workers. Occupationally, these two groups seem to be in the least favorable situation, since professionals, white-collar and skilled workers are few, and many of the immigrants are manual laborers and service workers. Mexicans have the additional characteristic of coming from a country of origin having a high fertility rate and rapid population growth.

In conclusion, it seems advisable to suggest measures which might be taken in order to have better knowledge of this topic in the future:

1. Special tabulations of the 1970 Census could be completed, either by request to the U.S. Bureau of the Census, or by way of the local use of the summary tapes which will become available during 1971 and 1972. These tabulations would concern the social and economic characteristics of the foreign-born population--ideally, by countries of origin. (This information will not appear in the published reports for California.)

2. A survey of the foreign-born population of the state could be undertaken, using school records as a means of identifying immigrant families. This procedure would not cover all of the foreign population, but it would focus on a major component--the group which is most likely to stand in need of public resources as it progresses through the family life cycle. If such a survey is not possible, simple tabulations of the available data on the school records of foreign children or children of foreign parents could be quite useful for policy formation.

3. A similar survey of economic distress and occupational displacement could be undertaken, using unemployment records as a means for drawing the sample. Again, if this is not possible, a simple tabulation of the information available on the unemployment records would be very helpful.

4. Information of a secondary nature (historical studies, descriptive materials, and so forth) could be organized in such a way as to be readily accessible for the understanding and interpretation of future research along the lines suggested.

MINORITIES IN CALIFORNIA'S POPULATION

Peter Uhlenberg

Among the most explosive social issues in the United States today is the relative deprivation of certain minority populations. The increasingly strident and threatening demands for social and economic equality by spokesmen for Blacks, Chicanos, Puerto Ricans, and Indians can be neither unnoticed nor disregarded by persons concerned with social policy. Underlying the wide gamut of particular issues being raised are two fundamental demands common to almost all of the diverse protesting groups. First is the demand for economic elevation of the entire group, irrespective of individual achievement, and second is the demand that the group be permitted to retain unique patterns of behavior. In support of these demands, representatives of the disadvantaged minorities offer a diagnosis of why their group occupies an inferior position, and they propose means for eliminating the gap between their group and the dominant society. In this paper the adequacy of the diagnoses being offered is challenged, and hence the adequacy of the solutions that are being proposed is questioned. In particular, the accuracy of externalizing all responsibility for the lower position of certain groups in the American status hierarchy is questioned, by demonstrating that the patterns of demographic behavior characteristic of many members of these groups virtually ensures a high degree of failure for the groups. This does not mean that governments are impotent to institute policies that may benefit disadvantaged groups, but it directs attention toward somewhat non-traditional types of policies.

The Social Stratification of Minorities

The population of California can be disaggregated into the dominant white population and the several other racial and ethnic groups present in the state. It is possible to rank these various minority groups, which together comprise over one-fifth of the total population of California, in a status hierarchy according to the average incomes or educations of their members. When this ranking is completed, one can compare the position of each minority group with that of the dominant white population, and those groups which fall below the dominant group can be considered relatively disadvantaged. Before proceeding to analyze some types of demographic behavior which retard the achievement of disadvantaged minorities, it is necessary to note several features of the social stratification of groups.

A first aspect of stratification is that the extent to which a group is classified as successful or unsuccessful is determined by its <u>relative</u> position in a particular status hierarchy, not by some absolute scale. Mexican-American males in California, for example, have a median income of less than three-fourths that of other white males, so the minority is considered seriously disadvantaged. If instead of this comparison Mexican-Americans are compared with Mexicans in Mexico or other populations throughout the world, they are found to be among the most advantaged groups. Their median income for adult males of $3,800 in 1960, their low mortality rates, their enrollment of 94 percent of their children aged seven to fifteen in school, and their position on other indicators of socio-economic status all reveal that Mexican-Americans rank high on a world basis. In fact, the median income of Mexican-Americans in California is only 7 percent below the median income of other whites in Texas. However, the social status of the group is determined by its position relative to its primary reference group--other whites in California--and this comparison establishes Mexican-Americans as a relatively disadvantaged group.

The relative nature of stratification leads to the second principle, which is that one group can advance in status only at the expense of others. One might conceive of a completely egalitarian society in which all groups have an identical economic position; but as long as there are identifiable groups with different patterns of behavior, it is reasonable to assume that differences in level of achievement will persist. Therefore, given the relative nature of stratification, one minority can improve its status only by moving ahead of some other minority which would consequently <u>lose</u> status (without suffering any loss in absolute well-being). Thus, while policies may be directed toward improving economic conditions for a particular group, it is unrealistic to expect to eliminate the existence of disadvantaged groups, since this would require the elimination of stratification.

A third feature of stratification is that while groups can be ranked, there is nevertheless wide variation between individuals within each group. For example, within the lowly ranked Negro population of California, 14 percent of the males in the labor force are employed in white-collar occupations. Likewise, "successful" groups contain individuals who are not "successful." These variations within groups indicate that irrespective of group membership, individuals will find that certain types of behavior are more highly rewarded by the American economic system than are others. Since groups ranked low in status have a disproportionate number of members in the lower class, it is possible that a policy aimed at altering the dysfunctional behavior of the lower class in general, without treating the various low-status groups differentially, would have the effect of producing the greatest economic improvement among the disadvantaged groups.

This last statement must be qualified by one additional characteristic of stratification, however, which is that the criteria which determine status vary between groups. Thus individuals may discover that behavior which is rewarded by their particular minority group conflicts with behavior rewarded in the larger American society. For example, conformance to ideal family roles for Mexican-Americans, which is a source of status within the minority, may conflict with educational achievement, which is essential for success in the larger society. This conflict between criteria for status becomes acute when individuals desire status in both their own minority and the larger society, as many members of minorities currently do. Therefore, a policy aimed at changing some aspect of lower class behavior may encounter great resistance from a minority which values that behavior as a part of its unique heritage. This brings us to the question of how much economic equality between groups is possible as long as groups are truly different in more than superficial ways.

Having noted these characteristics of stratification which apply to minorities in California, the crucial question concerning why some groups are more successful economically than the dominant society while others are less successful still remains. A complete answer to this question obviously exceeds the possibilities of this paper, but one important determinant can be explored--the demographic behavior of those who comprise the different groups. Most attention in the following discussion is on the largest minority in California--Mexican-Americans-- although other groups are brought in by way of comparison.

Demographic Behavior and Group Achievement

Most members of the Mexican-American, Negro, and Japanese-American minorities in California are descendants of migrants who arrived in the state after 1900. Overwhelmingly, immigrants from these minorities were greatly inferior in terms of education and occupational skills to the dominant population, and consequently they occupied the lowest economic positions in the state. For groups with an initial economic status at the bottom of the hierarchy, it is imperative that members of the second and third generations achieve substantial upward social mobility if the minorities are to become "successful." Japanese-Americans have made this transition; Mexican-Americans and Negroes have not.

Differences in family structure between groups provide an important clue as to why descendants of some immigrants have achieved upward mobility while others have failed to advance.

Kingsley Davis noted the critical importance of the family when he wrote: "It [the family] is the first, the most persistent, the most intimate, and the most complete agency dealing with the child."[1] In seeking to understand differences in levels of achievement, the significance of family structure must be considered. The analysis here focuses upon the size of families, the stability of families, and the pattern of family formation as they relate to opportunities for educational and occupational achievement.

Family Size. The size of family in which a child is reared has a significant bearing upon his future life chances, particularly if family income is low. A first effect of family size is amount of per capita investment in children that is possible. The greater the capitalization, particularly in education, the greater a child's chances to later achieve a rewarding position in society. Since the cost of higher education is substantial, especially if earnings foregone while attending school are included, families with few children have a decided advantage over those with many.[2] For a group with most of its families in the lower class, a pattern of large family size effectively precludes the next generation from obtaining the requisite skills for upward mobility.

In addition to its influence upon human capitalization, family size influences a child's future through its effect upon socialization. Socialization involves the complex transformation of a newborn child into a social person possessing the culture of his society or sub-society and motivated to perform roles required for its preservation. The socialization experience of a child is affected by the size of his family, because the more siblings one has, the less individual attention he receives and the less parent-child interaction there is. A lack of parental stimulation results in a diminution of achievement motivation in children, and this lower achievement motivation results in lower educational and occupational attainment. Bernard Rosen, among others studying this relationship, has found the effect of family size to be very important; in tests of achievement motivation, he found that children from small families scored, on average, twice as high as those from large families.[3] A recent

---

[1] Human Society (New York: Macmillan, 1949), p. 406.

[2] For an attempt to quantify the costs involved in educating a child, see Theodore W. Schultz, The Economic Value of Education (New York: Columbia University Press, 1963).

[3] "Family Structure and Achievement Motivation," American Sociological Review, Vol. 26 (October 1961), pp. 574-585.

study of the relationship between family structure and college attendance for young persons concluded: "Sibship size is an important factor related to educational chances, those from large families being substantially less likely to have attended college than those from smaller families."[4] Another large study found a similar relationship:

> The number of children of the head is a major factor influencing the level of education expected for children. Other things being equal, girls and boys in families with one or two children are expected to obtain a substantially higher level of education than those who are members of families having five or more children.[5]

Thus large families are seen to impede achievement of children both by restricting opportunities for obtaining skills and by reducing motivation to achieve.

Among those with low incomes, large families further retard the progress of children by producing crowded home environments. A careful study investigating the effects of housing upon physical and mental health found that morbidity among children is strongly influenced by housing conditions, and that independent of other factors, superior school adjustment and educational advancement by children are positively associated with better housing.[6] By producing deleterious physical environments for young people, large families further contribute to the low achievement of many children.

After reviewing these consequences of family size for individuals, the extreme significance of this demographic variable for the Mexican-American population becomes clear (see Table 1). One of every two Mexican-American children, in contrast to one in seven of other white children, is born into a family in which the mother will bear at least seven children. Except for the negligible effect of infant and childhood mortality, the data in Table 1 accurately reflect the number of siblings Mexican-American children have--siblings with whom they must share the attention,

---

[4] Bert N. Adams and Miles T. Meiden, "Economics, Family Structure, and College Attendance," American Journal of Sociology, Vol. 74 (November 1968), p. 238.

[5] Martin David et al., Educational Achievement--Its Causes and Effects (Ann Arbor, Michigan: Survey Research Center, Monograph #23, October 1961), p. 68.

[6] Daniel M. Wilner et al., The Housing Environment and Family Life (Baltimore: The Johns Hopkins Press, 1962).

Table 1

DISTRIBUTION OF MEXICAN-AMERICAN AND NATIVE WHITE CHILDREN
BORN TO WOMEN 40 TO 49 YEARS OLD IN 1960
BY CHILDREN EVER BORN TO THEIR MOTHERS

Number of Children Ever Born to Mother	Number and Percent of Children			
	Mexican-American		Native White	
	Number	Percent	Number	Percent
1	16,360	2.8%	1,660,106	7.4%
2	43,658	7.4	4,851,342	21.7
3	58,029	9.8	4,891,809	21.9
4	67,144	11.3	3,686,168	16.5
5	60,445	10.2	2,403,755	10.8
6	65,628	11.1	1,571,016	7.0
7+	281,473	47.5	3,274,906	14.7
Total Children	592,737	100.0	22,339,102	100.0

NOTE: The census report combines Spanish surname women with 5 and 6 children. The distribution of these women according to whether they had 5 or 6 was assumed to be the same as for nonwhite women aged 40-44 in rural, nonfarm areas (since their fertility schedule was very similar to Spanish surname women).

Source: Derived from U.S. Bureau of the Census, U.S. Census of Population: 1960, Subject Reports: Women by Number of Children Ever Born, Final Report PC(2)-3A, Tables 8 and 11.

affection, and resources of their parents. Only 29 percent of this minority's children are reared in families in which the mother has four or fewer live births, while 67 percent of other white children live in such families. On the other hand, among the successful Japanese-American minority an even larger percentage of the children are reared in small families than is the case for other whites.

The extent of overcrowding produced by the combination of low incomes and large families among Mexican-Americans is shown in Table 2. Nearly half of the Mexican-American youth, in contrast to less than one-tenth of all white children, are living in households which have more than 1.5 persons per room. To visualize what a density of more than 1.5 persons per room means, consider a family with seven members, which would be allowed four rooms. Assuming a kitchen and living room, the seven individuals would have available only two bedrooms. Similarly, a family of nine would be forced to share three bedrooms. Seven out of ten other white children live in households with a density of 1.0 or fewer persons per room, but only three out of ten Mexican-American children are in this advantaged category.

Table 2

PERCENT DISTRIBUTION OF MEXICAN-AMERICAN AND WHITE CHILDREN BY PERSONS PER ROOM IN THEIR HOUSEHOLD, BY AGE: 1960

Group and Persons per Room	Age	
	0-5	6-17
Mexican-American		
1.00 or less	33.0%	29.3%
1.01-1.50	20.9	24.3
1.51 or more	46.1	46.3
	100.0	100.0
White[a]		
1.00 or less	67.0	71.1
1.01-1.50	23.5	20.3
1.51 or more	9.5	8.6
	100.0	100.0

[a]Total white population of the United States.

Sources: U.S. Bureau of the Census, U.S. Census of Population: 1960, Subject Reports: Persons by Family Characteristics, Final Report PC(2)-4B, Table 3; and calculations from the one-in-one-thousand sample from the 1960 Census.

When discussing Mexican-Americans it is important to recognize variations within the group. The pattern of large families clearly applies to the lower class, but it does not characterize the segment of the Mexican-American minority that has achieved middle class status and no longer closely identifies with the ethnic group. Among families in which both husband and wife have attended less than eight years of school and the husband earns less than $3,000 per year, women average 6.1 children each. In contrast, the average number of children per woman in families where both husband and wife are high school graduates and the husband earns over $5,000 annually is only 2.0. This gross difference in fertility increases the proportion of children being reared in homes able to provide the fewest advantages. Since lower class Mexican-Americans are the ones who most identify with their ethnic communities, this differential fertility also indicates some negative consequences that may accrue from the call for increasing isolation of the group currently being made by many of the ethnic leaders.

Family Stability. In addition to family size, the stability of the family in which a child is reared affects his potential achievement. Since the "Moynihan Report"[7] appeared in 1965, there has been considerable discussion concerning obstacles to achievement among Negro youth created by unstable families, but little recognition has been given to the pattern among other minorities. Although precise measures of the effect of instability are not available, there is little doubt that, other things being equal, children reared in stable home environments have advantages over those from broken homes. Frequently the economic welfare of children is adversely affected when a family is broken. Particularly among low income families, the absence of a male head in the household leaves family members in an economically precarious condition. Another negative consequence for children in unstable families is the incomplete socialization that occurs when one of the parents is missing.[8] Research has revealed the kinds of deleterious consequences that disorganized families have upon children, and frequency of broken families is one indicator of the extent of family disorganization for a group.

---

[7] Daniel Patrick Moynihan, "Employment, Income, and the Ordeal of the Negro Family," Daedalus, Vol. 94 (Fall 1965), pp. 745-770.

[8] For example, see: Judson T. Landis, "The Trauma of Children When Parents Divorce," Marriage and Family Living, Vol. 22 (February 1960), pp. 7-13; Sheldon and Eleanor Glueck, Unraveling Juvenile Delinquency (New York: The Commonwealth Fund, 1951); and Thomas P. Monahan, "The Trend in Broken Homes Among Delinquent Children," Marriage and Family Living, Vol. 19 (November 1957), pp. 362-365.

MINORITIES IN CALIFORNIA'S POPULATION

The extent of family instability for Negroes, Japanese-Americans, Mexican-Americans, and other whites is presented in Table 3. The percent of ever-married women aged 45 to 64 still living with their first husband gives an indicator of how many families survive intact until the children have been reared. Among Negroes in California, nearly 70 percent of the ever-married women aged 45 to 64 are no longer living with their first husband, which indicates that relatively few children in this minority escape the handicap of experiencing a broken family. Using percent of females who are divorced, separated, or remarried as a measure of family disorganization, Japanese-Americans are seen to have the greatest stability. Only 15 percent of the Japanese-American females aged 45 to 64 are in these categories, compared to 20 percent of other whites, 25 percent of Mexican-Americans, and 48 percent of Negroes.

While family instability remains higher among Negroes than other groups, it should be noted that a trend toward increasing instability is developing among Mexican-Americans. Most studies of Mexican-Americans have commented upon the stability of families in the group. Sociologist John Berma, for example, writes: "Their interacting family structure is far superior in stability to our own divorce-ridden one"; elsewhere he states that among Mexican-Americans, "family ties are usually strong and divorce and desertion are more rare than among Anglo families."[9] This greater stability is clearly no longer the case in California, and a comparison of the different generations shows that the native-born have less stable families than the foreign-born. Among third generation Mexican-Americans in urban areas of California, less than half of all first marriages are still intact for females aged 45 to 64, and 37 percent of the women are divorced, separated, or remarried. The social and economic consequences of increasing numbers of females being left to rear children without male assistance will surely present additional problems to the next generation of Mexican-American children.

Family Formation. In the period of life from adolescence to young adulthood most individuals are forced to make decisions which determine their future levels of success, and family background influences the kinds of choices made. Among the important decisions made during this stage of life are those regarding the formation of a new family through marriage and the birth of children. To maximize potential for future advances an individual can postpone entrance into marriage and parenthood until after he has acquired an extended education and become established in an occupation. Particularly for males who lack access to resources

---

[9] John H. Berma, *Spanish-Speaking Groups in the United States* (Durham, N.C.: Duke University Press, 1954), pp. 33-84.

Table 3

PERCENT DISTRIBUTION OF EVER-MARRIED MEXICAN-AMERICAN, JAPANESE-AMERICAN, NEGRO, AND OTHER WHITE WOMEN BY MARITAL STATUS AND AGE: 1960

Group and Marital Status	Age 35-44	Age 45-64
Mexican-American		
Husband present, married once	71.1%	57.0%
Married more than once	13.5	13.6
Widowed	3.9	17.8
Other[a]	11.5	11.6
Total	100.0	100.0
Japanese-American		
Husband present, married once	87.1	65.3
Married more than once	5.7	8.8
Widowed	1.9	20.1
Other	5.2	5.8
Total	99.9	100.0
Negro		
Husband present, married once	45.6	30.7
Married more than once	22.2	24.0
Widowed	5.1	21.1
Other	27.0	24.2
Total	100.0	100.0
Other Whites		
Husband present, married once	78.0	65.3
Married more than once	12.3	12.2
Widowed	2.7	14.9
Other	7.0	7.6
Total	100.0	100.0

[a] Divorced, separated, or husband absent.

Sources: U.S. Bureau of the Census, U.S. Census of Population: 1960, Subject Reports: Persons of Spanish Surnames, Final Report PC(2)-1B, Table 7; and Marital Status, Final Report PC(2)-4E, Table 1; and Non-white Population by Race, Final Report PC(2)-1C, Tables 19 and 21.

MINORITIES IN CALIFORNIA'S POPULATION

which permit them to continue preparation for employment after marriage, early assumption of the responsibilities associated with being head of a family greatly restricts opportunities for future advances. Early marriage and motherhood for females generally limits their opportunities to prolong their education, to work outside of the home, and to engage in other non-familial activities which might produce lasting interests outside the family. For both males and females, early marriage and early childbearing reduce the opportunity to acquire a different approach to childrearing than the one they experienced as children.

The successful Japanese-American minority provides an example of the types of decisions that facilitate upward mobility. To a much greater extent than the rest of the population, Japanese-Americans extend the period of education and delay marriage. In 1960, 65 percent of all Japanese-Americans aged 18 or 19 were enrolled in school, compared to 43 percent for all whites of this age; twice as many Japanese-Americans as whites were enrolled at ages over 22. Comparing marital patterns (see Table 4), the median age at which Japanese-Americans marry is three to four years older than that for members of the dominant society. Although they delay their marriages, nearly the same proportion of Japanese-Americans as whites eventually marry. Thus Japanese-Americans have developed a pattern which does not weaken the importance of the family, but delays the formation of a new family to an older age in order to permit individuals to obtain greater educational preparation.

Age at marriage for the total white population followed a downward trend after World War II and is currently very low for an industrialized country, but Mexican-Americans marry at even younger ages. Combined with their other characteristics, early entrance into marriage severely limits the possibility of young Mexican-Americans to establish their families upon firm economic bases. Among those aged 25 to 34 in 1960, 28 percent of third generation Mexican-American females, compared to 17.5 percent of all white females, married when they were 17 years or younger--i.e., before the normal age for completion of high school. Two years later, before they were 20 years old, 53.9 percent of the Mexican-American females were married, compared to 10.0 percent of Japanese-American females. Third generation Mexican-American males are following a similar pattern of early age at marriage, with 21 percent marrying while in their teens and 43 percent by age 21. To compound the disadvantages of early marriages, childbearing tends to follow shortly after marriage. Among third generation Mexican-American males aged 20 to 24 who are married, 77 percent have at least one child. By following a pattern that reduces, if not eliminates, the interval between leaving the family in which they are reared and forming their own family, Mexican-Americans are preparing to socialize the next

Table 4

PERCENT DISTRIBUTION OF PERSONS AGED 25 TO 34 AND
35 TO 44 IN 1960, BY SEX, AGE, GROUP MEMBERSHIP,
MARITAL STATUS, AND AGE AT MARRIAGE

Sex, Age, and Group Membership	Un-married	Percent Married Before Age:					Median Age at Marriage[a]
		18	20	22	25	30	
Females, 25 to 34							
Mexican-American	11.7%	23.6	45.1	62.9	78.6	87.1	19.9
Native parents	7.3	28.0	52.9	71.0	84.8	91.5	19.5
Foreign parents	14.0	22.1	42.1	60.3	76.7	85.1	20.1
Foreign-born	17.3	15.6	31.1	47.3	66.1	80.1	21.3
White	8.0	17.5	43.1	65.8	83.5	91.1	20.2
Negro	20.9	22.9	40.9	55.7	69.2	77.9	19.8
Japanese-American	10.7	2.3	10.0	26.1	60.8	86.8	23.6
Females, 35 to 44							
Mexican-American	6.5	20.8	39.6	55.9	72.5	86.6	20.9
Native parents	2.0	24.0	45.2	62.8	79.5	92.6	20.4
Foreign parents	9.1	19.7	37.9	54.3	70.7	85.0	20.9
Foreign-born	10.3	16.1	31.3	44.8	61.5	77.1	22.0
White	6.0	13.7	32.5	52.5	74.4	88.4	21.4
Negro	7.0	23.3	40.2	54.4	70.3	84.4	20.9
Japanese-American	7.9	4.0	13.7	30.2	53.7	79.7	24.0
Males, 25 to 34							
Mexican-American	17.7	5.7	18.5	37.5	63.6	80.0	22.4
Native parents	13.5	6.8	21.2	43.0	69.3	84.6	22.0
Foreign parents	18.1	5.1	18.6	37.0	64.0	79.7	22.4
Foreign-born	25.1	4.8	12.8	27.1	50.7	71.1	23.3
White	15.5	3.4	15.0	36.6	65.6	82.6	22.5
Negro	28.6	5.9	17.3	33.9	54.5	69.1	22.3
Japanese-American	34.6	0.6	2.4	8.7	28.7	60.6	25.6
Males, 35 to 44							
Mexican-American	8.2	3.9	13.6	29.2	53.6	78.2	24.1
Native parents	6.1	4.5	15.6	33.3	59.4	82.2	23.6
Foreign parents	8.9	3.2	13.1	29.1	53.8	78.9	24.0
Foreign-born	10.1	4.1	11.7	23.6	45.0	71.5	25.0
White	7.7	2.4	10.6	26.2	55.1	81.6	24.1
Negro	11.0	6.2	16.9	32.2	52.9	74.6	23.8
Japanese-American	15.3	0.7	2.3	6.1	23.7	60.2	27.5

[a] Median age at first marriage of those who marry.

Source: U.S. Bureau of the Census, U.S. Census of Population: 1960, Subject Reports: Age at First Marriage, Final Report PC(2)-4D, Tables 1, 5, and 7.

generation under the self-perpetuating conditions that are currently fostering poverty and low educational attainment.

Conclusion

The modern state is faced with a growing problem as it assumes responsibility for the economic welfare of individuals and groups, without gaining corresponding control over their behavior. The preceding analysis has focused upon this dilemma by examining the role of demographic behavior in the stratification of minority populations. It is clear that certain types of behavior facilitate achievement in the United States, while other types impede upward social mobility. The extremely significant consequences of demographic behavior for achievement, and the demographic variations between groups, have been discussed. The findings of this study suggest that one approach to upgrading the economic position of disadvantaged minorities would be social policy directed at altering self-defeating types of behavior among the lower class.

Three specific areas in which policy could be considered have been suggested. Policies encouraging more limited reproduction, greater family stability, or postponement of marriage and childbearing could produce beneficial changes for disadvantaged minorities in California. To devise the most effective policies to bring about these desired results, an examination of what determines individual decisions regarding these demographic choices, and how they can be altered, is required. For example, one needs to ask why lower class Mexican-Americans and Negroes have large families, why they frequently experience unstable families, and why they rush into marriage and childbearing at young ages.

In this era of acute sensitivity to singling out particular minorities for special government attention, it is unlikely that a "population policy" directed toward specific minority groups would be politically acceptable, regardless of intentions. But since Mexican-Americans, Negroes, Indians, etc. are also members of the larger society and share many of its goals, no special policy may be required. A general population policy encouraging a reduction in dysfunctional behavior of the lower class could have significant consequences for those minorities that are overrepresented in the lowest social strata. Such an approach presupposes a continued effort to eliminate discrimination against minorities, in order that no additional barriers to success occur simply due to membership in a particular group. Through its power to selectively allocate rewards, the state can both encourage behavior that will produce greater achievement and apply pressure to eliminate discrimination. This approach would increase the opportunities for members of minority groups to follow patterns that result in greater achievement. Ultimately, however, members of disadvantaged minorities are left with the difficult choice between, on the one hand, making the required changes that will bring greater economic prosperity and, on the other, continuing existing patterns of behavior with their attendant disadvantages.

PART III

WHAT CALIFORNIANS THINK

CALIFORNIANS' VIEWS ON POPULATION AND
THE ENVIRONMENT: RESULTS OF A SURVEY

Judith Blake

At both the national and state levels, population policy is officially regarded as a politically sensitive issue. The politician is, therefore, judged to be well-advised if he keeps questions of demographic policy from coming into sharp focus, in order to avoid the need for action that might be controversial. Typically unexamined, however, is the basic assumption in terms of which such side-stepping occurs--namely, that explicit national or state action regarding fertility, birth control, migration, population distribution, population characteristics, and similar matters would be met with widespread public disaffection and resistance. It is usually considered axiomatic that Americans would not see population policies as being in their interest and for their betterment, but rather as serving the devious schemes of a monolithic, and probably fascist, state.

In this paper I shall discuss an attempt, in California, to take into account a broadly based segment of public opinion concerning policy-related demographic issues. With the encouragement and support of former Assembly Speaker Robert Monagan, I inserted in the November California Poll a set of questions designed to give a preliminary notion of how Californians view population growth and distribution as possible causes of environmental problems, what they think could be done to change patterns of growth and distribution, how nearly they are able to assess the population size of the state, what size family they prefer, and why.[1] Since the questions concerning population growth and distribution were phrased in terms of the relation of these issues to environmental problems, we naturally wish to know something of Californians' views about the environment. Fortunately, a prior California Poll (January 1970) provides data on the importance assigned by the public to ecological deterioration.

Concern with the Environment

The January poll allows us to obtain two kinds of information on the environmental issue. The first concerns its saliency

---

[1]The complete set of questions asked of respondents is presented in sequence in Appendix A, pp. 161-162.

when respondents are asked a general question about "the most important problem facing the country today." The second results from a direct question as to the importance of environmental problems. Throughout this discussion I shall deal with white respondents first and then discuss non-whites.

Saliency of the Issue

As might have been expected, the most salient issue for California respondents in January 1970 was not environmental problems, but Vietnam and peace. Almost 28 percent of all responses related to the war. However, pollution and problems of the environment tied for second place with the high cost of living and inflation--almost 11 percent of all responses were in each of these categories.

Whether a respondent did or did not mention environmental problems was strongly associated with the socio-economic indicators of education, occupation, and income (see Table 1). College-educated respondents were almost four times as likely to mention the issue as were the grade school-educated. The proportion mentioning it in the $15,000-and-over class was more than double that in the lowest income bracket. Men were more likely to bring the issue up than women, non-Catholics than Catholics, persons aged 30-39 than those under 30. Interestingly, there was virtually no relationship with political party, and the state showed little regional difference.

Responses to a Direct Question

Immediately after the question on "the most important problem facing the country today" (and a probe on "the next most important problem"), respondents were asked the following direct query:

There has been a lot of talk lately about problems of preserving man's environment, such as clean air and water, pure foods, amount of open space, and so on. Some people feel these problems are very urgent, while others don't see as much need for urgency. Which of the statements on this card best fits how urgent you feel it is that we deal with these problems?

1. The most important problem we have--the top priority.

2. Quite important--should have high priority.

3. Somewhat important--other things have higher priority.

Table 1

PERCENTAGE DISTRIBUTION OF WHITE RESPONDENTS WHO SPONTANEOUSLY MENTIONED POLLUTION AND ENVIRONMENTAL PROBLEMS IN ANSWER TO A QUESTION ON THE MOST IMPORTANT PROBLEM FACING THE COUNTRY TODAY: CALIFORNIA POLL, JANUARY 1970, TABULATED ACCORDING TO SELECTED CHARACTERISTICS

AGE		PARTY IDENTIFICATION	
Under 30	11%	Republican	12%
30-49	16	Democratic	10
40-59	10		
60+	6	EDUCATION	
SEX		Grade School	4
		High School	8
Male	13	College	15
Female	9		
RELIGION		OCCUPATION	
		White Collar	15
Catholic	8	Blue Collar	9
Non-Catholic	12	Farm	4
AREA		Other	9
So/Cal	11	INCOME	
No/Cal	10	Under $7,000	7
		$7,000-9,999	6
TIME IN STATE		$10,000-14,999	15
		$15,000+	16
Under 5 years	14		
5-14 years	12	TOTAL PERCENTAGE	11
15+ years	10		
		TOTAL SAMPLE (N)	(925)

4. Not too important--no need to worry unduly yet.

5. Not at all important--low priority.

When compared with the spontaneous designations of pollution and environmental problems as "most important," the results shown in Table 2 may seem surprising. In response to a direct question, well over three times as many respondents maintained that the problem had top priority as had mentioned it spontaneously in the previous query. Moreover, 49 percent of the respondents gave the issue second place in response to the direct question, whereas in response to an open-ended question on "the next most important problem," only 16 percent mentioned it. Thus, 87 percent of the respondents ranked this problem as having either first or second priority when questioned directly, although the issue was assigned first or second place by only 27 percent in an open-ended response.

The tabulations by socio-economic characteristics in Table 3, which show a blurring of the social-class gradient (as compared with Table 1), suggest that the direct question--phrased as attractively as it was--might have appealed to many respondents for whom this issue actually had low saliency--namely, the elderly, the poor, and the less-educated. Traditionally inarticulate respondents may have assented out of relief at being presented with a high-sounding issue they did not have to think of themselves. Even so, although the degree of positive consensus throughout the social structure may be inflated, it is nonetheless true that indifferent or negative views were proportionately negligible, albeit more prevalent among the less-educated. Quite clearly, there was at this time no structured antipathy to, or irritation with, the "ecological" problem. It should be noted here that the breakdowns shown in Table 3, when applied only to those under age 40, show clearer and more linear social-class gradients, suggesting that the independent appeal of this question to older respondents (and the association of old age with low educational level and low income) introduced a confounding element into the tabulations in Table 3.

Non-Whites

The saliency of environmental problems for non-whites was somewhat less than for whites--7 percent of non-whites (as against 11 percent of whites) spontaneously mentioned this issue when asked about the most important problem facing the country. In response to the direct question, the percentage among non-whites assigning "top priority" to the issue was the same as for whites, but fewer non-whites put it in second place, and there were more low priority and "don't know" responses (Table 2). However, 77 percent of the non-whites in the sample put the issue in first

Table 2

PERCENTAGE OF WHITE MEN AND WOMEN AND NON-WHITES GIVING, IN ANSWER TO A DIRECT QUESTION, VARIOUS RANKS TO ENVIRONMENTAL PROBLEMS: CALIFORNIA, JANUARY 1970

	Top Priority	High Priority	Other Things Higher Priority	No Need To Worry Yet	Low Priority	NA/DK*	Total	(N)
WHITES								
Men	42	46	11	1	0	0	100	(405)
Women	35	52	11	2	0	0	100	(520)
Total	38	49	11	2	0	0	100	(925)
NON-WHITES	38	39	13	2	1	7	100	(112)

*NA = No Answer; DK = Don't Know.

Table 3

PERCENTAGE OF WHITE MEN AND WOMEN AND NON-WHITES RANKING
ENVIRONMENTAL PROBLEMS AS HAVING TOP PRIORITY AND LOW PRIORITY,
ACCORDING TO AGE, EDUCATIONAL LEVEL, INCOME, RELIGION,
AREA OF RESIDENCE IN THE STATE, AND PARTY IDENTIFICATION:
CALIFORNIA, JANUARY 1970[a]

	Whites							Non-Whites		
	MEN		WOMEN		TOTAL			TOTAL		
	Top	Low	Top	Low	Top	Low	(N)[b]	Top	Low	(N)
AGE										
Under 30	41	10	34	10	37	10	(225)	41	10	(39)
30-39	42	15	35	10	38	12	(166)	38	25	(24)
40-59	39	14	33	13	36	14	(320)	35	16	(49)
60+	46	9	40	17	43	13	(211)			
EDUCATION										
Grade School	33	14	54	16	43	16	(76)	--[c]	--	--
High School	39	14	32	17	35	16	(448)	39	22	(64)
College	46	9	36	7	40	8	(396)	26	10	(31)
INCOME										
Under $7,000	42	12	37	15	40	14	(270)	36	20	(44)
$7,000-9,999	38	13	33	13	35	13	(183)	38	17	(24)
$10,000-14,999	43	11	38	16	40	14	(241)	32	11	(28)
$15,000+	44	11	33	6	38	9	(187)	--	--	--
RELIGION										
Catholic	41	7	36	14	38	11	(240)	56	8	(36)
Non-Catholic	42	14	35	13	38	13	(685)	29	20	(76)
AREA										
So/Cal	41	13	37	11	39	11	(525)	38	12	(73)
No/Cal	42	12	34	16	37	14	(400)	36	23	(39)
PARTY										
Republican	39	12	33	12	36	12	(354)	39	13	(23)
Democrat	43	14	38	13	40	13	(473)	34	18	(79)
Other	43	8	34	16	38	12	(98)	--	--	--
TOTAL	42	12	35	13	38	13	(925)	38	16	(112)

[a] "Low" priority includes all responses from "Other things have higher priority" down through "Low priority."

[b] Occasionally the total respondents within a category (such as age) will add up to fewer than 925 because of non-response on the independent variable.

[c] Fewer than 25 cases in total.

or second place in response to a direct question. These [text cut] not support the notion that non-whites generally view eco[logical] concerns as a red herring to divert attention from racial [prob]lems. On the other hand, as Table 3 shows, there appear to be important differences of opinion on this point among the non-white population--differences that can only be suggested here.

There was a clear split between Catholics and non-Catholics in the non-white population. Almost 60 percent of Catholics assigned "top priority" to the environment; fewer than 30 percent of non-Catholics did so. Moreover, less than 10 percent of Catholics gave it "low priority," as opposed to 20 percent of non-Catholics. Since the Catholic/non-Catholic break reflects a division primarily between Mexican-Americans and Negroes, we must conclude that there is a major difference of opinion concerning environmental deterioration between these two populations, and that Negroes are markedly less concerned about it than are whites or Mexican-Americans. Given this division of opinion between two important minority groups, socio-economic differentials are hard to interpret. However, as with whites, we see that respondents in the middle adult years were more likely than others to assign low priority. Young non-white respondents assigned the highest priority and were least likely to assign low priority. Political differences were not important, but northerners were proportionately less concerned than southerners.

Population Growth as a Cause of Environmental Problems

If environmental problems are important to Californians, how much weight is assigned by them to the growth of the state's population in creating these problems? The following question inserted in the November 1970 California Poll helps to provide an answer:

> As you know, there has been a lot of discussion in California recently about the state's environmental problems--things like rapidly using up our natural resources, air and water pollution, pressures on recreational space, and so on. Some people say that the growth of population in the state is an important cause of California's environmental problems, while other people feel this is not an important cause. Which of the statements on this card comes closest to describing how you feel?
>
> 1. One of the most important causes of environmental problems.
>
> 2. Quite important--ranks somewhere in the middle.
>
> 3. Not too important--may be important but I have doubts.

4. Not at all important--I don't think it has any influence on environmental problems.

5. I don't think California has any environmental problems.

In response to this question, over half of the respondents of each sex considered separately (53 percent) thought that population growth is one of the most important causes of environmental degradation. An additional 30 percent ranked population growth as "quite important." Interestingly, less than 5 percent believed that demographic increase has no effect on ecological deterioration, and only a little over one percent claimed that the state has no environmental problems. In sum, well over 80 percent of the respondents viewed population growth as having an important role in causing environmental difficulties.

Tables 4 and 5, giving--for men and women separately--tabulations of the responses by age, education, income, religion, area in the state, and time in the state, reveal some surprising similarities and interesting differences among subcategories of the state's population. With regard to similarities, the breakdown by age shows that a concern with population growth is not in the least preempted by the young. Among both sexes, there is very little difference by age in the proportions assigning high priority to population growth as a cause of ecological imbalance. Moreover, the lack of sharp religious cleavage in the state on this issue, perhaps surprising to some, appears to indicate that Californians have broad interests that transcend formally structured and particularistic influences on opinions.

Concerning differences among subgroupings, it seems important to emphasize that the data indicate no deep and decided splits in opinion. There is a tendency for lower-income, less-educated respondents to appear less frequently in the category that assigns high priority to population growth, and more frequently in the categories assigning low priority. However, if one takes into account the immense difference in life chances and perspective between a grade school-educated and college-educated person, the difference of a few percentage points in response to this question (at either the upper or lower end of the response continuum) seems remarkably small.

The amount of time that respondents had resided in California seems to have affected their views concerning the role of population growth in ecology. Recent arrivals were less likely to feel that growth is highly important and, among women at least, more likely to doubt its importance. Residents of the Bay Area were, on the whole, least likely to think that population growth is influential, and residents of Los Angeles and Orange counties most likely to think it so.

Table 4

PERCENTAGE DISTRIBUTION OF WHITE MEN ACCORDING TO THEIR EVALUATION OF POPULATION GROWTH AS A CAUSE OF ENVIRONMENTAL PROBLEMS, BY AGE, EDUCATIONAL LEVEL, INCOME, RELIGION, AREA OF RESIDENCE IN THE STATE, AND LENGTH OF TIME IN THE STATE: CALIFORNIA, NOVEMBER 1970

	One of Most Important Causes	Quite Important/Ranks in Middle	Not Too Important/I Have Doubts	Not at All Important/No Influence	State Has No Environmental Problems	Total[a]	(N)
AGE							
Under 30	50	30	16	3	0	100	(99)
30-44	55	31	10	3	1	100	(98)
45+	53	25	13	6	2	100	(162)
EDUCATION							
Grade School	45	24	17	12	2	100	(42)
High School	52	28	15	4	2	100	(137)
College	56	29	11	3	1	100	(180)
INCOME							
Under $5,000	47	29	18	4	2	100	(51)
$5,000-6,999	56	32	9	3	0	100	(34)
$7,000-9,999	52	25	15	4	3	100	(67)
$10,000-14,999	56	24	11	8	1	100	(80)
$15,000+	53	34	9	3	1	100	(107)
RELIGION							
Catholic	56	24	8	8	2	100	(82)
Non-Catholic	52	29	14	3	1	100	(277)
AREA							
LA/Orange	58	20	16	4	1	100	(147)
Other So/Cal	49	38	7	4	1	100	(73)
Bay Area	46	33	13	6	3	100	(70)
Other No/Cal	52	29	13	4	1	100	(69)
TIME IN STATE							
Under 5 years	43	46	8	0	3	100	(37)
5-14 years	58	26	9	7	0	100	(55)
15+ years	53	26	15	4	2	100	(267)
TOTAL	53	28	13	4	1	100	(359)

[a] Five men did not respond to this question.

Table 5

PERCENTAGE DISTRIBUTION OF WHITE WOMEN ACCORDING TO THEIR EVALUATION OF POPULATION GROWTH AS A CAUSE OF ENVIRONMENTAL PROBLEMS, BY AGE, EDUCATIONAL LEVEL, INCOME, RELIGION, AREA OF RESIDENCE IN THE STATE, AND LENGTH OF TIME IN THE STATE: CALIFORNIA, NOVEMBER 1970

	One of Most Important Causes	Quite Important/Ranks in Middle	Not Too Important/I Have Doubts	Not at All Important/No Influence	State Has No Environmental Problems	Total[a]	(N)
AGE							
Under 30	51	34	10	3	1	100	(140)
30-44	53	32	12	2	1	100	(164)
45+	55	31	9	4	2	100	(185)
EDUCATION							
Grade School	52	26	18	4	0	100	(27)
High School	50	35	10	3	2	100	(244)
College	57	30	10	3	0	100	(217)
INCOME							
Under $5,000	55	33	7	2	2	100	(85)
$5,000-6,999	48	31	10	10	2	100	(42)
$7,000-9,999	53	31	11	4	1	100	(102)
$10,000-14,999	54	31	13	1	0	100	(121)
$15,000+	57	31	9	2	1	100	(121)
RELIGION							
Catholic	52	29	13	6	0	100	(143)
Non-Catholic	54	33	9	2	2	100	(346)
AREA							
La/Orange	55	29	10	4	1	100	(201)
Other So/Cal	49	33	10	2	5	100	(87)
Bay Area	50	34	16	1	0	100	(95)
Other No/Cal	56	35	7	3	0	100	(106)
TIME IN STATE							
Under 5 years	41	35	20	3	2	100	(66)
5-14 years	56	30	9	4	1	100	(80)
15+ years	55	32	9	3	1	100	(343)
TOTAL	53	32	10	3	1	100	(489)

[a] Fourteen women did not respond to this question.

Because age is positively associated with the assignment of importance to population growth and yet diversely associated with other characteristics such as educational level and time in the state, it seems important to view our data with some control for age. In Tables 6 and 7 we see that, among younger men and women, there was a major sex differential in opinion among Catholics. Catholic men under age 45 assigned highest priority to population growth with considerably greater frequency than did non-Catholic men or Catholic women (65 percent of Catholic men are in the top priority category as against 49 percent of non-Catholic men and 47 percent of Catholic women). Among older respondents, on the other hand, Catholic men were least likely to assign top priority as compared with either non-Catholic men or Catholic women (42 percent of older Catholic men are in the top priority class as compared with 56 percent of non-Catholic men and 60 percent of Catholic women). There thus appears to be a major split between the generations among Catholic men, with the younger generation evincing an explicit concern for population growth. Among Catholic women, the generation gap runs in the opposite direction. Younger women are far less likely than older women to be concerned with population as a factor. This peculiar set of relationships is perhaps explicable in terms of the educational experiences and social roles of Catholic men and women. Although both young men and young women have been upgraded educationally, younger women are more likely to have received a Catholic education than are younger men. Young Catholic men as compared with older ones are not only more educated, but more secularized by virtue of their education. Comparing younger and older Catholic women, we can reasonably assume not only that more education among the younger has meant more Catholic education, but that younger women are unwilling to admit that the relatively high fertility to which they are presently contributing is detrimental. Such an admission would require a change in behavior. Nothing can change the past for older Catholic women.

Some association between length of time in the state and concern over population growth--particularly a lower proportion concerned among those in the state under 5 years--holds even when age is held constant. Regardless of age, Bay Area residents were the least anxious about population growth, and (with the exception of older women) Los Angeles-Orange county respondents were the most anxious. The similarity of opinion among the college-educated is noteworthy. Taking college-educated older and younger men and women, one finds almost complete consensus on this issue. The most pronounced "generation gap" within the educational and age breakdowns is between older grade school-educated men and younger college-educated men and women. It should be borne in mind, however, that older grade school-educated white men form a small percentage of the state's population.

Table 6

PERCENTAGE DISTRIBUTION OF WHITE MEN UNDER AGE 45 AND 45 AND OVER ACCORDING TO THEIR EVALUATION OF POPULATION GROWTH AS A CAUSE OF ENVIRONMENTAL PROBLEMS, BY EDUCATIONAL LEVEL, RELIGION, AREA OF RESIDENCE IN THE STATE, AND LENGTH OF TIME IN THE STATE: CALIFORNIA, NOVEMBER 1970

	One of Most Important Causes	Quite Important/Ranks in Middle	Not Too Important/I Have Doubts	Not at All Important/No Influence	State Has No Environmental Problems	Total	(N)
UNDER 45							
EDUCATION							
Grade School	--[a]	--	--	--	--	--	--
High School	49	30	16	4	1	100	(80)
College	56	32	10	3	0	100	(110)
RELIGION							
Catholic	65	22	4	6	2	100	(49)
Non-Catholic	49	33	16	2	0	100	(148)
AREA							
LA/Orange	59	24	14	3	0	100	(76)
Other So/Cal	46	40	12	2	0	100	(43)
Bay Area	45	40	10	2	2	100	(40)
Other No/Cal	55	24	16	5	0	100	(38)
TIME IN STATE							
Under 5 years	44	47	6	0	3	100	(32)
5-14 years	65	22	8	5	0	100	(37)
15+ years	52	29	16	3	0	100	(128)
TOTAL	53	30	13	3	1	100	(197)
45 AND OVER							
EDUCATION							
Grade School	43	26	14	14	3	100	(35)
High School	56	25	12	5	2	100	(57)
College	56	26	13	3	3	100	(70)
RELIGION							
Catholic	42	27	15	12	3	100	(33)
Non-Catholic	56	25	12	5	2	100	(129)
AREA							
LA/Orange	58	17	18	6	1	100	(71)
Other So/Cal	53	37	0	7	3	100	(30)
Bay Area	47	23	17	10	3	100	(30)
Other No/Cal	48	36	10	3	3	100	(31)
TIME IN STATE							
Under 5 years	--	--	--	--	--	--	--
5-14 years	--	--	--	--	--	--	--
15+ years	55	24	13	6	3	100	(139)
TOTAL	53	25	13	6	2	100	(162)

[a] Fewer than 25 cases in total.

Table 7

PERCENTAGE DISTRIBUTION OF WHITE WOMEN UNDER AGE 45 AND 45 AND OVER ACCORDING TO THEIR EVALUATION OF POPULATION GROWTH AS A CAUSE OF ENVIRONMENTAL PROBLEMS, BY EDUCATIONAL LEVEL, RELIGION, AREA OF RESIDENCE IN THE STATE, AND LENGTH OF TIME IN THE STATE: CALIFORNIA, NOVEMBER 1970

	One of Most Important Causes	Quite Important/Ranks in Middle	Not Too Important/I Have Doubts	Not at All Important/No Influence	State Has No Environmental Problems	Total[a]	(N)
			UNDER 45				
EDUCATION							
Grade School	--[a]	--	--	--	--	--	--
High School	49	36	12	2	2	100	(154)
College	56	32	9	3	0	100	(141)
RELIGION							
Catholic	47	33	15	4	0	100	(93)
Non-Catholic	54	33	10	2	1	100	(211)
AREA							
LA/Orange	57	26	12	4	2	100	(121)
Other So/Cal	47	38	10	3	2	100	(60)
Bay Area	49	37	14	0	0	100	(65)
Other No/Cal	52	38	9	2	0	100	(58)
TIME IN STATE							
Under 5 years	44	34	18	4	0	100	(55)
5-14 years	54	30	12	2	2	100	(59)
15+ years	54	33	9	3	1	100	(190)
TOTAL	52	33	11	3	1	100	(304)
			45 AND OVER				
EDUCATION							
Grade School	--	--	--	--	--	--	--
High School	52	33	7	4	3	100	(90)
College	59	26	10	4	0	100	(76)
RELIGION							
Catholic	60	22	10	8	0	100	(50)
Non-Catholic	53	34	9	2	2	100	(135)
AREA							
LA/Orange	52	35	8	5	0	100	(80)
Other So/Cal	56	22	11	0	11	100	(27)
Bay Area	50	27	20	3	0	100	(30)
Other No/Cal	60	31	4	4	0	100	(48)
TIME IN STATE							
Under 5 years	--	--	--	--	--	--	--
5-14 years	--	--	--	--	--	--	--
15+ years	56	31	9	3	1	100	(153)
TOTAL	55	31	9	4	2	100	(185)

[a] Fewer than 25 cases in total.

Non-Whites

Non-whites in the sample differed greatly from whites in their views concerning the role of population growth and the environment (Table 8). Only 29 percent of non-whites assigned highest priority to growth (as compared with more than half of whites), 26 percent said they "have doubts" (as compared with 13 percent of whites), 15 percent said growth has no influence (as compared with less than 5 percent of whites). More Catholics (presumably Mexican-Americans) assigned high priority than non-Catholics, but more Catholics also said that "no influence" exists. College education as compared with high school does not appear to have influenced the opinion of non-whites. Older non-whites were clearly the most negative toward assigning a role to population growth.

What the State Should Do to Stop Growth

The respondents had decided opinions about how to discourage population growth. Those who had maintained that population growth is "one of the most important" contributors to environmental problems, or is "quite important," were asked: "What do you think the State of California should do to discourage further population growth?"

Table 9 presents the range of responses for white men and women separately by age. From the point of view of policy, one of the most noteworthy features of these materials is the generally positive attitude toward the idea of a policy to discourage growth. Among whites, only 4 percent of the responses said that discouraging population growth is not a state function, 7 percent of the male and 3 percent of the female responses said that the state should cope with growth rather than discourage it, and 4 percent of the responses of both sexes said that "nothing can be done."

The suggestions about what should be done were heavily concentrated on restricting migration into the state. Approximately 50 percent of both white male and female responses favored restricting migration, but the sexes differed greatly in the youthful age category. At ages under 30, 28 percent of the female responses related to restricting migration as against 40 percent of the male responses. Moreover, only 9 percent among young women as against 28 percent among young men favored welfare cutbacks to achieve this goal. Among both men and women, the strongest support for restricting migration came from those age 45 and over. Fifty-seven percent of the male and 58 percent of the female responses in this age bracket favored this policy. Over a third of all replies within this age group concerned welfare cutbacks and reinstituting residency requirements as a means of discouraging migrants.

Table 8

PERCENTAGE DISTRIBUTION OF NON-WHITES ACCORDING TO THEIR EVALUATION OF POPULATION GROWTH AS A CAUSE OF ENVIRONMENTAL PROBLEMS, BY AGE, EDUCATIONAL LEVEL, INCOME, RELIGION, AND LENGTH OF TIME IN THE STATE: CALIFORNIA, NOVEMBER 1970

	One of Most Important Causes	Quite Important/Ranks in Middle	Not Too Important/I Have Doubts	Not at All Important/ No Influence	State Has No Environmental Problems	Total	(N)
AGE							
Under 30 years	--[a]	--	--	--	--	--	--
30-44 years	38	35	19	8	0	100	(26)
45+ years	19	15	42	19	4	100	(26)
EDUCATION							
Grade School	--	--	--	--	--	--	--
High School	30	30	22	18	0	100	(40)
College	32	32	24	12	0	100	(25)
INCOME							
Under $10,000	32	34	25	10	0	100	(41)
$10,000+	25	21	33	21	0	100	(28)
RELIGION							
Catholic	35	19	15	27	4	100	(26)
Non-Catholic	26	34	32	8	0	100	(47)
TIME IN STATE							
Under 15 years	--	--	--	--	--	--	--
15+ years	24	22	31	20	2	100	(49)
TOTAL	29	29	26	15	1	100	(73)

[a] Fewer than 25 cases in total.

Table 9

WHAT THE STATE OF CALIFORNIA SHOULD DO TO DISCOURAGE FURTHER POPULATION GROWTH: WHITE MEN AND WOMEN WHO SAID THAT GROWTH IS "ONE OF THE MOST IMPORTANT" CAUSES OF ENVIRONMENTAL PROBLEMS, OR "QUITE IMPORTANT," BY AGE, AND NON-WHITES: CALIFORNIA, NOVEMBER 1970

	Percentage Saying:												
	Restrict In-Migration				Provide/ Encourage Birth Control	Liberalize Abortion Laws	Educate About Population	No More Deductions/ Change Tax Laws	Cope Rather Than Discourage	Not State Function	Nothing Can Be Done	Other	Number of Responses
AGE	Cut Back Pub-Welfare	Stop Publicity	Restrict In-Migration	Total									
WHITE MEN													
Under 30	28	4	8	40	24	2	13	4	3	4	3	6	(97)
30-44	31	9	9	49	11	4	7	6	9	2	4	7	(99)
45+	36	12	9	57	14	1	4	2	8	5	4	4	(140)
TOTAL	28	10	11	49	25	4	6	2	3	3	4	4	(475)
WHITE WOMEN													
Under 30	9	12	7	28	31	9	12	4	4	2	4	5	(137)
30-44	35	12	11	57	25	2	2	2	1	2	5	2	(158)
45+	35	9	14	58	19	2	3	1	5	4	3	4	(180)
TOTAL	28	10	11	49	25	4	6	2	3	3	4	4	(475)
WHITE: BOTH SEXES													
TOTAL	30	10	10	50	21	4	7	3	5	4	4	5	(811)
NON-WHITES													
TOTAL	30	2	11	43	20	4	9	0	4	0	9	11	(46)

The only other major suggestion was the provision of birth control services and the encouragement of family limitation. However, the sexes differed in supporting this solution, as did the age groupings. Generally, women were more likely to mention birth control than men were--25 percent of female responses but only 16 percent of male responses were in this category. Young respondents of both sexes were more likely to mention birth control than older ones.

As between migration and fertility limitation, migratory restriction was clearly more salient, except among young women. It is possible that a structured question would have brought different weights in play, creating more of an emphasis on family limitation. However, given the balance of spontaneous responses, structured questions would doubtless have increased the proportions favoring a restriction of migration as well.

Differences in religion, education, or area of residence in the state did not deeply divide respondents in their views on policy to discourage growth (Tables 10 and 11). The virtual identity of responses by Catholics and non-Catholics suggests that a population policy for the state would not offend the sensibilities of its Catholic residents. Among both men and women the educational differences were minimal on the major issues of migration and birth control. Among men, those in the $7,000-15,000 income class were the most likely to mention migration, and particularly welfare changes, as a means of holding back the migratory stream. This income group among men was the least likely to mention birth control. These men appear to favor a policy that restricts growth at the same time that it reduces existing costs and incurs no additional ones. Among women, there was a greater tendency to phrase the suggestion to restrict migration in direct terms rather than in terms of welfare. When all the feminine answers regarding migration are totalled, however, the differences among income and educational categories are not great--approximately half of all the responses at each income and educational level favored policies restricting migration. Residents of the Bay Area, as compared with other areas in the state, were most likely to suggest birth control as a policy and least likely to suggest restricting migration. On the other hand, men and women of Northern California outside the Bay Area, along with men from Los Angeles and Orange counties, were most in favor of migratory restriction. Recent migrants into the state were much less likely to mention a restriction on migration than those who had resided here for 15 years or more. Recent migrants were also less inclined to suggest welfare cutbacks as a means of reducing migration.

Non-Whites

In considering the suggestions by non-whites as to how the state might stop further growth, we should bear in mind that

Table 10

PRINCIPAL SUGGESTIONS CONCERNING WHAT THE STATE OF CALIFORNIA SHOULD DO TO DISCOURAGE FURTHER POPULATION GROWTH: PERCENTAGE DISTRIBUTION OF WHITE MEN WHO SAID THAT GROWTH IS "ONE OF THE MOST IMPORTANT" CAUSES OF ENVIRONMENTAL PROBLEMS, OR "QUITE IMPORTANT," BY EDUCATIONAL LEVEL, INCOME, RELIGION, AREA OF RESIDENCE IN THE STATE, AND LENGTH OF TIME IN THE STATE: CALIFORNIA, NOVEMBER 1970

	Percentage Saying:						
	Restrict In-Migration				Provide/ Encourage Birth Control	Educate about Population	Number of Responses
	Cut Back Welfare	Stop Publicity	Restrict In-Migration	Total			
EDUCATION							
Grade School	30	9	12	51	18	3	(33)
High School	32	6	9	47	21	4	(108)
College	33	11	8	52	12	11	(195)
INCOME							
Under $5,000	23	7	14	44	27	7	(44)
$5,000-6,999	19	17	8	44	19	6	(36)
$7,000-9,999	39	7	9	55	7	9	(56)
$10,000-14,999	42	6	12	60	12	4	(73)
$15,000+	29	11	4	44	16	11	(115)
RELIGION							
Catholic	34	10	6	50	16	6	(73)
Non-Catholic	32	9	10	51	16	8	(263)
AREA							
LA/Orange	36	8	11	55	12	10	(143)
Other So/Cal	32	6	7	45	18	9	(68)
Bay Area	27	10	5	42	24	5	(63)
Other No/Cal	31	13	10	54	14	5	(62)
TIME IN STATE							
Under 5 years	20	9	7	36	20	16	(44)
5-14 years	32	13	8	53	15	4	(53)
15+ years	35	8	9	52	15	7	(239)
TOTAL	32	9	9	50	16	8	(336)

Table 11

PRINCIPAL SUGGESTIONS CONCERNING WHAT THE STATE OF CALIFORNIA SHOULD DO TO DISCOURAGE FURTHER POPULATION GROWTH: PERCENTAGE DISTRIBUTION OF WHITE WOMEN WHO SAID THAT GROWTH IS "ONE OF THE MOST IMPORTANT" CAUSES OF ENVIRONMENTAL PROBLEMS, OR "QUITE IMPORTANT," BY EDUCATIONAL LEVEL, INCOME, RELIGION, AREA OF RESIDENCE IN THE STATE, AND LENGTH OF TIME IN THE STATE: CALIFORNIA, NOVEMBER 1970

	Percentage Saying:						
	Restrict In-Migration				Provide/ Encourage Birth Control	Educate about Population	Number of Responses
	Cut Back Welfare	Stop Publicity	Restrict In-Migration	Total			
EDUCATION							
Grade School	--[a]	--	--	--	--	--	--
High School	29	8	14	51	24	6	(229)
College	25	13	8	46	26	6	(223)
INCOME							
Under $5,000	31	9	9	49	27	6	(44)
$5,000-6,999	12	12	19	43	21	10	(36)
$7,000-9,999	24	14	14	52	20	4	(56)
$10,000-14,999	25	9	12	46	30	7	(73)
$15,000+	36	10	6	52	23	4	(115)
RELIGION							
Catholic	31	8	13	52	23	6	(133)
Non-Catholic	26	11	10	47	25	6	(342)
AREA							
LA/Orange	27	9	12	48	23	5	(198)
Other So/Cal	27	13	7	47	29	7	(84)
Bay Area	20	8	12	40	30	8	(86)
Other No/Cal	35	14	11	60	20	4	(107)
TIME IN STATE							
Under 5 years	9	14	7	30	38	5	(56)
5-14 years	17	10	12	39	27	5	(82)
15+ years	33	10	11	54	22	6	(337)
TOTAL	28	10	11	49	25	6	(475)

[a] Fewer than 25 cases in total.

only 58 percent of non-whites, as compared with over 80 percent of whites, believed that p pulation growth is "one of the most important" causes of environmental problems, or "quite important." These 42 respondents form only a base for further inquiry concerning what should be done.

Perhaps the most interesting feature of the suggestions by non-whites is the virtual identity of the distribution of responses to those of whites (Table 9). Among non-white responses the suggestion to cut back welfare in order to stop migration occurred as often as among whites, as did the direct suggestion to restrict migration. It is unfortunate that the number of cases is so small, since there appears to be a major difference between Catholics (mostly Mexican-Americans) and non-Catholics (mostly Negroes) in the non-white population. Among the 16 Catholic responses, half favored cutting back welfare to restrict migration, and an additional 19 percent favored restricting migration without any mention of how. Among the non-Catholic responses, only 20 percent favored a welfare cutback, and 7 percent favored restricting migration. All responses that "nothing can be done" came from non-Catholics. The proportion of Catholics and non-Catholics suggesting birth control was the same--20 percent.

Population Distribution as a Cause of Environmental Problems

Since settlement in California is distributed so unevenly, it is of some interest to know how much weight Californians assign to the geographic distribution of population in contributing to problems of environmental quality. Respondents were asked:

> Some people also say that an important cause of California's environmental problems is the geographic distribution of the population in the state--that is, that people are overly concentrated in a few metropolitan areas of the state--while other people feel that this is not an important cause. Which of the statements on this card comes closest to describing how you feel?
>
> 1. One of the most important causes of environmental problems.
>
> 2. Quite important--ranks somewhere in the middle.
>
> 3. Not too important--may be important but I have doubts.
>
> 4. Not at all important--I don't think it has any influence on environmental problems.
>
> 5. I don't think California has any environmental problems.

CALIFORNIANS' VIEWS ON POPULATION AND THE ENVIRONMENT

In general, respondents were more doubtful about metropolitan and regional concentration as causes of environmental degradation than they were about growth as a cause. Approximately 40 percent of the white respondents felt that maldistribution is "one of the most important causes," as against over 50 percent who assigned this ranking to growth. This question--relating as it does to residents of metropolitan areas--evoked responses that differed consistently between the Los Angeles/Bay Area complexes and the rest of the state. The metropolitan area residents assigned top ranking to this cause less often and expressed doubts more often than did respondents in the remainder of the state. Consequently, I have tabulated separately the age, socio-economic, and religious differentials for respondents within these two categories--Los Angeles/Bay Area and the remainder of California.

In 16 of 18 possible comparisons (Tables 12 and 13), residents of the two large metropolitan areas were less likely to rank metropolitan concentration as most important, and in 13 of 18 comparisons were more likely to rank it of low importance than residents elsewhere in the state. There were no clearly patterned relationships by age, religion, education, or time in the state, but men were somewhat more likely than women to think that metropolitanization is important as a contributor to environmental degradation.

Non-Whites

Among the 65 non-whites who answered this question (out of a possible 77), 35 percent ranked distribution as "one of the most important causes" of environmental problems, and 25 percent ranked it as "quite important" (Table 14). No respondents claimed that the state has no environmental problems, but 12 percent thought that distribution is not influential. As between Catholics and non-Catholics (primarily distinguishing Mexican-Americans and Negroes), there was no difference in the proportion assigning a major role to distribution, but 31 percent of non-Catholics gave it second place, as against 15 percent of Catholics, and almost 20 percent of Catholics thought that it has no influence, compared with 8 percent of non-Catholics.

What the State Should Do to Change Population Distribution

Those respondents who claimed that metropolitan concentration is "one of the most important" contributors to environmental problems, or is "quite important," were asked: "What do you think the State of California should do to change the geographic distribution of the population?"

Table 12

PERCENTAGE DISTRIBUTION OF WHITE MEN RESIDING IN LOS ANGELES-ORANGE COUNTIES/BAY AREA AND IN THE REMAINDER OF CALIFORNIA ACCORDING TO THEIR EVALUATION OF POPULATION DISTRIBUTION AS A CAUSE OF ENVIRONMENTAL PROBLEMS, BY AGE, EDUCATIONAL LEVEL, RELIGION, AND LENGTH OF TIME IN THE STATE: CALIFORNIA, NOVEMBER 1970

	LA-Orange/Bay Area			Remainder of State		
	Most Important	Low Importance[a]	Total Responses	Most Important	Low Importance	Total Responses
AGE						
Under 30 years	27	37	(52)	49	21	(47)
30-44 years	50	27	(64)	53	21	(34)
45+ years	35	31	(97)	43	30	(60)
EDUCATION						
Grade School	--[b]	--	--	--	--	--
High School	43	29	(77)	45	22	(60)
College	38	30	(114)	54	25	(65)
RELIGION						
Catholic	42	33	(55)	40	36	(25)
Non-Catholic	36	31	(158)	49	22	(116)
TIME IN STATE						
Under 5 years	--	--	--	57	22	(37)
5-14 years	50	22	(36)			
15+ years	35	33	(158)	44	26	(104)
TOTAL	38	31	(213)	47	25	(141)

[a] "Low Importance" groups all answers assigning lower rank than "Quite Important."

[b] Fewer than 25 cases in total.

Table 13

PERCENTAGE DISTRIBUTION OF WHITE WOMEN RESIDING IN LOS ANGELES-ORANGE COUNTIES/BAY AREA AND IN THE REMAINDER OF CALIFORNIA ACCORDING TO THEIR EVALUATION OF POPULATION DISTRIBUTION AS A CAUSE OF ENVIRONMENTAL PROBLEMS, BY AGE, EDUCATIONAL LEVEL, RELIGION, AND LENGTH OF TIME IN THE STATE: CALIFORNIA, NOVEMBER 1970

	LA-Orange/Bay Area			Remainder of State		
	Most Important	Low Importance[a]	Total Responses	Most Important	Low Importance	Total Responses
AGE						
Under 30 years	31	26	(84)	32	19	(53)
30-44 years	37	27	(97)	42	29	(62)
45+ years	38	26	(109)	50	23	(74)
EDUCATION						
Grade School	--[b]	--	--	--	--	--
High School	29	30	(144)	47	23	(94)
College	44	20	(132)	37	23	(83)
RELIGION						
Catholic	38	32	(85)	41	33	(54)
Non-Catholic	35	24	(205)	43	20	(135)
TIME IN STATE						
Under 5 years	34	25	(44)	42	17	(43)
5-14 years	28	32	(54)			
15+ years	38	25	(192)	42	26	(146)
TOTAL	36	26	(290)	42	24	(189)

[a] "Low Importance" groups all answers assigning lower rank than "Quite Important."

[b] Fewer than 25 cases in total.

Table 14

PERCENTAGE DISTRIBUTION OF NON-WHITES ACCORDING TO THEIR
EVALUATION OF POPULATION DISTRIBUTION AS A CAUSE OF
ENVIRONMENTAL PROBLEMS, BY RELIGION: CALIFORNIA, NOVEMBER 1970

	One of Most Important Causes	Quite Important/Ranks in Middle	Not Too Important/I Have Doubts	Not at All Important/No Influence	State Has No Environmental Problems	Total[a]	(N)
RELIGION							
Catholic	35	15	31	19	0	100	(26)
Non-Catholic	36	31	26	8	0	100	(39)
TOTAL	35	25	28	12	0	100	(65)

[a] Twelve of 77 did not respond to this question.

CALIFORNIANS' VIEWS ON POPULATION AND THE ENVIRONMENT

As with the responses on growth, so with distribution; few responses said that a state policy on population is illegitimate--4 percent of white male and 3 percent of white female responses (Tables 15 and 16). The feeling that "nothing can be done" characterized about 10 percent of all responses, and the proportion of non-response was considerably higher than in the case of population growth. In general, we may say that this issue did not have the general saliency for respondents that the issue of growth had. Fewer respondents thought that the issue is of prime importance and, among those who considered it important, fewer had concrete suggestions concerning what should be done about it.

Most answers fell into two related categories--provide jobs and move industry to less developed areas of the state, on the one hand, and provide facilities (homes, model cities, transportation, etc.) in those areas, on the other. If one considers that the responses in terms of tax incentives to undeveloped areas and bringing water to the deserts are also related to the development of less developed areas, then three-fourths of all the responses concerned pulling population away from present centers of concentration by creating demographic magnets elsewhere in the state.

It is not without interest that respondents thought in terms of measures to create development away from existing centers, but did not think of concurrent measures to stop development in the metropolitan areas. Fewer than 10 responses related to preventing northern waters from going to the southern part of the state, and fewer than 10 were concerned with dividing the state. Understandably, the logistics of metropolitan deconcentration are, at this time, beyond the scope of the average respondent--in part because his experience with such matters is far more limited than is his experience with the migration pattern involved in growth. However, the lack of enthusiasm for redistribution is probably not simply a function of ignorance and lack of prior thought; it is also that such plans would involve changes for people who are already settled in the state--the respondents themselves. To them, it seems far less threatening to discourage additional in-migration than to engage in redistribution schemes.

Growth Versus Distribution

In view of the lesser importance assigned to distribution than growth, we may ask whether the question on growth predisposed respondents to assign a lesser role to distribution. In other words, having committed themselves on growth, did they feel less able to claim, in addition, that distribution is important? As Table 17 shows, this does not appear to be the case. Among white men, those respondents who claimed that growth is one of the most

Table 15

WHAT THE STATE OF CALIFORNIA SHOULD DO TO CHANGE THE GEOGRAPHIC DISTRIBUTION OF THE POPULATION: WHITE MEN WHO SAID THAT DISTRIBUTION IS "ONE OF THE MOST IMPORTANT" CAUSES OF ENVIRONMENTAL PROBLEMS, OR "QUITE IMPORTANT," BY AGE, EDUCATIONAL LEVEL, INCOME, RELIGION, AREA OF RESIDENCE IN THE STATE, AND LENGTH OF TIME IN THE STATE: CALIFORNIA, NOVEMBER 1970

Percentage Saying:

	Jobs/Industry to Undeveloped Areas	Facilities to Undeveloped Areas	Tax Incentives to Undeveloped Areas	Water to Deserts	Restrict Immigration	Not a State Function	Nothing Can Be Done	Other	Total Responses
AGE									
Under 30	45	15	9	6	0	6	11	8	(80)
30-44	44	12	5	11	6	1	10	10	(80)
45+	46	17	2	8	2	5	12	9	(102)
EDUCATION									
Grade School	--[a]	--	--	--	--	--	--	--	--
High School	50	16	3	8	3	3	11	7	(106)
College	42	11	7	10	2	6	10	12	(136)

INCOME								
Under $5,000	43	20	0	9	3	3	11	11	(35)
$5,000-6,999	42	25	4	0	4	12	8	4	(25)
$7,000-9,999	53	9	6	11	0	0	15	6	(53)
$10,000-14,999	44	17	7	7	3	4	9	9	(69)
$15,000+	45	11	6	10	3	6	10	11	(73)
RELIGION								
Catholic	52	19	3	5	2	0	5	14	(59)
Non-Catholic	43	14	5	9	3	5	13	7	(203)
AREA								
LA/Orange	51	13	5	10	2	4	9	6	(105)
Other So/Cal	41	11	4	11	2	9	11	11	(54)
Bay Area	35	21	12	6	2	2	8	15	(52)
Other No/Cal	47	16	0	4	6	2	20	6	(51)
TIME IN STATE								
Under 5 years	41	11	15	7	0	11	4	11	(27)
5-14 years	50	9	4	13	6	0	9	9	(46)
15+ years	44	17	4	7	2	4	13	9	(189)
TOTAL	45	15	5	8	3	4	11	9	(262)

aFewer than 25 cases in total.

Table 16

WHAT THE STATE OF CALIFORNIA SHOULD DO TO CHANGE THE GEOGRAPHIC DISTRIBUTION OF THE POPULATION:
WHITE WOMEN WHO SAID THAT DISTRIBUTION IS "ONE OF THE MOST IMPORTANT" CAUSES OF ENVIRONMENTAL PROBLEMS,
OR "QUITE IMPORTANT," BY AGE, EDUCATIONAL LEVEL, INCOME, RELIGION, AREA OF RESIDENCE IN THE STATE, AND
LENGTH OF TIME IN THE STATE: CALIFORNIA, NOVEMBER 1970

Percentage Saying:

	Jobs/Industry to Undeveloped Areas	Facilities to Undeveloped Areas	Tax Incentives to Undeveloped Areas	Water to Deserts	Restrict Immigration	Not a State Function	Nothing Can Be Done	Other	Total Responses
AGE									
Under 30	50	23	2	4	3	3	5	10	(113)
30-44	52	23	7	2	1	3	8	3	(122)
45+	53	16	2	4	5	3	12	5	(130)
EDUCATION									
Grade School	--a	--	--	--	--	--	--	--	--
High School	52	18	2	4	5	2	10	6	(158)
College	53	21	5	3	2	3	7	7	(196)

INCOME								
Under $5,000	45	18	0	8	2	4	14	10	(51)
$5,000-6,999	39	21	0	0	11	0	18	11	(28)
$7,000-9,999	59	20	3	3	1	4	7	3	(71)
$10,000-14,999	59	20	6	2	3	2	4	5	(106)
$15,000+	48	24	4	5	3	3	7	7	(102)
RELIGION								
Catholic	48	24	2	2	3	4	6	12	(104)
Non-Catholic	54	19	4	4	3	3	10	4	(261)
AREA								
LA/Orange	50	23	4	4	4	2	7	5	(151)
Other So/Cal	53	21	0	6	3	3	9	6	(68)
Bay Area	60	19	3	3	2	3	3	8	(67)
Other No/Cal	48	16	5	1	2	5	15	6	(79)
TIME IN STATE								
Under 5 years	40	29	2	6	2	4	8	10	(52)
5-14 years	64	17	2	3	0	3	7	3	(58)
15+ years	52	20	4	3	4	3	9	6	(255)
TOTAL	52	20	3	4	3	3	8	6	(365)

[a]Fewer than 25 cases in total.

Table 17

EVALUATION OF THE IMPORTANCE OF DISTRIBUTION TO THE ENVIRONMENT BY WHITE MEN AND WOMEN WHO SAID THAT POPULATION GROWTH IS "ONE OF THE MOST IMPORTANT" CAUSES OF ENVIRONMENTAL PROBLEMS, OR "QUITE IMPORTANT": CALIFORNIA, NOVEMBER 1970

Those Who Said That Growth Is:	Percentage Who Said That Distribution Is:						
	One of Most Important Causes	Quite Important/Ranks in Middle	Not Too Important/I Have Doubts	Not at All Important/No Influence	State Has No Environmental Problems	Total	(N)
WHITE MEN							
One of Most Important Causes	52	28	14	3	2	100	(185)
Quite Important	36	40	21	3	0	100	(100)
Total Respondents	42	30	20	6	2	100	(354)
WHITE WOMEN							
One of Most Important Causes	50	36	11	3	0	100	(257)
Quite Important	28	41	26	4	1	100	(151)
Total Respondents	38	36	20	4	1	100	(479)
WHITE TOTAL							
One of Most Important Causes	51	33	12	3	1	100	(442)
Quite Important	31	41	24	4	0	100	(251)
Total Respondents	40	34	20	5	2	100	(833)

important contributors to environmental problems also claimed, in higher proportions than the total male sample, that distribution is among the most important contributors. Moreover, among those who said "quite important" with respect to growth, the proportion saying that distribution is among the "most important" contributors was approximately the same as that for the white male sample as a whole, and the proportion saying that distribution is "quite important" exceeded the proportion of the total sample. The same was true for white women. In general, therefore, people who thought that growth is important were more likely to think that distribution is also important than were respondents generally.

How Informed Are Californians About the Size of Their State's Population?

Although more than half of all respondents said that population growth is one of the most important causes of environmental problems, and an additional 30 percent claimed that such growth is "quite important" as a cause, most Californians, as judged by this sample, do not have a clear picture of the demographic size of their state (Table 18). Only 36 percent of the men and a mere 17 percent of the women who ventured an answer were approximately correct--i.e., their answers fell in the range of 18 to 22 million. Twenty percent of the men and 35 percent of the women thought they lived in a state less than one half its actual size--that is, with fewer than 10 million inhabitants. Among men, the modal response was correct. Among women, it underestimated the population by fully one half. Moreover, 10 percent of the men and 25 percent of the women did not feel able to answer the question. Viewed according to age, educational level, religion, area of residence, and length of time in the state, there are certain striking relationships.

Among men, those under age 30 were less likely to give a correct answer and more likely to give extremely wrong answers than were older respondents. Among women, the same was true, but we should note additionally that women were markedly less informed than men on the subject and far more likely to underestimate the state's population in an extreme fashion. For example, almost half the women under age 30 thought that the state's population was fewer than 10 million. Only 12 percent gave a correct answer. Among men in that age group, 30 percent were correct. It would thus appear that however much the young claim "awareness" of issues such as population and the environment, they are actually less informed than their elders.

The college-educated were better informed than those with less education, particularly among women. When age is controlled (Table 19), the educational difference is really striking only among older women. Bay Area and other Northern California male

Table 18

ESTIMATES OF CALIFORNIA'S POPULATION SIZE BY WHITE MEN AND WOMEN ACCORDING TO AGE, EDUCATIONAL LEVEL, RELIGION, AREA OF RESIDENCE IN THE STATE, AND LENGTH OF TIME IN THE STATE: CALIFORNIA, NOVEMBER 1970

	MEN								WOMEN						
	Percentage Who Said That Size Is:								Percentage Who Said That Size Is:						
	Millions					Total	(N)	Percent DK & NA	Millions					Total	(N)	Percent DK & NA
	<10	10-17	18-22	23-30	31+				<10	10-17	18-22	23-30	31+			
AGE																
Under 30	26	25	30	8	11	100	(88)	12	46	22	12	9	11	100	(115)	18
30-44	20	29	40	4	6	100	(93)	6	29	22	16	10	23	100	(130)	22
45+	17	33	37	7	6	100	(147)	11	32	21	23	10	14	100	(136)	30
EDUCATION																
Grade School	28	26	33	8	5	100	(39)	9	--[a]	--	--	--	--	--	--	39
High School	22	31	33	5	9	100	(121)	13	40	21	14	8	17	100	(184)	27
College	17	30	38	7	7	100	(168)	8	30	22	22	11	15	100	(177)	19

RELIGION																
Catholic	26	32	31	5	5	100	(74)	12	33	22	16	11	18	100	(108)	26
Non-Catholic	19	29	37	7	8	100	(254)	9	36	21	18	9	16	100	(273)	24
AREA																
LA/Orange	22	36	32	5	5	100	(136)	9	40	24	14	9	13	100	(157)	25
Other So/Cal	17	30	27	11	16	100	(71)	5	23	24	18	13	23	100	(71)	20
Bay Area	23	19	48	3	7	100	(62)	11	33	18	18	10	21	100	(72)	26
Other No/Cal	19	27	42	7	5	100	(59)	14	40	19	22	7	12	100	(81)	25
TIME IN STATE																
Under 5 years	23	16	39	6	16	100	(31)	16	27	31	18	11	13	100	(55)	17
5-14 years	18	32	38	6	6	100	(50)	9	43	15	21	7	15	100	(61)	27
15+ years	21	31	35	6	7	100	(247)	9	35	21	16	10	17	100	(264)	25
TOTAL	20	30	36	6	8	100	(328)	10	35	22	17	9	16	100	(381)	24

[a] Fewer than 25 cases in total.

Table 19

ESTIMATES OF CALIFORNIA'S POPULATION SIZE BY WHITE MEN AND WOMEN WHO ARE UNDER AGE 45 AND 45 AND OVER ACCORDING TO EDUCATION AND AREA IN THE STATE: CALIFORNIA, NOVEMBER 1970

	MEN								WOMEN							
	Percentage Who Said That Size Is:								Percentage Who Said That Size Is:							
	Millions								Millions							
EDUCATION	<10	10-17	18-22	23-30	31+	Total	(N)	Percent DK & NA	<10	10-17	18-22	23-30	31+	Total	(N)	Percent DK & NA
								UNDER 45								
Grade School	--[a]	--	--	--	--	--	--	--	--	--	--	--	--	--	--	--
High School	28	28	29	6	10	100	(72)	11	39	20	13	9	19	100	(120)	24
College	20	28	37	7	9	100	(102)	8	34	23	17	10	16	100	(119)	16

AREA																
LA/Orange	26	33	34	4	3	100	(73)	5	40	22	14	11	12	100	(98)	21
Other So/Cal	17	23	28	12	20	100	(40)	9	28	28	15	11	19	100	(47)	22
Bay Area	25	19	47	0	8	100	(36)	10	35	17	13	9	26	100	(54)	17
Other No/Cal	22	28	31	9	9	100	(32)	16	44	20	15	4	17	100	(46)	22
TOTAL	23	27	35	6	9	100	(181)	9	37	22	14	9	18	100	(245)	20

<u>45 AND OVER</u>

EDUCATION																
Grade School	28	28	28	9	6	100	(32)	11	--	--	--	--	--	--	--	--
High School	14	35	39	4	8	100	(49)	15	42	22	17	6	13	100	(64)	33
College	14	35	39	8	5	100	(66)	7	21	21	31	14	14	100	(58)	26
AREA																
LA/Orange	17	40	29	6	8	100	(63)	14	41	25	14	5	15	100	(59)	31
Other So/Cal	16	39	26	10	10	100	(31)	10	12	17	25	17	29	100	(24)	17
Bay Area	19	19	50	8	4	100	(26)	13	28	22	33	11	6	100	(18)	44
Other No/Cal	15	26	56	4	0	100	(27)	13	34	17	31	11	6	100	(35)	29
TOTAL	17	33	37	7	6	100	(147)	11	32	21	23	10	14	100	(136)	30

[a] Fewer than 25 cases in total.

residents were markedly better informed than residents of the South (Table 18). Almost half of Bay Area men gave the correct answer, as against not quite one-third of Los Angeles/Orange county residents, and just over a quarter of those residing in the remainder of Southern California. When age is controlled, as in Table 19, older Northern California men are seen to be particularly well-informed. It is interesting to note that long-term residence in the state did not give respondents an advantage in knowing their state's population (Table 18). Religious differences apparently had some effect on male responses, with non-Catholics being somewhat better informed than Catholics. For women, no such relationship is apparent.

It is thus quite clear that however large a role respondents assigned to population growth as an environmental hazard, their evaluation did not rest on an exaggerated view of the state's demographic size and density; insofar as incorrect answers were given, most underestimated the state's size. As Table 20 shows, respondents who expressed the most concern over population growth and the environment were not likely to be more correct than respondents generally in estimating the state's size. Moreover, 50 percent of the men and 56 percent of the women who said that population growth is one of the most important causes of environmental problems believed that the state had fewer than 18 million people. We are led to suspect that population figures per se have little meaning for most people in the state at this time.

Non-Whites

Among the 77 non-whites in the sample, 17 did not reply to this question. The remaining 60 do not afford a basis for cross-tabulations, since the non-whites are further divided into at least two distinct populations--Mexican-Americans and Negroes. However, the overall distribution of responses of non-whites was fairly close to the distribution for white women. A third of non-whites believed the state had fewer than 10 million people, 35 percent placed the population at 10-17 million, and 12 percent gave a correct answer--18-22 million. It is perhaps of interest that non-whites tended, even more than white women, to underestimate the state's size rather than overestimate it.

Ideal Family Size

It is often thought that a population can achieve a zero rate of increase simply by cutting down to two the number of children per woman. In this fashion, a couple just about replaces itself in a society where everyone lives through the reproductive years. Unfortunately, the situation is not so simple. The annual

Table 20

ESTIMATES OF THE SIZE OF CALIFORNIA'S POPULATION BY WHITE MEN AND WOMEN WHO SAID THAT POPULATION GROWTH IS "ONE OF THE MOST IMPORTANT" CAUSES OF ENVIRONMENTAL PROBLEMS, OR "QUITE IMPORTANT": CALIFORNIA, NOVEMBER 1970

Those Who Said That Growth Is:	Percentage Who Said That Size Is: Millions							Percent DK & NA
	<10	10-17	18-22	23-30	31+	Total	(N)	
MEN								
One of Most Important Causes	17	33	37	6	6	100	(171)	10
Quite Important	22	27	33	8	10	100	(90)	10
Total Respondents	20	30	36	6	8	100	(328)	10
WOMEN								
One of Most Important Causes	33	23	19	10	15	100	(201)	23
Quite Important	39	22	16	6	18	100	(125)	20
Total Respondents	35	22	17	9	16	100	(381)	24

birth rate is not only a function of the rate at which women are reproducing, but is also heavily influenced by the proportion of women in the population available for reproduction. This proportion is, of course, affected by past peaks and troughs in the birth rate and by migration. It is thus disturbingly true for the country as a whole, and for California in particular, that the achievement of zero population growth implies not only a cessation of net increase by migration, but also a very small input of births per woman to compensate for a feminine age structure favorable to reproduction. A recent monograph on California's population has shown that, in order to achieve zero population growth by 1990, California would have to have no migration and a decline of lifetime fertility to 1.1 births per woman.[2]

The achievement of an average of 1.1 births per woman does not, of course, necessarily imply that mothers have extremely small families. Other ways of arriving at such an average are possible. For example, it could be achieved by high proportions unmarried, a large proportion childless, and a moderate size family for those having children. However, as yet we have no indication that many Americans will wish to withdraw altogether from family life, and hence it is of some importance to know how large a family people believe to be desirable. For this reason, I inserted a question on respondents' family-size ideals in the November California Poll along with the other questions on population. The question was worded in the same way as the one I have used in the Gallup Poll for the United States as a whole every six or eight months during the 1960's. (Prior to that, it had been used frequently extending back to the 1930's.) In order to provide a comparison of the nation with California, I have tabulated the results of the data for the United States from the Gallup survey of October 1970 along with those from the November California Poll, taken only a few weeks later (Tables 21 and 22).

The data in Tables 21 and 22 show that white Californians did not come close to approaching the family-size ideal of 1 child per woman. However, compared to the country as a whole, Californians preferred atypically small families. Moreover, they consistently maintained smaller family-size ideals than respondents in the same age, religious, and socio-economic categories in the nation. Among white men, Californians preferred an average of 2.4 children as compared with 2.7 for the total country; among white women the comparison was 2.6 for California as against 3.0 for the nation. Tables 23 and 24, which show family-size

---

[2] Eduardo E. Arriaga and Kingsley Davis, The Magnitude and Character of California's Population Growth (Berkeley: Institute of International Studies--forthcoming).

CALIFORNIANS' VIEWS ON POPULATION AND THE ENVIRONMENT

Table 21

MEAN IDEAL FAMILY-SIZE AND PERCENTAGE SAYING TWO CHILDREN OR FOUR OR MORE CHILDREN: WHITE MEN IN CALIFORNIA, NOVEMBER 1970, AND IN THE UNITED STATES, OCTOBER 1970, BY AGE, EDUCATIONAL LEVEL, INCOME, RELIGION, AREA OF RESIDENCE IN THE STATE, AND LENGTH OF TIME IN THE STATE

	CALIFORNIA November 1970				UNITED STATES October 1970			
		Percent				Percent		
	$\bar{X}$	2	4+	(N)	$\bar{X}$	2	4+	(N)
AGE								
Under 30	2.3	74	7	(99)	2.6	59	13	(124)
30-44	2.3	64	8	(97)	2.6	55	18	(157)
45+	2.5	58	16	(160)	2.8	43	23	(377)
EDUCATION								
Grade School	2.8	54	23	(43)	3.0	38	36	(123)
High School	2.4	65	11	(136)	2.7	48	18	(324)
College	2.3	66	8	(177)	2.6	56	13	(209)
INCOME								
Under $5,000	2.6	59	20	(51)	2.8	33	27	(114)
$5,000-6,999	2.5	57	17	(35)	2.8	52	25	(80)
$7,000-9,999	2.3	67	8	(67)	2.8	50	22	(135)
$10,000-14,999	2.3	74	10	(80)	2.7	55	17	(98)
$15,000+	2.4	58	9	(105)	2.6	52	14	(224)
RELIGION								
Catholic	2.6	58	17	(83)	2.9	42	26	(188)
Non-Catholic	2.3	66	10	(273)	2.6	52	18	(471)
AREA								
LA/Orange	2.4	67	10	(146)	--	--	--	--
Other So/Cal	2.6	53	19	(74)	--	--	--	--
Bay Area	2.2	67	4	(70)	--	--	--	--
Other No/Cal	2.3	67	12	(66)	--	--	--	--
TIME IN STATE								
Under 5 years	2.5	62	14	(37)	--	--	--	--
5-14 years	2.4	57	13	(53)	--	--	--	--
15+ years	2.4	66	11	(266)	--	--	--	--
TOTAL	2.4	64	11	(356)	2.7	49	20	(659)

Table 22

MEAN IDEAL FAMILY-SIZE AND PERCENTAGE SAYING TWO CHILDREN OR FOUR OR MORE CHILDREN: WHITE WOMEN IN CALIFORNIA, NOVEMBER 1970, AND IN THE UNITED STATES, OCTOBER 1970, BY AGE, EDUCATIONAL LEVEL, INCOME, RELIGION, AREA OF RESIDENCE IN THE STATE, AND LENGTH OF TIME IN THE STATE

	CALIFORNIA November 1970				UNITED STATES October 1970			
		Percent				Percent		
	$\bar{X}$	2	4+	(N)	$\bar{X}$	2	4+	(N)
AGE								
Under 30	2.4	64	15	(141)	2.7	56	23	(132)
30-44	2.7	52	23	(161)	3.2	37	41	(216)
45+	2.7	47	21	(191)	3.0	35	34	(343)
EDUCATION								
Grade School	2.9	52	26	(31)	3.3	35	49	(105)
High School	2.6	54	19	(247)	3.0	37	34	(437)
College	2.6	53	20	(214)	2.8	49	23	(152)
INCOME								
Under $5,000	2.7	48	27	(90)	3.1	37	39	(165)
$5,000-6,999	2.7	50	20	(46)	3.1	36	41	(91)
$7,000-9,999	2.6	50	19	(101)	3.1	39	32	(138)
$10,000-14,999	2.6	55	18	(118)	3.0	40	34	(101)
$15,000+	2.5	62	20	(118)	2.8	44	28	(190)
RELIGION								
Catholic	3.0	42	32	(142)	3.3	26	47	(193)
Non-Catholic	2.5	58	16	(351)	2.9	45	29	(501)
AREA								
LA/Orange	2.7	52	23	(204)	--	--	--	--
Other So/Cal	2.5	53	14	(85)	--	--	--	--
Bay Area	2.7	55	21	(97)	--	--	--	--
Other No/Cal	2.5	57	19	(107)	--	--	--	--
TIME IN STATE								
Under 5 years	2.5	47	18	(66)	--	--	--	--
5-14 years	2.7	62	21	(80)	--	--	--	--
15+ years	2.6	53	20	(346)	--	--	--	--
TOTAL	2.6	54	20	(493)	3.0	40	34	(694)

Table 23

MEAN IDEAL FAMILY-SIZE AND PERCENTAGE SAYING TWO CHILDREN OR FOUR OR MORE CHILDREN: WHITE NON-CATHOLIC MEN, WHITE MEN UNDER AGE 45, AND WHITE NON-CATHOLIC MEN UNDER AGE 45 IN CALIFORNIA, NOVEMBER 1970, AND IN THE UNITED STATES, OCTOBER 1970, BY EDUCATIONAL LEVEL AND INCOME

	CALIFORNIA November 1970				UNITED STATES October 1970			
	$\bar{X}$	Percent 2	4+	(N)	$\bar{X}$	Percent 2	4+	(N)
				Non-Catholic Men				
EDUCATION								
Grade School	2.6	59	17	(29)	3.0	40	34	(96)
High School	2.4	66	10	(105)	2.5	54	13	(213)
College	2.2	68	8	(139)	2.6	57	13	(159)
INCOME								
Under $5,000	2.4	65	12	(40)	2.8	33	26	(93)
$5,000-6,999	2.6	52	18	(27)	2.8	52	26	(54)
$7,000-9,999	2.3	65	8	(52)	2.6	63	16	(91)
$10,000-14,999	2.3	79	10	(61)	2.6	60	16	(68)
$15,000+	2.3	61	5	(77)	2.5	53	11	(160)
TOTAL	2.3	66	10	(273)	2.6	52	18	(471)
				Men Under Age 45				
EDUCATION								
Grade School	--[a]	--	--	--	--	--	--	--
High School	2.4	67	9	(81)	2.7	54	18	(148)
College	2.2	69	6	(108)	2.6	62	12	(122)
INCOME								
Under $5,000 / $5,000-6,999	2.3	68	10	(40)	2.6	56	13	(52)
$7,000-9,999	2.3	76	4	(45)	2.8	55	20	(74)
$10,000-14,999	2.3	75	9	(44)	2.7	54	20	(46)
$15,000+	2.3	62	5	(61)	2.5	60	11	(107)
TOTAL	2.3	69	8	(196)	2.6	57	16	(281)
				Non-Catholic Men Under Age 45				
EDUCATION								
Grade School	--	--	--	--	--	--	--	--
High School	2.4	68	7	(60)	2.5	63	12	(86)
College	2.1	72	6	(82)	2.5	64	14	(87)
INCOME								
Under $5,000 / $5,000-6,999	2.1	69	7	(29)	2.6	53	13	(38)
$7,000-9,999	2.3	74	6	(35)	2.5	75	11	(44)
$10,000-14,999	2.2	82	9	(33)	2.6	57	18	(28)
$15,000+	2.2	64	2	(45)	2.5	62	12	(69)
TOTAL	2.2	71	7	(147)	2.6	62	13	(180)

[a] Fewer than 25 cases in total.

Table 24

MEAN IDEAL FAMILY-SIZE AND PERCENTAGE SAYING TWO CHILDREN OR FOUR OR MORE CHILDREN: WHITE NON-CATHOLIC WOMEN, WHITE WOMEN UNDER AGE 45, AND WHITE NON-CATHOLIC WOMEN UNDER AGE 45 IN CALIFORNIA, NOVEMBER 1970, AND IN THE UNITED STATES, OCTOBER 1970, BY EDUCATIONAL LEVEL AND INCOME

	CALIFORNIA November 1970				UNITED STATES October 1970			
	$\bar{X}$	Percent 2	4+	(N)	$\bar{X}$	Percent 2	4+	(N)
Non-Catholic Women								
EDUCATION								
Grade School	--[a]	--	--	--	3.3	35	49	(74)
High School	2.5	63	14	(171)	2.9	43	27	(307)
College	2.4	55	16	(158)	2.7	55	20	(120)
INCOME								
Under $5,000	2.5	52	22	(67)	3.1	39	35	(127)
$5,000-6,999	2.7	48	23	(31)	3.1	41	36	(69)
$7,000-9,999	2.4	56	12	(72)	2.9	44	26	(97)
$10,000-14,999	2.6	60	16	(83)	2.8	47	26	(68)
$15,000+	2.2	68	10	(87)	2.6	53	22	(133)
TOTAL	2.4	58	16	(351)	2.9	45	29	(501)
Women Under Age 45								
EDUCATION								
Grade School	--	--	--	--	--	--	--	--
High School	2.5	60	18	(154)	3.1	39	37	(228)
College	2.5	54	21	(138)	2.9	56	23	(99)
INCOME								
Under $5,000	2.6	53	22	(64)	3.2	39	45	(84)
$5,000-6,999								
$7,000-9,999	2.5	58	18	(66)	3.2	43	34	(86)
$10,000-14,999	2.6	55	17	(82)	3.1	37	35	(57)
$15,000+	2.4	66	21	(80)	2.8	52	26	(117)
TOTAL	2.5	58	19	(302)	3.0	44	34	(348)
Non-Catholic Women Under Age 45								
EDUCATION								
Grade School	--	--	--	--	--	--	--	--
High School	2.4	70	12	(105)	2.9	46	31	(150)
College	2.3	55	16	(100)	2.6	64	17	(75)
INCOME								
Under $5,000	2.7	51	22	(45)	3.2	41	43	(61)
$5,000-6,999								
$7,000-9,999	2.2	63	11	(46)	3.0	50	28	(58)
$10,000-14,999	2.5	62	14	(58)	2.9	43	23	(35)
$15,000+	2.2	72	12	(58)	2.5	66	17	(77)
TOTAL	2.4	63	14	(211)	2.9	52	27	(231)

[a] Fewer than 25 cases in total.

preferences by educational and income breakdowns for non-Catholics, persons in the reproductive ages, and non-Catholics in the reproductive ages, demonstrate that the smaller family-size ideals of Californians as compared with the nation as a whole were maintained within all subcategories shown.

The substantial difference between the family-size ideals in California and the nation leads us to ask about the relation of the West to the nation and of California to the West. Table 25 gives this comparison of family-size preferences among all whites by sex--and by sex, among non-Catholics, persons in the reproductive ages, and non-Catholics in the reproductive ages. Clearly, family-size ideals in the West were not, by and large, lower than those of the nation and, when factors such as age and religion are controlled, the Western ideal was as high or even higher than the nation's. The ideals in the West were typically higher than in the East, especially when age and religion are controlled. Hence, family-size ideals in California differed more from those in the Western region than from those in the East or the total country. This divergence from the Western ideal may seem reasonable in view of the greater degree of urbanization in California than in the other Western states. However, urbanization is obviously not the entire answer, since Californians' preferred smaller families than Easterners also. These data lead us to ask whether, regardless of socio-economic background, age, or religious persuasion, migrants to California have not been self-selected according to characteristics that are related to small-family preferences--a lack of traditional kinship ties, an abhorrence of high densities, and a desire to pursue forms of recreation that are not well-suited to large families and continued childbearing.

California is by no means homogeneous with regard to family-size preferences. Tables 21-24 show that respondents of lower income and education preferred larger families than did those in the highest educational and income brackets. An intriguing phenomenon is the sex difference in family-size preferences when viewed in relation to age, for both California and the nation. Although women invariably preferred larger families than men did, this difference was small among those under 30 and those age 45 and over. The biggest difference between the sexes occurred in the 30-44 year old bracket--where, in both California and the country, men preferred families as small as did their counterparts under age 30, but women wanted families approximately half a child larger. One can only surmise that this age group of women, unlike younger ones, had already committed itself to reproduction as a major enterprise, and did not feel free to publicly change its views. The men, however, were feeling ever more free to express the smaller

Table 25

MEAN IDEAL FAMILY-SIZE FOR THE EASTERN AND WESTERN REGIONS OF
THE UNITED STATES, AND CALIFORNIA, AMONG WHITES, BY SEX FOR
VARIOUS AGE AND RELIGIOUS CATEGORIES: UNITED STATES,
OCTOBER 1970, AND CALIFORNIA, NOVEMBER 1970

Region[a]	Men	Women	Non-Catholic Men	Non-Catholic Women	Under 45 Men	Under 45 Women	Non-Catholic Under 45 Men	Non-Catholic Under 45 Women
UNITED STATES								
East	2.6	2.9	2.5	2.7	2.6	2.9	2.4	2.7
West	2.9	2.9	2.7	2.8	3.0	3.0	3.1	2.9
Total	2.7	3.0	2.6	2.9	2.6	3.0	2.6	2.9
CALIFORNIA	2.4	2.6	2.3	2.5	2.3	2.5	2.2	2.4

[a] Included in the Eastern Region are: Maine, New Hampshire, Vermont, Massachusetts, Rhode Island, Connecticut, New York, New Jersey, Pennsylvania, Maryland, Delaware, West Virginia, District of Columbia. The Western Region includes: California, Oregon, Washington, Montana, Arizona, Colorado, Idaho, Wyoming, Utah, Nevada, New Mexico.

family-size preferences they have maintained throughout the entire series of data for the United States since the 1930's.[3]

So far we have discussed only average family-size ideals. However, as previously noted, it is important for us to look also at the distribution of family-size preferences in the population, since it is the distribution that tells us whether, for example, many people prefer childlessness, or only one child, thereby leaving others free to have larger families. The data show that Californians, like other Americans, had no preferences for childlessness and, if they were going to have children, typically wanted at least two. Only 3 percent of our sample favored childlessness, and 2 percent preferred one child. There was a remarkable concentration on the two-child family. Almost two-thirds of the white men in the state gave two as their ideal, and, among those under age 30 (as well as among those in the highest income bracket), the proportion rose to three-fourths. Among women, 54 percent favored two children, and among young women (and those in the highest income bracket), the proportion was two-thirds. When Catholics were excluded, the two-child preference rose to 71 percent for men in the reproductive ages and 63 percent for women.

It is thus clear that, although Californians desired smaller families than Americans generally, like the rest of the country they had an antipathy to childlessness and a definite threshold below which they judged it undesirable for family-size to fall. (On the basis of national data I have collected concerning the upper and lower limits of family-size preferences, I have concluded it would be unwise to believe that this lower threshold will change without marked social changes. In October 1970, I inserted the following two questions in a national sample survey conducted by the Gallup Poll: "According to your personal tastes and preferences, what size family do you think is too small? Too large?" The average family-size judged to be too small by Americans was 1.4 children. Seventy-six percent of respondents said that one child was too few. The average family-size judged to be too large was 5.5 children. Only 17 percent said that three children were too many.) Family-size preferences

---

[3] Judith Blake: "Ideal Family Size Among White Americans: A Quarter of a Century's Evidence," *Demography*, Vol. 3, No. 1, 1966, pp. 154-173; "The Americanization of Catholic Reproductive Ideals," *Population Studies*, Vol. 20 (July 1966), pp. 27-43; "Reproductive Ideals and Educational Attainment Among White Americans," *Population Studies*, Vol. 21 (September 1967), pp. 159-174; "Income and Reproductive Motivation," *Population Studies*, Vol. 21 (November 1967), pp. 185-206.

in the country as a whole have dropped significantly during the
recent recession, and it is possible that the absolute levels of
Californians' responses have been similarly influenced. Unfortunately, we do not have trend data for California. However, it
appears certain that Californians--even during the recession--have
not come close to preferring families small enough to give zero
population growth, and it is likely that in normally prosperous
times their family-size preferences will be larger. With this in
mind, let us look at their reasons for preferring two children.

Why Two Children?

Respondents who replied that they favored the two-child
family were asked: "Why do you say two children rather than more?
What considerations do you have in mind?"

Perhaps the most significant feature of the responses
shown in Table 26 is the reasons that were not given for wanting
only two children. For example, respondents do not appear to
have thought in terms of alternative activities in which they
could engage, alternative roles they could play, non-economic
opportunity-costs of larger families. The parental role was
apparently taken for granted, and if not, scaling it down was
not something about which the respondents were vocal. It is also
significant that, with the exception of a few respondents mentioning love and affection, they did not reply in terms of the two-child family as a better child-rearing unit than a larger one.
From Table 26, we see that the most salient reasons given for
having a two-child family were economic. Despite the state's
affluence, almost 40 percent of the responses concerned the
difficulty of having more than two children if parents are to
provide the basic necessities of food, clothing, and shelter.
Obviously, the respondents' standards for these necessities were
luxurious. An additional 20 percent of the responses concerned
the provision of advantages to children--higher education, special
training, etc. Aside from these responses, only one other category was important--the desirability of attaining zero population
growth, and the need to stop growth because of environmental
problems. In general, therefore, one has the impression that
the respondents had backed into the preference for two children
because of their high standards of living, which had been particularly challenged during the recession period.

On the other hand, when one looks at the responses by
age, one sees that there may be small family-size desires emerging
that are independent of either a sudden sense of deprivation, or
a shift to prosperity. For example, there is a striking difference
in the responses of older and younger, and college-educated and
less-educated, men. Whatever their actual reason may have been
for preferring two children, young, highly educated men were much

Table 26

FOUR PRINCIPAL REASONS FOR PREFERRING TWO CHILDREN: WHITE MEN AND WOMEN BY AGE, EDUCATIONAL LEVEL, INCOME, AND RELIGION: CALIFORNIA, NOVEMBER 1970

	Percentage Saying:				
	Afford Basics	Afford Advantages	Population/ Environment	Large Family Less Love & Attention	Total Responses
Men					
AGE					
Under 30	33	10	28	10	(99)
30-44	41	17	20	5	(75)
45+	38	25	19	4	(111)
EDUCATION					
Grade School	28	31	14	3	(29)
High School	47	14	16	8	(110)
College	32	18	30	6	(146)
INCOME					
Under $5,000 $5,000-6,999	33	15	25	10	(60)
$7,000-9,999	39	18	20	10	(61)
$10,000-14,999	39	14	18	6	(71)
$15,000+	36	21	29	3	(77)
RELIGION					
Catholic	38	21	18	7	(61)
Non-Catholic	37	17	24	7	(224)
TOTAL	37	18	22	7	(285)
Women					
AGE					
Under 30	36	23	20	9	(132)
30-44	40	22	21	5	(108)
45+	39	27	15	7	(118)
EDUCATION					
Grade School	--[a]	--	--	--	--
High School	40	27	14	8	(189)
College	35	22	26	5	(149)
INCOME					
Under $5,000	54	20	11	9	(55)
$5,000-6,999	32	27	8	11	(37)
$7,000-9,999	42	20	18	4	(77)
$10,000-14,999	36	26	20	7	(83)
$15,000+	32	27	26	6	(96)
RELIGION					
Catholic	41	24	12	7	(87)
Non-Catholic	37	24	21	7	(271)
TOTAL	38	24	19	7	(358)

[a] Fewer than 25 cases in total.

less likely to justify the two-child family in terms of either economic necessities or ec 1omic advantages than were those over 30 and of less education. One may believe that the emphasis by this group on population growth and ecology was solely a function of their greater "enlightenment." However, the fact is that this echelon has maintained smaller family-size preferences for the entire 35-year-period for which we have data.[4] Hence it seems more reasonable to assume that the population-ecology movement has provided these men with the first genuine, socially acceptable antidote to motherhood that has come their way. One has the suspicion that, although they may want some family, they do not wish to enslave themselves in the syndrome of attempting to provide an upper-status American way of life for a wife and three or four children. At the same time that some highly educated women are "liberating" themselves, a fair share of highly educated men are expressing a wish to avoid heavy commitments to a family.

It is noteworthy that women were more likely than men to mention economic reasons for a small family (particularly the provision of "advantages" for children). Women were similar throughout the age groups in their concern for "advantages"--approximately a quarter of the responses in each age group spoke to this point. But among men, provision of "advantages" for children was rarely mentioned by those under 30, although among older men (age 45 and over) this response was as frequent as among women. Ecological/population reasons were more salient among the young than the old of both sexes, but among young men such considerations were almost as important as being able to afford the basics of child support. Women differed greatly in mentioning population and ecology depending on level of education and income. Highly educated women and those in high income brackets were almost as likely as men to mention population growth and ecology. One may surmise that this group of women in California is heavily weighted by those who are, or wish to be, career-oriented, and who are rapidly beginning to take advantage of the society's greater alternative roles and activities. They have found an unselfish reason to justify and give status to what they have wanted to do all along.

What of the future? The respondents were interviewed during a bleak period of high unemployment and tight credit. In view of their concentration on economic problems, it is likely that their family-size preferences will drift upward with prosperity and easy money. However, the sexes differed. Not only did more men than women want small families, but young men appeared to be searching for a justification that would not disappear with the advent of prosperity--namely, population growth and ecology.

---

[4] See footnote 3.

Among women, there was clearly more interest in small families among the more highly educated--an interest that may be sustained if the society genuinely opens up alternatives to motherhood. However, if the promise to women that has recently emerged forecloses--if we clamp down on jobs, opportunity, and education for them--then there may again be a retreat into motherhood. Clearly, the avant-garde of women does not have, as yet, broadly based support.

Why Three or More?

Respondents who idealized three or more children were asked: "What do you think are the advantages of this size family rather than a smaller one?" Table 27 shows that (excluding the answers in terms of why the respondent did not prefer more than three) most responses were in terms of the child-rearing advantages of a larger family, and the greater viability of the family group when it is larger. Few respondents mentioned any expectations of help from children--either concurrently or in old age. Rather, respondents who desired a larger family viewed it primarily as instrumental to success in achieving its own ends--the rearing of offspring. And, like respondents who indicated a desire for only two children, they offered rationalizations in terms of the children's welfare, or the public good. In neither case did the average adult think of a response in terms of his own interests, statuses, or activities--or, if he thought of one, he did not deem it appropriate.

Conclusions

What may we conclude from these results? Bearing in mind that one survey does not make a policy, it seems to me that some of the implications are nonetheless important.

There is clearly a broadly based concern in the state about environmental degradation. Although the issue has high saliency only for an elite, its significance is averred by almost all respondents replying to a direct question. Further, as yet the issue has no structured opposition.

Most respondents believe not only that population growth in the state is a major contributor to environmental problems, but also that the state is justified in having a policy to discourage further demographic increase. There is, at present, little spontaneous aversion to the idea of a policy to discourage demographic expansion. On the contrary, there is opposition to policies that are believed to encourage in-migration, such as lack of residency requirements for welfare and publicity about the state. Non-whites appear to be no more in favor of attracting

Table 27

FOUR PRINCIPAL REASONS FOR PREFERRING THREE OR MORE CHILDREN: WHITE MEN AND WOMEN BY AGE, EDUCATIONAL LEVEL, INCOME, AND RELIGION: CALIFORNIA, NOVEMBER 1970

	Percentage Saying:				
	Togetherness/ Companionship	Not Spoiled, Selfish	More Socially Adjusted	Can't Afford More than 3	Total Responses
	Men				
AGE					
Under 30	41	11	11	15	(27)
30-44	32	21	15	12	(34)
45+	29	9	9	19	(75)
EDUCATION					
Grade School	--[a]	--	--	--	--
High School	32	9	9	15	(54)
College	37	17	15	12	(60)
INCOME					
Under $5,000 $5,000-6,999	25	8	11	19	(36)
$7,000-9,999 $10,000-14,999	33	11	9	11	(45)
$15,000+	36	17	14	17	(52)
RELIGION					
Catholic	37	5	8	11	(38)
Non-Catholic	31	15	12	18	(98)
TOTAL	32	12	11	16	(136)
	Women				
AGE					
Under 30	36	23	15	11	(53)
30-44	29	22	18	15	(82)
45+	29	20	8	16	(116)
EDUCATION					
Grade School	--	--	--	--	--
High School	30	22	12	14	(125)
College	30	22	16	15	(108)
INCOME					
Under $5,000 $5,000-6,999	32	22	9	18	(77)
$7,000-9,999	35	19	11	11	(57)
$10,000-14,999	35	24	16	14	(58)
$15,000+	21	19	19	11	(47)
RELIGION					
Catholic	34	18	11	15	(98)
Non-Catholic	29	23	14	14	(153)
TOTAL	31	21	13	15	(251)

[a] Fewer than 25 cases in total.

migrants than are whites. This can doubtless be explained in terms of the immediate individual aspirations of non-whites already resident in the state. The fulfillment of their aspirations is not rendered more probable by the continued influx of additional impoverished migrants.

It is of interest that Californians have not been as actively considering redistribution of population in the state as they have growth. There is an indication that metropolitan area residents are reluctant to regard metropolitan concentration as a major cause of problems like pollution. The uncertainty of respondents is understandable, since it is by no means clear that spreading smaller-scale urban development more evenly over the state would improve the environment generally, whatever it might do for Los Angeles and the Bay Area.

The consistent underestimation of the state's population by respondents suggests that population figures per se are not very meaningful, but that people nonetheless assign to numerical increase the blame for problems associated with it--increased densities in metropolitan areas, air pollution, tax increases, escalation of crime, violence, and social diseases such as VD and drug addiction, high rates of illegitimacy, and problems in the educational system. Were high densities arrived at gradually and with few startling social pathologies accompanying them, tolerance for the increase in numbers would doubtless be much greater. Witness, for example, the far more tightly packed countries of Belgium and France, where there is an emphasis on population expansion rather than curtailment.

Finally, it is significant that the family-size desires of Californians are, within numerous sub-groupings, lower than those for the nation as a whole. This suggests that respondents are consistent in desiring a cessation of growth. To be sure, even during the present recession, family-size desires are substantially larger than would produce zero growth in the absence of migration. There is virtual consensus on the desirability of at least two children, and respondents do not seem predisposed to give up parenthood altogether in favor of pursuing alternative personal goals. The desire for larger families among the less-advantaged argues for policy that rapidly upgrades these groups educationally and occupationally--having special concern for the advancement of their women as well as their men, since the women are particularly pressured into traditional maternal roles. Similarly, the justification for small families in demographic/ecological terms offered by young respondents suggests that state policy should specifically direct itself to opening up demanding and fulfilling alternatives to family involvement--again particularly for women, since they are especially vulnerable to backsliding into the pattern of existing roles if viable alternatives are not presented. The high standards of living of California residents and the state's basic affluence have resulted in critical shortages in the service sector--medicine and dentistry being prime examples. The state has the opportunity to divert individuals from redundant reproduction into rewarding occupations where they are desperately needed.

Acknowledgements

I acknowledge support from the California State Assembly to cover the costs of obtaining the data discussed in this paper. Grants from the Ford Foundation and the National Institute of Child Health and Human Development have contributed to its completion. Particular thanks are due to individuals without whose assistance this paper could not have been written: Joie B. Hubbert of the Field Research Corporation provided expertise in the data collecting stage; Heidi Nebel and Bronia Johnson were most helpful in the task of data processing; and Ann Harrington contributed her excellent typing skills. I wish also to thank Frederick G. Styles of the California State Assembly for his advice and administrative help during the course of the project.

CALIFORNIANS' VIEWS ON POPULATION AND THE ENVIRONMENT

Appendix A

QUESTIONS ASKED ON NOVEMBER, 1970 CALIFORNIA POLL

1. In your opinion, what do you think is the ideal size of a family--a husband, wife, and how many children?

2. IF "TWO CHILDREN" ON QUESTION 1, ASK:

    Why do you say two children rather than more? What considerations do you have in mind? (PROBE: What other reasons are there?)

3. IF "THREE OR MORE" CHILDREN ON QUESTION 1, ASK:

    What do you think are the advantages of this size family rather than a smaller one? (PROBE: What other reasons are there?)

4. Approximately how many million people would you say there are in California now?

5. As you know, there has been a lot of discussion in California recently about the state's environmental problems--things like rapidly using up our natural resources, air and water pollution, pressures on recreational space and so on. Some people say that the growth of population in the state is an important cause of California's environmental problems, while other people feel this is not an important cause. Which of the statements on this card comes closest to describing how you feel?

    1. One of the most important causes of environmental problems.

    2. Quite important--ranks somewhere in the middle.

    3. Not too important--may be important but I have doubts.

    4. Not at all important--I don't think it has any influence on environmental problems.

    5. I don't think California has any environmental problems.

6. IF "ONE OF THE MOST IMPORTANT CAUSES" OR "QUITE IMPORTANT" IN QUESTION 5, ASK:

   What do you think the State of California should do to discourage further population growth? (PROBE: What else?)

7. Some people also say that an important cause of California's environmental problems is the geographic distribution of the population in the state--that is, that people are overly concentrated in a few metropolitan areas of the state--while other people feel that this is not an important cause. Which of the statements on this card comes closest to describing how you feel?

   1. One of the most important causes of environmental problems.

   2. Quite important--ranks somewhere in the middle.

   3. Not too important--may be important but I have doubts.

   4. Not at all important--I don't think it has any influence on environmental problems.

   5. I don't think California has any environmental problems.

8. IF "ONE OF THE MOST IMPORTANT CAUSES" OR "QUITE IMPORTANT" IN QUESTION 7, ASK:

   What do you think the State of California should do to change the geographic distribution of the population? (PROBE: What else?)

PART IV

REPRODUCTIVE PATTERNS, PROBLEMS, AND POLICIES

MARRIAGE REGULATION AND THE CALIFORNIA BIRTH RATE

June Sklar

When future historians look back upon mid-twentieth-century California and characterize the citizenry, they may be tempted to label us, with all due respect to the Spanish padres, as The Early Californians. For in the past several decades, Californians have married earlier than at any time in their recorded history. Yet never has there been more of a necessity to marry later than at present. In what follows, I will show how the early age at marriage of Californians acts to aggravate the population growth we are experiencing, and how through a policy of increasing the age at which couples marry we can reduce this growth. I will also suggest that even with the tangible benefits of delayed marriage, certain demographic and personal costs may cause Californians to hesitate to accept such regulation upon their marital behavior.

To analyze the impact of marriage regulation on the birth rate and the consequences of such regulation, this paper focuses on four basic questions. First, what is the present marriage situation in California? At what age do Californians typically enter matrimony, and how do they compare in this respect with people in the rest of the United States and other countries? Second, what difference does it make if Californians marry early or late? In terms of fertility levels and other demographic and non-demographic factors, what kinds of "benefits" can be obtained by changing the age at marriage in California? Third, what are the means by which the age at marriage can be regulated? What kinds of deprivations or "costs" will Californians have to endure in order to achieve these "benefits"? Finally, given the

---

The research for this paper was supported partly by a contract that International Population and Urban Research (IPUR) and the California State Department of Public Health have jointly with the National Institute of Child Health and Human Development, Center for Population Research (NIH-70-2196); by a grant to IPUR from the same agency (1 R02 HD04602-02); and by a Ford Foundation Grant to the Department of Demography, University of California, Berkeley. The author wishes to thank Arlene Guerriero and Sarah Tsai, both on the staff of IPUR, for their research assistance in preparing this paper, and Eduardo E. Arriaga and Fred Sklar for their advice.

"benefits" and "costs" of marriage regulation, what is the possibility of actually changing marriage behavior in California? Let us begin with a delineation of the present marriage situation in California.

Marriage in California

California is very similar to the rest of the United States with respect to marriage behavior. Regardless of which indicator of age at marriage is used--the median ages of brides and grooms marrying for the first time (see Table 1), or the age at which exactly half of the population has ever been married (see Table 2)--we see that both California and the United States are early marriage regions, especially compared to the West European countries. No matter what measure we look at, California women first marry at about age 20, and California men at about age 23--ages that are very comparable to those of the United States,[1] but that are in sharp contrast to the West European countries, where women on the average do not first marry until their 22nd birthday or later, and men not until their 24th birthday or later. While the marital age in both California and the United States has risen slightly in the past decade (Table 1), this rise is insufficient to change the basically early marriage pattern of either the state or the nation.[2] In fact, if we turn from summary measures such as the median, and examine the distribution of brides and grooms marrying for the first time by age (see Table 3), the tendency toward early marriage in both California and the United States appears even more pronounced. Between 1958 and 1967, for example, the most common age of brides marrying for the first time was 19 or younger.[3]

---

[1] An early age at marriage is associated with a fairly early age at remarriage in both California and the United States. (See Appendix Table A. Also see pp. 192ff. below for a further discussion of age at remarriage.)

[2] This is not to say that there are no areas in the United States where marriage occurs relatively late, or that California is necessarily the earliest marrying state in the union. The Northeast region, for example, typically has later marriages than the rest of the country, and women in Wyoming marry substantially earlier than women in California (see Appendix Table B). In spite of these variations, however, the early marriage pattern of Californians and most Americans is unmistakable.

[3] During every year between 1958 and 1967, 40 to 50 percent of all brides marrying for the first time fell into the age group under 20.

Table 1

MEDIAN AGES OF BRIDES AND GROOMS MARRYING FOR THE FIRST TIME, IN CALIFORNIA, U.S. MARRIAGE-REGISTRATION AREA (USMRA),[a] AND WESTERN EUROPE: 1958-1967

	Year	Brides California	Brides USMRA	Grooms California	Grooms USMRA
California-USMRA	1958	19.8	20.2	23.1	23.2
	1959	19.8	20.2	23.1	23.2
	1960	19.6	20.2	23.0	23.1
	1961	19.8	20.2	23.2	23.1
	1962	20.3	20.3	23.1	23.0
	1963	20.4	20.5	23.1	23.0
	1964	20.4	20.6	23.0	23.0
	1965	20.4	20.5	22.9	22.9
	1966	20.4	20.5	22.8	22.8
	1967	20.7	20.8	22.9	22.9
Western Europe					
Finland	1965	22.0		23.9	
Austria	1967	22.3		24.9	
Netherlands	1967	22.6		24.3	
West Germany	1966	22.7		25.3	
Sweden	1967	22.7		24.4	
Portugal	1967	23.0		25.8	
Italy	1966	23.3		27.3	
Switzerland	1966	23.3		25.6	
Spain	1967	23.8		27.3	
Ireland	1967	24.1		27.0	

[a] The Marriage-Registration Area was established in 1957 for the collection of marriage statistics, and includes states with sufficiently complete and adequate programs for collecting marriage statistics. When established, the USMRA included 28 states and, in addition, all of New York except New York City, Alaska, Hawaii, Puerto Rico, and the Virgin Islands. In 1967, it included 38 states, the District of Columbia, Puerto Rico, and the Virgin Islands. Marriages in the USMRA accounted for 75 percent of all marriages in the United States in 1967. For further information, see Technical Appendix of the **Vital Statistics of the United States: 1967**.

Sources: U.S. Department of Health, Education and Welfare: **Vital Statistics of the United States: 1967**, Vol. III, **Marriage and Divorce**, pp. 1-14, 1-15; **Vital Statistics...1966**, III, pp. 1-14, 1-15; **Vital Statistics...1965**, III, pp. 1-17, 1-19; **Vital Statistics...1964**, III, pp. 1-18, 1-20; **Vital Statistics...1963**, III, pp. 1-17, 1-19; **Vital Statistics...1962**, III, p. 1-21; **Vital Statistics...1961**, III, p. 2-12; **Vital Statistics...1960**, III, pp. 2-16, 2-17; **Vital Statistics...1959**, I, p. 61; **Vital Statistics...1958**, I, p. 80.

Table 2

AGE AT WHICH HALF OF THE POPULATION HAS EVER BEEN MARRIED, IN CALIFORNIA, THE UNITED STATES, AND SELECTED WESTERN EUROPEAN COUNTRIES: C. 1960

State or Country	Age	
	Female	Male
California 1960		
Total	20.2	22.9
White	20.2	22.8
Nonwhite	20.6	24.4
United States 1960		
Total	20.6	23.0
White	20.5	22.9
Nonwhite	21.0	23.7
Belgium 1961	21.9	24.8
Norway 1960	22.5	26.3
Denmark 1960	22.1	25.5
Netherlands 1960	23.7	26.1
Sweden 1965	23.5	26.1
Ireland 1966	25.8	29.9

Sources: U.S. Bureau of the Census, United States Census of Population: 1960, Vol. I, Characteristics of the Population, Pt. 1, United States Summary, p. 436; United Nations Demographic Yearbook: 1968, Special Topic: Marriage and Divorce Statistics, pp. 248, 249, 256-263; United Nations Demographic Yearbook: 1963, Special Topic: Population Census Statistics II, pp. 728-731.

Table 3

PERCENTAGE DISTRIBUTION OF BRIDES AND GROOMS MARRYING FOR THE FIRST TIME, BY AGE, IN CALIFORNIA AND THE U.S. MARRIAGE-REGISTRATION AREA: 1958-1967[a]

Year	Percent of All Brides Who Are:				Percent of All Grooms Who Are:			
	<20	20-24	25-29	30+	<20	20-24	25-29	30+
				California				
1958	51.8	33.5	8.5	6.2	18.4	50.4	19.4	11.8
1959	51.7	33.6	8.5	6.2	18.2	51.0	18.8	12.0
1960	53.0	32.4	8.1	6.5	20.4	48.6	18.9	12.1
1961	51.1	33.9	8.6	6.4	17.9	49.9	20.6	11.6
1962	47.6	40.5	7.8	4.1	16.4	54.2	19.0	10.4
1963	46.5	40.0	7.7	5.8	17.3	53.4	18.2	11.1
1964	47.0	39.7	8.3	5.0	16.0	56.9	17.4	9.7
1965	46.8	40.2	7.9	5.1	18.2	54.1	17.4	10.3
1966	47.2	39.8	8.3	4.7	19.6	53.4	18.2	8.8
1967	44.0	43.4	8.1	4.5	18.5	53.8	18.2	9.5
				U.S. Marriage-Registration Area				
1958	48.4	37.7	7.6	6.3	15.6	53.5	19.3	11.6
1959	48.6	37.8	7.4	6.2	16.1	53.5	18.6	11.8
1960	48.4	38.0	7.3	6.3	16.9	53.2	18.3	11.6
1961	48.3	38.8	7.0	5.9	16.8	54.4	17.5	11.3
1962	48.0	39.8	6.9	5.3	17.4	54.2	17.6	10.8
1963	45.4	42.6	6.7	5.3	16.3	56.3	16.7	10.7
1964	45.3	42.9	6.7	5.1	15.9	57.7	16.3	10.1
1965	45.5	42.2	7.0	5.2	17.7	55.9	16.4	10.0
1966	46.0	42.0	7.1	5.0	20.0	53.2	17.1	9.7
1967	42.6	45.3	7.4	4.7	18.2	55.1	17.1	9.6

[a] Percentages for all brides total 100 percent for each year; percentages for all grooms total 100 percent for each year.

Sources: See Sources for Table 1 above.

The early marriage pattern of California is a phenomenon of only the last several decades. As Table 4 and Figure 1 indicate, although Americans around the beginning of this century generally married later than they do today, Californians married even later than most Americans. In 1900, California women did not wed until their mid-twenties, and California men not until their early thirties. These marital ages were about one and a half years older than that for all American women combined, and about four and a half years older than that for all American men. By 1920, California women had reduced their marital age to the same level as in other states, and by 1940, California men had done so as well. Since then, age at marriage in both California and the United States has declined in concert to the very young levels noted earlier.

Marriage, Fertility, and the California Birth Rate

Why, one may ask, should California be concerned about early marriage? Californians should be concerned about their early marriage behavior because such behavior is extremely pronatalist. Because fecundity, or a woman's ability to conceive and produce a live birth, is highest in her early 20's, late marriage postpones a woman's childbearing to her less fecund years, while early marriage advances it to her most fecund period.

Table 4

AGE AT WHICH EXACTLY HALF OF THE POPULATION HAS EVER BEEN MARRIED, IN CALIFORNIA AND THE UNITED STATES: 1900-1960

Census Year	Females		Males		Difference Between Males and Females	
	California	U.S.	California	U.S.	California	U.S.
1900	24.4	22.8	31.4	26.8	7.0	4.0
1910	22.6	22.3	30.2	26.4	7.6	4.1
1920	21.9	22.0	27.2	25.8	5.3	3.8
1930	21.7	22.0	26.4	25.5	4.7	3.5
1940	21.5	22.2	25.7	25.6	4.2	3.4
1950	20.4	20.8	23.7	23.8	3.3	3.0
1960	20.2	20.6	22.9	23.0	2.7	2.4

Source: U.S. Bureau of the Census, United States Census of Population: 1960, Vol. I, Characteristics of the Population, Pt. 1, United States Summary, pp. 436-438.

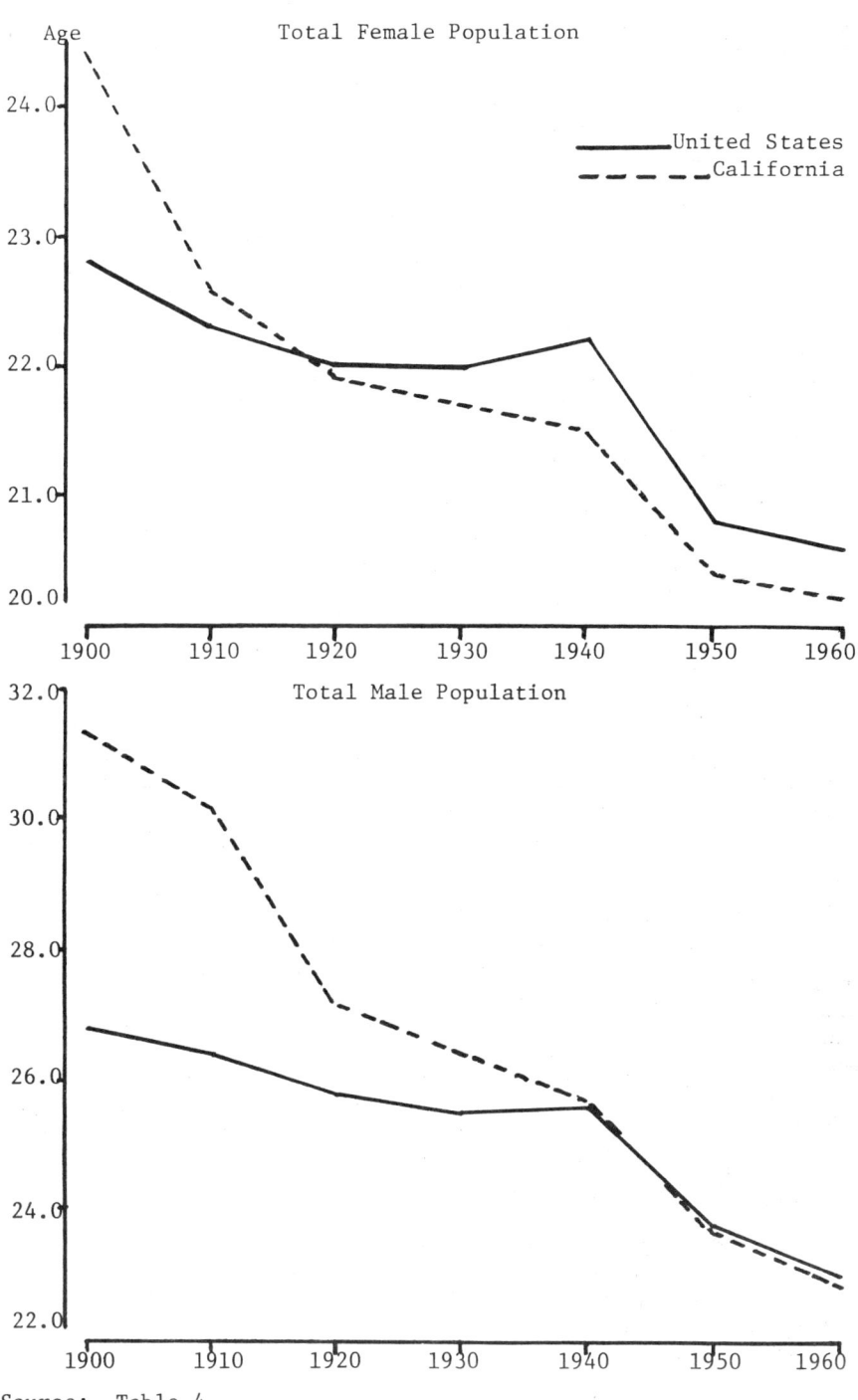

Figure 1
AGE AT WHICH EXACTLY HALF OF THE POPULATION HAS EVER BEEN MARRIED
IN CALIFORNIA AND THE UNITED STATES, 1900-1960

Source: Table 4.

The precise figures on the effect of young marriage in California are presently unavailable. We do know from United States data, however, that young marriage is supportive of high fertility in two major ways: it lessens the risk of childlessness, and increases the number of children ever born by those women who become mothers. Delayed or late marriage has exactly the opposite effect: it increases the proportion of women who cannot have a child, and reduces the family size of those who can have children. For example, Table 5 shows that among American women aged 45-54 who were married once and whose husbands were present in 1960, less than 8 percent of those women who wed in their early teens were childless by the end of their reproductive years. The comparable percentage for women who married at 30 or over was 45 percent, or almost six times as great. Among American women who became mothers, the impact of age at marriage on family size is equally significant: the number of children ever born among mothers who married before their 18th birthday was almost twice as large as among those who delayed marriage until their 30's. The very early marriers had a completed family size of a little over four children, compared to a little over two children for the very late marriers. Even if we ignore the very early and late marriers, and confine the comparison to women who married within a more reasonable age range--i.e., women who wed in their early 20's compared to women who wed in their late 20's--the difference in both childlessness and completed family size is still substantial.

One might argue, however, that the relationship between age at marriage and fertility has been oversimplified. In this regard, one could point to factors that are related to age at marriage, such as level of education and urban-rural residence, which may be producing the fertility differences. For example, highly educated urbanized women usually marry later and want fewer children than less educated rural women. In such a case, socioeconomic factors rather than late marriage per se would seem to be responsible for the low birth levels. But while it is true that women from higher socioeconomic groups generally have less children and higher proportions of childlessness than other women, Table 6 shows that <u>within</u> each socioeconomic group, women who marry late still have less children and higher levels of childlessness than women who marry early. Even among urban women whose husbands are college-educated professionals, those who did not marry until their 22nd birthday or later had slightly smaller families and a much greater percentage of childlessness than those who married before their 22nd birthday.

Nor does late marriage produce low fertility simply because women who marry late are more "realistic" about their potential reproductive behavior, and thus do not try as hard as those who marry early. According to this argument, the low family size of late marriers would not be due to the fact that

Table 5

CHILDREN EVER BORN AND PERCENT CHILDLESS AMONG WOMEN 45-54 WHO ARE MARRIED ONCE, HUSBAND PRESENT, BY RACE AND AGE AT FIRST MARRIAGE: UNITED STATES, 1960

Age at First Marriage	Children Ever Born Per:		Percent Childless
	1,000 Mothers[a]	1,000 Women[b]	
All Females			
14-17	4,069	3,757	7.7
18-19	3,349	3,057	8.7
20-21	2,980	2,648	11.1
22-24	2,694	2,307	14.4
25-26	2,548	2,074	18.6
27-29	2,409	1,828	24.1
30-44	2,130	1,171	45.0
White Females			
14-17	3,932	3,657	7.0
18-19	3,250	2,979	8.3
20-21	2,898	2,589	10.7
22-24	2,637	2,272	13.9
25-26	2,504	2,050	18.1
27-29	2,360	1,811	23.3
30-44	2,066	1,140	44.8
Nonwhite Females			
14-17	5,356	4,631	13.5
18-19	5,002	4,264	14.8
20-21	4,605	3,720	19.2
22-24	3,981	3,005	24.5
25-26	3,503	2,523	28.0
27-29	3,289	2,077	36.8
30-44	2,730	1,447	47.0

[a] Excludes all childless women.

[b] Includes childless women.

Source: U.S. Bureau of the Census, United States Census of Population: 1960, Women by Number of Children Ever Born, Final Report, PC(2)-3A, pp. 61, 67.

Table 6

CHILDREN EVER BORN AND PERCENT CHILDLESS AMONG WOMEN 45-54 WHO ARE MARRIED ONCE, HUSBAND PRESENT, BY RACE, AGE AT FIRST MARRIAGE, AND SOCIOECONOMIC STATUS: UNITED STATES, 1960

Residence of Woman and Occupation and Education of Husband	Women First Married at Ages 14-21			Women First Married at Age 22 and Over		
	Children Ever Born Per:		Percent Childless	Children Ever Born Per:		Percent Childless
	1,000 Mothers	1,000 Women		1,000 Mothers	1,000 Women	
White						
Resides in Urban Area; Husband Has Some College and in Professional Occupation	2,420	2,163	10.6	2,329	1,858	20.2
Resides in Rural Area; Husband Has No High School and Is in Laboring Occupation[a]	4,538	4,272	5.9	3,315	2,613	21.2
Nonwhite						
Resides in Urban Area; Husband Has Some College and in Professional Occupation	2,911	2,160	25.8	2,365	1,571	33.6
Resides in Rural Area; Husband Has No High School and Is in Laboring Occupation[a]	6,294	5,853	7.0	4,632	3,550	23.4

[a] Laborers excluding farm and mine.

Source: U.S. Bureau of the Census, United States Census of Population: 1960, Women by Number of Children Ever Born, Final Report, PC(2)-3A, pp. 202-217, 226-233.

they married late, but to the fact that after marriage they had lower age-specific fertility than women who married early. To test this possibility, we need age-specific fertility rates for women who marry after given ages. Unfortunately, such data is presently unavailable. However, we can obtain some idea of whether the childbearing performance of late marriers is lagging behind that of early marriers by examining the number of children ever born by age and marital duration at first marriage. As Table 7 demonstrates, among white women who had been married five years in 1960, those who married at 25-29 had almost the same number of children as those who married at 15-19: 2,142 and 2,250 respectively. Thus, at least in the early years of wedlock, the late marriers seem to be keeping abreast of the early marriers in terms of childbearing performance. Although they married late, there is nothing anemic about their fertility behavior. It is at the longer durations of marriage that the late marriers fall behind. By the 15th year of marriage, the gap between the early and late marriers has grown from one-tenth of a child to over half a child, and the difference is even greater if we look at all women instead of just mothers (Table 7). The extent to which the large gap at the longer marital durations is due to the greater "realism" of the late marriers, and the extent to which it is due to their lack of fecundity, is difficult to say. But no matter how realistic the late marriers may be, by the 15th year of their marriage they have little choice in the matter. By the time they reach their 15th wedding anniversary, women who first married at 25-29 are 40-44 and entering menopause.

Thus we see that regardless of their "realism," marital duration, or socioeconomic status, late-marrying women have higher levels of childlessness and smaller completed families than their early-marrying cohorts. And because Californians are an early- rather than late-marrying population, their behavior is supportive of high rather than low birth performance. The early marriage of most Californians in effect operates as a "built-in" tendency toward high fertility.

But it is precisely this kind of "built-in" pronatalist tendency that California does not need. Between 1960 and 1970, the population in California increased by approximately 4.3 million, or by about 2.5 percent annually. Such a growth rate, if continued indefinitely into the future, would double California's population within 29 years. While it is true that slightly more than half of this growth--or 53 percent--was due to in-migration, the remaining 47 percent was due to natural increase, or the surplus of births over deaths.[4] Hence, any attempt to control

---

[4] Eduardo Arriaga and Kingsley Davis, The Magnitude and Character of California's Population Growth (Berkeley: Institute of International Studies--forthcoming).

Table 7

CHILDREN EVER BORN TO WOMEN MARRIED ONCE, HUSBAND PRESENT, OF DIFFERENT MARITAL DURATIONS, BY RACE AND AGE AT FIRST MARRIAGE: UNITED STATES, 1960

Age at First Marriage	White Women with Marital Durations of:			Nonwhite Women with Marital Durations of:		
	5 Years	10 Years	15 Years	5 Years	10 Years	15 Years
Children Ever Born Per 1,000 Mothers						
15-19	2,250	3,028	3,253	2,927	4,208	4,631
20-24	2,149	2,796	2,931	2,743	3,668	3,861
25-29	2,142	2,609	2,638	2,573	3,080	3,215
Children Ever Born Per 1,000 Women						
15-19	2,090	2,905	3,113	2,681	3,916	4,222
20-24	1,902	2,586	2,735	2,353	3,178	3,298
25-29	1,751	2,223	2,243	1,997	2,393	2,471

Source: U.S. Bureau of the Census, United States Census of Population: 1960, Women by Number of Children Ever Born, Final Report, PC(2)-3A, pp. 84, 85, 92, 93.

future population growth in California must be directed not only at migration, but also at those elements supporting high birth performance in the state. Since young marriage is an element supporting high birth performance, one judicious way to regulate California's population growth is to control or, preferably, change this early marriage pattern.

If marriage could be delayed, the savings in fertility for Californians would be considerable. Data are presented in Table 8 which show what the California birth situation would be if no women were married before the ages of 20, 25, and 30, and if the age-specific fertility rates remain the same, regardless of age at marriage.[5] As the table shows, the influence of such

---

[5] Such an assumption might not seem realistic, since if women did not marry until their 30th birthday it is unlikely they would keep exactly the same pattern of age-specific fertility they had when they married at age 20. But such an assumption allows us to see the influence that shifts in the marital distribution alone would have on fertility levels.

Table 8

BIRTHS AND BIRTH RATES IN CALIFORNIA IF NO WOMEN WERE MARRIED BEFORE THE AGES OF 20, 25 AND 30: 1960-1969[a]

Year and Fertility Measure	Actual Marital Distribution	Hypothetical Marital Distribution No Women Married Before the Age of:		
		20	25	30
1966				
Total Births	337,623	292,930	202,810	150,615
General Fertility Rate[b]	89.3	77.5	53.7	40.0
Crude Birth Rate[c]	18.4	16.0	11.0	8.2
1967				
Total Births	336,584	294,720	203,585	152,169
General Fertility Rate	86.3	75.6	52.2	39.0
Crude Birth Rate	18.0	15.7	10.9	8.1
1968				
Total Births	339,221	299,804	210,495	157,171
General Fertility Rate	85.4	75.5	53.0	39.6
Crude Birth Rate	17.9	15.8	11.1	8.3
1969				
Total Births	352,907	314,480	223,829	165,667
General Fertility Rate	87.2	77.7	55.3	40.9
Crude Birth Rate	18.3	16.3	11.6	8.6

[a] Births and birth rates under the actual and hypothetical marital distributions are calculated using the observed age-specific fertility schedule for each year.

[b] Number of births per 1,000 females 15-44.

[c] Number of births per 1,000 total population.

Source: Age-specific fertility rates and marital distributions in Appendix Tables C and D.

shifts in the marital distribution would be substantial. For example, looking at the actual 1969 marital distribution, we see that Californians had 352,907 births, a general fertility rate of 87.2 births per 1,000 women aged 15-44, and a crude birth rate of 18.3 births per 1,000 population. If we change the marital distribution, and assume that in 1969 no women were married before the age of 20, with everything else remaining the same, Californians would have had much lower fertility. The total number of births in 1969 would have dropped by 10 percent (from 352,907 to 314,480), the general fertility rate by 11 percent (from 87.2 to 77.7), and the crude birth rate by 11 percent (from 18.3 to 16.3). Had there been no married women before the age of 25, the number of total births would have declined by almost 40 percent (from 352,907 to 223,829), the general fertility rate by more than 60 percent (from 87.2 to 55.3), and the crude birth rate by more than 60 percent (from 18.3 to 11.6). The reduction in fertility would of course be even greater if we assume there were no married women before the age of 30.

A substantial reduction in fertility is itself reason enough to seriously consider marriage regulation as a part of California policy. But there are also other important benefits that can be derived from delayed marriage. For one thing, we know that divorce is likelier to occur among persons who marry young than among persons who marry late. Young marriages, often impetuously and hastily arranged affairs, are high divorce risks.[6] Given the high divorce risk of young marriages, to the extent that we can reduce the number of very young marriages, we will also reduce the amount of divorce and marital disruption.

In addition to a reduction in divorce, a further benefit of late marriage is likely to be a better educated and more economically active population than is currently the case. A later age at marriage allows young people to remain in school or in the labor force for a longer period of time. And with higher levels of education and longer periods of time in the labor market before marriage, people will be better prepared--in terms of psychological maturity and financial security--to assume the responsibilities and burdens of marriage and parenthood when they do marry.

In short, some form of marriage regulation that would postpone wedlock to the middle or late twenties would undoubtedly be in the best interests of California.[7] Delayed marriage would

---

[6] See U.S. Department of Health, Education and Welfare, Divorce Statistics Analysis: United States, 1963, Series 21, p. 15.

[7] It may be argued that increased contraceptive use within marriage is just as effective as delayed marriage. After all,

not only significantly reduce fertility levels--an extremely important item given our current rapid rate of growth--but it is also likely to help improve the divorce situation, raise the educational level, and provide a more sound mental and financial basis for matrimony. I must make it clear, however, that such a policy would also involve certain demographic and personal costs, and that Californians may hesitate to accept these costs.

The "Costs" of Marriage Regulation in California

One cost that Californians will have to face is a demographic by-product of delaying marriage. I am speaking of illegitimacy. By postponing marriage we decrease the number of married females who are exposed to legitimate conceptions, but at the same time we increase the number of unmarried females. Consequently, we expose a larger population of women to the "risk" of illegitimate conception. And not only does the population at "risk" increase with delayed marriage, but one might say that the "risk" itself also increases. By this I refer to the fact that many young women who are premaritally pregnant legitimize their pregnancies through marriage. Thus a policy of delayed marriage would raise the "risk" of having an illegitimate birth because births that are premaritally conceived by very young women could no longer be legitimized by a hasty wedding ceremony. Figures presented in Table 9 indicate that illegitimacy would indeed increase with postponed marriage. However, this increase would be more than compensated for by an even greater decrease in legitimate fertility obtained by such a postponement, a decrease sufficient to produce a substantial net "savings" in total births. In addition, were abortion to be further liberalized, many potential illegitimate births

---

delayed marriage on the one hand, and early marriage plus extensive contraceptive use on the other hand, are functionally equivalent--both help postpone childbearing to the less fecund years. However, delayed marriage has certain advantages over mere contraceptive use. First, even with efficient contraceptive use, late marriage lengthens the time period between generations of reproducers and hence puts an "independent brake on long range population growth," even if there is no change in completed family size. Second, even in the most urban and educated groups (see Table 6)--the sections of the population most likely to use contraception and use it effectively--those who delay marriage still have higher levels of childlessness and lower completed family sizes than those who marry early. Third, besides fertility savings, delayed marriage also has the advantage of "improving" the divorce situation and raising the level of education and economic productivity.

Table 9

TOTAL, ILLEGITIMATE, AND LEGITIMATE BIRTHS IN CALIFORNIA
IF NO WOMEN WERE MARRIED BEFORE THE AGES OF
20, 25 AND 30: 1966[a]

Legitimacy Status of Births	Actual Marital Distribution	Hypothetical Marital Distribution No Women Married Before the Age of:		
		20	25	30
Ignoring Premarital Conceptions That Result in Marriage[b]				
Illegitimate	31,804	33,809	56,209	82,745
Legitimate	305,819	259,121	146,601	67,870
Total Births	337,623	292,930	202,810	150,615
Taking Into Account Premarital Conceptions That Result in Marriage[c]				
Illegitimate	31,804	50,330	92,656	123,156
Legitimate	305,819	259,121	146,601	67,870
Total Births	337,623	309,451	239,257	191,026

[a] Births and birth rates under the actual and hypothetical marital distributions are calculated using the observed age-specific fertility schedule for each year.

[b] Here we assume that there are no premarital conceptions which are legitimized by a subsequent marriage--i.e., that all legitimate births were conceived after marriage.

[c] Here we assume that a proportion of California women legitimize their premarital conceptions by a subsequent marriage: (1) California women have the same level and pattern of legitimate premarital conceptions as the United States, 1964-1966 (see Appendix Table E); (2) when marriage is delayed to age 20, 25, or 30, premaritally pregnant women who originally would have legitimized pregnancy by marriage would be forced to have an illegitimate birth instead.

Sources: Appendix Tables C, D, and E.

resulting from delayed marriage would be prevented through this means. In fact, it could be argued that the state's present reluctance to make abortion more easily available is pushing many young, unmarried pregnant women into early matrimony, and hence into a high fertility as well as a high divorce situation.

In the last analysis, however, acceptance of a policy of postponed marriage will probably not hinge very much on the demographic costs, but rather on certain personal costs or deprivations that are directly linked to the regulative mechanisms needed to achieve a policy of delayed marriage.[8]

Undoubtedly the first regulative mechanism that comes to people's minds is that of direct legislation--i.e., they will be forced by law to delay marriage.[9] They incorrectly assume that the only way to control the age at marriage is through legal restrictions on when people marry. In fact, however, the average age at marriage has rarely if ever had much relationship to the legal age in both the United States and other countries.[10] In California, for example, the minimum legal age at which women can marry without parental consent is 18, and for men, 21. Yet the average age at first marriage in California, as noted earlier, is much higher--about 20 for women and about 23 for men. California is not unique in this respect; in most other states the average age at marriage is higher than the minimum legal age.[11]

---

[8] Of course if the age at marriage, and hence the age at childbearing, is delayed to the older ages, there is also the additional "cost" of an increased probability of birth defects, pregnancy complications, etc. However, while it is true that this probability rises with the age of the mother, even with this rise the probability would still be low.

[9] As Kingsley Davis has pointed out: "Any suggestion that age at marriage can be raised as a part of population policy is usually met with the argument that even if a law were passed, it would not be obeyed" ("Population Policy: Will Current Programs Succeed?" Science, Vol. 158, p. 737).

[10] For example, Roman Catholic countries in Western Europe generally follow canon law in stipulating 12 years as the minimum legal age at which females may wed, but the average age at marriage in these countries has been more like 24 and 25 (Davis, ibid.).

[11] In Alaska in 1967, the minimum legal age at marriage (without parental consent) was 18 for women and 21 for men; the average age at first marriage was 20 and 23 respectively. In Hawaii, the minimum legal age was 20 for women and 20 for men; the average

Legal restriction on the age at matrimony would probably not be the most effective method to achieve marriage regulation in California. California could raise the minimum legal age at marriage to perhaps 25 for females and 28 for males. Should this occur, the most likely reaction would be an increase in out-of-state marriages by Californians. That such an increase is likely is seen in the fact that a substantial proportion of Californians are already marrying outside the state. Exactly how many migrate out of the state to marry is uncertain, but Table 10 provides some estimates for the years 1949 to 1969. We assume that if there were no migration, Californians would have experienced the marriage rate of the Western region as a whole (Column 1). Under this assumption, California should have had an estimated 242,488 marriages in 1969 (Column 3). Yet only 166,832 marriages actually occurred in the state that year, giving it a "deficit" of 75,656 marriages (Columns 4 and 5). This "deficit" represents an estimate of how many marriages of Californians occurred outside the state in 1969. These 75,656 marriages comprise 31.2 percent of all estimated marriages of Californians in 1969, regardless of where they married (Column 6). In other words, 3 out of every 10 Californians who married in 1969 did so out of the state. In fact, for every year of the 20-year period between 1949 and 1969, between 30 and 40 percent of all marriages involving Californians did not occur in California.

As one might assume, a substantial proportion of these out-of-state marriages have occurred in neighboring Nevada. While it is impossible to say precisely how many Californians marry in Nevada each year, a rough estimate can be made. Assuming that if Nevada had no migration it would experience the marriage rate of the Western states as a whole, it is estimated that Nevada would have had 5,713 marriages in 1969 (see Table 11). However, Nevada actually had 94,699 marriages, or more than 16 times the estimated number under conditions of no migration. In other words, there was a huge "excess" of marriages in Nevada that was due to people migrating into the state to marry. Nor was 1969 a unique year, because for every year between 1949 and 1969 Nevada had more than 16 to 20 times the estimated number of marriages it would have had if there had been no migration.

---

age at first marriage was 22 and 24 respectively. In New Jersey, the minimum legal age was 18 for women and 21 for men; the average age at first marriage was 22 and 23.5 respectively. Etc. See Appendix Table B and Stephen S. Kaplan, Marriage and Divorce: Principal Provisions of the Marriage and Divorce Laws of the U.S., District of Columbia, Commonwealth of Puerto Rico, and Territories (International Institute of Municipal Clerks: Chicago, Illinois, 1967), pp. 4ff.

MARRIAGE REGULATION AND THE CALIFORNIA BIRTH RATE

Now if we assume that <u>all</u> of California's estimated migratory marriages took place in Nevada, then from 80 to 90 percent of all "excess" marriages in Nevada between 1957 and 1969 involved Californians (Column 8). This is of course a maximum estimate, since obviously not all Californians who marry out of state marry in Nevada. In fact, prior to 1957, not all Californians who married out of state <u>could</u> have married in Nevada, since the estimated number of out-of-state marriages from Californians exceeds the estimated number of "excess" marriages in Nevada.[12]

It is not known precisely why so many Californians marry in Nevada, but the ease and convenience of Nevada weddings are certainly important factors. Unlike California, Nevada requires no physical examination or blood test to obtain a marriage license.[13] Marriage licenses themselves may be obtained twenty-four hours a day in Carson City or Las Vegas, and a multitude of wedding chapels in these cities await the opportunity to marry couples. Add to these factors the relatively short distance between metropolitan areas in California and Nevada, the glamour and excitement of Las Vegas and Reno, and the fact that many persons who get divorced in Nevada remain long enough to remarry there, and one can see why so many California couples go to Nevada to marry.[14]

Thus, comparison of the actual and legal ages at marriage, as well as the evidence on migratory marriages, indicates that legal restrictions on the age of matrimony are probably not the best way to achieve marriage regulation in California. As we have seen, the age at which Californians <u>actually</u> marry has little relationship to when they can legally marry, and persons who currently desire to evade the technicalities of California marriage law--such as the blood test or physical examination--can and do escape over the border to marry. Instead of regulating the age at marriage through marriage laws alone, I suggest that we must

---

[12] If we estimate the number of marriages that would have occurred under conditions of no migration in another neighboring state--Arizona--we find that Arizona had an annual "excess" number of marriages prior to 1957, suggesting that during this period some of California's migratory marriages that cannot be explained by Nevada's "excess" took place in Arizona. (See Appendix Table H.)

[13] Kaplan, pp. 4ff.

[14] It does not appear that California couples marry in Nevada in order to escape California's minimum legal age at marriage, since the two states have the same requirements (18 for women and 21 for men, without parental consent).

Table 10

ESTIMATED MIGRATORY MARRIAGES IN CALIFORNIA, 1949-1969[a]

Year	Western Marriage Rate[b] (1)	Population in California (2)	Estimated Number of Marriages in California Under Conditions of No Migration: (1) x (2) (3)	Actual Number of Marriages in California (4)	Estimated Number of Migratory Marriages: (4) - (3) (5)	Migratory Marriages as Percent of All Estimated Marriages (5)/(3) (6)
1949	12.5	10,337,000	129,313	77,873	-51,340	39.7%
1950	13.1	10,586,223	138,680	79,360	-59,320	42.8
1951	12.2	11,130,000	135,786	76,648	-59,138	43.6
1952	11.8	11,638,000	137,328	78,833	-58,495	42.6
1953	11.7	12,101,000	141,582	79,662	-61,920	43.7
1954	10.9	12,517,000	136,435	77,947	-58,488	42.9
1955	10.6	13,004,000	137,842	81,939	-55,903	40.6
1956	11.2	13,581,000	152,107	87,452	-64,655	42.5
1957	10.0	14,177,000	141,770	92,607	-49,163	34.7
1958	9.5	14,741,000	140,040	96,034	-44,006	31.4
1959	9.8	15,288,000	149,822	101,314	-48,508	32.4
1960	9.8	15,717,204	154,029	105,352	-48,677	31.6

Year				
1961	9.8	16,453,000	161,239	109,699	-51,540	32.0
1962	9.9	17,044,000	168,736	114,128	-54,608	32.4
1963	10.2	17,670,000	180,234	121,359	-58,875	32.7
1964	10.4	18,183,662	189,110	129,104	-60,006	31.7
1965	10.9	18,390,541	200,457	136,090	-64,367	32.1
1966	11.3	18,958,684	214,233	144,086	-70,147	32.7
1967	11.5	18,987,342	218,354	150,000	-68,354	31.3
1968	12.1	19,201,882	232,343	163,216	-69,127	29.8
1969	12.5	19,399,070	242,488	166,832	-75,656	31.2

a Estimates are based on crude marriage rates (number of marriages per 1,000 population). For estimates based on refined marriage rates, see Appendix Table F. There is little difference in results using crude or refined rates.

b The combined marriage rate for states in the Western U.S., including Montana, Idaho, Wyoming, Colorado, New Mexico, Arizona, Utah, Nevada, Washington, Oregon, California, Alaska, and Hawaii.

Sources: U.S. Department of Health, Education and Welfare: Vital Statistics--Special Reports, National Summaries, Vol. 37, No. 3, "Summary of Marriage and Divorce Statistics: United States, 1950," pp. 58, 59; Vital Statistics...Summaries, Vol. 40, No. 3, "Summary...1952," pp. 52, 53; Vital Statistics...Summaries, Vol. 48, No. 3 (1958), p. 59; Vital Statistics of the United States: 1958, Vol. I, p. 3; Vital Statistics...1959, I, p. 2-26; Vital Statistics...1962, III, Marriage and Divorce, p. 1-7; Vital Statistics...1967, III, Marriage and Divorce, p. 1-7; Monthly Vital Statistics Report, Provisional Statistics, Vol. 18, No. 3, "Annual Summary for the United States, 1969: Births, Deaths, Marriages, and Divorces," p. 13; California State Department of Public Health, California Health Trends, Vol. II, Trends in Family Patterns, 1965, p. A10.

Table 11

ESTIMATED MIGRATORY MARRIAGES IN NEVADA, 1949-1969, AND THE PERCENT OF SUCH MARRIAGES INVOLVING CALIFORNIANS[a]

Year	Western Marriage Rate[b] (1)	Population in Nevada (2)	Estimated Number of Marriages in Nevada under Conditions of No Migration: (1) x (2) (3)	Actual Number of Marriages in Nevada (4)	"Deficit" or "Excess" Marriages= Estimated Number of Migratory Marriages: (4) - (3) (5)	Migratory Marriages as Percent of All Estimated Marriages: (5)/(3) (6)	Number of "Deficit" or "Out-of-State" Marriages Involving Californians[c] (7)	California's "Deficit" as a Percent of Nevada's "Excess": (7)/(5) (8)
1949	12.5	158,996	1,987	45,155	+43,168	2,172.5	51,340	118.9
1950	13.1	160,103	2,096	49,872	+47,776	2,279.4	59,320	124.2
1951	12.2	166,980	2,037	49,209	+47,172	2,315.8	59,138	125.4
1952	11.8	185,000	2,183	50,209	+48,026	2,200.0	58,495	121.8
1953	11.7	196,017	2,293	51,729	+49,436	2,156.0	61,920	125.3
1954	10.9	211,973	2,311	49,432	+47,121	2,039.0	58,488	124.1
1955	10.6	244,953	2,597	52,420	+49,823	1,918.5	55,903	112.2
1956	11.2	254,001	2,845	54,915	+52,070	1,830.2	64,655	124.2
1957	10.0	262,041	2,620	58,042	+55,422	2,115.3	49,163	88.7

1958	9.5	268,940	2,555	55,832	+53,277	2,085.2	44,006	82.6
1959	9.8	278,951	2,734	60,365	+57,631	2,107.9	48,508	84.2
1960	9.8	285,310	2,796	59,373	+56,577	2,023.5	48,677	86.0
1961	9.8	316,982	3,106	63,967	+60,861	1,959.5	51,540	84.7
1962	9.9	350,072	3,466	68,404	+64,938	1,873.6	54,608	84.1
1963	10.2	390,993	3,988	73,233	+69,245	1,736.3	58,875	85.0
1964	10.4	419,072	4,358	75,894	+71,536	1,641.5	60,006	83.9
1965	10.9	433,980	4,730	81,024	+76,294	1,613.0	64,367	84.4
1966	11.3	453,917	5,129	86,335	+81,206	1,583.3	70,147	86.4
1967	11.5	436,054	5,015	86,426	+81,411	1,623.3	68,354	84.0
1968	12.1	449,055	5,434	90,799	+85,365	1,570.9	69,127	81.0
1969	12.5	457,042	5,713	94,699	+88,986	1,557.6	75,656	85.0

[a] Estimates are based on crude marriage rates (number of marriages per 1,000 population). For estimates based on refined marriage rates, see Appendix Table G. There is little difference in results using crude or refined rates.

[b] The combined marriage rate for states in the Western U.S., which includes Montana, Idaho, Wyoming, Colorado, New Mexico, Arizona, Utah, Nevada, Washington, Oregon, California, Alaska, and Hawaii.

[c] Taken from Column 5 of Table 10.

Sources: See Sources for Table 10 above (excluding last entry).

look toward certain social and economic conditions if we are to successfully achieve a goal of marital control.

It is my opinion that certain social and economic conditions have permitted and motivated couples to wed at the relatively young ages that they presently do, virtually irrespective of legal age restrictions on marriage. Consequently, if we wish to see marriage postponed to a later age, these conditions must be such that couples are motivated to marry late. With this in mind, let us now examine the social and economic conditions affecting marriage behavior in California, the kinds of changes that would have to be made if postponed marriage were to be adopted as a part of population policy in the state, and the kinds of deprivations that Californians would have to endure as a result of these changes.

First, certain major social and economic changes have occurred in both California and the United States which permit couples to marry earlier than previously. Until very recently in our history, a couple would not consider marriage until the man had a steady job and sufficient savings to set up a proper household and support himself and his family. Since it was not customary for women, especially married women, to work outside the home, women could contribute very little financially, and marriage was often delayed beyond the age that couples might otherwise have desired. In recent years, certain changes have occurred which make such postponement no longer necessary, and which consequently allow and support a pattern of early matrimony.[15]

Foremost among such changes has been the increasing tendency for women, particularly married women, to enter the labor force. As Table 12 shows, in California in 1920, only 11 percent of all married women aged 15-44 were engaged in gainful occupations. By 1960, more than a third, or 34 percent, of all married women in the childbearing ages were engaged in the labor force. This increasing ability and willingness of women to bring home part of the family income has helped many young couples decide that they can "afford" to get married sooner than they thought.

Another socioeconomic change that has facilitated early marriage in the United States has been the movement toward subsidized housing. In West European countries, one of the most important reasons why couples have delayed marriage has been the great difficulty in finding adequate housing facilities.[16] In

---

[15] Kingsley Davis, "The Early Marriage Trend," *What's New*, No. 207 (Fall 1958).

[16] See Alva Myrdal, *Nation and Family* (Cambridge, Mass.: MIT Press, 1941).

Table 12

PERCENT OF MARRIED WOMEN IN THE LABOR FORCE BY AGE: CALIFORNIA, 1920, 1940, AND 1960[a]

Census Year	Age	Number of Married Women (1)	Number of Married Women in Labor Force[b] (2)	Percent of Married Women in Labor Force: (2)/(1)
1920	15-44	503,148	55,492	11.0%
	15-24	84,034	9,433	11.2
	25-34	219,732	24,074	11.0
	35-44	199,382	21,985	11.0
1940	14-44	1,013,414	190,139	18.8
	14-24	182,444	28,881	15.8
	25-34	437,328	85,057	19.4
	35-44	393,642	76,201	19.4
1960	14-44	2,217,815	744,473	33.6
	14-24	401,722	119,404	29.7
	25-34	867,036	254,842	29.4
	35-44	949,057	370,227	39.0

[a] 1920 figures refer to all married women; 1940 and 1960 figures refer to married women, spouse present.

[b] There have been some changes in the definition of labor force participation. Prior to 1940, data were collected on the basis of the gainfully employed: "'Gainful workers' were persons reported as having a gainful occupation, that is, an occupation in which they earned money or a money equivalent, or in which they assisted in the production of marketable goods, regardless of whether they were working or seeking work at the time of the census. A person was not considered to have had a gainful occupation if his activity was of limited extent." Since 1940, however, the labor force concept has been used, which is "defined on the basis of activity during the reference week only and includes all persons who were employed, unemployed, or in the Armed Forces during the week. Certain classes of persons, such as retired workers, and seasonal workers neither working nor seeking work at the time of the census, were frequently included among gainful workers; but in general, such persons are not included in the labor force. On the other hand, the census included in the labor force for 1940, 1950, and 1960 persons without previous work experience who were seeking work, that is, new workers. Such

California and the rest of the United States, however, the federal subsidy of home ownership in terms of extremely low-interest loans enables young couples with very limited resources to obtain a home, with the result that early marriage is permitted and encouraged.

Certain changes in our educational system have also made early marriage more economically feasible. At one time, it was extremely rare for students to be married. While men were in school, they customarily did not marry, simply because they had no means of supporting their wives and families. Marriage was more often than not delayed until after one's education was completed.[17] But this situation has been radically altered, particularly with the advent of the postwar GI educational benefits. Young couples increasingly find that going to school need not mean the postponement of marriage. The entry of student wives into the labor market along with other married women, the increasing tendency for fellowships to provide living expenses not only for the student but for his spouse and dependents as well, and the very inexpensive student housing that is often available for married couples and their families--all enable education-minded couples to advance rather than postpone marriage. While data on California are unavailable, data on the country as a whole indicate that many young people are taking full advantage of the situation. Table 13 shows that between 1959 and 1969, almost one-fifth of all persons and almost one-quarter of all males 18-29 who were enrolled in college in the United States were married.

---

[17] This was apparently one reason for the late average age at marriage in Sweden (ibid., p. 35).

(Table 12 continued)
new workers were not reported as gainful workers in the Censuses of 1920 and 1930." For further information, see: U.S. Bureau of the Census, United States Census of Population: 1960, Subject Reports, Employment Status and Work Experience, Final Report PC(2)-6A, p. ix.

Sources: U.S. Bureau of the Census: United States Census of Population: 1960, Vol. I. Characteristics of the Population, Pt. 6, California, p. 6-622; Sixteenth Census of the United States, 1940: Population, Vol. III, The Labor Force, Pt. 2, Alabama-Indiana, p. 212, and Vol. IV, Characteristics by Age, Pt. 2, Alabama-Indiana, p. 190; Fourteenth Census of the United States, 1920: Population, Vol. II, General Report and Analytical Tables, p. 413, and Vol. IV, Occupations.

Table 13

PERCENT OF ALL PERSONS AGES 18-29 ENROLLED IN COLLEGE
WHO ARE MARRIED, SPOUSE PRESENT, BY SEX:
UNITED STATES, 1959-1969

Year	Percent of All Persons Attending College Who Are Married	Percent of Males Attending College Who Are Married	Percent of Females Attending College Who Are Married
1959	21.3	26.9	10.3
1960	20.7	24.2	13.8
1961	16.0	18.9	10.8
1962	19.0	23.9	9.8
1963	19.9	22.8	14.9
1964	17.7	21.1	12.3
1965	19.3	22.4	14.1
1966	18.8	22.1	13.2
1967	19.9	23.6	14.2
1968	19.4	23.2	13.4
1969	20.0	23.4	15.0

Sources: U.S. Bureau of the Census, Current Population Reports, Series P-20: No. 101, "School Enrollment: October 1959," p. 12; No. 110, "School Enrollment and Education of Young Adults and Their Fathers: October 1960," p. 13; No. 117, "School Enrollment: October 1961," p. 11; No. 126, "School Enrollment: October 1962," p. 10; No. 129, "School Enrollment: October 1963," p. 11; No. 148, "School Enrollment: October 1964," p. 13; No. 162, "School Enrollment: October 1965," p. 11; No. 167, "School Enrollment: October 1966," p. 14; No. 190, "School Enrollment: October 1968 and 1967," pp. 26, 50; No. 206, "School Enrollment: October 1969," p. 24.

Not only is early marriage more economically feasible than before, but the motivation to marry and to marry fairly early has remained strong. Despite the liberalization of social attitudes, marriage and parenthood are still socially prescribed roles for men and women. The man who remains a bachelor is still perceived and treated as an "oddball" of society. So too is the woman who embarks on a career at the expense of marriage and a family. There are a whole host of positive and negative sanctions--such as denigration of the single person, the tendency to label unmarried persons as potential homosexuals or lesbians, and the corresponding support and praise for those who marry and have children--which subtly but effectively bring people around to the altar.

The desire to wed and to wed at fairly young ages is motivated not merely by positive sanctions for conforming and negative sanctions for deviating; it is also buttressed by the lack of viable and rewarding alternatives to matrimony, especially for women. Even the increased female labor force participation in recent years does not reflect a real outlet for women besides marriage. Most women in the labor force are concentrated in "dead end jobs of the middle white collar range"--jobs which do not require high levels of education or commitment, and which are thus supportive of early marriage. For example, in 1960, of all employed American women 25-34, over half (52 percent) were in clerical, sales, and service occupations while only 17 percent were employed in professional and managerial occupations.[18] Yet data indicate that it is precisely the women in professional occupations who delay marriage to the older ages. Among ever-married women 45-54, for example, those employed in professional positions first married on the average at age 25. Those employed in sales occupations, however, first married at a much younger age--at a little over 21.[19] In other words, it is the woman who has a rewarding alternative to marriage and motherhood who tends to put off wedlock to the older ages. The fact that most women participating in the labor force are in mediocre, low-level jobs means that such participation supports rather than discourages early matrimony.

The motivation to marry and to marry relatively early has also been buttressed by the increasing ease of divorce. Couples are willing to marry young because they know--at least implicitly--that if the marriage does not work out they can easily obtain a divorce and try again. Table 14 shows that in the United States, for example, both the number and rate of divorce have increased substantially in recent years. Moreover, as Table 15 indicates, divorced persons do not stay unmarried for long: the marriage rate among divorced brides and grooms is two to three times that of all unmarried persons. This tendency to remarry can be seen in the fact that a high percentage of all marriages that occur are _remarriages_. Of all brides marrying in California in 1967, as shown in Table 16, almost one quarter, or 24.4 percent, were women entering a second or later marriage, and of those women who remarried, almost all--79.7 percent--were divorcees hitting the matrimonial road again. The comparable figures for

---

[18] U.S. Bureau of the Census, U.S. Census of Population: 1960, Subject Reports, Marital Status, Final Report PC(C)-4E, Table 5, pp. 92-100.

[19] U.S. Bureau of the Census, U.S. Census of Population: 1960, Subject Reports, Age at First Marriage, Final Report PC(2)-4D, Table 11, pp. 136ff.

Table 14

DIVORCES AND ANNULMENTS IN THE UNITED STATES, 1922-1967

Year	Number of Divorces and Annulments	Rate per 1,000 Married Women, Age 15 and Over
1922	148,815	6.6
1925	175,449	7.2
1930	195,961	7.5
1935	218,000	7.8
1940	264,000	8.8
1945	485,000	14.4
1950	385,144	10.3
1955	377,000	9.3
1960	393,000	9.2
1961	414,000	9.6
1962	413,000	9.4
1963	428,000	9.6
1964	450,000	10.0
1965	479,000	10.6
1966	499,000	10.9
1967	523,000	11.2

Source: U.S. Department of Health, Education and Welfare, Vital Statistics of the United States: 1967, Vol. III, Marriage and Divorce, p. 2-5.

grooms are equally high: 23.9 percent of all grooms in 1967 were entering a remarriage, and of these, 80.7 percent had been divorced. Furthermore, a high proportion of those who remarry do so at fairly young ages. As Table 17 indicates, more than one-fifth of all brides and almost one-tenth of all grooms who remarried in California in 1967 were below the age of 25.

Hence, marriages which cannot stand the acid test are fairly easily dissolved. Divorced persons quickly move on to remarriage, so that for many, relatively little time and energy is expended on ridding themselves of an unhappy situation. It is the realization of this possibility that makes people more willing to enter marriage quickly. It is interesting to note

Table 15

MARRIAGE RATES BY PREVIOUS MARITAL STATUS FOR THE POPULATION 14 YEARS OLD AND OVER: U.S. MARRIAGE-REGISTRATION AREA, 1967[a]

Previous Marital Status	Bride	Groom
All Marriages	64.0	77.4
First Marriages	85.2	71.0
All Remarriages	34.2	107.9
Widowed	10.1	37.4
Divorced	129.8	206.8

[a] Based on sample data; for frequencies, see source, Tables 1-15 and 1-16; for population bases, see Tables 3-14, Section 3. Rates per 1,000 population in specified group. Rates for all marriages are based on unmarried population, those for first marriages are based on single population, and those for remarriages are based on widowed and divorced population. Figures for widowed and divorced, but not for all remarriages, exclude data for Michigan and Ohio. All marriages include previous marital status not stated; all remarriages include widowed and divorced not stated.

Source: U.S. Department of Health, Education and Welfare, Vital Statistics of the United States: 1967, Vol. III, Marriage and Divorce, p. 1-9.

in this regard that in those Western countries where divorce cannot be obtained or can be obtained only with great difficulty—Ireland, Spain, Portugal, and Italy—age at marriage is fairly late. Women in these countries do not first marry on the average until their 23rd birthday, and men not until their 26th or 27th birthday (see Tables 1 and 2).

In sum, many social and economic features of our society now permit and motivate early wedlock. Given this fact, it is likely that age at marriage in California can be increased by removing or weakening these features. Reduce low-cost housing, make fellowships less generous, revoke some educational and housing benefits, allow women alternative roles to marriage and motherhood by raising their occupational level, liberalize abortion, do not force pregnant unwed women into a marriage situation, make divorce more difficult to obtain—and Californians will think twice before marrying.

Table 16

MARRIAGES AND REMARRIAGES BY PREVIOUS MARITAL STATUS:
CALIFORNIA, 1967

Number of Marriages, Remarriages, and Previous Marital Status	Brides		Grooms	
	Number	Percent	Number	Percent
Total Marriages	149,900	100.0	149,900	100.0
First Marriages	113,300	75.6	114,060	76.1
Remarriages	36,600	24.4	35,840	23.9
Marital Status of Remarriages				
All Statuses	36,600	100.0	35,840	100.0
Divorced	29,200	79.7	28,940	80.7
Widowed	6,420	17.5	6,120	17.1
Not Stated	1,040	2.8	780	2.7

Source: U.S. Department of Health, Education and Welfare, Vital Statistics of the United States: 1967, Vol. III, Marriage and Divorce.

In addition to these more long-term social and economic changes, California might consider more immediate measures, such as imposing certain economic levies upon couples entering the marital arena. For example, couples might be required to prove financial solvency in order to obtain a marriage license. In the same vein, the state might consider imposing a tax on newly married couples, with the level of the tax increasing with each subsequent marriage, if any. Finally, the marriage license fee itself could easily be raised: at its present low level of $6.00, it is in many cases cheaper for a couple to obtain a marriage license than to attend a first-run movie.

I must emphasize, however, that these financial levies would merely be stop-gap measures. In order to be truly effective, they would have to be accompanied by a vigorous attempt to remove or weaken the currently pervasive social and economic supports of early matrimony. In the absence of any effort to change these supports, the imposition of levies would be more likely to result in increased out-of-state marriages than in an increased age at marriage.

All this is not to say that achieving any of these changes would be either a simple or a pleasant task. It is very possible

Table 17

PERCENTAGES OF BRIDES AND GROOMS REMARRYING IN CALIFORNIA AND U.S. MARRIAGE-REGISTRATION AREA, 1958-67[a]

Year	Percent of All Brides Who Are:					Percent of All Grooms Who Are:				
	<25	25-29	30-34	35-44	45+	<25	25-29	30-34	35-44	45+
California										
1958	17.2	16.2	15.9	25.2	25.5	7.9	14.1	15.6	26.6	35.8
1959	17.0	16.3	15.6	25.5	25.6	7.7	14.3	15.6	26.7	35.8
1960	19.2	21.4	16.2	18.5	24.7	8.4	13.4	14.7	24.0	39.5
1961	17.4	18.7	16.5	21.8	25.6	8.1	16.2	18.1	27.2	30.4
1962	19.0	18.7	13.2	22.3	26.7	8.8	10.0	16.0	27.6	37.6
1963	19.2	15.3	13.5	26.0	26.0	7.9	13.7	13.7	29.2	35.6
1964	19.4	16.1	14.7	24.6	25.2	7.4	15.3	14.3	28.8	34.1
1965	18.0	18.4	15.4	23.3	24.9	7.7	14.9	16.7	28.1	32.7
1966	17.9	19.4	15.2	23.9	23.5	8.6	16.2	16.2	27.0	32.0
1967	20.7	18.3	13.2	22.4	25.4	8.7	16.9	15.0	24.9	34.6
U.S. Marriage-Registration Area										
1958	18.1	15.8	15.0	24.2	26.9	8.1	14.4	14.7	24.6	38.2
1959	18.1	15.7	14.8	24.5	26.9	8.0	14.2	14.6	24.8	38.3
1960	18.3	15.9	13.8	24.1	27.8	8.4	12.9	14.6	24.2	39.9
1961	18.8	15.9	14.1	24.3	26.8	8.6	14.9	15.5	24.4	36.7
1962	18.6	15.5	13.9	24.7	27.3	8.2	13.9	14.5	26.2	37.2
1963	18.9	15.5	14.0	24.1	27.4	8.3	14.5	13.7	25.9	37.5
1964	19.3	15.9	13.3	23.6	27.9	8.6	15.2	13.4	25.9	36.9
1965	19.0	16.3	13.4	23.3	28.0	8.7	15.2	14.1	25.2	36.8
1966	18.8	17.1	13.4	23.2	27.4	9.1	15.6	14.3	24.9	36.1
1967	19.4	17.5	13.2	23.1	26.9	9.4	16.4	14.0	24.5	35.7

[a]Percentages for all brides total 100 percent for each year; percentages for all grooms total 100 percent for each year.

Sources: See sources for Table 1 above.

that Californians would resent any additional financial levies, especially on what many would feel is none of the state's business. Furthermore, many of the social and economic supports of early marriage are now deeply rooted in our society, and many people have come to enjoy them and to take them as given. Californians must recognize, however, that they enjoy these supports at a price, and this price is the potential for very high fertility in a state that does not need it.

In any event, it is certain that California should place some limit on its expanding population. Although sharp reaction is to be expected from any consideration of marital regulation regardless of how it is to be achieved, regulation in some form should be seriously considered. Californians are noted for their ability to try the unusual: hopefully their inclination toward innovativeness will extend to the arena of marriage behavior.

Appendix Table A

MEDIAN AGE OF BRIDES AND GROOMS AT FIRST MARRIAGE AND REMARRIAGE, IN CALIFORNIA AND U.S. MARRIAGE-REGISTRATION AREA: 1958-1967

Year	Brides		Grooms	
	First Marriage	Remarriage	First Marriage	Remarriage

California

Year	First Marriage	Remarriage	First Marriage	Remarriage
1958	19.8	35.3	23.1	39.3
1959	19.8	35.4	23.1	39.2
1960	19.6	32.9	23.1	40.5
1961	19.8	34.2	23.2	37.4
1962	20.3	34.7	23.1	39.6
1963	20.4	35.8	23.1	40.1
1964	20.4	34.9	23.0	39.5
1965	20.4	34.4	22.9	38.8
1966	20.4	34.2	22.9	38.3
1967	20.7	34.2	22.9	38.8

U.S. Marriage-Registration Area

Year	First Marriage	Remarriage	First Marriage	Remarriage
1958	20.2	35.4	23.2	39.8
1959	20.2	35.5	23.2	39.9
1960	20.2	35.7	23.1	40.7
1961	20.2	35.4	23.1	39.4
1962	20.3	35.8	23.0	40.0
1963	20.5	35.6	23.0	40.2
1964	20.6	35.6	23.0	40.0
1965	20.5	35.5	22.9	39.8
1966	20.5	35.3	22.8	39.4
1967	20.8	35.0	22.9	39.2

Sources: See Sources for Table 1 above.

Appendix Table B

MEDIAN AGES OF BRIDES AND GROOMS WHO ARE MARRYING FOR THE FIRST TIME IN CALIFORNIA AND SELECTED WESTERN AND EASTERN STATES: 1960-1967

	California	Western States					Eastern States		
		Oregon	Utah	Wyoming	Alaska	Hawaii	Conn.	New York	New Jersey
Brides
1960	19.6	18.8	18.8	18.7	19.5	21.5	21.9	21.4	21.8
1961	19.8	18.4	19.2	18.7	19.2	21.8	21.7	20.6	21.7
1962	20.3	19.3	19.0	19.2	20.0	22.0	21.8	21.3	21.4
1963	20.4	19.9	19.9	19.8	20.2	21.8	22.1	21.2	21.8
1964	20.4	20.1	20.3	19.8	20.2	21.8	22.0	21.3	21.8
1965	20.4	20.8	20.1	19.8	20.0	22.0	21.9	21.9	21.7
1966	20.4	20.0	20.0	19.9	20.0	22.0	21.8	21.9	21.8
1967	20.7	20.2	20.2	19.9	20.2	22.0	22.1	22.0	22.0
Grooms
1960	23.0	22.7	22.4	22.8	23.8	24.0	24.1	23.7	23.9
1961	23.2	22.5	22.4	22.8	23.6	24.3	23.9	23.2	23.8
1962	23.1	22.6	22.3	22.8	24.8	24.0	24.0	23.7	23.8
1963	23.1	22.6	22.5	22.9	23.7	23.9	23.8	23.4	23.7
1964	23.0	22.6	22.5	22.9	23.6	23.8	23.6	23.3	23.5
1965	22.9	22.6	22.4	22.8	23.6	24.0	23.6	23.7	23.5
1966	22.8	22.5	22.4	22.7	23.5	23.8	23.6	23.8	23.6
1967	22.9	22.4	22.2	22.7	23.3	23.6	23.6	23.7	23.5

Sources: U.S. Department of Health, Education and Welfare: Vital Statistics of the United States: 1967, Vol. III, Marriage and Divorce, pp. 1-15 through 1-17; Vital Statistics,..1966, III, pp. 1-15 through 1-17; Vital Statistics,..1965, III, pp. 1-19 through 1-21; Vital Statistics,..1964, III, pp. 1-20 through 1-22; Vital Statistics,..1963, III, pp. 1-19 through 1-21; Vital Statistics,.. 1962, III, pp. 1-21, 1-23; Vital Statistics,..1961, III, pp. 2-12, 2-14; Vital Statistics,..1960, III, pp. 2-17 through 2-19.

Appendix Table C
AGE-SPECIFIC FERTILITY RATES IN CALIFORNIA: 1966-1969

Year and Age	Age-Specific Birth Rate	Age-Specific Illegitimate Birth Rate	Age-Specific Legitimate Birth Rate
1966			
15-19	74.4	18.5	431.8
20-24	197.4	52.6	264.0
25-29	147.0	54.6	161.9
30-34	77.5	37.8	82.4
35-39	36.8	17.4	39.4
40-44	10.2	4.4	11.1
1967			
15-19	72.1	20.6	394.6
20-24	176.8	49.5	239.1
25-29	142.6	54.4	157.4
30-34	73.5	35.3	78.4
35-39	34.1	18.4	36.3
40-44	9.5	4.7	10.3
1968			
15-19	69.6	22.1	396.1
20-24	171.2	52.3	234.1
25-29	145.0	57.3	160.0
30-34	70.6	38.1	74.9
35-39	31.5	17.8	33.4
40-44	8.6	4.6	9.2
1969			
15-19	68.8	23.8	383.8
20-24	170.1	54.5	233.1
25-29	150.6	59.0	167.6
30-34	72.0	39.2	76.4
35-39	30.6	18.7	32.3
40-44	8.1	4.8	8.6

Sources: Births in denominators supplied by State of California, Department of Public Health Records; population estimates in denominators obtained from Department of Finance estimates for California; U.S. Bureau of the Census, United States Census of Population: 1960, Vol. I, Characteristics of the Population, Pt. 1, United States Summary, Table 176, and Pt. 6, California, Table 105; Vital Statistics of the United States: 1966, Vol. I, Natality, Tables 1-6, 1-7; Vital Statistics...1967, Vol. I, Natality, Table 1-17; National Center for Health Statistics, "Monthly Vital Statistics Report," Vol. 17, No. 9, Supplement, Tables 1, 3, 4; U.S. Bureau of the Census, Current Population Reports, Series P-20, No. 187, "Marital Status and Family Status: March 1968," Table 1, and No. 211, "Marital Status and Family Status: March 1969," Table 1.

For a discussion of the method used to estimate denominators, see Beth Berkov and Paul W. Shipley, Illegitimate Births in California, 1966-1967, State of California, Department of Public Health, Berkeley, 1971, pp. 6-8.

Appendix Table D

FEMALE MARITAL DISTRIBUTIONS IN CALIFORNIA: 1966-1969

Year and Age	Total Female Population	Actual Proportion Married	Hypothetical Proportion Married No Married Females Before Age:		
			20	25	30
1966					
15-19	799,622	13.5	.0	.0	.0
20-24	622,098	68.5	68.5	.0	.0
25-29	564,601	86.1	86.1	86.1	.0
30-34	560,378	89.1	89.1	89.1	89.1
35-39	589,572	88.1	88.1	88.1	88.1
40-44	642,819	85.9	85.9	85.9	85.9
1967					
15-19	813,311	13.8	.0	.0	.0
20-24	716,185	67.1	67.1	.0	.0
25-29	582,941	85.7	85.7	85.7	.0
30-34	567,034	88.5	88.5	88.5	88.5
35-39	582,380	87.8	87.8	87.8	87.8
40-44	638,896	85.6	85.6	85.6	85.6
1968					
15-19	829,791	12.7	.0	.0	.0
20-24	751,062	65.4	65.4	.0	.0
25-29	608,590	85.3	85.3	85.3	.0
30-34	572,924	88.4	88.4	88.4	88.4
35-39	576,529	87.5	87.5	87.5	87.5
40-44	631,165	85.3	85.3	85.3	85.3
1969					
15-19	853,973	12.5	.0	.0	.0
20-24	784,430	64.7	64.7	.0	.0
25-29	634,941	84.3	84.3	84.3	.0
30-34	580,810	88.3	88.3	88.3	88.3
35-39	573,104	88.0	88.0	88.0	88.0
40-44	619,530	86.2	86.2	86.2	86.2

Sources: Estimates of female population by marital status obtained from Department of Finance estimates for California. For remaining sources, see sources for Appendix Table C above.

Appendix Table E

ANNUAL AVERAGE NUMBER OF LEGITIMATE FIRST BIRTHS TO WOMEN AGES 15-44, ACCORDING TO AGE OF MOTHER AND PERCENT DISTRIBUTION BY INTERVAL FROM FIRST MARRIAGE TO FIRST BIRTH: UNITED STATES, 1964-1966

Interval from First Marriage to First Birth	Total	Age of Mother at First Birth				
		15-19	20-24	25-29	30-34	35-44
Number of Mothers (000's)	1,008	335	481	136	38	17
All Intervals	100.0	100.0	100.0	100.0	100.0	100.0
Under 12 Months	43.2	70.0	35.3	17.0	15.4	13.4
Under 8 Months	21.6	42.4	14.5	3.7	1.7	1.9
8-11 Months	21.6	27.2	20.8	13.3	13.7	11.5
12-23 Months	28.7	25.6	34.9	19.7	15.3	15.4
12-17 Months	17.6	17.7	20.9	9.1	9.3	7.7
18-23 Months	11.1	8.0	14.0	10.6	5.9	7.7
24-35 Months	11.6	3.3	17.3	14.3	5.1	6.1
36-47 Months	5.8	0.6	8.0	10.4	8.6	1.9
48-59 Months	2.9	0.3	2.0	11.6	5.1	5.8
60 Months or More	7.8	0.2	2.6	26.9	50.5	57.4
60-119 Months	5.6	--[a]	--	23.0	28.3	11.5
120 Months or More	2.2	--	--	3.9	22.3	45.9

[a] Figure does not meet standards of reliability or precision.

Source: U.S. Department of Health, Education and Welfare, Monthly Vital Statistics Report; National Natality Survey Statistics, Vol. 18, No. 12, "Interval Between First Marriage and Legitimate First Birth, United States, 1964-1966," p. 1.

Appendix Table F

ESTIMATED MIGRATORY MARRIAGES IN CALIFORNIA, 1950 AND 1960, USING REFINED MARRIAGE RATES

Year and Rate	Marriage Rate in Western States (1)	Female Population (2)	Estimated Number of Marriages in California Under Conditions of No Migration: (1) x (2) (3)	Actual Number of Marriages in California (4)	Estimated Number of Migratory Marriages: (4) - (3) (5)	Migratory Marriages as Percent of All Estimated Marriages: (5)/(3) (6)
Using Refined Rate #1[a]						
1950	36.3	4,010,505	145,581	79,360	-66,221	45.5
1960	28.4	5,546,733	157,527	105,352	-52,175	33.1
Using Refined Rate #2[b]						
1950	117.9	1,287,270	151,769	79,360	-72,409	47.7
1960	92.5	1,761,318	162,922	105,352	-57,570	35.3
Using Refined Rate #3[c]						
1950	227.9	623,080	142,000	79,360	-62,640	44.1
1960	181.5	857,620	155,658	105,352	-50,306	32.3

[a] Refined Rate #1 = Number of marriages per 1,000 females age 15 and over.
[b] Refined Rate #2 = Number of marriages per 1,000 unmarried females age 15 and over.
[c] Refined Rate #3 = Number of marriages per 1,000 unmarried females age 15-44.

Sources: For sources see p. 206.

Appendix Table G

ESTIMATED MIGRATORY MARRIAGES IN NEVADA: 1950 AND 1960

Year and Rate	Marriage Rate in Western States (1)	Female Population (2)	Estimated Number of Marriages in Nevada Under Conditions of No Migration: (1) x (2) (3)	Actual Number of Marriages in Nevada (4)	"Deficit" or "Excess" Marriages= Estimated Number of Migratory Marriages: (4) - (3) (5)	Migratory Marriages as Percent of All Estimated Marriages: (5)/(3) (6)
Using Refined Rate #1[a]						
1950	36.3	54,725	1,987	49,872	+47,885	2409.9
1960	28.4	94,951	2,697	59,373	+56,676	2101.4
Using Refined Rate #2[a]						
1950	117.9	14,320	1,688	49,872	+48,184	2854.5
1960	92.5	31,521	2,916	59,373	+56,457	1936.1
Using Refined Rate #3[a]						
1950	227.9	7,845	1,788	49,872	+48,084	2689.3
1960	181.5	21,505	3,903	59,373	+55,470	1421.2

[a] See Appendix Table F for definitions of Refined Rates 1-3.

Sources: For sources see p. 206.

Appendix Table H

ESTIMATED MIGRATORY MARRIAGES IN ARIZONA, 1949-1969[a]

Year	Western Marriage Rate[b] (1)	Population in Arizona (2)	Estimated Number of Marriages in Arizona Under Conditions of No Migration: (1) x (2) (3)	Actual Number of Marriages in Arizona (4)	"Deficit" or "Excess" Marriages = Estimated Number of Migratory Marriages: (4) - (3) (5)
1949	12.5	714,167	8,927	23,139	+14,212
1950	13.1	750,225	9,828	20,031	+10,203
1951	12.2	792,078	9,663	20,198	+10,535
1952	11.8	846,642	9,990	22,436	+12,446
1953	11.7	893,536	10,454	23,500	+13,046
1954	10.9	931,584	10,154	20,588	+10,434
1955	10.6	1,029,764	10,915	21,831	+10,916
1956	11.2	1,017,103	11,392	25,631	+14,239
1957	10.0	1,072,444	10,724	9,652	-1,072
1958	9.5	1,195,366	11,356	9,805	-1,551
1959	9.8	1,265,556	12,402	10,251	-2,151
1960	9.8	1,301,667	12,756	10,153	-2,603
1961	9.8	1,428,219	13,997	10,426	-3,571
1962	9.9	1,489,444	14,745	10,724	-4,021
1963	10.2	1,522,667	15,531	11,420	-4,111
1964	10.4	1,541,579	16,032	11,716	-4,316
1965	10.9	1,573,117	17,147	12,113	-5,034
1966	11.3	1,626,386	18,378	13,499	-4,879
1967	11.5	1,633,667	18,787	14,703	-4,084
1968	12.1	1,659,208	20,076	16,758	-3,318
1969	12.5	1,699,626	21,245	18,186	-3,059

[a] Estimates are based on crude marriage rates (number of marriages per 1,000 population).

[b] The combined marriage rate for states in the Western U.S., which includes Montana, Idaho, Wyoming, Colorado, New Mexico, Arizona, Utah, Nevada, Washington, Oregon, California, Alaska, and Hawaii.

Sources: See Sources for Table 10 above (excluding last entry).

Sources for Appendix Tables F and G

(pp. 203-204 above)

U.S. Bureau of the Census, <u>United States Census of Population: 1960</u>, Vol. I, <u>Characteristics of the Population</u>: Pt. 3, Alaska, pp. 3-138 through 3-142; Pt. 4, Arizona, pp. 4-158 through 4-163; Pt. 6, California, pp. 6-539 through 6-541; Pt. 7, Colorado, pp. 7-230 through 7-235; Pt. 13, Hawaii, pp. 13-141 through 13-145; Pt. 14, Idaho, pp. 14-178 through 14-181; Pt. 28, Montana, pp. 28-198 through 28-201; Pt. 30, Nevada, pp. 30-138 through 30-141; Pt. 33, New Mexico, pp. 33-176 through 33-180; Pt. 39, Oregon, pp. 39-199 through 39-203; Pt. 46, Utah, pp. 46-168 through 46-171; Pt. 49, Washington, pp. 49-225 through 49-231; Pt. 52, Wyoming, pp. 52-142 through 52-145; AND U.S. Department of Health, Education and Welfare, <u>Vital Statistics of the United States: 1960</u>, Vol. III, <u>Marriage and Divorce</u>, p. 1-22; <u>Vital Statistics . . .1958</u>, I, p. 3; <u>Vital Statistics. . .1950</u>, p. 67; AND California State Department of Public Health, <u>California Health Trends</u>, Vol. II, <u>Trends in Family Patterns</u>, 1965, p. A10.

ILLEGITIMATE FERTILITY IN CALIFORNIA'S POPULATION

Beth Berkov

In the study of illegitimacy, one encounters many serious obstacles. Not the least of these is that the term itself produces differing emotional reactions in various segments of the population. At the same time, the credible data available about illegitimacy have been limited and confusing. The principal object of this paper is to present new demographic information on illegitimate births in California, but it is necessary to refer briefly to some of the prevailing sociological theories regarding the concept of illegitimacy.

Illegitimate fertility is childbearing outside the socially prescribed and legally contracted arrangement of marriage.[1] The concept of "illegitimacy" has always existed because marriage has always been the only socially sanctioned setting for reproduction.[2] Anthropologists have found this to be true of all surviving societies, from the most primitive to the most advanced.[3] While it is often assumed that a permissive attitude toward sexual intercourse outside of marriage is a comparatively recent development and peculiar to our society, such permissiveness has in fact been common in most human societies. This

---

[1] For a comprehensive definition, see Kingsley Davis, "The Forms of Illegitimacy," Social Forces, Vol. 18, No. 1 (October, 1939).

[2] Kingsley Davis, "Illegitimacy and the Social Structure," American Journal of Sociology, Vol. 45, September 1939, pp. 215-233.

[3] G.P. Murdock, Social Structure (New York: Macmillan, 1949).

The data on illegitimate births reported in this paper were developed as part of a cooperative project between the University of California and the California State Department of Public Health. The project is supported, in part, by a contract with the National Institute of Child Health and Human Development, Center for Population Research (NIH-70-2196). The author is a demographer in the Bureau of Maternal and Child Health, California State Department of Public Health.

sexual permissiveness, however, has not carried with it social approval of childbirth outside of marriage. On the contrary, every society has exerted strong moral and social force to prevent illegitimate births.[4] The rise in illegitimacy in recent history appears to indicate an important change in social sanctions related to reproductive behavior. The unique aspect of the change is not in the degree of acceptance of extramarital sexual intercourse, but in the apparent loosening of the social restraints on out-of-wedlock childbirth.

The implications of such a change in attitude are of the greatest importance to our social well-being. While we appear to be more willing to accept the fact that increasing numbers of children are born outside of marriage, we have not, as a society, altered our traditional methods of child rearing. We still expect each child to be supported and reared to maturity by a family with a responsible father as well as mother. No human society has survived without a form of the nuclear family as the predominant child-rearing unit. In fact, the classical sociological analysis of marriage identifies it as the licensing of parenthood rather than the licensing of sexual intercourse.[5]

The high incidence of illegitimacy among certain disadvantaged groups within the population has led many observers to assume the existence in these groups of living arrangements which are functional equivalents of legal marriage. According to this theory, the illegitimate child is reared in a home with a responsible father as well as mother, even though they are unmarried. It is further assumed that when this is not the case, it is usually the poverty of the parents which has prevented it. In some cases, however, it is believed that the absence of the child's biological father is the result of the mother's decision to seek a more desirable husband as a permanent head of the family--a search in which she is frequently successful. These hypotheses appear not to be supported by studies of illegitimacy and family formation in our country.

Incidence of Illegitimacy in California

I will return later to a further discussion of the relationship of illegitimacy to poverty. But before doing this, I

---

[4]Kingsley Davis, "Sexual Behavior" in Robert K. Merton and Robert Nisbet, eds., Contemporary Social Problems (3rd ed.; New York: Harcourt Brace Jovanovich, 1971), pp. 313-340.

[5]Bronislaw Malinowski, "Parenthood, The Basis of Social Structure" in Rose L. Coser, ed., The Family: Its Structure and Functions (New York: St. Martins, 1964).

ILLEGITIMATE FERTILITY IN CALIFORNIA'S POPULATION

shall discuss some data that have recently become available relating to illegitimate fertility in California.

The bulk of the data is found in a report entitled "Illegitimate Births in California, 1966 and 1967."[6] Since about 1916, the California birth certificate has not required information regarding the legitimacy of the birth or the marital status of the mother. However, an inferential method has been developed by statisticians for the classification of births by their apparent legitimacy status. This method has been applied since 1966. The methodology and results for the first two years are comprehensively set forth in the report previously cited. This paper extends the main data through 1969 and, on the basis of the first half of 1970, estimates the data for that full year (Tables 1-3 below).

It is generally assumed that the California Therapeutic Abortion Law has produced a decline in illegitimacy. This has not been demonstrated by the data for the first half of 1970. During this period, illegitimate births in California continued the upward trend that has characterized the four-and-one-half years for which we now have information (see Tables 1 and 2). Further, we can reasonably assume that a part of the pregnancies in unmarried women which were aborted within the provisions of the law would have otherwise resulted in illegitimate births.

In examining the data that are now available, it is important to distinguish between the various measurements of illegitimacy. The "illegitimacy ratio" is the proportion of illegitmate births to total births. The "illegitimacy rate," however, is a very different measure. The "rate" is the number of illegitimate births per 1,000 unmarried women in the reproductive ages. Ratios are more readily available figures than are rates because ratios are calculated from births alone and do not require estimation of the size and characteristics of the population of childbearing women. However, precisely because they do not separate the influence of changes in population from changes in fertility, ratios can be quite misleading if they are used to determine trends or measure differences between population groups. For example, if only illegitimacy _ratios_ were available for California, it would be assumed that illegitimacy among black women had increased between 1966 and 1970 by approximately the same amount as among white women (Table 1). _Rates_ are available, however (Table 2), and they show that while illegitimacy is

---

[6] Beth Berkov and Paul W. Shipley, _Illegitimate Births in California 1966-1967_ (State of California, Department of Public Health, Berkeley, 1971).

Table

ILLEGITIMATE AND TOTAL LIVE BIRTHS AND ILLEGITIMACY
1966-1969 AND

(By place of

Race and Age of Mother	Illegitimate					Number
	1970[b]	1969[c]	1968[c]	1967	1966	1970[b]
All Races	46,619	42,085	38,053	35,215	31,804	361,000[e]
White	30,785	27,943	25,820	23,774	21,122	311,752
Under 15	312	256	262	258	202	421
15-17	5,573	4,859	4,284	3,810	3,306	16,209
18-19	6,807	6,191	5,883	5,435	4,879	34,181
20-24	10,991	10,158	9,421	8,457	7,293	119,523
25-29	4,054	3,726	3,322	3,076	2,850	86,756
30-34	1,849	1,639	1,534	1,526	1,478	36,203
35 and Over	1,183	1,103	1,109	1,205	1,113	18,416
Black	14,608	13,027	11,348	10,640	9,965	34,123
Under 15	314	291	286	267	264	337
15-17	3,344	3,187	2,741	2,609	2,365	4,172
18-19	3,214	2,693	2,375	2,308	2,029	5,552
20-24	4,658	4,005	3,333	2,905	2,748	12,128
25-29	1,759	1,647	1,384	1,339	1,326	6,670
30-34	864	740	756	727	762	3,403
35 and Over	448	458	470	484	471	1,818
Other Races	1,226	1,115	885	801	717	15,125
Am. Indian	--[f]	421	--	302	287	--
Chinese	--	68	--	67	44	--
Japanese	--	122	--	100	101	--
Other	--	504	--	332	285	--

[a] Illegitimate live births as percent of total live births.
[b] Annual estimate based on certificates received January-August 1970 (estimate prepared February 1971).
[c] Figures for illegitimate births adjusted for comparability with coding rules applied for 1966, 1967, and 1970. Adjustment based on special coding of certificates received October-December 1969.

NOTE: Totals include births with age of mother unknown.

Source: State of California, Department of Public Health, Birth

ILLEGITIMATE FERTILITY IN CALIFORNIA'S POPULATION

1

RATIOS BY RACE AND AGE OF MOTHER: CALIFORNIA, ESTIMATED 1970

residence)

All Live Births				Illegitimacy Ratio[a]				
1969[d]	1968	1967	1966	1970[b]	1969	1968	1967	1966
352,907	339,221	336,584	337,623	12.9	11.9	11.2	10.5	9.4
305,313	295,075	293,261	293,989	9.9	9.2	8.8	8.1	7.2
336	342	345	277	74.1	76.2	76.6	74.8	72.9
14,694	13,975	13,697	13,378	34.4	33.1	30.7	27.8	24.7
33,234	33,691	34,934	36,690	19.9	18.6	17.5	15.6	13.3
117,539	114,317	112,895	109,253	9.2	8.6	8.2	7.5	6.7
84,611	78,104	73,323	72,762	4.7	4.4	4.3	4.2	3.9
35,713	34,511	35,761	37,259	5.1	4.6	4.4	4.3	4.0
19,153	20,114	22,278	24,348	6.4	5.8	5.5	5.4	4.6
33,494	31,169	31,151	31,539	42.8	38.9	36.4	34.2	31.6
328	316	286	284	93.2	88.7	90.5	93.4	93.0
3,991	3,736	3,717	3,489	80.2	79.9	73.4	70.2	67.8
5,429	5,103	5,136	4,928	57.9	49.6	46.5	44.9	41.2
11,840	10,686	10,372	10,370	38.4	33.8	31.2	28.0	26.5
6,657	6,061	6,118	6,487	26.4	24.7	22.8	21.9	20.4
3,305	3,336	3,402	3,702	25.4	22.4	22.7	21.4	20.6
1,936	1,916	12,114	2,279	24.6	23.7	24.5	22.9	20.7
14,100	12,977	12,172	12,095	8.1	7.9	6.8	6.6	5.9
1,799	1,687	1,705	1,735	--	23.4	--	17.7	16.5
2,726	2,652	2,534	2,511	--	2.5	--	2.6	1.8
3,105	3,277	3,397	3,586	--	3.9	--	2.9	2.8
6,470	5,361	4,536	4,263	--	7.8	--	7.3	6.7

[d]Figures may differ slightly from those published in <u>Vital Statistics of California 1969</u> because data by legitimacy status exclude 30 live births.
[e]Final count for 1970 will be approximately 363,000 live births (revised estimate prepared April 1971).
[f]Not available.

Records.

Table

ESTIMATED BIRTH RATES[a] BY LEGITIMACY
1966-1969 AND

(By place of

Race and Age of Mother	Illegitimate					
	1970[b]	1969	1968	1967	1966	1970[b]
All Races, 15-44[c]	31.7	29.9	28.2	27.1	25.4	111.4
White, 15-44[c]	24.4	23.1	22.1	21.1	19.3	111.6
15-19	17.8	16.4	15.4	14.3	12.7	409.4
20-24	39.1	39.5	39.7	39.0	37.7	223.6
25-29	44.1	43.2	41.0	40.6	39.3	153.8
30-34	29.2	26.8	25.9	26.1	26.7	71.1
35-44[c]	9.2	8.5	8.6	9.3	8.5	18.8
Black, 15-44[c]	110.2	106.7	101.4	103.1	105.8	105.7
15-19	117.5	108.1	97.2	95.5	87.9	345.4
20-24	153.6	151.1	144.2	144.1	163.4	206.5
25-29	125.3	134.8	131.0	144.6	167.0	124.2
30-34	77.8	78.0	99.6	115.0	151.7	67.5
35-44[c]	21.1	23.5	26.1	30.3	32.7	22.1
Black,[e] 15-44[c]	89.9	86.1	80.8	81.4	82.7	126.2
15-19	114.9	105.8	95.1	93.4	86.0	399.2
20-24	127.4	123.4	115.5	113.4	125.8	249.6
25-29	84.4	88.2	82.6	88.4	97.9	150.0
30-34	50.0	47.5	56.7	61.5	75.0	80.8
35-44[f]	14.6	15.8	17.0	19.0	19.8	26.0

[a] Denominators of rates estimated by using methods described in *Illegitimate Births in California, 1966-1967*, but applying revised estimates of number of women by age and race. The revised estimates, though partly based on "first tape" 1970 census counts, will need further revision when more detailed 1970 census data become available.

[b] Numerators estimated on basis of birth certificates received January-August 1970.

[c] Rates computed by relating total births, regardless of age of mother, to estimated women age 15-44.

NOTE: Rates are per 1,000 unmarried (illegitimate), married (legitimate), and total women. Except as noted, unmarried women are those single, widowed, or divorced.

Sources: State of California, Department of Finance, Financial prepared April 1971); B. Berkov and P. Shipley, *Illegitimate* of Public Health, Berkeley, 1971): see sources and references Health, Birth Records.

ILLEGITIMATE FERTILITY IN CALIFORNIA'S POPULATION

STATUS, RACE AND AGE OF MOTHER: CALIFORNIA, ESTIMATED 1970

residence)

Legitimate				All Live Births				
1969	1968	1967	1966	1970[b]	1969	1968	1967	1966
111.4	108.8	109.8	113.2	84.1[d]	84.1	82.4	83.3	85.4
111.7	109.5	110.4	113.6	82.5	82.7	81.4	82.2	84.1
394.0	390.5	381.0	413.9	64.0	62.5	63.0	64.9	67.3
226.9	225.8	230.0	238.0	155.9	161.0	162.9	168.3	175.7
157.8	151.7	148.3	151.8	137.8	141.3	136.1	133.4	136.5
71.6	71.0	75.4	80.0	66.3	66.5	65.9	69.8	74.1
19.4	20.2	22.1	24.1	17.6	18.1	18.8	20.5	22.2
109.1	104.3	108.5	116.2	107.6	108.1	103.2	106.6	112.7
393.2	420.4	423.1	467.0	149.6	148.6	143.7	145.6	143.6
212.3	194.1	196.8	208.4	182.4	186.8	175.2	178.5	194.2
129.5	122.7	129.0	142.7	124.4	130.8	124.5	132.1	147.1
66.8	68.6	72.3	82.9	69.9	69.0	73.8	78.6	91.4
22.9	21.4	24.1	26.2	21.8	23.0	22.4	25.3	27.4
129.2	122.7	127.0	135.3					
454.0	484.3	483.1	536.3					
253.2	228.7	229.9	241.5					
155.5	146.4	153.4	168.9					
79.3	81.0	85.0	96.9					
26.8	25.0	28.0	30.4					

[d]Rate calculated using revised estimate of 363,000 live births = 84.5.

[e]Alternate set of rates considering separated women living apart from husband as unmarried and included with single, widowed, and divorced women. For discussion, see Illegitimate Births in California, 1966-1967, pp. 6-8.

[f]Rates computed by relating births to mothers age 35 and over to estimated women age 35-44.

and Population Research Section (July 1 population estimates Births in California, 1966-1967 (State of California, Department Tables 10, 11, J; State of California, Department of Public

increasing among young black women, it is at the same time falling for older black women. The rate for all unmarried black women in the childbearing ages increased by less than 10 percent between 1966 and 1970.[7] The increase for white unmarried women in the same period was 26 percent. If rates were not available, these trends would not be apparent.

And now, I would like to call to your attention some of the principal facts which emerge from a study of the data.

The level of the illegitimate birth rate is high in California. This was true for 1966 and 1967, when a detailed comparison was made with estimates for the United States as a whole.[8] The rate in California was found to be particularly high for white women; it was two-thirds above the rate for white women in the United States in general. The rate for black women was roughly comparable to that for black women in the rest of the nation.

The analysis made for 1966 and 1967 indicated that while Spanish surname women had relatively high illegitimate (as well as legitimate) birth rates, this was only part of the explanation for the high white illegitimacy rate in California. Compared to the nation as a whole, California white women not of Spanish surname appeared to have a relatively high incidence of illegitimacy. However, this incidence was approximately the same as reported for white women in the other Pacific Coast states and Hawaii.[9] It probably is associated with high migration rates and high divorce rates, and merits further study.

---

[7] The rate calculated by the "standard" method (used by the National Center for Health Statistics in the estimation of United States rates) rose 4.2 percent between 1966 and 1970, while the rate calculated by the alternate method rose 8.7 percent (Table 2). Because the alternate method includes separated women among those at risk of bearing an illegitimate child, it yields substantially lower and probably more accurate estimates of illegitimate birth rates for black women than does the "standard" method. For further discussion, see ibid., pp. 6-8.

[8] Ibid., pp. 8-12, 30-37.

[9] Interstate comparisons based on inferences from illegitimacy ratios rather than rates and will need further study when 1970 illegitimacy data for other states become available and can be related to 1970 census findings. See ibid., pp. 12-15.

ILLEGITIMATE FERTILITY IN CALIFORNIA'S POPULATION

There are large differences in illegitimate birth rates by race. In 1966, the rate for black women in California was from four to five-and-a-half times the rate for white women, depending on the method used to estimate the rate for black women (Table 2). In 1970, despite declines in illegitimacy for older black women, the most conservative estimate of the rate was still nearly four times the rate for white women.

The number of illegitimate births in California was estimated at 46,600 in 1970, an increase of almost 50 percent over the 32,000 recorded in 1966 (Table 1). In this five-year period, illegitimate births increased faster than did legitimate births, which also rose. In 1970, nearly 13 percent of all births in California were illegitimate, compared to 9.4 percent in 1966.

The rate of illegitimate births--the measurement that describes the trend independent of changes in the number of unmarried women of childbearing age--rose 25 percent. (As has already been stated, the rise was 26 percent for white women and less than 10 percent for black.)

With respect to the age distribution of unmarried mothers, we find that the main change in 1970 from 1966 was a reduction in the proportion over age 30. In 1970, as in 1966, women under age 20 comprised about 40 percent of the white unmarried mothers and almost half of the black. In terms of _rates_ of illegitimacy, however, increases between 1966 and 1970 had occurred for all age groups of white women and for younger black women.

The relative decline in births to women age 30 and over, and a greater concentration of births among women in their 20's, is a trend that applies also to legitimate fertility. The trend reflects changes in the timing and spacing of births, and cannot be interpreted to mean that completed family size is necessarily falling. What has happened is that women about age 35 and over now have had, on the average, a relatively large number of children--for most of these women, as many children as they want. Younger women, on the other hand, are in most instances just starting their childbearing. This is evident from the rapid decline in recent years in higher order births, accompanied by a rapid rise in first and second births. The shift for California between 1966 and 1970 is shown in Table 3 and Chart 1.

I wish to emphasize that the trend in illegitimate fertility needs to be interpreted in relation to the trend in legitimate fertility. It appears that the downward course since 1957 in the general fertility rate and in the legitimate fertility rate came to a halt in California in 1968 and turned up in 1969 (Table 2).

For some time it has been clear to demographers that a new wave of births was inevitable. The only questions were when

Table 3

PERCENT DISTRIBUTION OF LIVE BIRTHS AND BIRTH RATES BY LEGITIMACY STATUS AND LIVE BIRTH ORDER: CALIFORNIA, 1966 AND ESTIMATED 1970
(By place of residence)

Live Birth Order	Percent Distribution of Births				Estimated Birth Rate				Ratio: 1970 Rate/ 1966 Rate	
	White		Black		White		Black		White	Black
	1970[a]	1966	1970[a]	1966	1970[a]	1966	1970[a]	1966		
Illegitimate	(30,785)	(21,122)	(14,608)	(9,965)						
All Birth Orders	100.0	100.0	100.0	100.0	24.4	19.3	89.9	82.7	1.264	1.087
1	64.9	60.1	52.0	46.5	15.8	11.6	46.7	38.5	1.362	1.213
2	14.8	14.6	21.2	19.0	3.6	2.8	19.1	15.7	1.286	1.217
3	8.1	8.7	10.2	10.4	2.0	1.7	9.3	8.6	1.176	1.081
4	4.6	6.3	6.6	7.2	1.1	1.2	5.9	6.0	.917	.983
5 and Over	7.6	10.3	10.0	16.9	1.9	2.0	9.0	14.0	.950	.643
Legitimate	(280,967)	(272,867)	(19,515)	(21,574)						
All Birth Orders	100.0	100.0	100.0	100.0	111.6	113.6	126.2	135.3	.982	.933
1	38.5	34.4	30.6	26.8	43.0	39.1	38.6	36.3	1.100	1.063
2	29.9	27.0	27.6	23.2	33.4	30.7	34.8	31.4	1.088	1.108
3	15.8	16.7	17.0	16.9	17.6	19.0	21.5	22.9	.926	.939
4	7.7	9.8	10.0	11.5	8.6	11.1	12.6	15.6	.775	.808
5 and Over	8.2	11.9	14.7	21.6	9.1	13.5	18.6	29.2	.674	.637

[a] Estimate based on certificates received January-August 1970.

NOTE: Rates are per 1,000 unmarried (illegitimate) and married (legitimate) women ages 15-44; rates for black women assume that separated women, as well as those single, widowed, or divorced, are unmarried.

Sources: State of California, Department of Finance, Financial and Population Research Section (population estimates prepared April 1971); State of California, Department of Public Health, Birth Records.

ILLEGITIMATE FERTILITY IN CALIFORNIA'S POPULATION

Chart 1

ESTIMATED BIRTH RATES IN CALIFORNIA
BY LEGITIMACY STATUS AND LIVE BIRTH ORDER

1970*
1966

First and Second Births   Third and Higher Order Births

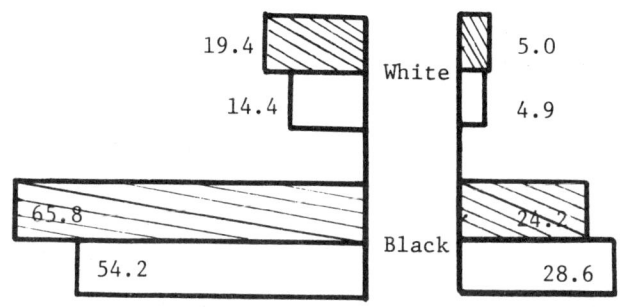

ILLEGITIMATE BIRTHS PER 1000 UNMARRIED WOMEN AGES 15-44

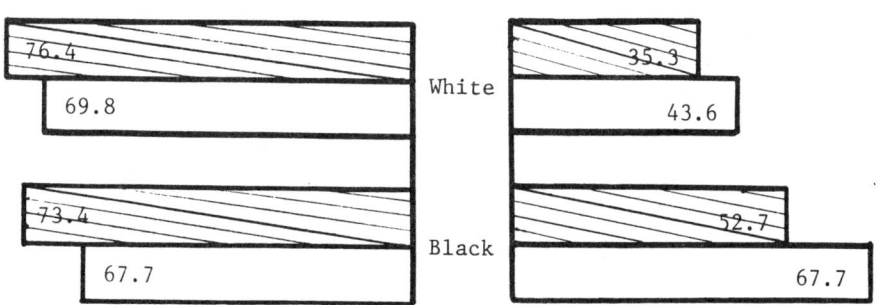

LEGITIMATE BIRTHS PER 1000 MARRIED WOMEN AGES 15-44

*Estimate based on certificates received January-August 1970.

Source: Table 3.

it would start and whether its size could be limited. It is now evident that the wave has started in California, with a larger part than of the previous wave comprised of illegitimate births. A crucial question is to what extent the young women having first babies now will go on to second, third, and higher order births, either within marriage or outside it. Another such question is what childbearing patterns will be adopted by the increasing numbers of women who will be entering the childbearing years throughout the 1970's.

Illegitimacy and Public Assistance

The public policies adopted in the immediate future, particularly in the area of welfare benefits, may have considerable influence on the decisions young women make with respect to family size. Unfortunately, many of the policies which might influence fertility are being debated and determined without understanding or consideration of the need to restrain population growth. An extremely important and controversial matter for consideration in the determination of these policies is the relationship of illegitimacy to poverty, and to the increasing number of families receiving public assistance.

It is appropriate to examine some of the information relating to this subject presently available. This information has been derived from two sources. One is a special study of infant mortality which includes information about births in 1967 paid for under the Medi-Cal Program or with public funds provided through county hospital services. The data from this study (see Table 4) demonstrate that illegitimate births comprise a disproportionately large share of public-expense deliveries (32 percent of these were illegitimate, whereas among all California births in 1967 the proportion illegitimate was only 10 percent). Further, the data show that unmarried mothers are very much more likely to require financial assistance than married mothers. Among all California births in 1967, 69,000 or 20.5 percent of the annual total of about 337,000 births, were delivered at public expense. The proportion for illegitimate births was 63 percent, while for legitimate births it was 16 percent. As would be expected, the proportions of all births at public expense were high for Spanish surname births and black births but, within each of these groups, the public-expense proportion among illegitimate births was approximately double that for legitimate births.

The second source of information is the Department of Social Welfare's sampling of its active Aid to Families with Dependent Children caseload (see Tables 5 and 6). The total AFDC caseload has risen rapidly in recent years. Between 1962 and 1970, it rose faster for legitimate than for illegitimate children, but the increases in both categories were substantial. In

Table 4

NUMBER AND PERCENT OF LIVE BIRTHS BY LEGITIMACY STATUS, COUNTY HOSPITAL OR MEDI-CAL DELIVERY, RACE, SPANISH SURNAME, AND AGE OF MOTHER: CALIFORNIA, 1967
(By place of residence)

Race, Spanish Surname, and Age of Mother	Illegitimate			Legitimate			All Live Births		
	Total Number	County Hospital or Medi-Cal Delivery		Total Number	County Hospital or Medi-Cal Delivery		Total Number	County Hospital or Medi-Cal Delivery	
		Number	Percent		Number	Percent		Number	Percent
All Races	35,215	22,036	62.6	301,369	47,118	15.6	336,584	69,154[a]	20.5
White, Not Spanish Surname	17,296	8,974	51.9	212,860	21,280	10.0	230,156	30,254	13.1
Under 20	7,413	3,773	50.9	30,460	5,788	19.0	37,873	9,561	25.2
20-24	6,342	3,367	53.1	84,164	8,520	10.1	90,506	11,887	13.1
25 and Over	3,535	1,823	51.6	98,219	6,965	7.1	101,754	8,788	8.6
White, Spanish Surname	6,478	4,527	69.9	56,627	16,543	29.2	63,105	21,070	33.4
Under 20	2,090	1,517	72.6	9,013	3,724	41.3	11,103	5,241	47.2
20-24	2,115	1,472	69.6	20,274	5,622	27.7	22,389	7,094	31.7
25 and Over	2,272	1,531	67.4	27,336	7,192	26.3	29,608	8,723	29.5
Black	10,640	8,060	75.8	20,511	8,158	39.8	31,151	16,218	52.1
Under 20	5,184	3,997	77.1	3,955	2,189	55.4	9,139	6,186	67.7
20-24	2,905	2,195	75.6	7,467	3,002	40.2	10,372	5,197	50.1
25 and Over	2,550	1,861	73.0	9,084	2,963	32.6	11,634	4,824	41.5
Other Races	801	475	59.3	11,371	1,137	10.0	12,172	1,612	13.2

[a] Excludes 2,812 Medi-Cal deliveries in community hospitals for which birth records not located.

NOTE: Totals include births with age of mother unknown.

Source: State of California, Department of Public Health, Birth Records and Special Study of Matched Birth, Infant Death, and Medi-Cal Records.

Table 5

CHILDREN IN FAMILIES RECEIVING AFDC[a] BENEFITS
BY LEGITIMACY STATUS:
CALIFORNIA, SELECTED DATES 1960-1970

Date	Total Number of Children	Illegitimate	Legitimate	Percent Illegitimate
September 1970	975,666	241,964	733,702	24.8
June 1968	602,475	165,317	437,158	27.4
July 1962	249,318	85,259	164,059	34.2
March 1960	208,637	60,919	147,718	29.2

[a] Aid to Families with Dependent Children program, including Family Group and Unemployed Parent benefits; Unemployed Parent benefits available since February 1, 1964.

Sources: State of California, Department of Social Welfare, Research Series Reports Numbers 17, 20, 26; unpublished data for September 1970; data derived from periodic samples of active cases.

Table 6

ESTIMATED PROPORTION OF CHILDREN UNDER AGE 7
RECEIVING AFDC BENEFITS BY LEGITIMACY STATUS:
CALIFORNIA, SEPTEMBER 1970

	Total	Illegitimate	Legitimate
Population of Children Under Age 7	2,485,000	247,000[a]	2,238,000
Children Under Age 7 on AFDC	401,880	99,665[b]	302,215
Percent of Children Under Age 7 on AFDC	16.2	40.4	13.5

[a] Illegitimate births as classified from birth certificates for 1966-1970 (ages 0-4) and estimated for 1964-1965 (ages 5 and 6).

[b] Estimate assuming age distribution of illegitimate children on AFDC same as age distribution of all children on AFDC; excludes unborn children.

Sources: State of California, Department of Finance, population estimate prepared December 1970; State of California, Department of Social Welfare, sample survey of cases; State of California, Department of Public Health, Birth Records.

ILLEGITIMATE FERTILITY IN CALIFORNIA'S POPULATION

September 1970, 975,666 (or nearly a million) children in California were in families receiving welfare. Of these, 242,000 (or about one-fourth) were illegitimate.

An effort has been made to estimate the proportions of legitimate and illegitimate children under age 7 in the population who find their way onto welfare (Table 6). Again the results show that illegitimate children are much more likely to require aid. Approximately 40 percent of the illegitimate children under age 7 were estimated to be on welfare as of September 1970, while for legitimate children the figure was approximately 14 percent.

The initial estimate of 40 percent of illegitimate children under age 7 on welfare may be refined by certain adjustments to exclude children on welfare born outside the state. These refined estimates show, however, that at least 30 percent of illegitimate children born in California in the past seven years were on the welfare rolls in September 1970.[10] The figure is at least 42 percent on welfare if we limit consideration to illegitimate children born in the state who were not adopted.[11]

Historical Perspective

The possible causal relationship between illegitimacy and welfare should be viewed in the light of the changes which have occurred in the social factors which previously acted to minimize illegitimacy. One very important change has been that in modern times, when the family fails, society assumes a much

---

[10] The figure of 30 percent was obtained by subtracting 25,913 from the numerator--an estimate of the number of children under age 7 born outside the state. This can be considered a high estimate, since it was obtained by assuming that the proportion of children under age 7 born outside the state was the same as the proportion of family heads on welfare residing in the state less than 7 years. (Data on the place of birth of children on welfare is not available.) It is probable that many of the estimated 25,913 children were born in California.

[11] In the seven-year period 1964-1970, an estimated 72,000 children (29 percent of the estimated total of 247,000 illegitimate children born in the state) were adopted by nonrelatives. This estimate of children adopted by nonrelatives is based on State of California, Department of Social Welfare, agency and independent adoption statistics, and Research Series Report No. 25, 1969.

more protective role than in the past. In previous eras, illegitimacy was reduced not only by moral stigma, but also by meager or nonexistent charity that increased an already high infant death-rate. Dramatic evidence of this comes to us from the historical statistics of Sweden. These show that in the first decade of the nineteenth century, when about 20 percent of legitimate babies in Sweden died in infancy (183 per 1,000), almost half the illegitimate babies (439 per 1,000) failed to survive the first year of life.[12]

How far we have come from this situation is shown by data recently compiled for California (Table 7). While illegitimate babies still have a lower rate of survival, which is important from a humanitarian standpoint and as an indicator of the disadvantages suffered by the family to whom the child is born, the difference in the survival-rate is not really significant as a factor in reducing population. Among all babies born in California in 1966 and 1967, 97.1 percent of the illegitimate and 98.3 percent of the legitimate survived infancy. For black babies, the survival-rate was 96.8 percent for the illegitimate and 97.3 percent for the legitimate. It is evident that infant mortality no longer has a significant impact on the growth of either the total population or the illegitimately born population.

From the standpoint of history, it becomes clear that what has happened is that the restraints on illegitimacy have been released while the reasons for its existence have remained. Humanitarian welfare services have largely removed the moral and economic punishments, and modern medicine has solved the technical problems, that previously held down the size of the population born illegitimately. But the social rewards for motherhood, and the social pressures that push women to motherhood allowing some to miss the link of marriage, have remained. We have not offered alternatives to motherhood; in fact, we have blocked many--particularly the alternative of abortion. In these circumstances, we should not be surprised if illegitimacy rises and increasing numbers of mothers and babies require welfare services.

Policies and Recommendations

The growing tax burden and the increasing number of children raised in disadvantaged circumstances are of great

---

[12] June Sklar, "Illegitimacy: An Historical Comparison of Ireland and Sweden," unpublished paper, March 1968; source cited by Sklar, *Historisk Statistik for Sverige*, Vol. 1, 1720-1950 (Stockholm, 1955), p. 60.

concern to all. The frustration produced by these problems has led many to seek simplistic solutions. I cannot believe that we can today effectively control extramarital sexual intercourse, particularly between consenting adults. Nor can there be a return to previous callous attitudes toward poverty. We must assume that once a child is born, society will, if necessary, accept responsibility for reasonable support and medical care and will seek, in general, to promote the child's full growth and development.

If a constructive and humane welfare policy is to be adopted, we must recognize that the very existence of welfare aid contributes to the growth of illegitimacy. This is not to say that women consciously plan to have a baby in order to obtain welfare benefits. We know that the pattern of behavior in women which results in extramarital pregnancy is the product of a number of psychological, social, and economic pressures which were not instigated by the welfare program. Nevertheless, in the total framework of rewards and punishments which surround the choice of action faced by the woman, the availability of even minimal financial support makes it possible, and in many cases most immediately satisfying, to choose motherhood even without marriage.

Our dilemma, then, is that in developing policies, we must seek to deter illegitimate childbearing without causing harm to children already born. Nor is it sufficient to convert illegitimate births into legitimate ones by encouraging early marriage, because the results are likely to be unfortunate, including an increase in total fertility and in marital disorganization.

I have no illusions that these problems can be dealt with easily. Difficult choices will be required. Better choices will be made, however, if they are based on factual information. While we have made a beginning by measuring the extent to which illegitimate fertility contributes to overall fertility and population growth, we remain ignorant about many important aspects of the problem. For example, while it is generally recognized that poverty increases the risk of illegitimacy, we have not studied the extent to which illegitimacy establishes a chain of circumstances which result in the family's impoverishment. There are no definitive studies of what happens to illegitimate children in later life. We have only fragmentary information on the number of illegitimate children born to mothers who themselves were illegitimate.

A wide variety of proposals have emerged in the recent debate on welfare policy in California. It seems likely that one of these--the proposal for a more stringent attempt to enforce support of the child by the father--might not only reduce welfare costs, but might serve to encourage a greater use of contraception

Table 7

RATE AND NUMBER OF INFANT DEATHS[a] BY LEGITIMACY STATUS, BIRTH ORDER, RACE AND AGE OF MOTHER FOR SINGLE LIVE BIRTHS OCCURRING IN CALIFORNIA IN 1966 AND 1967

Race and Age of Mother	All Live Births[b]			First Births[c]			Second and Higher Order Births[d]		
	Total	Illegitimate	Legitimate	Total	Illegitimate	Legitimate	Total	Illegitimate	Legitimate
	INFANT DEATH RATE								
All Races, Total[e]	18.2	28.7	17.1	15.5	23.1	14.1	19.2	36.3	18.0
Under 20	22.3	26.4	21.0	18.9	23.2	17.3	34.0	44.0	32.1
20-29	16.1	29.2	15.1	12.7	21.9	11.7	17.9	35.2	16.7
30-39	19.0	35.6	18.0	21.9	35.7[b]	20.9	18.6	35.3	17.6
40 and Over	22.4	29.4[f]	21.9	28.4[f]	--[g]	23.5[f]	22.1	25.4[f]	21.9
White, Total[e]	17.1	26.9	16.2	14.7	21.9	13.6	18.0	35.0	17.2
Under 20	20.8	24.1	20.1	17.9	21.6	17.0	31.9	46.0[c]	30.5
20-29	15.3	27.4	14.5	12.1	21.5	11.2	17.0	33.4	16.2
30-39	17.6	35.5	16.8	20.7	32.7[f]	19.9	17.3	35.6[f]	16.5
40 and Over	22.7	28.0[f]	22.4	28.6[f]	--[g]	24.6[f]	22.4	23.5	22.3
Black, Total[e]	28.6	32.2	26.8	24.5	26.3	22.9	28.5	37.7	25.3
Under 20	30.7	30.9	30.6	25.4	27.1[h]	22.6	42.2	42.4[h]	42.0
20-29	24.7	33.7	21.8	21.4	21.8[h]	21.3	25.8	38.3	21.9
30-39	29.1	33.5[h]	27.9	47.6[f]	--[g]	--[g]	27.9	32.0[h]	26.8[f]
40 and Over	22.2[f]	--[g]	21.0[b]	--[g]	--[g]	--[g]	21.8[f]	--[g]	21.6[f]

NUMBER INFANT DEATHS

All Races, Total[e]	12,043	1,907	10,136	3,775	889	2,886	8,009	1,013	6,996
Under 20	2,623	745	1,878	1,721	556	1,165	901	188	713
20-29	6,561	892	5,669	1,774	301	1,473	4,782	589	4,193
30-39	2,332	246	2,086	258	27	231	2,070	217	1,853
40 and Over	276	24	252	20	5	15	256	19	237
White, Total[e]	9,824	1,208	8,616	3,141	611	2,530	6,518	594	5,924
Under 20	2,044	435	1,609	1,392	350	1,042	651	84	567
20-29	5,514	593	4,921	1,521	237	1,284	3,990	356	3,634
30-39	1,864	164	1,700	208	20	188	1,652	142	1,510
40 and Over	243	16	227	18	4	14	225	12	213
Black, Total[e]	1,747	648	1,099	512	257	255	1,142	389	753
Under 20	539	299	240	303	198	105	236	101	135
20-29	802	272	530	179	51	128	621	219	402
30-39	293	71	222	29	7	22	264	64	200
40 and Over	22	6	16	1	1	0	21	5	16

[a] Deaths under one year of age.
[b] Includes birth order unknown.
[c] No previous live births or fetal deaths.
[d] One or more previous live births or fetal deaths.
[e] Includes age of mother unknown.

[f] Rate based on 500-999 live births.
[g] Rate not calculated (less than 500 live births).
[h] Rate based on 1,000-2,999 live births.

NOTE: Rates per 1,000 single, live births.

Source: State of California, Department of Public Health, Matched Birth and Infant Death Records.

by males. A recent study of illegitimacy levels in Norway and England indicates that such public enforcement of support in Norway was one important reason for a much lower illegitimacy rate in that country.[13] The current controversy over unwed pregnant minors granted AFDC or Medi-Cal eligibility demonstrates how a policy may be self-defeating. One proposed policy is aimed at preventing abortion paid for under Medi-Cal, but its effect may be to encourage illegitimate births and a continuing burden on AFDC. The proposed policy may also discourage early and adequate prenatal care.

In addition to the increase of illegitimate children on welfare, an even greater increase has occurred in families with legitimate children receiving public assistance. This is a result in large part of the breakup of marriages contracted at very early ages, frequently because of pregnancy.

Clearly, concern with welfare policy should not be focused solely on illegitimacy. Welfare policy, as well as public policy in general, should be aimed at an overall reduction in fertility. The measures which must be developed if illegitimate births are to be reduced are not necessarily different in kind from those needed to limit legitimate fertility. Although we have not as yet seen a reduction in fertility associated with the Therapeutic Abortion Act, it must be recognized that the Act does not give ready access to abortion for many women. It is not, therefore, truly the alternative to motherhood it might be. In addition to contraception and abortion, more positive incentives are needed to limit births. In the long run, there will need to be profound changes in the social attitudes toward motherhood and the availability of other satisfying roles for women.

NOTE

Final 1970 birth counts for California became available as this volume was going to press. The data show that during the second half of 1970 a small but definite decline had occurred in the incidence of illegitimacy. The decline applied to white

---

[13] S. Hartley, "Comparative Differences and Changes in Levels of Illegitimacy," unpublished doctoral dissertation, University of California, Berkeley, 1969.

ILLEGITIMATE FERTILITY IN CALIFORNIA'S POPULATION

births only. Measurements for 1970 based on final counts as compared to the estimates presented in this paper based on experience in the first half of the year are shown below. Major patterns by age of mother and birth order are not changed by use of the final data.

MEASUREMENTS OF FERTILITY BY LEGITIMACY STATUS:
CALIFORNIA, 1970

(By place of residence)

Measurement	All Races		White		Black	
	Final	Estimate	Final	Estimate	Final	Estimate
Number of Live Births, Total	362,652	361,000	312,140	311,752	35,147	34,123
Illegitimate	45,593	46,619	29,546	30,785	14,865	14,608
Legitimate	317,059	314,381	282,594	280,967	20,282	19,515
Estimated Birth Rate, Total	84.5	84.1	82.6	82.5	110.8	107.6
Illegitimate	31.0	31.7	23.5	24.4	91.5	89.9
Legitimate	112.4	111.4	112.2	111.6	131.1	126.2
Illegitimacy Ratio	12.6	12.9	9.5	9.9	42.3	42.8

Note: For definitions and sources, see Tables 1, 2, and 3.

CALIFORNIA'S ABORTION LEGISLATION AND ITS DEMOGRAPHIC EFFECTS

Edwin W. Jackson

Introduction

The Law. The Therapeutic Abortion Act became effective November 1967. Its basic provisions are that a woman may obtain an abortion if (a) there is a substantial risk that continuance of the pregnancy would gravely impair her physical or mental health, or (b) if the pregnancy resulted from rape or incest. The law also outlines the mechanisms and procedures for determining individual eligibility. Specifically it requires that a medical committee be established in each hospital in order to determine an applicant's qualifications under the physical or mental health categories. Applications based on rape or incest grounds are referred to the District Attorney. The law sets guidelines for the operation of the medical committees, certain procedures are detailed, and definitions are given. (For the text of the complete law, see Appendix A.)

Data Needs. The question under consideration here is "What demographic effects have occurred, and what can be expected as a result of the application of this law?" There are several basic pieces of information which are needed in order to answer this question properly. The first item needed is a sound projection of therapeutic abortion trends. Second, the relationship between illegal and therapeutic abortion experience must be known in order to place the therapeutic component in proper perspective. Third, the outcome of pending operational and legal decisions affecting application of the law should be known in order to determine whether present abortion trends will be dampened or reinforced.

Data Limitations. It must be admitted that at this point in time these elements are either not precisely known, or at best, tenuously estimated. Therapeutic abortions are such a recent entrant into the scene that sound projections cannot be made based solely on the figures accumulated to date. In addition, there is a lack of firm data on illegal abortions in California, which makes it difficult to determine if total abortions are increasing or if the illegal procedures are simply shifting into the therapeutic abortion category. Monitoring of abortion deaths provides a rough index to gauge illegal abortion trends, but special studies would be required to provide precise information on this practice. The result of pending court and

CALIFORNIA'S ABORTION LEGISLATION AND ITS DEMOGRAPHIC EFFECTS

administrative action about the abortion act can be tentatively predicted on the basis of earlier decisions and current experience. The prediction can be dignified as "educated," but it is subject to the wide range of human and institutional response in this area.

If abortion is to have any demographic effect, it will ultimately be measured in terms of fertility. Abortion is only one means of affecting fertility, and other factors affecting childbearing patterns must be measured in order to determine the independent effect of abortion. Because fertility patterns change slowly and therapeutic abortions have been available only a short time, no attempt is made here to assess their influence on fertility.

For these reasons, much of the material presented here must be considered tentative. However, the current information on therapeutic abortions is reliable, and there are indicators as to their future direction. The approach taken here will consist of a projection of abortions based on trends in both the performance of abortions and decisions affecting abortion practices. In light of that projection, the effect of therapeutic abortions on childbearing and its demographic consequences will be considered.

Therapeutic Abortion Experience and Trends

Between November 1967 and December 31, 1970, there were over 84,000 therapeutic abortions performed in California. In the first full calendar year of experience--1968--there were approximately 5,000 therapeutic abortions. In 1969, there was more than a threefold increase, with some 16,200 procedures reported. In 1970, there were 62,672 abortions reported, nearly four times that of 1969, giving a ratio of 172 therapeutic abortions per 1,000 live births. The most conservative projection would be that the number reported in the last quarter of 1970 would be repeated in each quarter of 1971. With this model, over 90,000 terminations would be anticipated in 1971. A more expansive view is to assume that the magnitude of increase in mid-1970 will remain constant. Using this assumption, some 120,000 abortions would be expected. It seems likely that the 1971 figure will fall somewhere in the mid-range of these two projections--that is, between 100,000 to 110,000.

Current Demographic Effects

To assess the present demographic impact of the abortion law, the past and present experience with illegal abortion should be known. The question to be answered is "Are abortions (i.e., the total abortion rate) more frequent under the new law, or is there a more or less simple substitution of therapeutic abortion for illegal procedures?"

Although the rate of illegal abortions for California women is not known, a survey of induced abortions in urban North Carolina[1] provides a reasonable basis to estimate the total number of abortions in California. The survey showed that the proportion of women in the 18-44 age group having induced abortions was 13.9 per 1,000 white women and 68.1 per 1,000 nonwhite women. Applying these rates to the number of California women ages 15-44 in 1970, the estimated total induced abortions would be over 78,500.

Assuming that each therapeutic abortion resulted in one less illegal abortion, there still would have been some 16,000 illegal procedures in 1970. There is evidence that up to this time a simple one-for-one replacement of therapeutic abortion for illegal abortion has been the dominant operating mechanism. Perhaps the most important observation sustaining such a view is that illegitimacy rates are rising.[2] One would expect that any substantial increase in the total abortion rate would be reflected in lower illegitimacy figures.

There is also other information consistent with this view. Deaths due to illegal abortions have decreased from 35 in 1966-67 to 21 in 1968-69. In addition, there are signs that many Mexican-based abortionists have closed up, and many hospitals have noted that their intake of patients with septic abortions has decreased markedly. These facts all support the view that the advent of therapeutic abortions has not resulted in a higher total abortion rate than existed in the period before the law became effective.

The Therapeutic Abortion Act: Operational and Legal Issues

One difficulty in projecting abortion trends and future population effects is that pending operational and legal decisions could either reinforce or dampen the upward trend. In order to assess the possibilities, the tenor of the recent actions of organized medicine and the courts should be noted. Dissatisfaction with the present legal requirements is seen in the stand of

---

[1] J.R. Abernathy, B.G. Greenberg, and D.G. Horvitz, "Estimates of Induced Abortion in Urban North Carolina," Demography, 7 (1970), pp. 19-29.

[2] B. Berkov, "Illegitimate Fertility in California's Population," pp. 207 - 227 above.

CALIFORNIA'S ABORTION LEGISLATION AND ITS DEMOGRAPHIC EFFECTS

organized medicine on abortion. In March 1970, the California Medical Association House of Delegates approved a resolution which reads, in part, as follows:

WHEREAS, abortion is a surgical procedure, and, like other surgical procedures is governed by the Medical Practice Act contained in the California Business and Professions Code; and,
WHEREAS, recent appellate decisions are to the effect that the performance of abortions should be determined by medical consideration; and,
WHEREAS, statutory restrictions inconsistent with good medical practice unfairly threaten patients and physicians; now, be it
RESOLVED, that it be the policy of the California Medical Association that abortion should be governed by medical standards of sound clinical judgment, and informed patient consent, according to the merits of each individual case, and be it further
RESOLVED, that the California Medical Association shall seek reformation of the law consistent with this resolution; and the sense of this resolution be introduced by its delegation to the American Medical Association.[3]

In addition to the action of organized medicine, the abortion act faces a number of court challenges. The first decision weighing indirectly on the Therapeutic Abortion Act was that of the California Supreme Court in the case of the People v. Bellous, which invalidated an earlier anti-abortion law (September 1969). The 4 to 3 decision was based on two findings: (1) the phrase "necessary to preserve life" in the anti-abortion law was vague and in violation of the due process requirements for a criminal law, and (2) the law was in violation of women's fundamental rights to life and to choose whether to bear children. The court ruled that the state had no compelling interest which would justify so deep an infringement on the fundamental rights of women.

The Supreme Court would not rule on the Therapeutic Abortion Act. It has been argued that the present law could be found invalid on these same grounds, and indeed, two recent municipal court decisions have followed this course. Some details of pending cases both in California and elsewhere in the United States can be found in a recent article by Roemer.[4] To illustrate

---

[3] California Medical Association ad hoc Committee on Therapeutic Abortion, Final Report (CMA, San Francisco, California, March 1970).

[4] R. Roemer, "Abortion Law Reform and Repeal: Legislative and Judicial Developments," American Journal of Public Health, 61 (March 1971), pp. 500-509.

the tenor of the court, portions from the opinion of the court in the People v. Robb are quoted below:

> This brings us to the primary underlying problem. Does a woman have a constitutional right to make a free choice whether or not to bear children, i.e., whether or not to have an abortion? This Court rules, that unless the State has a compelling State interest which permits it to interfere in this area, that the total freedom of choice as to whether or not to bear children, including the unrestricted right to have an abortion, is such a fundamental right .... It has been suggested that there is a State interest in preserving the morals of the State and controlling promiscuity. Beside the obvious fact that laws such as this have no effect whatsoever on sexual attitudes of the community, the Griswold case makes it clear that private sexual relations are beyond the purview of the State. The State has no compelling interest in controlling promiscuity. . . . The State no longer has, if it ever had, a compelling interest in increasing the population of the State. We need not consider this argument further, as the decision is abundantly clear. Thus, the Court can find no compelling interest of the State, and concludes that the right to choose to bear or not to bear children is a fundamental right of the individual woman to be exercised in any manner she chooses and which may not in any way be abridged by law.[5]

In the case of the People v. Barksdale, the Municipal Court of Alameda County also held the Therapeutic Abortion Act unconstitutional. The reasoning followed that of the Robb decision. In summary, the court held that the Therapeutic Abortion Act (a) violated the equal protection clause of the Fourteenth Amendment, (b) is a vague and improper delegation of authority to the Joint Commission on Hospital Accreditation, (c) is discriminatory between rich and poor, and (d) violates the fundamental right of women to make a free choice whether or not to bear children.[6]

In addition to the legal issue of a compelling state interest, there is the question of the state's ability to effectively enforce abortion statutes. The existence of an

---

[5] People v. Robb, Nos. 149005 & 159061 (California Municipal Court Orange County, January 9, 1970) (Mast. J.)

[6] People v. Barksdale, No. 33237c (California Municipal Court Alameda County, March 24, 1970) (Foley, J.)

abortion law implies that the state is able to control the abortion practices of its citizens. Currently and historically both states and nations have been relatively ineffective in this area. In California, for example, an estimated 70,000 to 80,000 illegal abortions a year were obtained by state residents under the old anti-abortion law. Now there are other states with unrestrictive abortion statutes. These are being used by residents of states with restrictive abortion laws to obtain legal abortion. These facts indicate that anti-abortion laws do not prevent abortion. What has been affected by the new California law is the setting in which abortions are carried out. The question now is "What can we expect in the future?"

Future Demographic Effects

The court decisions and the attitude of organized medicine suggest that future changes will reinforce present trends and that abortion will become increasingly available and acceptable. Under such circumstances the predicted immediate effect of abortion will be to reduce the level of "unwanted births." Hopefully other means to prevent unwanted pregnancies will prevail, leaving abortions as an infrequent backup procedure. However, assuming that no marked changes occur in contraceptive practices, it is likely that abortion will be the method used in the 1970's to reduce unwanted births from previous levels.

The implication of the term "unwanted birth" is not always clear; however, the assumption made here is that if abortion were safe and available it would be chosen over continuance of pregnancy by a large proportion of women who now have unwanted births. It follows, then, that the incidence of unwanted births would provide a basis to estimate the upper limit of abortions in an unrestricted abortion setting. Bumpas and Westoff have estimated that 20 percent of the births in the United States are unwanted.[7] Applying these percentages to California's estimated 364,000 births in 1970 indicates that some 72,000 infants were in this category. Thus, the potential upper limit for abortion in California appears to be more than twice that experienced in 1970. The implication is that if abortions were fully available and acceptable, upwards of 137,000 terminations would be expected in 1971. This projection is too simplified, and as such, is an overestimate. It does not account for the proportion of women who for personal and moral reasons find abortion unacceptable, even though the birth is unwanted.

---

[7]L. Bumpas and C. Westoff, "The 'Perfect Contraceptive' Population," Science, 169 (September 1970), pp. 1177-1182.

Even though actual abortions in 1971 fall short of this potential, it is reasonable to believe that there will be an increase in the therapeutic abortion rate beyond that of 1970. This would result in total abortions exceeding past levels and dampen recent upward birth-rate trends.

There are other demographic consequences implicit in an increasing abortion rate. One is that the selective reduction of unwanted births will reduce the number of infants available for adoption. The number of infants available for adoption in California has already decreased in 1969 and 1970. It has been suggested that contraceptive and abortion practices account for this; however, this is not necessarily the case. Total abortions have not increased, and most significantly, the rate and number of illegitimate births--the basic source of adopted infants--has increased. From this it is concluded that much of the decrease in the number of infants available for adoption is due to single mothers choosing to keep their child.

Increasing abortion rates may also reduce the marriage rate in the age group under 20. Forty-two percent of the California women who marry before age 20 are pregnant at the time of the ceremony.[8] In 1968 there were 55,000 marriages of women under 20 years of age; an estimated 23,000 were pregnant at the time of marriage. Presumably some of these couples would choose abortion to marriage if abortion services were readily available.

Conclusion

From the limited data and information available at this time a few conclusions about therapeutic abortion can be made:

First, in the period November 1967 to December 1970, therapeutic abortions appear to have been largely a substitution for illegal procedures. Total abortions did not increase, and no demographic effects are postulated for this period.

Second, a continued increase in the therapeutic abortion rate is to be expected in 1971. If this occurs, the total abortion rate will rise above previous levels, and the immediate effect will be a dampening of the birth rate. Secondary effects may be a reduction in the number of infants available for adoption, and possibly a lowering of the marriage rate in the group under age 20.

---

[8]"Interval between First Marriage and Legitimate First Birth, United States 1964-66," Monthly Vital Statistics Report, National Mortality Survey Statistics; National Center for Health Statistics, 18:12 Suppl., March 27, 1970.

Finally, if therapeutic abortion is going to have a fundamental demographic effect, it will ultimately be measured in terms of fertility. There are many factors affecting fertility. For this reason any definitive study of an "abortion effect" will require consideration of the dynamics of the major factors weighing on fertility.

EDWIN W. JACKSON

APPENDIX A

Senate Bill No. 462

CHAPTER 327

An act to add Chapter 11 (commencing with Section 25950) to Division 20 of the Health and Safety Code, to amend Section 2377 of the Business and Professions Code, and to amend Sections 274, 275, and 276 of the Penal Code, relating to abortion.

(Approved by Governor June 15, 1967. Filed with Secretary of State June 15, 1967.)

The people of the State of California do enact as follows:

Section 1. Chapter 11 (commencing with Section 25950) is added to Division 20 of the Health and Safety Code, to read:

Chapter 11. Abortion

25950. This chapter shall be known and may be cited as the Therapeutic Abortion Act.
25951. A holder of the physician's and surgeon's certificate, as defined in the Business and Professions Code, is authorized to perform an abortion or aid or assist or attempt an abortion, only if each of the following requirements is met:
 (a) The abortion takes place in a hospital which is accredited by the Joint Commission on Accreditation of Hospitals.
 (b) The abortion is approved in advance by a committee of the medical staff of the hospital, which committee is established and maintained in accordance with standards promulgated by the Joint Commission on Accreditation of Hospitals. In any case in which the committee of the medical staff consists of no more than three licensed physicians and surgeons, the unanimous consent of all committee members shall be required in order to approve the abortion.
 (c) The Committee of the Medical Staff finds that one or more of the following conditions exist:
 (1) There is substantial risk that continuance of the pregnancy would gravely impair the physical or mental health of the mother;
 (2) The pregnancy resulted from rape or incest.
25952. The Committee of the Medical Staff shall not approve the performance of an abortion on the ground that the pregnancy resulted from rape or incest except in accordance with the following procedure:

CALIFORNIA'S ABORTION LEGISLATION AND ITS DEMOGRAPHIC EFFECTS

(a) Upon receipt of an application for an abortion on the grounds that the pregnancy resulted from rape or incest, the committee shall immediately notify the district attorney of the county in which the alleged rape or incest occurred of the application, and transmit to the district attorney the affidavit of the applicant attesting to the facts establishing the alleged rape or incest. If the district attorney informs the committee that there is probable cause to believe that the pregnancy resulted from a violation of Section 261 or Section 285 of the Penal Code, the committee may approve the abortion. If, within five days after the committee has notified the district attorney of the application, the committee does not receive a reply from the district attorney, it may approve the abortion. If the district attorney informs the committee that there is no probable cause to believe the alleged violation did occur, the committee shall not approve the abortion, except as provided in subdivision (b) of this section;

(b) If the district attorney informs the committee that there is no probable cause to believe the alleged violation did occur, the person who applied for the abortion may petition the superior court of the county in which the alleged rape or incest occurred, to determine whether the pregnancy resulted from a violation of Section 261 or Section 285 of the Penal Code. Hearing on the petition shall be set for a date no later than one week after the date of filing of the petition.

The district attorney shall file an affidavit with the court stating the reasons for his conclusion that the alleged violation did not occur, and this affidavit shall be received in evidence. The district attorney may appear at the hearing to offer further evidence or to examine witnesses.

If the court finds that it has been proved, by a preponderance of the evidence, that the pregnancy did result from a violation of Section 261 or Section 285 of the Penal Code, it shall issue an order so declaring, and the committee may approve the abortion. Any hearing granted under this section may, at the court's discretion, be held in camera. The testimony, findings, conclusions or determinations of the court in a proceeding under this section shall be inadmissible as evidence in any other action or proceeding, although nothing herein shall be construed to prevent the appearance of any witness who testified at a proceeding under this section, or to prevent the introduction of any evidence that may have been introduced at a proceeding under this section, in any other action or proceeding.

(c) Notwithstanding any other provision of this section, an abortion shall be approved on the ground of a violation of subdivision 1 of Section 261 of the Penal Code only when the woman at the time of the alleged violation, was below the age of 15 years.

(d) Notwithstanding any other provision of this section, the testimony of any witness in a proceeding under this section shall be admissible as evidence in any prosecution of that witness for perjury.

25953. The committee of the medical staff referred to in Section 25951 must, in all instances, consist of not less than two licensed physicians and surgeons, and if the proposed termination of pregnancy will occur after the 13th week of pregnancy, the committee must consist of at least three such licensed physicians and surgeons. In no event shall the termination be approved after the 20th week of pregnancy.

25954. The term "mental health" as used in Section 25951 means mental illness to the extent that the woman is dangerous to herself or to the person or property of others or is in need of supervision or restraint.

Sec. 2. Section 2377 of the Business and Professions Code is amended to read:

2377. The procuring or aiding or abetting or attempting or agreeing or offering to procure an abortion constitutes unprofessional conduct within the meaning of this chapter, unless such an act be done in compliance with the provisions of the Therapeutic Abortion Act, Chapter 11 (commencing with Section 25950) of Division 20 of the Health and Safety Code.

Sec. 3. Section 274 of the Penal Code is amended to read:

274. Every person who provides, supplies, or administers to any woman, or procures any woman to take any medicine, drug, or substance, or uses or employs any instrument or other means whatever, with intent thereby to procure the miscarriage of such woman, except as provided in the Therapeutic Abortion Act, Chapter 11 (commencing with Section 25950) of Division 20 of the Health and Safety Code, is punishable by imprisonment in the state prison not less than two nor more than five years.

Sec. 4. Section 275 of the Penal Code is amended to read:

275. Every woman who solicits of any person any medicine, drug, or substance whatever, and takes the same, or who submits to any operation, or to the use of any means whatever, with intent thereby to procure a miscarriage, except as provided in the Therapeutic Abortion Act, Chapter 11 (commencing with Section 25950) of Division 20 of the Health and Safety Code, is punishable by imprisonment in the state prison not less than one nor more than five years.

Sec. 5. Section 276 of the Penal Code is amended to read:

276. Every person who solicits any woman to submit to any operation, or to the use of any means whatever, to procure a miscarriage, except as provided in the Therapeutic Abortion Act, Chapter 11 (commencing with Section 25950) of Division 20 of the Health and Safety Code, is punishable by imprisonment in the county jail not longer than one year or in the state prison not longer than five years, or by fine of not more than five thousand dollars ($5,000). Such offense must be proved by the testimony of two witnesses, or of one witness and corroborating circumstances.

NUMBER OF CHILDREN AND FEMALE JOBS:
SOME EVIDENCE FROM CALIFORNIA

Samuel H. Preston

Long overdue attention is now being directed toward ways of reducing fertility levels in the United States. Ironically, the focus on population policy issues has resulted less from population growth itself than from economic growth. Rapidly rising living standards have permitted additional population members to consume ever-larger quantities of exhaustible natural resources and leave behind increasing amounts of unpleasant or noxious byproducts. The impact of added members on congestion and crowding became perceptibly greater after the concentration of population which accompanied industrialization. And the costs of equipping new members of the labor force, borne principally by society at large, have grown in step with the increasingly technical needs of a modern economy.

This paper will attempt to evaluate the potential effectiveness of a special type of fertility policy, one which would operate on the conditions under which women can work or find jobs. We will thus be dealing with indirect policy measures, in the sense that they would achieve a modification in fertility by altering conditions presumed to be influential in a couples' fertility decision, rather than directly imposing limits on family size.

The Relationship Between Fertility and Female Labor Force Participation

The reason for pursuing the present line of inquiry is that, in modern industrial societies, a very strong inverse association exists between the number of children a woman has borne and the amount of time she has spent working. According to Judith Blake, "Female labor force participation has long been known to bear one of the most impressive relationships to family

---

Research for this paper was supported by training grants to the Department of Demography, University of California, Berkeley, from the National Center for Health Services Research and Development (8 T01 HS00059), National Institute of General Medical Sciences (8 T01 GM1240), and the Ford Foundation.

size of any variable--typically in Western countries it has been equalled or exceeded in strength only by Catholic-non-Catholic religious affiliation."[1] The extensive evidence which documents this statement will not be reproduced here.[2] The data are most exhaustive and convincing for women in the United States during recent decades. Particularly illuminating have been cross-sectional, or moment-of-time, studies of the relationship between fertility and labor force status for individuals[3] and for areas.[4]

Table 1 presents data generated for a 5 percent sample of the whole country by the 1960 U.S. Census of Population. In each category of age, color, and residence status (not presented), ever-married women had fewer children the more actively they were or had been involved in employment. The negative relationship between fertility and female employment persists even when the levels of wife's education, husband's income, and areal unemployment rates are held constant.[5]

It is clear that women behave as though motherhood and employment were competitive activities. Confirmation is provided by Current Population Survey data on women who are leaving or remaining withdrawn from the labor force. Fifty-six percent of married women aged 25-34 who withdrew from the labor force in 1963 listed the reason as pregnancy;[6] 79.9 percent of all women

---

[1]Mindel C. Sheps and Jeanne Clare Ridley, eds., "Demographic Science and the Redirection of Population Policy" in Public Health and Population Change (Pittsburgh: University of Pittsburgh Press, 1965), pp. 62-63.

[2]For a brief summary and bibliography of international data, see Murray Gendell, "The Influence of Family-Building Activity on Women's Rate of Economic Activity" in Proceedings, United Nations World Population Conference (Belgrade, 1965), Vol. 4, pp. 283-287.

[3]William G. Bowen and T. Aldrich Finegan, The Economics of Labor Force Participation (Princeton: Princeton University Press, 1969); Glen C. Cain, Married Women in the Labor Force (Chicago: University of Chicago Press, 1966); James A. Sweet, "Family Composition and the Labor Force Activity of American Wives," Demography, Vol. 7, No. 2 (May 1970), pp. 195-209; Ronald Freedman, Pascal K. Whelpton, and Arthur A. Campbell, Family Planning, Sterility, and Population Growth (New York: McGraw-Hill, 1959).

[4]Bowen and Finegan; Cain.

[5]Bowen and Finegan.

[6]U.S. Department of Labor, Bureau of Labor Statistics, "Why Women Start and Stop Working: A Study in Mobility," Monthly Labor Review, September 1965, pp. 1077-1082.

NUMBER OF CHILDREN AND FEMALE JOBS: CALIFORNIA

Table 1

RELATIONSHIP BETWEEN THE EXTENT OF LABOR FORCE INVOLVEMENT AND AVERAGE NUMBER OF CHILDREN EVER-BORN, MARRIED WOMEN: UNITED STATES, 1960

Age	Employment Status	Average Number of Children Ever-Born per 1000 Women Ever-Married	
		White	Non-White
20-24	In labor force	809	1612
	Worked less than 35 hours/wk	1124	1858
	Not in labor forced	1647	2235
	Never worked	1929	2283
25-29	In labor force	1498	2179
	Worked less than 35 hours/wk	1907	2579
	Not in labor force	2424	3216
	Never worked	2806	3314
30-34	In labor force	1993	2506
	Worked less than 35 hours/wk	2344	2983
	Not in labor force	2811	3766
	Never worked	3233	4003
35-39	In labor force	2145	2519
	Worked less than 35 hours/wk	2454	2970
	Not in labor force	2893	3833
	Never worked	3391	4141
40-44	In labor force	2132	2483
	Worked less than 35 hours/wk	2388	2867
	Not in labor force	2788	3635
	Never worked	3333	4028
45-49	In labor force	2042	2408
	Worked less than 35 hours/wk	2245	2698
	Not in labor force	2602	3336
	Never worked	3168	3854
50-64	In labor force	2096	2401
	Worked less than 35 hours/wk	2305	2579
	Not in labor force	2670	3288
	Never worked	3201	3693

Source: United States Census of Population, 1960. Subject Reports. Women by Number of Children Ever-Born. Final Report PC(2) - 3A. Based on a 5 percent sample.

not in the labor force in 1968 attributed their status to "home responsibilities," a percentage which peaks at 92.2 among women aged 25-34, who are most likely to have young children at home to care for.[7]

Explaining the Inverse Association Between Fertility and Employment

Several reasons have been suggested for the apparent antagonism between female employment and motherhood. Westoff, Potter, and Sagi, in the second publication from the Princeton Fertility Study, hypothesize that "Fertility as a value is incompatible with values supporting extrafamilial identifications such as employment."[8] Others have argued in a similar vein that employment fosters a more acute awareness of the hidden costs of motherhood.

However, the hypothesis that family and employment values are in opposition is not sustained by available evidence. The Princeton study found no "statistically significant correlation between liking for children and months of employment or future work intentions."[9] Earlier data from the well-known Indianapolis study indicated that white, Protestant, fecund married women who had worked for a longer period of time evinced a slightly higher degree of interest in and liking for children.[10] Finally, the Growth of the American Family study found that the average number of children considered "ideal" for the average American family by white married women in 1960 was 3.5 if a woman had never worked and 3.4 if she had.[11] It seems quite doubtful that employment engenders a distaste for children and that women are impelled by valuing work highly to value family-formation less.

---

[7]U.S. Department of Labor, Bureau of Labor Statistics, "Persons Not in the Labor Force," Special Labor Force Report No. 110 (1969).

[8]Charles Westoff, Robert G. Potter, and Philip Sagi, The Third Child (Princeton: Princeton University Press, 1965), p. 187.

[9]Westoff, Potter, Sagi, and Elliot Mishler, Family Growth in Metropolitan America (Princeton: Princeton University Press, 1961), p. 304.

[10]Lois Pratt and P.K. Whelpton, "Extra-familial Participation of Wives in Relation to Interest in and Liking for Children, Fertility Planning, and Actual and Desired Family Size," Milbank Memorial Fund Quarterly, Vol. 34, No. 1 (January 1956), p. 50.

[11]P.K. Whelpton, Arthur A. Campbell, and John E. Patterson, Fertility and Family Planning in the United States (Princeton: Princeton University Press, 1966), p. 110.

NUMBER OF CHILDREN AND FEMALE JOBS: CALIFORNIA

A more persuasive explanation of the antagonism between motherhood and work is based upon the amount of time required by each activity and the finite number of hours available to a woman in a week. Time spent in employment is time which cannot be devoted to childraising. The two are difficult to combine without a substantial sacrifice of leisure time or a less satisfactory performance of one or both tasks. Time-budget studies are explicit about the drain on a woman's time posed by additional children. In urban areas of France, where the most satisfactory studies have been performed, the first child was found to add an average (not considering his age) of 17.8 hours of household work a week for the mother, and the second child another 12.1 hours.[12] The only study of budget-times in the U.S. which provides roughly comparable data indicates that an additional child in 1965 increased total hours of housework per week (for both husbands and wives) by an average of 5.2 hours, which increases to 10.4 hours for the first child while he is under age 4.[13] These figures understate considerably the total burden of an added child, since the hours of outside help received by the family increased substantially with the number of children. The great difficulty of combining employment and motherhood at some stages is signalled by the increase in average hours of outside help from two per week if the wife doesn't work or three if she has no children to 19 if she works more than 20 hours and has a child under age 6.[14] Evidently the pressure on a woman's time when the two activities are combined in their most intense form is such that this combination is elected only when the safety valve of abundant outside help is available.

It seems reasonable to conclude that the source of the apparent competition between motherhood and employment is the competing demands which the two activities place upon a woman's limited supply of time. Against the backdrop of this tension, an inverse association between fertility and labor force participation in a population could result from:

---

[12]Alain Girard, "Le Budget-temps de la femme mariée dans les agglomerations urbains," Population (Paris), Vol. 13, No. 4 (1958), p. 613.

[13]James N. Morgan, Ismail Serageldin, and Nancy Baerwaldt, Productive Americans (University of Michigan Institute for Social Research, Ann Arbor, 1966). Figures compiled from p. 108. The average hours spent on a child is computed by dividing the difference in hours spent between those families with at least one child under 18 and those with no children by the average number of children under age 18 in families with children under 18 (2.40), compiled from page 400.

[14]Ibid., pp. 167-168.

243

(1) A lack of control over fertility, releasing those whose fertility is, by chance, low into the labor force and restraining those who prove most fertile from working;

(2) A lack of control over employment, so that those fortunate enough to find jobs voluntarily restrict their fertility, while those less successful withdraw into the home and pursue family-building activity;

(3) Effective control over both fertility and employment, combined with relative preferences for the two activities which vary from woman to woman. Rational planning by the couple, which would necessarily take cognizance of the difficulty of combining the two activities, will in this case ensure that women who have a preference for employment will restrict their fertility. Similarly, women who opt for large families will limit their economic activity.

The policy implications of the fertility/employment association obviously depend upon which of these three mechanisms is operative. If a woman's fertility determines her participation, changing employment opportunities would have scant effect on fertility. Measures would achieve maximum effect when employment opportunities exclusively determine participation and fertility. Finally, in the situation of free choice we must ascertain the important factors which mutually govern participation and fertility before any policy conclusions can be drawn.

The relative importance of the first mechanism can be studied by reference to the 1955 Growth of the American Family survey data on white married women aged 18-39 with husband present.[15] Thirty-one percent of all women in the survey were classified as "subfecund" or "sterile,"[16] and the labor force participation rate of this group was somewhat higher than that of "fecund" women.[17] Similarly, 13 percent of fecund contraceptors had "excess fertility," and these women had a reduced labor force participation rate.[18] However, the principal group

---

[15] Freedman, Whelpton, and Campbell.

[16] Ibid., p. 42.

[17] Ibid., p. 51.

[18] Ibid., p. 138. Ascribing all "excess fertility" to chance or to faulty contraceptive devices would clearly be incorrect. To the extent that women are motivated to practice contraception more efficiently by a desire to work, the inverse association between fertility and employment results from conditions which precede, rather than follow, experience with contraception.

NUMBER OF CHILDREN AND FEMALE JOBS: CALIFORNIA

accounting for the inverse association between employment and
fertility was fecund women who were efficient contraceptors. For
example, about 70 percent of the difference in the average number
of children ever-born between women who had never worked and women
who worked 1-4 years since marriage was due to differences in
fertility rates among the fecund women in the two groups.[19]

Evidently, the difference in the average number of children ever-born between labor force participants and non-participants
is not principally a result of uncontrolled fertility among one or
both of the groups. The first mechanism listed above is an incomplete explanation of the association.

The Influence of Employment Opportunities on Fertility and Wife's Labor Force Participation

We will now consider the possibility that a woman's employment opportunities are a prime determinant of her fertility
and labor force behavior. We will not attempt to distinguish
between mechanisms 2 and 3, but rather to show instead that if 3
is pertinent, then one of the principal factors affecting a woman's
relative preferences for children and work is her employment
opportunities.

Virtually all of the available studies relate to the effect of employment opportunities on labor force participation,
rather than on fertility. These investigations have unanimously
concluded that employment opportunities exert a powerful influence
over the proportion of married women who are economically active.
One of the earliest studies examined 1940 U.S. Census data on
Standard Metropolitan Statistical Areas.[20] Female participation
rates were shown to be highest in areas where light industries,
such as textile, apparel, tobacco, and electrical machinery,

---

[19] Derived from data in ibid., pp. 51 and 303. The procedure was
to weight the difference between the fertility rates in the two
work categories for fecund women by the average proportion in the
two groups who were fecund. When this procedure is applied to
the difference in average fertility between those working more
than 5 years and those never working, less than half of the total
difference can be attributed to fertility variations among fecund
women. However, only 17 percent of women who reported working
had done so for more than 5 years (ibid., p. 139).

[20] Nora Belloc, "Labor Force Participation and Employment Opportunities for Women," Journal of the American Statistical Association, Vol. 45 (1950), pp. 400-410.

dominated. Conversely, female activity rates were lowest in areas like Gary, Indiana, where iron and steel, or automobile, or rubber manufacturing was predominant.

Two separate studies have demonstrated that similar relationships continued to hold in Metropolitan Areas in 1960.[21] In addition, the level of female earnings in an area was shown to exert a strong and significant positive effect on participation. In one study, Growth of the American Family data on individuals (not areas) was reexamined and a variable constructed that was designed to represent a wife's potential earnings.[22] This variable also showed a close positive association with a woman's labor force participation.

Finally, time series data indicate that, like other "secondary workers," married women's labor force participation rates are very responsive to the business cycle. They exhibit high values when unemployment is low and low values when it is high.[23]

In light of the responsiveness of married women's economic activity to employment opportunities, and of the antagonism between employment and motherhood, it is quite reasonable to expect a woman's fertility to be negatively related to her employment opportunities. Surprisingly, this matter has received almost no attention. One exception is a 1938 study of fertility in England and Wales. Charles and Moshinsky noted the "fertile coalfield area" and the "infertile textile towns," and attributed their differences to the fact that "In mining districts there are practically no avenues of employment open to women outside the home, whereas in textile districts the bulk of the work is carried on by women."[24] In fact, however, the variation was due mainly to differences in the proportion married, which was low in textile areas, for example, because single women seeking work were attracted there. The resulting sex ratio of the population was heavily weighted with women, who were consequently more likely to remain single.

The same relationships may be perceived today in the United States. In a separate paper I have examined the average

---

[21] Bowen and Finegan; Cain.

[22] Cain, p. 98.

[23] Bowen and Finegan, p. 187.

[24] Enid Charles and Pearl Moshinsky, "Differential Fertility in England and Wales During the Past Two Decades" in Lancelot Hogben, ed., Political Arithmetic (New York: MacMillan, 1938), p. 143.

NUMBER OF CHILDREN AND FEMALE JOBS: CALIFORNIA

number of children ever-born to married women in the 100 largest Standard Metropolitan Statistical Areas of the U.S., 1960.[25] The factor which was by far the most closely associated with this quantity was the ratio of female to male earnings in an area. The "femaleness" of the industrial structure also contributed significantly to the explanation of fertility variation.

Here I will attempt to show that similar relationships hold in California by examining the average number of children ever-born to ever-married women aged 25-34 in the various counties of California. This age group has accumulated sufficient marital experience to produce substantial variations among the counties, while it is young enough that current behavior will have an important effect on completed family size.

Our hypothesis--that a greater availability of attractive employment opportunities for women should depress the average number of children ever-born to married women in an area--receives striking confirmation from the data. The coefficients of correlation between fertility in California counties and various socioeconomic indicators for the counties are shown in Table 2. It is clear that the two variables most closely associated with an area's average fertility are the percentage of the total labor force in clerical jobs--used to indicate whether the configuration of occupations in an area is favorable or unfavorable to female work-- and the median earnings of females in the area. In both cases the variables are negatively related to fertility. The close relationship between children ever-born and female work opportunities is obviously not caused by their mutual association with one of the other variables listed, since none has as high a degree of explanatory power as employment opportunities.

In Table 3, the 22 counties larger than 100,000 are arranged according to the level of median female earnings. The number of children ever-born, averaged over the grouped data, declines monotonically as the level of female earnings increases. Figure 1 shows the scatter plot of median female earnings against children ever-born for all 52 counties.

Table 4 shows the average number of children ever-born in California counties cross-classified by the median female earnings and the proportion of the county population which is rural. The level of female earnings continues to exert a strong effect on fertility within each class of rural proportion. However, the rural proportion no longer affects fertility in a significant fashion within a given earnings level. The partial correlation

---

[25]"Marital Fertility and Female Employment Opportunities, United States, 1960," presented at Population Association of America annual meeting, 1971; Washington, D.C.

Table 2

COEFFICIENTS OF CORRELATION BETWEEN AVERAGE NUMBER OF CHILDREN EVER-BORN TO EVER-MARRIED WOMEN AGED 25-34 IN CALIFORNIA, 1960, AND SOCIO-ECONOMIC INDICATORS

	52 Counties with Population > 10,000	22 Counties with Population > 100,000
General Socio-Economic Indicators		
Median years of school completed, females 25+, 1960	-.611	-.674
Total county population, 1960	-.380	-.305
Percentage of families with annual income > $3,000, 1959	.528	.672
Percentage foreign-born, 1960	-.298	-.627
Percentage non-white, 1960	-.329	-.456
Median earnings, males with earnings, 1959	-.692	-.658
Percent of population residing in "rural" areas, 1960	.571	.786
Indicators of Female Employment Opportunities		
Percentage of total labor force in clerical jobs, 1960	-.855	-.871
Median earnings, females with earnings, 1959	-.819	-.877
Ratio, median female to male earnings, 1959	-.522	-.664
Ratio, employed females to males, 1960	-.679	-.630
Significant at 5%	±.268	±.406
Significant at 1%	±.348	±.516

NUMBER OF CHILDREN AND FEMALE JOBS: CALIFORNIA

Table 3

AVERAGE NUMBER OF CHILDREN EVER-BORN TO EVER-MARRIED WOMEN IN THE 22 LARGEST CALIFORNIA COUNTIES, 1960, CLASSIFIED ACCORDING TO MEDIAN EARNINGS OF THE FEMALE WORK FORCE

Range of Median Female Earnings, 1959	Number of Counties	Names	Mean, Average Number of Children Ever-Born to Ever-Married Women Aged 25-34 (unweighted)
> $3,300	1	San Francisco	1.902
$2,9000 - 3,300	5	Alameda, Los Angeles, Marin, Sacramento, San Mateo	2.206
$2,500 - 2,900	5	Contra Costa, Orange, San Diego, Santa Clara, Solano	2.388
$2,200 - 2,500	4	San Bernadino, Santa Barbara, Sonoma, Ventura	2.485
$1,900 - 2,200	5	Fresno, Humboldt, Monterey, Riverside, San Joaquin	2.589
< $1,900	2	Stanislaus, Tulare	2.682

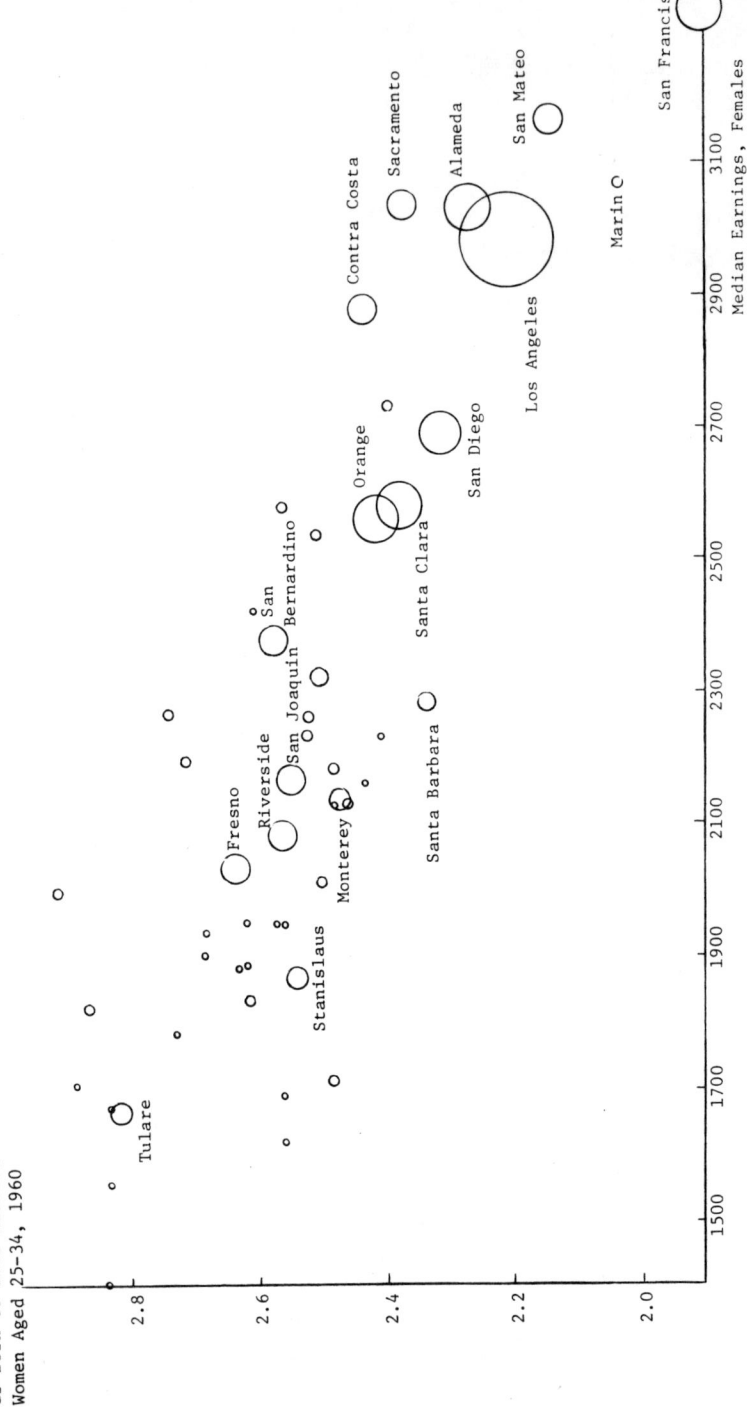

FIGURE 1. SCATTER-PLOT OF FERTILITY AND FEMALE EARNINGS, 52 CALIFORNIA COUNTIES

(Area of circle roughly proportional to population)

Table 4

AVERAGE NUMBER OF CHILDREN EVER-BORN, EVER-MARRIED WOMEN AGED 25-34 IN CALIFORNIA COUNTIES, 1960, CROSS-CLASSIFIED BY MEDIAN FEMALE EARNINGS AND PROPORTION RURAL

Median Earnings, Females with Earnings, 1959	Proportion of Total Population Living in Rural Areas[a]			
	< .33	.33 - .60	> .60	Total
> 2500	2.262 (11)	-- (0)	2.540 (2)	(13)
2150 - 2500	2.487 (4)	2.575 (5)	2.528 (3)	(12)
1950 - 2149	2.617 (3)	2.577 (7)	2.619 (5)	(15)
< 1950	-- (0)	2.736 (5)	2.719 (7)	(12)
Totals	(18)	(17)	(17)	(52)

[a] Number of cases in parentheses.

coefficient between rural proportion and average children ever-born, holding constant the level of female earnings, is an insignificant -.03. This suggests that one of the most important factors in current rural-urban fertility differentials is the relative absence of job opportunities for women in rural areas.

Similarly, it is possible to reinterpret the importance of a female's education for her fertility behavior. It may not be a "taste" for children which changes as education advances, but rather the opportunity cost of children. Women with higher educational attainment have, in general, higher potential earnings and a greater access to comfortable jobs. For this reason, children clearly represent a greater economic sacrifice for these women than for those having less education.

It is important to note that an alternative explanation of the negative association between fertility and the proportion of the labor force in clerical jobs is ruled out by the supplementary evidence on earnings. Conceivably, women first decide to have small families and then begin to look for work, thereby swelling a county's clerical work force. In this case, however, we would expect a negative relation between the clerical proportion and average female earnings; the unusually large female labor supply released to the market would drive down the average female wage level. In point of fact the correlation coefficient between average female earnings and the clerical proportion is an extraordinarily high +.905 for the 52 counties and +.929 for the largest 22. Furthermore, the ratio of female to male earnings is correlated with the ratio of the size of the female to male labor force at +.490 and +.778 in the two cases. Evidently, the proportion of females in labor force, and its occupational composition, are principally determined by the structure of demand for labor in an area.

Policy Implications

Our strong suspicion that female employment opportunities should affect fertility in a negative direction has been confirmed by evidence for California, as well as for other areas. There is obviously good reason to believe that policies to increase the availability and attractiveness of jobs for married women would serve to reduce fertility. The question must still be asked, "How much change in female employment opportunities would be required in order to reduce fertility by a certain desired amount?"

The answer can be given with precision (not to say accuracy) only for a policy of paying a subsidy to married women who work, or to their employers for hiring them. In this case, the answer is supplied by the slope of the line relating average number of children ever-born to the female earnings level. The slopes are quite similar for the two groups of counties: -.371 for the 52 counties and -.406 for the 22 largest counties. However, a portion of the latter figure is due to the activity of other variables having a significant effect on fertility.[26] The least-squares multiple regression with all significant variables included is:

$$\begin{array}{l}\text{Average Number}\\ \text{of Children}\\ \text{Ever-Born to}\\ \text{Ever-Married Women}\end{array} = 3.560 - \frac{.3790}{(.0390)} \cdot \begin{array}{l}\text{Median Female}\\ \text{Earnings (in}\\ \text{thousands of}\\ \text{dollars)}\end{array} - \frac{.0331}{(.0067)}$$

$$+ \frac{.0111}{(.0048)} \cdot \text{Percentage Foreign-Born} \cdot \text{Percentage Non-White}$$

$$N = 22 \quad R^2 = .903$$

All coefficients are significant at 5 percent. The positive effect of the non-white proportion agrees with our information about the behavior of these groups in California's largest cities. The negative effect of the foreign-born population reflects primarily the large size of this population in San Francisco and the city's exceptionally low fertility.

The slopes imply that if median female earnings were raised by $1000, or about 40 percent in 1960 dollars, then the average number of children ever-born would be reduced by .375, or approximately 16 percent.[27] A reduction of 16 percent would bring California's total fertility rate in 1970 slightly below the replacement level.[28] The cost of such a program would be staggering,

---

[26] In the case of the 52 counties, only the proportion of the labor force in clerical jobs contributed significantly to explain variation in fertility, once the effect of female earnings was accounted for.

[27] For the 22 largest counties, the average number of children ever-born to ever-married women ages 25-34 in 1960 was 2.41, and the average median female earnings in 1959 were $2,508.

[28] California's total fertility rate in 1970 is estimated to be 2.414 children. (I am grateful to Eduardo Arriaga of International Population and Urban Research, University of California, Berkeley, for this estimate based on data supplied by Beth Berkov, State Department of Public Health.) A 16 percent reduction would bring this down to 2.02, below the replacement level of approximately 2.14.

however: somewhat above $1 billion annually, in 1960 dollars, even if the subsidy were paid only to employed married women with husband present.[29] This figure represents about 20 percent of total current state expenditures from the general fund annually, but only about 1 percent of annual personal income.[30] Whether or not such a large expenditure would be justified by the benefits to be derived from replacement level fertility cannot be evaluated in this paper.

One additional economic policy for affecting fertility by changing female employment conditions would be to alter the manner in which married women are taxed. At present, the wife's earnings are usually considered to be the marginal, or extra, earnings in a household, and are consequently viewed as being taxed at the higher rates pertaining to higher incomes. There seems to be no valid reason for discriminating against married women vis-à-vis single women in this manner. The effect of such an alteration in tax policy would, in view of the above calculations, undoubtedly not be sufficient to reduce fertility to replacement levels.

The most promising non-economic technique to increase female labor force participation is probably to attack existing discrimination in hiring or promotion and in admission to educational institutions. Sex discrimination in hiring, firing, or compensation has, of course, already been outlawed by Section 703, Title VII, of the U.S. Civil Rights Act of 1964. However, the scope for new and more rigid laws for states, or more rigorous enforcement policies, is undoubtedly still considerable.

Two important side effects might be expected from a policy of forceful governmental intervention in the sex structure of job opportunities. One is a reduction of or compensation for existing discrimination which women face in the job market. A certain portion of this discrimination is undoubtedly "rational," in the sense that it reflects greater rates of absenteeism, higher turnover rates, and in some cases the expense of paid maternity leave. Yet women unquestionably face discrimination for "irrational"

---

[29] There were 1,156,478 employed married women with husbands present in California in 1960 (U.S. Census of Population, 1960, PC (93)-1A, pp. 136-138). If the program were successful, the final figure would be greater than $1 billion, since more women would have been induced to work.

[30] Estimated budget for 1970-71: $4.8 billion (State of California, State Budget of California for Support and Local Assistance, 1970-71, Vol. I, p. A-3. Estimated personal income, 1970: $90 billion (State of California, Department of Finance, California Personal Income, 3rd quarter, 1970).

reasons as well: employers', employees', or customers' preference for association with males rather than females.[31] As it has in other cases in the past, society may deem it desirable to eliminate or reduce the effect of such discriminatory conditions on the affected group.

Second, the effect of intervention would be to reorder, perhaps only marginally, the relative economic positions of males and females in the home. Such a reordering is unlikely to be enthusiastically welcomed by social scientists, who have already noted the difficult adjustments required when the same consequence was produced by the introduction of cotton-spinning and weaving machinery in nineteenth-century England, or by the growth of employment opportunities for Negro women in the 1950's.[32]

It should be noted that any fertility policy is bound to have side effects. The most serious would probably issue from the most popular policy suggestion, i.e., to increase the costs of children. The effect of this policy on children already born, or who manage to be born in the future, and of the redistribution of income away from the group which is responsible for feeding, clothing, and socializing the next generation in society, needs to be carefully explored. Before any policy is adopted, its costs and its unfavorable side effects must be carefully weighed against the favorable side effects and the costs of fertility rates continuing at levels well above replacement.

Summary and Conclusion

It is argued that the source of the inverse association between fertility and female employment is the competing demands placed by the two activities on a woman's limited supply of time. The relationship does not appear to result from a change in values consequent upon a woman's pursuit of either activity itself.

For the most part, women are not impelled into or out of employment by uncontrolled fertility. Instead, they are able to

---

[31] See, in particular, International Labor Office, "Discrimination in Employment or Occupation on the Basis of Marital Status," I: *International Labor Review*, Vol. 85 (1962), pp. 262-282, and II: Vol. 85 (1962), pp. 368-389.

[32] Neil J. Smelser, *Social Change in the Industrial Revolution* (Chicago: University of Chicago Press, 1959), ch. 9, and United States Department of Labor, Office of Planning and Research, *The Negro Family* (Washington, D.C.: Government Printing Office, March 1965 [The "Moynihan Report"]), chs. 3 and 4.

select voluntarily their quotas of children and work, keeping in mind the fundamental antagonism between the two. In this situation, it is reasonable to expect that the availability and attractiveness of female employment opportunities will have an important effect on fertility. This expectation is verified by analysis of fertility variation in California. The average level of female earnings and the proportion of the labor force in clerical jobs are shown to bear an extremely close, negative relationship to an area's average fertility. This relationship is stronger than that between fertility and educational level, population size, ethnic or racial composition, incidence of poverty, proportion rural, or male earnings.

Judging from this analysis, an increase in female work opportunities would in all probability effect a reduction in fertility rates in California. Policies designed to alter these opportunities may prove to be too expensive after a point to allow this to be the only approach to the problem of excessively high fertility. However, these policies represent an important potential weapon in the considerable arsenal of devices that may ultimately be required to constrain rates of childbearing to socially desirable levels.

P A R T   V

THE NATION'S MOST URBANIZED STATE

CALIFORNIA'S URBAN POPULATION: PATTERNS AND TRENDS

Staff: University of Southern California, Department of Sociology and Anthropology, Population Research Laboratory, Los Angeles, California*

Introduction

The State of California displays in exaggerated form several national population trends (see Table 1). These include rapid numerical growth and movement to coastal areas, as well as urban aggregation into metropolitan areas and regions (see Figure 1). By 1950 California's population was 81 percent urban. The percent urban has continued to increase, reaching 91 in 1970.[1] California has been the most urban state in the nation since 1960. Increasingly Californians live in large cities, and these cities and their suburbs now run together forming vast urban concentrations.

Population concentrations have modified California's environment and aggravated its economic, social, and political problems. The concentration of growth has produced more drastic changes than simple population increments would bring about. If

---

[1]The urban population includes all persons living in (a) incorporated or unincorporated places of 2,500 inhabitants or more, (b) the densely settled urban fringe, whether incorporated or unincorporated, of urbanized areas, and (c) towns which have no incorporated municipalities within their boundaries and have a density of 1,500 persons or more per square mile. (Category "c" was dropped for 1970 Census.) Source: U.S. Bureau of the Census, 1970 Census Users' Guide (Washington, D.C.: U.S. Government Printing Office, 1970).

---

*Rodger R. Rice, Judith J. Friedman, Maurice D. Van Arsdol, Jr., Mary Beth Olsen, John E. Lawson, Jr., Douglas MacKinnon, Charles F. Hohm, Alexandra Andriola, Leo A. Schuerman, Roger Ingram, Ann A. Woods, Nancy Edwards, Sara Saucier and Barbara Cook. Research for this paper was supported by the National Institute of Mental Health Demography of Social Disorganization Training Program, Training Grant MH 10243-06, and Grant (GH 89) from the National Sea Grant Program, U.S. Department of Commerce, to the University of Southern California.

Table 1

POPULATION AND POPULATION CHANGE, CONTINENTAL UNITED STATES AND CALIFORNIA: 1860-1970

Year	Continental United States		California		California as Percent of Continental United States	Index of Relative Differential Growth for California[b]
	Population	Percent Change[a]	Population	Percent Change[a]		
1860	31,443,321	--	379,994	--	1.2%	--
1870	39,818,449	26.6	560,247	47.7	1.4	78
1880	50,155,783	26.0	864,694	54.3	1.7	109
1890	62,947,714	25.5	1,213,398	40.3	1.9	58
1900	75,994,575	20.7	1,485,053	22.4	2.0	8
1910	91,972,266	21.0	2,377,549	60.1	2.6	186
1920	105,710,620	14.9	3,426,861	44.1	3.2	196
1930	122,775,046	16.1	5,677,251	65.7	4.6	308
1940	131,669,275	7.2	6,907,387	21.7	5.2	201
1950	150,697,361	14.5	10,586,223	53.3	7.0	268
1960	178,464,236	18.4	15,717,204	48.5	8.8	163
1970	199,251,668	11.6	19,953,134	27.0	10.0	133

[a] Percent change from previous date.

[b] Numerical differences between percent change of California and United States expressed as percent of percent change for United States in given period.

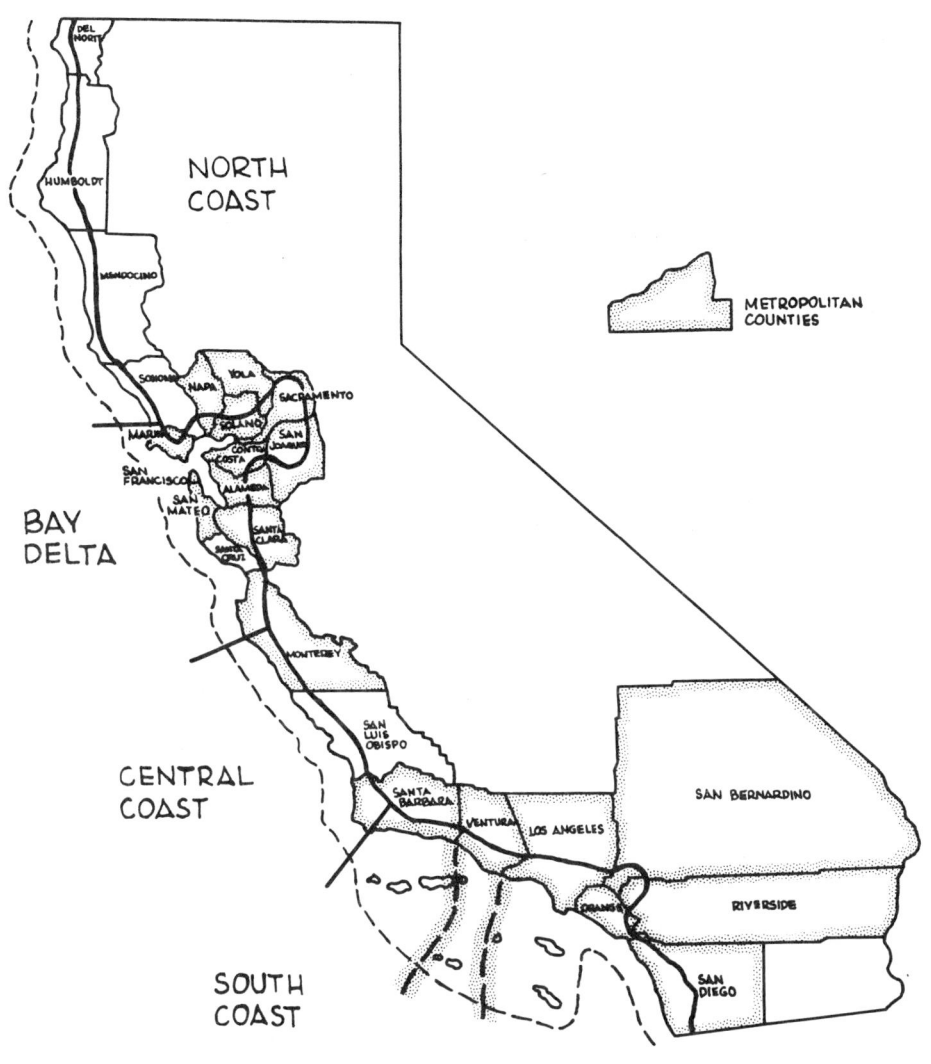

FIGURE I - COASTAL STRIP AREAS, CALIFORNIA

STAFF: POPULATION RESEARCH LABORATORY, USC

population growth and aggregation in California stopped today, urban problems would neither end nor diminish in severity. Population growth can be regarded as "an intensifier or modifier of many problems impairing the quality of life in the United States."[2] We will consider some implications of trends in California's urban population for the California environment and the problems of California's urban, metropolitan, and megalopolitan areas.

The Character of California's Population Growth

Both the rate and the composition of California's population growth changed in the 1960's. Between 1950 and 1960 California's population grew by 48 percent; for the 1960's its growth rate was nearly half that much--28 percent (see Table 2). The components of growth--natural increase[3] and net migration[4]--both declined in the 1960's, though net migration to California declined somewhat more than did natural increase (see Table 3). Net migration accounted for 61 percent of the state's net population growth in the 1950's; in the 1960's it accounted for 51 percent. The change in numbers is more dramatic: California added 3.1 million persons through net migration in the 1950's, but only 2.1 million in the 1960's. In contrast, natural increase totaled 2.2 million in the 1950's and 2.0 million in the 1960's. In the past, California has held unusual attraction for persons from other parts of the nation, but for the next decade natural increase will be its major source of population growth.

California in-migrants during the past two decades have tended to settle in metropolitan areas.[5] Since many were young adults, they contributed significantly to natural increase.

---

[2]Commission on Population Growth and the American Future, *An Interim Report to the President and the Congress from the Commission on Population Growth and the American Future* (Washington, D.C.: U.S. Government Printing Office, March 16, 1971).

[3]Natural increase refers to the excess of births over deaths in a given population during a specified time period.

[4]Net migration refers to the excess of in-migrants over out-migrants (or vice versa) in a given population during a specified time period.

[5]A metropolitan area (Standard Metropolitan Statistical Area--SMSA) consists of a county or group of counties containing at least one city (or twin cities) with a population of 50,000 or more, plus adjacent counties which are metropolitan in character and are economically and socially integrated with the central city.

CALIFORNIA'S URBAN POPULATION: PATTERNS AND TRENDS

Between 1950 and 1960 California's metropolitan areas gained 32 persons through net migration for every 100 persons living in such areas at the beginning of the decade (Table 3). During the 1960's this declined to 19 persons per 100 original residents. In both decades the non-metropolitan areas gained about 10 per 100 population through net migration. Natural increase in metropolitan areas decreased from 19 per 100 residents in the 1950's to 13 per 100 residents in the 1960's. In the non-metropolitan areas the comparable decrease was from 16 to 13 per 100 population.

During the 1960's, natural increase rates for metropolitan and non-metropolitan areas have become nearly equal. Differential growth through migration resulted in more rapid growth in metropolitan than non-metropolitan areas. This meant increasing concentration of population in areas which already held the largest populations. The metropolitan areas were not gaining equally, however. Over half the state's 13 million population increase between 1940 and 1970 occurred in only three metropolitan counties--Los Angeles, Orange, and San Diego (see Table 4). Eight other metropolitan counties--Alameda, Contra Costa, Riverside, Sacramento, San Bernardino, San Mateo, Santa Clara, and Ventura-- added another 4 million persons over the last three decades. These 11 counties alone, then, accounted for about 82 percent of California's total population gain. During the 1960's these 11 counties gained over 3.5 million persons, accounting for 83 percent of the state's growth. These changes generally represent population redistribution towards coastal areas and towards Southern California (see Figure 2).

Patterns of Population Aggregation in California

Increasing population concentrations within California and the nation are linked with transformations in economic activity.[6] As California's and the nation's population have become increasingly concentrated within cities, and as intra-urban communication systems have expanded, manufacturing and some service activities have moved away from the center of cities.[7] Their decentralization as well as increasing dependence upon the automobile have facilitated population decentralization within large metropolitan areas. Urban areas composed of diverse neighborhoods

---

[6]Colin Clark, The Conditions of Economic Progress (3rd ed; London: Macmillan and Company, Ltd., 1957).

[7]Georges Sabagh, Maurice D. Van Arsdol, Jr., and Hamid Zahedi, "Urban Population Concentration and Occupational Structure in the United States: 1900-1950," 1960 Proceedings of the Social Statistics Section, American Statistical Association, pp. 166-171.

Table 2

POPULATION AND PERCENT CHANGE IN METROPOLITAN AREAS (SMSA'S), AND AREA OUTSIDE SMSA'S: CALIFORNIA AND UNITED STATES, 1940-1970

Area	Population				Percent Change		
	1940	1950	1960	1970	1940-50	1950-60	1960-70
California SMSA's[a]							
Anaheim-Santa Ana-Garden Grove	130,760	216,224	703,925	1,420,386	65.4	225.6	101.8
Bakersfield	135,124	228,309	291,984	329,162	69.0	27.9	12.7
Fresno	178,565	276,515	365,945	413,053	54.9	32.3	12.9
Los Angeles-Long Beach	2,785,643	4,151,687	6,038,771	7,032,075	49.0	45.5	16.4
Oxnard-Ventura	69,685	114,647	199,138	376,430	64.5	73.7	89.0
Sacramento	225,684	309,429	625,503	800,592	37.1	102.1	27.9
Salinas-Monterey	73,032	130,498	198,351	250,071	78.7	52.0	26.1
San Bernardino-Riverside-Ontario	266,632	457,688	809,782	1,143,146	69.4	79.3	41.1
San Diego	289,348	556,808	1,033,011	1,357,854	92.4	85.5	31.4
San Francisco-Oakland	1,412,686	2,126,939	2,648,762	3,109,519	50.6	24.5	17.4
San Jose	174,949	290,547	642,315	1,064,714	66.1	121.1	65.8
Santa Barbara	70,555	98,220	168,962	264,324	39.2	72.0	56.4

Stockton	134,207	200,750	249,989	290,208	49.6	24.5	16.1
Vallejo-Napa	77,621	151,436	200,487	249,081	95.1	32.4	24.2
Total California	6,907,387	10,586,223	15,717,204	19,953,134	53.3	48.5	26.9
Total SMSA's	--	9,303,692	14,176,925	18,100,615	--	52.4	27.6
Total Outside SMSA's	--	1,282,531	1,540,279	1,852,519	--	20.1	20.2
Total U.S. (Continental)	131,669,215	150,697,361	178,464,236	199,251,668	14.5	18.4	11.6
Total SMSA's	--	--	118,414,860	136,330,525	--	--	15.1
Total Outside SMSA's	--	--	60,049,376	62,921,143	--	--	4.8

[a] 1970 SMSA's of California consist of the following counties:

Anaheim-Santa Ana-Garden Grove SMSA: Orange County
Bakersfield SMSA: Kern County
Fresno SMSA: Fresno County
Los Angeles-Long Beach SMSA: Los Angeles County
Oxnard-Ventura SMSA: Ventura County
Sacramento SMSA: Placer, Sacramento, Yolo Counties
Salinas-Monterey SMSA: Monterey County
San Bernardino-Riverside-Ontario SMSA: Riverside, San Bernardino Counties
San Diego SMSA: San Diego County
San Francisco-Oakland SMSA: Alameda, Contra Costa, Marin, San Francisco, San Mateo Counties
San Jose SMSA: Santa Clara County
Santa Barbara SMSA: Santa Barbara County
Stockton SMSA: San Joaquin County
Vallejo-Napa SMSA: Napa, Solano Counties

Table 3

COMPONENTS OF POPULATION CHANGE, METROPOLITAN AREAS (SMSA'S) AND AREA OUTSIDE SMSA'S: CALIFORNIA, 1950-1960 AND 1960-1970

Area	1950-1960						1960-1970					
	Net Population Change	Natural Increase		Net Migration			Net Population Change	Natural Increase		Net Migration		
		Amount	Rate[a]	Amount	Rate[a]			Amount	Rate[a]	Amount	Rate[a]	
SMSA's												
Anaheim-Santa Ana-Garden Grove	487,701	76,347	35.3	411,354	190.2		716,461	166,600	23.7	549,861	78.1	
Bakersfield	63,675	54,732	24.0	8,943	3.9		37,178	42,181	14.4	-5,003	-1.7	
Fresno	89,430	58,852	21.3	30,578	11.1		47,108	48,678	13.3	-1,570	-0.4	
Los Angeles-Long Beach	1,887,084	715,760	17.2	1,171,324	28.2		993,304	730,666	12.1	262,638	4.3	
Oxnard-Ventura	84,491	29,341	25.6	55,150	48.1		177,292	45,855	23.0	131,437	66.0	
Sacramento	266,074	81,134	22.6	184,940	51.5		175,089	82,687	13.2	92,402	14.8	
Salinas-Monterey	67,853	33,544	25.7	34,309	26.3		51,720	32,279	16.3	19,441	9.8	
San Bernardino-Riverside-Ontario	358,094	105,650	23.4	252,444	55.9		333,364	113,873	14.1	219,491	27.1	

Area										
San Diego	476,203	150,356	27.0	325,847	58.5	324,843	149,100	14.4	175,743	17.0
San Francisco-Oakland	512,828	321,630	15.1	191,198	9.0	460,757	260,816	9.8	199,941	7.5
San Jose	351,768	80,686	27.8	271,082	93.3	422,399	139,225	21.7	283,174	44.1
Santa Barbara	70,742	16,142	16.4	54,600	55.6	95,362	30,629	18.1	64,733	38.3
Stockton	49,239	31,417	15.6	17,822	8.9	40,219	24,900	10.0	15,319	6.1
Vallejo-Napa	49,051	30,855	13.1	18,196	12.0	48,594	29,385	8.8	19,209	9.6
All SMSA's	4,814,233	1,786,446	19.3	3,027,787	32.3	3,923,690	1,896,874	13.3	2,026,816	14.3
Outside SMSA's	316,748	199,512	16.3	117,236	9.6	312,240	163,965	13.4	148,275	9.6
Total State	5,130,981	1,985,958	18.8	3,145,023	29.7	4,235,930	2,060,839	13.1	2,175,091	13.8

^aExpressed as percent of population size at beginning of period.

Sources: Data for 1950-60 from U.S. Bureau of the Census, "Components of Population Change 1950-60, for Counties, SMSA's, SEA's, and Economic Subregions," Current Population Reports, Series P-23, No. 7, November 1962. Data for 1960-70 from Walter P. Hollman, Chief, Population Research, Budget Division, Department of Finance of State of California. For 1960-70 estimates of natural increase, natural increase data available for 1960-69 were added to a natural increase estimate for 1970 to obtain an overall estimate for the decade.

STAFF: POPULATION RESEARCH LABORATORY, USC

Table 4

POPULATION SIZE OF COUNTIES BY METROPOLITAN STATUS:
CALIFORNIA, 1940, 1950, 1960, AND 1970

County by Metropolitan Status, 1970	Rank by Size, 1970	Population			
		1940	1950	1960	1970
(1)	(2)	(3)	(4)	(5)	(6)
Metropolitan					
Alameda	4	513,011	740,315	908,209	1,073,184
Contra Costa	9	100,450	298,984	409,030	558,389
Fresno	12	178,565	276,515	365,945	413,053
Kern	14	135,124	228,309	291,984	329,162
Los Angeles	1	2,785,643	4,151,687	6,038,771	7,032,075
Marin	18	52,907	85,619	146,820	206,038
Monterey	17	73,032	130,498	198,351	250,071
Napa	29	28,503	46,603	65,890	79,140
Orange	2	130,760	216,224	703,925	1,420,386
Placer	31	28,108	41,649	56,998	77,306
Riverside	11	105,524	170,046	306,191	459,074
Sacramento	8	170,333	277,140	502,778	631,498
San Bernardino	7	161,108	281,642	503,591	684,072
San Diego	3	289,348	556,808	1,033,011	1,357,854
San Francisco	6	634,536	775,357	740,316	715,674
San Joaquin	15	134,207	200,750	249,989	290,208
San Mateo	10	111,782	235,659	444,387	556,234
Santa Barbara	16	70,555	98,220	168,962	264,324
Santa Clara	5	174,949	290,547	642,315	1,064,714
Solano	22	49,118	104,833	134,597	169,941
Ventura	13	69,685	114,647	199,138	376,430
Yolo	28	27,243	40,640	65,727	91,788
Subtotal		6,024,491	9,362,692	14,176,925	18,100,615

CALIFORNIA'S URBAN POPULATION: PATTERNS AND TRENDS

Table 4 (continued)

(1)	(2)	(3)	(4)	(5)	(6)
Non-Metropolitan					
Alpine	58	323	241	397	484
Amador	51	8,973	9,151	9,990	11,821
Butte	26	42,840	64,930	82,030	101,969
Calaveras	49	8,221	9,902	10,289	13,585
Colusa	50	9,788	11,651	12,075	12,430
Del Norte	48	4,745	8,078	17,771	14,580
El Dorado	36	13,229	16,207	29,390	43,833
Glenn	45	12,195	15,448	17,245	17,521
Humboldt	27	45,812	69,241	104,892	99,692
Imperial	32	59,740	62,975	72,105	74,492
Inyo	46	7,625	11,658	11,684	15,571
Kings	33	35,168	46,768	49,954	64,610
Lake	43	8,069	11,481	13,786	19,548
Lassen	47	14,479	18,474	13,597	14,960
Madera	38	23,314	36,964	40,468	41,519
Mariposa	55	5,605	5,145	5,064	6,015
Mendocino	34	27,864	40,854	51,059	51,101
Merced	25	46,988	69,780	90,446	104,629
Modoc	54	8,713	9,678	8,308	7,469
Mono	56	2,299	2,115	2,213	4,016
Nevada	41	19,283	19,888	20,911	26,346
Plumas	52	11,548	13,519	11,620	11,707
San Benito	44	11,392	14,370	15,396	18,226
San Luis Obispo	24	33,246	51,417	81,044	105,690
Santa Cruz	23	45,057	66,534	84,219	123,790
Shasta	30	28,800	36,413	59,468	77,640
Sierra	57	3,025	2,410	2,247	2,365
Siskiyou	39	28,598	30,733	32,885	33,225
Sonoma	19	69,052	103,405	147,375	204,885
Stanislaus	20	74,866	127,231	157,294	194,506
Sutter	37	18,680	26,239	33,380	41,935
Tehama	40	14,316	19,276	25,305	29,517
Trinity	53	3,970	5,087	9,706	7,615
Tulare	21	107,152	149,264	168,403	188,322
Tuolumne	42	10,887	12,584	14,404	22,169
Yuba	35	17,034	24,420	33,859	44,736
Subtotal		882,896	1,223,531	1,540,279	1,852,519
State Total		6,907,387	10,586,223	15,717,204	19,953,134

FIGURE 2- POPULATION DISTRIBUTION BY COUNTY, CALIFORNIA: 1970

CALIFORNIA'S URBAN POPULATION: PATTERNS AND TRENDS

linked by communication networks have coalesced into "metropolitan communities" (see Figure 2). Older California cities within metropolitan communities form the nuclei of expanding urban settlements. They contain the units which regulate the economic export activity necessary for maintaining the entire metropolitan community, and they are centers for governmental activity and for specialized service, shopping, and recreation for the entire areas.

Populations of the state's 14 metropolitan areas are growing at different rates and in different ways (Tables 2 and 3). The growth rate for all California metropolitan areas was 28 percent during the 1960's, as compared with 12 percent for all metropolitan areas in the United States. Metropolitan areas with highest growth rates during the 1960's were Anaheim-Santa Ana-Garden Grove (102 percent), Oxnard-Ventura (89 percent) and San Jose (65 percent). These three metropolises had the highest rates for both natural increase and net migration. The Bakersfield and Fresno metropolitan areas grew at approximately the national rate (13 percent), although both areas experienced net migration losses. Santa Barbara was the only metropolitan area with a higher rate of natural increase in the 1960's than the 1950's, and only Oxnard-Ventura had higher net migration rates in the 1960's than in the 1950's.

The two oldest and largest metropolitan areas, Los Angeles-Long Beach and San Francisco-Oakland, have attracted fewer migrants each decade (Tables 2 and 3). The Los Angeles-Long Beach metropolitan area added 1.2 million persons through net migration in the 1950's, but only 263 thousand in the 1960's. The County of San Francisco lost population in the 1960's. Migrants are drawn instead to newer and smaller metropolitan areas located adjacent to Los Angeles and San Francisco. In Southern California during the 1960's large numbers of migrants were absorbed into the Anaheim-Santa Ana-Garden Grove, Oxnard-Ventura, San Bernardino-Riverside-Ontario, San Diego, and Santa Barbara metropolitan areas, as well as into the suburban portions of Los Angeles County (Table 3). In Northern California, major migrant destinations were the San Jose metropolitan area and Alameda and Contra Costa Counties within the San Francisco-Oakland metropolitan area.

The Emergence of California Megalopolitan Areas

California's population, then, is concentrating in the areas around Los Angeles and San Francisco. New metropolitan areas are developing around each of these older metropolitan areas. These newer areas are growing by natural increase and, especially, by their unusually high attraction for migrants. Los Angeles and San Francisco-Oakland are emerging as centers of vast megalopolitan areas. Presumably they serve as economic, social, and political coordinating centers for these megalopolises.

STAFF: POPULATION RESEARCH LABORATORY, USC

The megalopolis around Los Angeles includes the metropolitan areas of Anaheim-Santa Ana-Garden Grove, Los Angeles-Long Beach, Oxnard-Ventura, San Bernardino-Riverside-Ontario, San Diego, and Santa Barbara. In 1970 these six metropolitan areas together contained 11.6 million people. The megalopolis around San Francisco includes the metropolitan areas of Sacramento, San Francisco-Oakland, San Jose, Stockton, and Vallejo-Napa, with a combined population of 5.5 million in 1970. Together the Los Angeles and San Francisco megalopolises contained over 94 percent of the state's total metropolitan population and over 80 percent of the state's total population in 1970.

Growth patterns within metropolitan areas paralleled megalopolitan patterns in the 1960's. This is apparent when growth of their central cities is compared with growth in the "urban fringes" or rings around these cities and with growth in the rest of the counties defining the metropolitan areas (see Table 5). Taken as a whole, the state's urban areas, its urbanized areas, its central cities,[8] and its urban fringes each grew more rapidly than the rural parts of the state in the 1960's. Some of the growth in urban areas is attributable to rural-to-urban classification changes between 1960 and 1970. Also a portion of central city population growth accrued from the designation of new central cities. Between 1960 and 1970, for example, the population in central cities of metropolitan areas increased from 5.5 to 7.1 million.[9] More than 38 percent of the increase, however, is attributable to the populations of nine cities which became central cities for the first time in 1970.

Among the different "kinds" of urban population, the urban fringes grew the most rapidly in the 1960's, followed by the population in "isolated" urban places and then by the population

---

[8] The U.S. Bureau of the Census defines a central city as the major city or cities located in a metropolitan area, while a ring refers to the area's residual. For example, central cities in the Los Angeles-Long Beach Standard Metropolitan Statistical Area (SMSA) are Los Angeles and Long Beach (as indicated by the SMSA title). The metropolitan area boundaries are here coterminous with Los Angeles County. The population ring is determined by subtracting the central city populations from that of the total county. Some metropolitan areas include more than one county. Metropolitan area boundaries always follow county lines: the Sacramento metropolitan area, for instance, includes Placer, Sacramento, and Yolo Counties.

[9] The expansion of corporate central cities from 1950 to 1970 was not taken into account in our analysis; central city boundaries were not standardized to 1970 definitions.

CALIFORNIA'S URBAN POPULATION: PATTERNS AND TRENDS

within central cities (Tables 6 and 7). The "newer" central cities grew more rapidly than those which were central cities in 1960, and the fringe areas of these new central cities grew more rapidly than any other part of the urban population.

Only a small part of California's urban population lives in isolated cities. Of the state's total urban population, 89 percent resided in urbanized areas by 1970. While the fringes of these urbanized areas are growing more rapidly than their centers, the percent of the population residing within the central cities has been decreasing. In 1970, almost 56 percent of the populations of urbanized areas lived in the urban fringe.

Stages of California Metropolitan Growth

Cities expand into metropolitan areas, and the stages in this growth process are reflected by the shifting location of highest growth rates outward from central cities with little regard for political boundaries. Highest growth rates occur initially in central cities of emerging metropolitan areas. This growth pattern is currently observable in some of the moderately urban counties such as El Dorado, Kings, Napa, San Luis Obispo, Santa Cruz, and Sonoma. Here growth is occurring within the city limits of South Lake Tahoe; Hanford and Lemoore; Napa and Yountville; Arroyo Grande and Pismo Beach; Capitola, Petaluma, Santa Rosa, and Sebastopol. There are rapid percentage increments in the city populations with little in the "urban fringe" areas. Eventually population expansion exceeds the city's corporate boundaries. Although the city population continues to grow, more rapid growth occurs outside its boundaries.

Population increases from 1950 to 1970 in the Anaheim-Santa Ana-Garden Grove metropolitan area (Orange County) illustrate metropolitan growth stages. After 1950 agricultural land was rapidly converted to residential and other urban uses. The population residing in the three central cities--Anaheim, Santa Ana, and Garden Grove--increased from 29.5 percent of the county's population in 1950 to 41 percent in 1960, then decreased to 31 percent in 1970. County population grew rapidly in the 1960's, but newly developed areas outside the three central cities absorbed much of this growth.

We have traced metropolitan growth stages for Los Angeles in more detail. We found that as the metropolis grew it expanded both upward and outward. Its growth appeared to follow a cycle described by the economists Edgar M. Hoover and Raymond Vernon: subdivision and building up, transition to more intensive land use, downgrading, thinning out of housing units, and

Table 5

PERCENTAGE DISTRIBUTION OF CALIFORNIA METROPOLITAN AREAS (SMSA'S) BY CENTRAL CITIES AND RINGS: 1950-1970

SMSA	1950		1960		1970	
	Population	Percent of Total	Population	Percent of Total	Population	Percent of Total
Anaheim-Santa Ana-Garden Grove SMSA	216,224	100.0%	703,925	100.0%	1,420,386	100.0%
Central Cities	63,851	29.5	288,772	41.0	445,826	31.4
Ring	152,373	70.5	415,153	59.0	974,560	68.6
Bakersfield SMSA	228,307	100.0	291,984	100.0	329,162	100.0
Central City	34,784	15.2	56,848	19.5	69,515	21.1
Ring	193,523	84.8	235,136	80.5	259,647	78.9
Fresno SMSA	276,515	100.0	365,945	100.0	413,053	100.0
Central City	91,669	33.2	133,929	36.6	165,972	40.2
Ring	184,846	66.8	232,016	63.4	247,081	59.8
Los Angeles-Long Beach SMSA	4,151,687	100.0	6,038,771	100.0	7,032,075	100.0
Central Cities	2,221,125	53.5	2,823,183	46.8	3,174,694	45.2
Ring	1,930,562	46.5	3,215,588	53.2	3,857,381	54.8
Oxnard-Ventura SMSA	114,647	100.0	199,138	100.0	376,430	100.0
Central Cities	38,101	33.2	69,379	34.8	127,022	33.7
Ring	76,546	66.8	129,759	65.2	249,408	66.3
Sacramento SMSA	309,429	100.0	625,503	100.0	800,592	100.0
Central City	137,572	44.5	191,667	30.6	254,413	31.8
Ring	171,857	55.5	433,836	69.4	546,179	68.2

Salinas-Monterey SMSA	130,498	100.0	198,351	100.0	250,071	100.0
Central Cities	30,122	23.1	51,575	26.0	85,198	34.1
Ring	100,376	76.9	146,776	74.0	164,873	65.9
San Bernardino-Riverside-Ontario SMSA	457,688	100.0	809,782	100.0	1,143,146	100.0
Central Cities	132,694	29.0	222,871	27.5	308,458	27.0
Ring	324,994	71.0	586,911	72.5	834,688	73.0
San Diego SMSA	556,808	100.0	1,033,011	100.0	1,357,854	100.0
Central City	334,387	60.1	573,224	55.5	696,769	51.3
Ring	222,421	39.9	459,787	44.5	661,085	48.7
San Francisco-Oakland SMSA	2,126,934	100.0	2,648,762	100.0	3,109,519	100.0
Central Cities	1,159,932	54.5	1,107,864	41.8	1,077,235	34.6
Ring	967,002	45.5	1,540,898	58.2	2,032,284	65.4
San Jose SMSA	290,547	100.0	642,315	100.0	1,064,714	100.0
Central City	95,280	32.8	204,196	31.8	445,779	41.9
Ring	195,267	67.2	438,119	68.2	618,935	58.1
Santa Barbara SMSA	98,220	100.0	168,962	100.0	264,324	100.0
Central City	44,854	45.7	58,768	34.8	70,215	26.6
Ring	53,366	54.3	110,194	65.2	194,109	73.4
Stockton SMSA	200,750	100.0	249,989	100.0	290,208	100.0
Central City	70,853	35.3	86,321	34.5	107,644	37.1
Ring	129,897	64.7	163,668	65.5	182,564	62.9
Vallejo-Napa SMSA	151,436	100.0	200,487	100.0	249,081	100.0
Central Cities	39,617	26.2	83,047	41.4	102,711	41.2
Ring	111,819	73.8	117,440	58.6	146,370	58.8

Table 6

URBAN AND RURAL POPULATION AND PERCENTAGE DISTRIBUTION: CALIFORNIA, 1950-1970

Areas	1950		1960		1970	
	Population	Percent of Total	Population	Percent of Total	Population	Percent of Total
Total State	10,586,223	100.0%	15,717,204	100.0%	19,953,134	100.0%
Urban[a]	8,539,420	80.7	13,573,155	86.4	18,136,045	90.9
Rural	2,046,803	19.3	2,144,049	13.6	1,817,089	9.1
Urban	--	100.0	--	100.0	--	100.0
Urbanized Areas	7,219,444	84.5	11,943,983	88.0	16,147,770	89.0
Central Cities	3,923,109	54.3	5,526,028	46.3	7,131,451	44.2
Urban Fringe	3,296,335	45.7	6,417,955	53.7	9,016,319	55.8
Other Urban	1,319,976	15.5	1,629,172	12.0	1,988,275	11.0
Rural	--	100.0	--	100.0	--	100.0
Places of 1,000-2,500	249,664	12.2	241,237	11.3	201,857	11.1
Other Rural	1,797,139	87.8	1,902,812	88.7	1,615,232	88.9

[a]Current urban definition of U.S. Bureau of Census used in all cases. (See footnote 8.)

Table 7

URBAN AND RURAL POPULATION CHANGE AND PERCENT CHANGE: CALIFORNIA, 1950-1970

Areas	1950-1960			1960-1970		
	Population Change	Percent Change	Index of Relative growth[a]	Population Change	Percent Change	Index of Relative Growth[a]
Total State	5,130,981	48.5	--	4,235,930	27.0	--
Urban	5,033,735	58.9	21	4,562,890	33.6	24
Rural	97,246	4.8	-90	-326,960	-15.3	-157
Urban	--	--	--	--	--	--
Urbanized Areas	4,724,539	65.4	35	4,203,787	35.2	30
Central Cities	1,602,919	40.9	-16	1,605,423	29.1	8
Urban Fringe	3,121,620	94.7	95	2,598,364	40.5	50
Other Urban	309,196	23.4	-52	359,103	22.0	-19
Rural	--	--	--	--	--	--
Places of 1,000-2,500	-8,427	-3.4	-107	-39,380	-16.3	-160
Other Rural	105,673	5.9	-88	-287,580	-15.1	-156

[a] Difference of category growth rate and growth rate of state expressed as percent of growth rate of state in period. Minus sign (-) indicates growth rate less than that of state.

finally urban renewal.[10] For any given area the rate of population growth is highest in the first stage and decelerates through the succeeding stages. Metropolitan neighborhoods with intensive land use have a more limited growth potential than outlying areas with large tracts of undeveloped land. Furthermore, we found that current patterns of intra-metropolitan population changes can be understood only in terms of past development, because current metropolitan form reflects past changes.[11] When there is a housing shortage, as was the case during World War II and in the last years of the 1960's, growth tends to be vertical or to include more intensive use of existing housing. When new residences and adequate consumer financial resources are available, growth tends to be horizontal, and suburbanization becomes virtually synonymous with metropolitan growth.

The aforementioned relations, which were substantiated for Los Angeles, were investigated for 160 metropolitan areas in the United States. It was found that in the 1940's, rapid metropolitan growth and a densely populated central city were conducive to rapid suburbanization, but that a large metropolitan population size inhibited suburbanization.[12] This suggests that "growth tends to take the form of outward expansion until the spread of the city begins to present a barrier to internal transport and communication, at which juncture growth takes the form of upward expansion near the metropolitan core."[13] Suburbanization population movements, then, are not without limit. Given existing social, economic, and political restrictions on metropolitan transport technologies, forces leading to more dense settlement begin to operate as residential development reaches the effective limits of a metropolis. These limits, however, may be so extensive that metropolitan areas run into each other. This leads to an intertwining of functions and to the development of megalopolitan areas.

The megalopolises of Southern and Northern California contain past cityscape features as well as new urban functions. They contain centrally located industrial, commercial, governmental, and transportation centers, slums and aging suburbs,

---

[10] *Anatomy of a Metropolis* (Cambridge, Mass.: Harvard University Press, 1950), chapter viii.

[11] Beverly Duncan, Georges Sabagh, and Maurice D. Van Arsdol, Jr., "Patterns of City Growth," *American Journal of Sociology*, Vol. LXVII, No. 4 (January 1962), p. 418.

[12] *Ibid.*, p. 428.

[13] *Ibid.*

obsolete housing stock, and other relics of unplanned growth. Continued population aggregation means that urban settlements grow upward through high-rise construction--at both the core and outer reaches.

Megalopolitan sprawl appears to encompass many former non-urban functions, including retirement, resort, and other specialized residential communities, peripheral locations for agricultural and other extractive activity, as well as for industry and commerce, and forests, wildlife preserves, and recreation areas. As residential and non-residential uses compete for space, newly constructed residential communities are more dense than those built earlier. Changes in the economics, organization, and technology of land development have decreased the time it takes to create urban complexes from raw land. Unrelieved demands for public use intensify the environmental, social, political, and economic problems of urban populations in California.

Metropolitan Employment Trends in California

Metropolitan Employment. California urbanization is closely related to employment trends.[14] Shifts from primary extractive activity to factory-centered manufacturing accompany increasing urbanization, and the subsequent emergence of service and consumption-orientated industries accompanies metropolitan expansion.[15] California employment during the past decade continued previous shifts away from primary activities (agriculture, mining, forestry, and fisheries) and into service industries (government, finance, insurance, real estate, and other services). Moreover, the percent of the labor force employed in manufacturing declined slightly (see Table 8).

Employment outside metropolitan areas emphasizes the urban nature of all California economic activity; the non-metropolitan labor force distribution among industries is similar to that for the metropolitan labor force. Employment patterns of the various metropolitan areas are becoming more alike (see Table 9). Eight metropolises had an employment "profile" more like that for the labor force of all fourteen combined in 1970 than they had had in 1960.[16] Service and government employment

---

[14]Clark, The Conditions of Economic Progress.

[15]Sabagh, Van Arsdol, and Zahedi, "Urban Population Concentration. . ."

[16]The Oxnard-Ventura and Vallejo-Napa metropolitan areas underwent the greatest changes toward the norm: each declined in the

STAFF: POPULATION RESEARCH LABORATORY, USC

Table 8

PERCENTAGE DISTRIBUTION OF THE CALIFORNIA LABOR FORCE
BY INDUSTRY, 1960 AND 1969, AND PERCENT CHANGE
IN EACH INDUSTRY, 1960-1969

Industry	Percent of Employed 1960	1969	Change in Percent, 1960-1969
Agriculture, Forestry, Mining, Fisheries	6.1	3.9	-2.2
Construction	5.7	4.4	-1.3
Manufacturing	21.6	20.4	-1.2
Transportation, Communications, Public Utilities	5.9	5.7	-0.2
Retail, Wholesale Trade	19.9	20.2	0.3
Finance, Insurance, Real Estate	4.5	4.9	0.4
Services	16.5	19.4	2.9
Government	13.9	16.6	2.7
Total Employed	94.2	95.5	1.3
Unemployed	5.8	4.5	-1.3
Total Work Force	100.0	100.0	--
Total Number (000's)	6,299	8,367	2,068

Source: Department of Industrial Relations, "Estimated Civilian Employment, Unemployment, and Labor Force: California 1940-1969" (January 1970).

grew faster than other sectors of the labor force between 1960 and 1970, and therefore accounted for a larger share of the total employment in each metropolitan area (see Table 10). The percentage employed in primary industries declined in each area. Despite these similarities, California metropolises are at various "stages" of the shift to service employment. Some are still moving from primary industries into manufacturing, although

proportion of employment in agriculture and increased in the proportion in manufacturing. Sacramento, on the other hand, became more distinctive because of a 6 percent increase in the proportion employed by government, as did Anaheim-Santa-Ana-Garden Grove through an increase in manufacturing. Bakersfield continued to have unusually high agricultural employment and relatively little manufacturing. Vallejo-Napa had relatively little manufacturing and relatively high government employment.

CALIFORNIA'S URBAN POPULATION: PATTERNS AND TRENDS

Table 9

INDEX OF DISSIMILARITY COMPARING EACH METROPOLITAN AREA (SMSA) DISTRIBUTION WITH THAT OF ALL CALIFORNIA SMSA'S, 1960 AND 1969, AND CHANGE IN THIS INDEX, 1960-1969

SMSA[a]	Index of Dissimilarity[b]		Change in Index, 1960-1969
	1960	1969	
Los Angeles-Long Beach	8.0	7.3	-0.7
San Francisco-Oakland	8.6	8.8	0.2
San Diego	5.4	7.5	2.1
San Bernardino-Riverside-Ontario	12.6	9.0	-3.6
Sacramento	16.6	19.5	2.9
San Jose	9.5	10.8	1.3
Anaheim-Santa Ana-Garden Grove	6.3	9.3	3.0
Fresno	22.8	19.3	-3.5
Bakersfield	24.7	23.8	-0.9
Stockton	19.9	16.2	-3.7
Oxnard-Ventura	25.0	16.4	-8.6
Vallejo-Napa	28.9	23.1	-5.8
Salinas-Monterey	19.9	17.4	-2.5
Santa Barbara	14.5	14.7	0.2

[a] Ordered by size of labor force in 1960.

[b] Index of Dissimilarity summarizes disparities in two percentage distributions. The formula is: $I.D. = \dfrac{\Sigma(p_i - q_i)}{2}$, where p_i is the percent employed in industry within an SMSA and q_i is the percent employed in industry for all state SMSA's combined.

service and government employment also are becoming more important.[17] The three largest metropolitan areas, however, have a smaller proportion of their labor force in manufacturing now than they had in 1960.[18]

---

[17] These metropolitan areas are: Anaheim-Santa Ana, Monterey, Oxnard, and San Bernardino-Riverside. Fresno, Bakersfield, San Jose and Stockton have virtually a constant proportion of their labor forces in manufacturing; services and government are expanding.

[18] Sacramento and Santa Barbara also show declines in manufacturing and increases in services and government; they are, however, still undergoing shifts out of the primary industries. The

STAFF: POPULATION RESEARCH LABORATORY, USC

Table 10

INDEX OF DISSIMILARITY COMPARING EACH CALIFORNIA METROPOLITAN AREA (SMSA) DISTRIBUTION IN 1960 WITH THAT IN 1969, AND CHANGE IN PERCENT EMPLOYED IN SELECTED INDUSTRIES, 1960-1969

SMSA[a]	Index of Dissimilarity[b] 1960 vs. 1969	1960-1969 Change in Percent Employed in:		
		Manufacturing	Services	Government
Los Angeles-Long Beach	4.9	-1.9	2.6	1.8
San Francisco-Oakland	6.0	-2.9	2.5	2.9
San Diego	10.4	-3.1	3.5	4.4
San Bernardino-Riverside-Ontario	8.2	1.4	4.4	1.1
Sacramento	10.4	-5.4	3.6	6.0
San Jose	7.4	0.9	3.5	2.0
Anaheim-Santa Ana-Garden Grove	9.3	4.6	1.4	1.7
Fresno	8.2	0.4	3.2	4.0
Bakersfield	4.0	-0.3	2.2	1.3
Stockton	9.3	1.0	2.9	4.6
Oxnard-Ventura	13.7	3.2	3.9	3.7
Vallejo-Napa	6.1	0.5	2.9	-0.4
Salinas-Monterey	8.5	1.9	2.1	3.5
Santa Barbara	10.0	-2.2	3.1	6.8
California	6.2	1.2	-2.8	-2.7
SMSA's	5.8	1.5	-2.8	-1.6
Non-SMSA's	8.5	0.5	-2.4	-5.5

[a] Ordered by size of labor force in 1960.

[b] See Table 9 for Index formula. Here p_i refers to the SMSA in 1960 and q_i to the same SMSA in 1969.

CALIFORNIA'S URBAN POPULATION: PATTERNS AND TRENDS

Changes in Employment Distribution within Metropolitan Areas. Manufacturing, wholesaling, retailing, and service decentralization in the past three decades[19] has changed internal commuting patterns and intra-metropolitan transportation demands. The extent of manufacturing, wholesaling, and service decentralization in California metropolises was examined by comparing the percent of employment within central cities in 1967 with that in 1958.[20] Each industry type showed a tendency to decentralize, but there is a wide range in the amount of decentralization and a few cases of centralization. San Francisco-Oakland and San Diego have the most centralized manufacturing. Sacramento and Oxnard-Ventura each added more manufacturing employment within the city limits than outside the central city; all other SMSA's decentralized. Almost 100 percent of wholesale employment in the San Francisco-Oakland metropolitan area was within the central cities' limits in 1958. San Francisco-Oakland and San Jose metropolitan areas underwent the greatest decentralization. There is some tendency for the smallest metropolises to have the greatest decentralization of service establishments.

Intra-Metropolitan Employment in Los Angeles. It is possible to trace employment decentralization in some detail for Los Angeles County during the past five years.[21] The "labor market" containing Los Angeles' central business district has a slightly higher percent of the county's manufacturing than any other labor market area. Finance employment shifted to the north

---

three largest metropolitan areas had a pattern similar to that for the total, as did an assortment of other SMSA's: San Jose, Fresno, and Stockton. All industries, including agriculture, grew in Santa Barbara. Sacramento had fewer employed in manufacturing in 1970 than in 1960. By contrast, four SMSA's had their fastest growth in manufacturing: Anaheim-Santa Ana, Oxnard, Monterey, and San Bernardino-Riverside.

[19] John Kain, "The Distribution and Movement of Jobs and Industry" in James Q. Wilson, ed., The Metropolitan Enigma (Cambridge, Mass.: Harvard University Press, 1968).

[20] The U.S. Census of Business publishes such information for current city boundaries only; annexations, then, may reduce apparent decentralization. Los Angeles is considered separately, using California Labor Market Areas data.

[21] The material in this section is based on published employment information concerning twenty-two labor market areas within Los Angeles County. There have been various boundary changes, but adjacent labor market areas are enough alike that these data reflect broad trends in industry location between 1965 and 1970.

and west of the city's center between 1965 and 1970. Manufacturing became more evenly spread through the county, although with the exception of the central area, it tends to be high where finance employment is low--that is, to the south, southwest, and east of the city's center. In addition to decentralization, then, there is a tendency for different types of employment to shift in opposite directions.

Intra-Metropolitan Residential Mobility in California

The significant contribution of in-migration to California's population growth from the end of World War II until 1960 is well-known. Once within the state, metropolitan Californians continue their restlessness. Los Angeles has often been cited as exemplifying a highly mobile metropolitan population. The 1960 Census showed that within the Los Angeles-Long Beach metropolitan area (then including both Los Angeles and Orange Counties) the five year intra-metropolitan residential mobility rate for the population aged five years and over was 38.2 percent, as contrasted with 30.0 percent for all U.S. metropolitan areas with more than one million inhabitants.[22] Similar rates of residence change also occurred in other Western and California metropolitan areas.[23]

Information available for Los Angeles County suggests that residential mobility rates within California metropolises have decreased during the past decade. These data show type of residence of the population one-year-old and over by mobility status for all United States metropolitan areas and for the Los Angeles-Long Beach metropolitan area (the County of Los Angeles) for 1963-64 and 1969-70 (see Table 11). Rates of residence change decreased during this time in Los Angeles-Long Beach. These declines included interstate and intrastate migration, as well as intra-metropolitan mobility. In 1963-64, in-migration rates to Los Angeles-Long Beach from outside the state were greater than the rate for all U.S. metropolitan areas combined; by 1969-70 they had decreased to a level below the rate for all U.S. metropolitan areas combined. During these years, Los Angeles-

---

[22] U.S. Bureau of the Census, U.S. Census of Population: 1960, Selected Area Reports, Standard Metropolitan Statistical Areas, Final Report PC(3) 1D, Table 4; and U.S. Census of Population: 1960, Vol. 1, Characteristics of the Population, Part 6, California; Part 39, Oregon; Part 49, Washington; Table 72.

[23] Maurice D. Van Arsdol, Jr., Georges Sabagh, and Edgar W. Butler, "Retrospective and Subsequent Metropolitan Residential Mobility," Demography, Vol. 5, No. 1 (1968), p. 252.

Table 11

PERCENT DISTRIBUTION OF THE POPULATION ONE-YEAR-OLD AND OVER BY MOBILITY STATUS: ALL U.S. STANDARD METROPOLITAN AREAS (SMSA'S) AND LOS ANGELES-LONG BEACH SMSA, 1963-1964 AND 1968-1969

Area	Total	Same House (Non-Movers)	Different House in the United States (Movers)					
			Total	Same County	Different Country (Migrants)			
					Total	Within a State	Between States	Abroad One Year Earlier
U.S. Metropolitan, 1964	100.0	79.2	20.3	13.9	6.4	3.0	3.4	0.5
In Central Cities	100.0	77.8	21.7	16.2	5.5	2.3	3.1	0.5
Outside Central Cities	100.0	80.5	19.0	11.6	7.4	3.7	3.7	0.6
U.S. Metropolitan, 1969	100.0	80.7	18.4	12.2	6.2	2.7	3.5	0.9
In Central Cities	100.0	79.8	19.3	14.1	5.2	2.3	2.9	0.9
Outside Central Cities	100.0	81.4	17.7	10.7	7.0	3.1	3.9	0.9
Los Angeles-Long Beach SMSA, 1964	100.0	70.3	28.8	20.9	7.9	3.6	4.5	1.0
In Central Cities	100.0	68.3	30.9	21.3	9.7	4.0	5.1	0.7
Outside Central Cities	100.0	71.4	27.5	20.7	8.8	3.4	3.5	1.1
Los Angeles-Long Beach SMSA, 1969	100.0	77.3	21.5	16.0	5.4	2.6	2.8	1.3
In Central Cities	100.0	78.7	19.8	16.0	3.8	1.4	2.4	1.5
Outside Central Cities	100.0	76.5	22.4	16.1	6.3	3.3	3.0	1.1

Sources: U.S. Bureau of the Census, "Mobility of the Population of the United States: March 1963 to March 1964," Current Population Reports, Population Characteristics, Series P-20, No. 141 (September 11, 1965), Table 3; and U.S. Bureau of the Census, "Mobility of the Population of the United States, March 1969 to March 1970," Current Population Reports, Population Characteristics, Series P-20, No. 210 (January 15, 1971), Table 12.

Long Beach in-migration rates from within the state also changed from greater to less than that for all U.S. metropolitan areas combined. Furthermore, in-migration rates increased for all U.S. metropolitan areas combined from 1963-64 to 1969-70, but decreased for Los Angeles-Long Beach. In-migration rates from abroad increased in both Los Angeles-Long Beach and in all U.S. metropolitan areas.

In contrast to the aforementioned changes, intra-metropolitan residential mobility remainded greater for Los Angeles-Long Beach than for all U.S. metropolitan areas combined. Nevertheless, intra-metropolitan residential mobility rates in Los Angeles-Long Beach declined from 20.9 percent in 1963-64 to 16.0 percent in 1969-70, as compared with a decline from 13.9 percent to 12.2 percent for all U.S. metropolitan areas combined. Survey data compiled by the Population Research Laboratory for Los Angeles and Orange Counties show that in 1961-62, 35.0 percent of the heads of households who had moved into these counties during the previous year moved again within these counties, as compared with 14.4 percent for non-movers during the previous year.[24] Declines in employment opportunities in the Los Angeles-Long Beach metropolitan area probably produced declines in in-migration rates and then declines in intra-metropolitan residential mobility. However, the spaciousness of the Los Angeles-Long Beach metropolitan area would suggest that job shifts are often associated with residence change.

In sum, migration rates in the United States and migration to California have declined during the past decade. The 1970 Census could show that migration rates to California metropolitan areas are as low as for all U.S. metropolitan areas combined. If this is the case, intra-metropolitan residential mobility probably will be less pronounced in California during the 1970's than it was during the 1950's and 1960's. Nevertheless, the state now has high rates of population growth and in-migration. This will mean a slow dampening of the unusually high residential mobility rates within California metropolises. In this respect, changes in family life cycles, occupations, and metropolitan environments are expected to be closely associated with future residence changes.[25]

Intra-Metropolitan Ethnic Shifts in California

Despite high residential mobility rates, California metropolitan areas continue to have residential segregation. Other

---

[24] Van Arsdol, Sabagh, and Butler, "Retrospective. . ."

[25] Sabagh, Van Arsdol, and Butler, "Some Determinants of Intra-metropolitan Residential Mobility: Conceptual Considerations," Social Forces, Vol. 48, No. 1 (September 1969), pp. 88-97.

CALIFORNIA'S URBAN POPULATION: PATTERNS AND TRENDS

California population trends assume added importance when linked with residential segregation. First, the fertility, mortality, and age structures of Black and Mexican-American populations mean that these populations will more than share in future growth. Current nonwhite and Mexican-American excesses of births over deaths are from 50 to 100 percent higher than those for Anglos.[26] This differential has increased the proportion of each ethnic group which resides in California, and has increased their proportions of the state's population. Second, the historical out-migration from the South is linked to movement of Negroes to California urban areas. During the 1940's and 1950's Negroes and Mexican-Americans accounted for increasing proportions of the total migrants to California. Negro migration probably has peaked, but the rates of natural increase still indicate a growing urban Negro population.

The racial pattern of population change within California metropolitan areas must be inferred from limited data. Figure 3 shows percent Negro and other nonwhite populations for selected California metropolitan central cities and rings for 1950, 1960, and 1970. (The central city boundaries are political boundaries at each census date and are not standardized.) Recent population increments in suburbs represent largely in-migration of whites from non-metropolitan and other metropolitan areas and the coming of age of post-World War II baby boom cohorts. With the exception of San Francisco-Oakland, metropolitan white populations are numerically increasing in both central cities and rings. Negroes and other nonwhites are accounting for increasing proportions of central city populations. These changes are attenuated in Los Angeles-Long Beach and San Francisco-Oakland. On the other hand, the percentages of Negroes and other nonwhites in metropolitan rings is increasing slowly.

Numerical and percentage increments of nonwhites in rings do not necessarily mean that residential segregation is dissipating; central city-ring distinctions do not permit an accurate assessment of such changes. In Los Angeles County, for example, neighborhoods in the later phases of the housing cycle experienced percentage increments of Negroes from 1940 to 1960, while areas of newer Negro settlement were developing "ghetto" characteristics by 1960.[27] Historical patterns of Negro residential segregation

---

[26] Michael Roof, "Ethnic Composition of the Population of Los Angeles County, April 1970: An Estimate Based Upon School Enrollment Data," Poverty Population Series, No. 1 (Los Angeles: Economic and Youth Opportunities Agency, December 1970).

[27] This section is abstracted from Maurice D. Van Arsdol, Jr., and Leo A. Schuerman, "Redistribution and Assimilation of Ethnic Populations: The Los Angeles Case," Demography (in press).

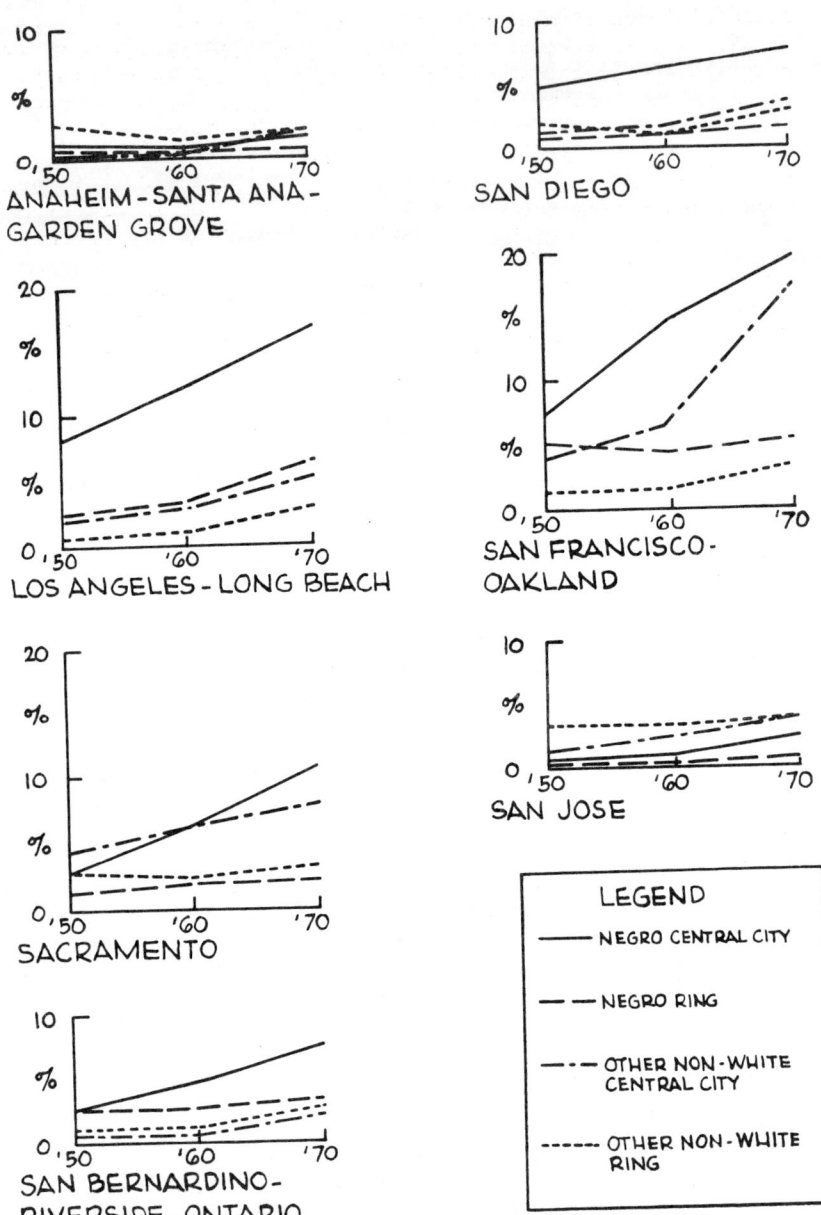

FIGURE 3 - PER CENT NEGRO AND OTHER NON-WHITE POPULATION - SELECTED CALIFORNIA SMSA CENTRAL CITIES AND RINGS: 1950-1970.

appear to have solidified in the past decade. White policies of residential containment and continued Negro population increments suggest that additional sections of aging suburbs, as well as the "gray areas" of cities, will become ghettos during the 1970's. Anglos are not really abandoning the central city; they are instead continuing to move into new neighborhoods, i.e., those at the beginning stages of the neighborhood housing cycle, wherever they may be located. Furthermore, the Anglo movement to newer areas is associated with employment decentralization, so that the ethnic populations left in the central city have more difficulty locating work and have longer commuting times.

We expect that 1970 Census reports will emphasize that suburbanization now applies to ethnic as well as to Anglo populations. However, our data for Los Angeles County from 1940 to 1960 suggest that such suburbanization in California is more illusory than real. The spreading out of ethnic populations over expanding older neighborhoods of Los Angeles County from 1940 to 1960 was a precursor of reported population declines in central city poverty areas in the 1960's and "rapid growth in the adjacent inner suburbs."[28] The recent redistribution of Negroes from one enclave to another is forecast from Los Angeles data reflecting ethnic population redistribution from 1940 to 1960. In addition, the bunching up of Negroes within enclaves in newer neighborhoods in Los Angeles is more pronounced than in the older areas of traditional Negro occupancy. Ethnic residential segregation pervades the entire metropolis and is growing in the wake of metropolitan expansion. As a result, the growth processes involved in California metropolitan-megalopolitan sprawl probably will continue to forge successive "iron rings" of residential segregation.[29]

Environmental Encroachment of Population and Technology in California

Reduction of Open Space.[30] An expanding metropolitan population necessarily means less open space. Eighty-four percent

---

[28]David L. Birth, "The Economic Future of City and Suburb," CED Supplementary Paper No. 30 (New York: Committee for Economic Development, 1970).

[29]Wallace Mendelsohn, Discrimination (Englewood Cliffs, N.J.: Prentice-Hall, 1962).

[30]This section is based on "Land Use" in California's Coastal Zone, by Bendix Bradbury Associates and Copley International, a report to the California Advisory Commission on Marine and Coastal Resources, 1968.

STAFF: POPULATION RESEARCH LABORATORY, USC

of all Californians live along a thin coastal strip[31] which we have subdivided into four main areas: the North Coast, extending from the Oregon border to Marin County; the Bay Delta, encompassing the San Francisco area; the Central Coast; and the South Coast, including the heavily populated Southern California coastal basin (Figure 1). The population growth throughout this strip has meant the steady disappearance of agricultural, recreational, and vacant land.

Three categories of land use in the coastal strip are considered. The first is urban, including residential, commercial, industrial, and public and military (other than publicly owned recreational land). The second is publicly owned recreational. The amount of land in recreational use is determined by policy decisions rather than by population growth and is assumed to remain constant. In contrast, land in urban use normally expands as a direct result of population increments. The third category is the open space residual that includes agricultural land and vacant and otherwise unusable land.

Space in the coastal strip available in 1967 and the amount that probably will be available in 1990 can be estimated (see Table 12).[32] Slow development in the North and Central

---

[31]The landward limit of this strip was established so as to include in it those areas that are recreationally, climatically, or topologographically influenced by proximity to the ocean. The strip is largely the California coastal plain. The landward line runs about twenty miles back from the coast and generally parallels the shore, although it swings far inland up the delta to include Stockton and Sacramento and the areas bordering San Francisco Bay. It also bulges inland to include the San Bernardino-Riverside portion of the Southern California metropolitan area ("Summary," California's Coastal Zone, 1968).

[32]The 1967 figures are based on the records of various state and local planning boards. 1990 estimates are based on population projections for that year supplied by the California Department of Finance. It was assumed in projecting 1990 acreages that per capita acreage requirements for different uses would remain constant. These 1990 population projections may be somewhat high, since California Department of Finance projections for that year assume a considerably larger California population increase in the 1960-70 decade than actually occurred. Thus, the figures in Table 12 may overestimate the acreage that will be devoted in 1990 to urban purposes and may underestimate the acreage that will be available in 1990 for agricultural and recreational purposes (U.S. Department of Commerce, 1970 Census of Population Preliminary Report (PC(P3)-1).

CALIFORNIA'S URBAN POPULATION: PATTERNS AND TRENDS

Table 12

ESTIMATED AND PROJECTED LAND USE, CALIFORNIA COASTAL STRIP:
1967 AND 1990

Coastal Areas	1967 Acres (000's)	1990 Acres, Current Rations (000's)	Percent Change, 1967-1990
North Coast	1,152	1,152	0.0%
Urban[a]	56	68	21.4
Recreational[b]	38	38	0.0
Vacant[c]	1,058	1,046	-1.1
Bay Delta	3,118	3,118	0.0
Residential	410	689	68.0
Industrial	90	154	71.1
Commercial	35	63	80.0
Public	115	199	73.0
Recreational[b]	119	119	0.0
Vacant[c]	2,349	1,894	-19.4
Central Coast	752	752	0.0
Urban[a]	115	126	9.6
Recreational[b]	10	10	0.0
Vacant[c]	627	616	-1.8
South Coast	2,624	2,624	0.0
Residential	590	1,006	70.5
Industrial	114	210	76.3
Commercial	62	110	77.4
Public	333	567	70.3
Recreational[b]	108	108	0.0
Vacant[c]	1,417	632	-56.0

[a] Includes residential, industrial, commercial, military, and public (other than recreational) land uses.
[b] Held constant.
[c] Includes agricultural, open, and unusable lands.

Source: Bendix Bradbury Associates and Copley International Corporation for California Advisory Commission on Marine and Coastal Resources, "Land Use," California's Coastal Zones.

Coast areas will mean little decline in open space there. These
are the least populated coastal areas and will probably remain
so. The Bay Delta and the South Coast areas, on the other hand,
are expected to experience major declines in open space due to
urban expansion--19.4 percent and 56.0 percent, respectively.
Open space reductions will reduce agricultural productivity and
will likely result in price increases of potential public recreational land.

The acreage needed to meet coastal strip recreational
needs is estimated on the assumption that every 1000 persons
require fifteen to eighteen acres of recreational land.[33] While
the Bay Delta area has sufficient publicly held recreational land
to meet current needs, the South Coast area is already estimated
deficient by 52,000 acres. By 1990 recreational land use needs
will have increased greatly. In the Bay Delta area alone, 17,000
additional acres will be needed for this purpose. South Coast
area recreational land use could consume as much as 80 percent
of the usable vacant land still available.

Hazards of California Environments. The utilization of
urban habitats leads to the intrajection of man-made features
into the air, earth, and water of California metropolitan areas.
These features include water supply and sewage systems; aircraft
landing, street, freeway, and railway patterns; and land utilized
for commercial, industrial, recreational, residential, and transportation functions. Such modifications are incorporated into
metropolitan settings, result in further changes in metropolitan
habitats, and influence and are influenced by the net migration,
fertility, mortality, and composition of population. Some of
the current hazards of California metropolitan environments include air pollution, pesticide residues, and water pollution, as
well as air traffic noise, brush fires, floods, and slides. These
hazards are generated by the technologies and resource organizations utilized to convert land to urban use.

Air Pollution. "Smog," or air pollution, is related both
to the size of metropolitan areas and to level of technology.
Three major components of smog--hydrocarbons, carbon monoxide,
and nitrogen oxides--are associated with motor vehicles. As
California population and motor vehicle registration has increased,
so has smog. Smog affects almost every part of the state,[34]
though it is of course a more intense problem in urban areas due

---

[33] These comments are based on "Land Use" in California's Coastal
Zone.

[34] Air Pollution Foundation, The Air Pollution Problem, 1960.
In 1960 a specialist from the University of California, Berkeley,

to greater concentrations of motor vehicles and industry there than in rural areas. In the County of Los Angeles, for example, 1969 motor vehicle exhaust polluted the air basin with more than 2,000 tons of hydrocarbons, 12,000 tons of carbon monoxide, and 1,000 tons of nitrogen oxides each day.[35]

Los Angeles County, the San Francisco Bay Area, San Diego County, and Sacramento County experienced increasing levels of carbon monoxide pollution from 1963 to 1965.[36] In the subsequent three years carbon monoxide pollution decreased slightly in all areas except Sacramento County, where it remained stable. Hydrocarbon pollution grew more slowly in the years 1963 to 1965, and, in fact, decreased in Los Angeles County. Since 1965 hydrocarbon pollution has decreased markedly in all four areas. These declines occurred in spite of an increasing number in California motor vehicles, and were presumably due to the introduction of exhaust control in 1966 and greater compliance with already existing crankcase control regulations.

Air pollution does not necessarily increase with population growth. Of the four metropolitan areas considered, San Diego experienced the greatest increase in pollution from 1963 to 1965 but the least numerical increase in population. San Francisco rated third in smog increase but first in population increase during that period. The second time period (1965-1968) showed similar reversals in rankings of pollution and population increases. If it is assumed that air pollution control boards accurately estimate pollution levels, increments in smog do not occur concurrent with population growth. Air pollution will likely lag behind metropolitan population increases.[37]

Pesticides. California acreage represented almost 10 percent of all national acreage treated at least once with pesticides in 1964, yet California contained less than 3 percent of

---

testified before a California legislative committee that in 1959 he had recorded smog damage to vegetation in all but three California counties.

[35] California Air Resources Board 1968 Annual Report, Sacramento, pp. 33-35.

[36] Ibid.

[37] Maurice D. Van Arsdol, Jr., "Population and the United States Urban Environment: The Los Angeles Case," International Population Conference, London 1969, Tome IV (Dorchester, 1971), pp. 2861-2871.

all U.S. harvested cropland.[38] Within the state a more extensive use of pesticides is made in metropolitan than in non-metropolitan counties. In 1964 twenty-two metropolitan counties accounted for slightly more than half (58 percent) of all California acreage sprayed with pesticides, although these counties included only 43 percent of all California harvested cropland. Farmers sprayed the cropland in metropolitan counties an average of 2.2 times per year and cropland in non-metropolitan counties an average of 1.2 times per year.[39]

The higher percentage of sprayed or dusted acres in metropolitan counties undoubtedly is due both to incidence and prevalence of treatment. Urban expansion into agricultural land leads to intensive farming and to land price rises near cities.[40] Increased land values force small-scale inefficient farmers to sell out, allowing large-scale efficient farmers to expand their operations. The greater prevalence of large-scale modern farming near cities than in more isolated areas may well be responsible for the greater use of pesticides in metropolitan areas. Such use of pesticides may be an important source of water pollution.

Water Pollution. Studies of marine life in waters near urban areas indicate that pollution by sewage, pesticides, and other wastes is responsible for the destruction of many marine species.[41] In the San Francisco area, commercial fishermen suspect that pesticides from irrigation drainage waters are responsible for the decline in crab catches from an average yield of 5.4 million pounds during 1953-1960 to a .9 million pound average during 1963-1968. In contrast, the crab catch in the Fort Bragg area, 150 miles north of San Francisco, increased over these two periods from 328,000 pounds to 504,000 pounds. A preliminary study in October 1967 found that DDE (a toxic metabolic compound of DDT) concentrations in crabs decreased as distance from the San Francisco Bay increased. Further research is needed to

---

[38] U.S. Bureau of the Census, U.S. Census of Agriculture, 1964, Vol. II, Chapter 9, Table 15, and Vol. I, Part 48, Table 9.

[39] Ibid. Also State of California, Department of Agriculture, March 29, 1960; mimeo.

[40] Edward Higbee, "Land and the Demand for Space," Farms and Farmers in an Urban Age (New York: The Connecticut Printers, 1963 [The Twentieth Century Fund]), pp. 98-101.

[41] See, for example, John C. Modin, "Chlorinated Hydrocarbon Pesticides in California Bays and Estuaries," Federal Subcommittee on Pest Control, Pesticide Monitoring Journal, Vol. 3, No. 1 (June 1969), p. 6.

determine whether the levels of DDE found in crabs could account for the severe drop in their population size.[42]

Major changes have occurred in marine life of the coastal waters of Southern California in the last decade. A 1969 oceanographic survey by the Biology Department of the University of Southern California indicated 63 percent fewer intertidal seaweed species than were found in 1959, and animal species which depend upon intertidal seaweed for food or shelter may well have declined proportionately.[43] The seaweed species that remain are characteristic of areas where high concentrations of organic and inorganic materials are present. This suggests that the heavy pollution of coastal waters with sewage and other waste has meant the elimination of many seaweed species and the flourishing of others.

Approximately one billion gallons of assorted wastes are discharged into Southern California shallows each day. These shallows have a restricted capacity to flush old waters with new. The waters surrounding the Channel Islands are not subjected to such heavy pollution and have not suffered the destruction of seaweed that the coastal waters have. The degree to which changes in intertidal seaweed populations reflect similar changes in deep waters is not known. However, there are indications that deep water life forms are adversely affected by water pollution. Giant bladder kelp has disappeared from the Los Angeles and Ventura regions. This kelp forms the major structure of the kelp forests of Pacific North America. At least 125 species of fish are known to be associated with these submarine forests.

Another indication of disturbance of the deep water ecology near urban centers is fish body malformations. Bottom fish such as Dover sole caught near Long Beach are soft and discolored compared with bottom fish caught further from urban centers. Some bottom fish caught in Santa Monica Bay have inflamed sores on their bodies. White sea bass in Southern California have been found with mouth papillomas (tumors). Papillomas identical to those on wild fish have been induced by exposing unaffected fish to a 6 percent solution of water from Dominguez Channel which empties into the Port of Los Angeles. Finally, a variety of skeletal malformations have been found in Southern California fish. All of these anomalies indicate that even life forms in

---

[42]Ibid.

[43]This section is drawn from a report by Nancy L. Nicholson, "Factors Affecting the Distribution and Health of Marine Organisms in Southern California," unpublished paper, Los Angeles: University of Southern California, Department of Urban Affairs Research Needs Conference and the Development and Management of the Coastal Zone of California, 1971.

deep waters are not safe from the effects of urban centers. We are now beginning to learn how such changes in fish affect human metropolitan populations in turn.

Summary

U.S. population trends are accentuated in the West and in California. The state's population has almost tripled in size since 1940, and is increasingly urban. Of greater significance is that California is now metropolitan and megalopolitan in character. Since 1940, eleven metropolitan counties have accounted for more than four-fifths of the state's growth, and a number of metropolitan counties have merged into the San Francisco and the Los Angeles megalopolitan regions. Urban fringe areas of metropolitan areas contain the fastest growing residential sections of the state. Older metropolitan areas have emerged as functional centers of the two megalopolitan regions. New metropolitan areas appear to be the foci of population increase for megalopolitan regions, and are growing by natural increase and especially by net migration.

California urbanization has been linked with relative declines in extractive activity, a shift to factory-centered manufacturing, and the emergence of service employment. Manufacturing, wholesaling, retailing, and service decentralization in the past three decades has changed metropolitan commuting patterns and transportation needs. California metropolitan areas may have higher rates of intra-metropolitan residential mobility than other metropolitan areas in the United States. While 1970 Census reports could indicate suburbanization of ethnic populations in California metropolises, such suburbanization may reflect primarily differential ethnic growth in older segments of outlying areas. Work-residence separation problems for ethnic populations are likely to remain severe during the 1970's.

The concentration of California's population in metropolises along the coastal strip has created major problems with respect to the availability of open space. Metropolitan development has also created or aggravated a number of environmental hazards, including air pollution, pesticide residues, and water pollution. These hazards are most apparent in metropolitan areas, but there is also severe contamination of rural areas and of the waters adjacent to population aggregations.

The aggregation of California populations into metropolitan areas and megalopolitan regions has caused financial and organizational difficulties for governments, and contributed to serious social and economic divisions among the residents. If we do not act now to deal with these problems, they will continue to increase in scope and intensity for at least the remainder of this century.

IMPACT OF STATE POLICY AND PROBLEMS ON CALIFORNIA'S DEVELOPMENT

Robert E. Grunwald

Introduction

In 1970 the California Legislature adopted one of the best written and potentially most important pieces of state planning legislation in the country. The legislation to which I refer was A.B. 2070 creating the Office of Planning and Research (OPR) in the Governor's office and replacing Chapter 1.5 of the Planning and Zoning law relating to the state's responsibility for planning.

It is ironic that a state which had developed such a fine law concerning the state's responsibilities for planning would also, during the same year, take a set of budgetary actions which all but eliminated the state's capability for planning within the new Office of Planning and Research--a capability which, in terms of manpower, is less than that of the County Planning Department in the rural county where I reside.

Since 1959, the state's ability to produce through its state planning function can be characterized as much like the critical path computer analysis which finds a loop in a program which prevents a product from ever being delivered. I submit that this condition must be identified as one of the great dilemmas of state development. I hope to place the eleven-year period of events surrounding the state's planning function in a perspective of some of the more important dimensions of state policy and problems which have an impact on California's development.

Policies and Programs Having a Significant Impact

First, let us examine some of the more important existing policies and programs of the state and federal governments which influence statewide patterns of population distribution, land use, resource management, and urbanization. Policies in these four interrelated areas of concern already are explicit in the new state planning law passed in 1970--at least to the extent that the law spells out what the state's planning function ought to be vis-à-vis these areas of concern. But since the state's planning function is barely operative at this point, it is perhaps more important to look at those policies which are implicit in the body of laws and plans and programs governing the present operations of many state and federal agencies. In the field of resources

management, the state's water, open-space preservation, and
nuclear power plant-siting programs serve as examples. Other
examples include the state freeway and expressway development
program, the statewide air transportation planning program, and
policies of the Coordinating Council on Higher Education concerning the location of state colleges and universities. Examples at
the federal level include programs of water development, interstate highway construction, military defense, and coastal resource
development. There are virtually dozens of state and federal
activities which directly or indirectly provide the existing
policy framework for the character and pattern of development
within the state and its regions.

Substantial evidence of this influence is provided in the
series of reports prepared as part of the State Development Plan
Program during the 1960's--evidence which points to a vacuum in
land-use policy resulting from fragmented and unilateral approaches to functional planning, and evidence which illustrates
the urgency for a means by which the collective actions of government and the private sector can be focused toward carrying out a
more deliberate set of development objectives.

In my judgment, the closest the State of California has
come to the development of a comprehensive land-use policy was
with the preparation of the California Water Plan, its adoption
in 1957, and the subsequent authorization of the California State
Water Project now nearing completion. The Water Plan was developed in response to urgent problems of regional imbalances in
water supply. The plan was prepared without the benefit of an
overall framework of goals, policies, and programs for general
statewide development. Flexibility was therefore built-in as an
essential characteristic of the plan. Estimates of future economic growth, changes in land use, and population distribution
were geared essentially to understanding the order of magnitude
of growth and consequent requirements for water. But such flexibility is more academic than real, for the fact remains that
through the first stage of implementation of the water program,
the state has committed itself largely to the continued enlarge-
ment of the patterns of urbanization and agricultural development
which existed 25 years ago, without examining the consequences
of such patterns except in relation to water.

With authorization of the State Water Project, the state
government set into motion political and economic forces which
are not likely to lend themselves to significant change for
twenty or more years--even if the state wished to encourage
faster rates of urbanization or new centers of urbanization within
less developed regions of the state. This is because water
planning must take place within a multi-decade perspective with
a lag in project development which may be as high as thirty years
from the date of project conception. Therefore, existing major

IMPACT OF STATE POLICY ON CALIFORNIA'S DEVELOPMENT

patterns and rates of urbanization tend to be locked-in to the year 1990, and flexibility is apparent primarily only over the longer haul--that is, provided that we begin now to reexamine and reevaluate priorities.

The water program illustrates that any approach to the subject of the state's responsibility for land-use policy must consider the fundamental and long-term impact of state and federal water development programs on the state's urban development process. Because of the long-range perspective required, it offers significant opportunities to assist and identify regional growth alternatives, for understanding their probable consequences, and for permitting a more deliberate selection of actions in formulating and achieving overall state development goals.

At this point in the state's water program, there is some encouragement that the limited focus of previous planning effort will not be continued. In its recently published Bulletin No. 160-70, which updates the California Water Plan, the Department of Water Resources included a chapter which represents a major departure in the investigation of alternatives for water development in the future. This chapter (Chapter 8) of the Bulletin is entitled "Population Dispersal--Impact on Resources Development." The purpose of the chapter is to explore, at least superficially, some of the pertinent ramifications of possible alternative patterns of population and urbanization for water management. With assistance from the State Office of Planning (now OPR), the Department of Water Resources developed three different models of future population distribution throughout the state's regions, and analyzed the possible impact of each model for water management. The results are not conclusive with respect to all questions posed by population dispersal within undeveloped and underdeveloped regions--even with respect to water. However, they certainly vindicate the viewpoint that substantial benefits might accrue from a population and urbanization policy which would seek variations in the magnitude and spatial distribution of regional growth from that otherwise anticipated by an extrapolation of existing trends.

The logical next step would be to expand the scope and depth of study presented in Chapter 8 of Bulletin 160-70. The perfect opportunity is presented by the two years of intensive water basin management studies to be undertaken by the State Water Resources Control Board in July, and by the two-phased study of Land Use and Population Policy proposed by the Office of Planning. Properly coordinated, these studies would provide a more thorough grasp of the issues and opportunities posed by alternative future patterns of population and urbanization in the state. Whether such coordination will take place is subject to speculation because the need and opportunity is not reflected in the Water Resources Control Board's study format, and the timing

of the Land Use and Population Policy Study of OPR has not yet
been announced.

A further opportunity is presented by the joint federal-
state and interstate river basin planning studies now being conducted under the auspices of the National Resources Council. Even
though these studies have been underway for several years, it is
not too late to build in considerations of alternative patterns
of population distribution within California, and indeed within
the Western States region. Federal and interstate water planning
and operations programming will have an enormous influence on the
future of California, just as they have in the past.

This call for a broadened scope of the water basin management studies is not new. Such recommendations were raised by the
very units of state government most directly involved six years
ago. During the period 1963-1966, the California Resources Agency
and all of its constituent units undertook what has to be considered one of the most bold internal evaluations of policies and
programs ever undertaken by a major public agency anywhere in the
country. This effort resulted in a report entitled "Resource
Policy Directions for California." The report was developed as
part of the State Development Plan Program of the Office of
Planning. It developed the rationale for relating water studies
to strategies and alternatives for population distribution and
land use. It examined every functional aspect of resource management in this context and went deeply into the interrelated aspects
of resource management activities and the collective relationship
of these activities to the task of statewide development planning
and programming. The report called for bold and imaginative and
yet realistic steps to assure environmental quality in the state,
and yet I doubt that it has been seen by more than a few legislators, or that it is being used and updated in any systematic way
by the agencies which participated in its conception. I ask this
question: Must we spend so much of our time re-inventing wheels,
and in the process rob ourselves of precious time required for the
public debate of issues which have already been identified and
which are still relevant today?

Now to the subject of transportation. In a major reorganization effort a few years ago, the state created the Transportation Agency to overcome gaps and deficiencies in state transportation policy which resulted from an over-reliance on highway
planning and construction. To date, however, we find:

(1) Alternatives probably will not be forthcoming in the short
term;

(2) The state still lacks the ability to perform integrated
transportation planning;

IMPACT OF STATE POLICY ON CALIFORNIA'S DEVELOPMENT

(3) A major statewide air transportation study is so narrowly oriented that it is not likely to produce much insight into the logical relationships required between all modes of air and ground transportation;

(4) Freeways continue to be constructed into further reaches of our metropolitan fringe areas, encouraging a continuation of the spatial distribution of the urban and metropolitan pattern which has evolved over the past 25 years;

(5) The state is unable to respond to the proposed Railpax System in terms of the implications of Railpax for long-term transportation requirements of the state;

(6) The state is not in a position to present a view of the facilities required or opportunities posed for shipping goods by ship, conveyor, or pipeline; and

(7) We are trapped by federal and state public investment policy which emphasizes highway transportation to points of ridiculous extreme and fosters the creation of transportation problems within our metropolitan areas faster than our ability to find solutions even for that single mode--the freeway.

As in the case of water development policy, considerable attention was given to this subject during the early and middle 1960's as part of the Phase I and II State Development Plan Program studies. But most of that information is still buried in reports which have never been published.

For a decade, the state has been engaged in the planning and construction of the first interregional freeway ever planned as such by the State of California--Interstate 5 extending from the Mexican border to the Oregon border. What will be the impact of this facility on population and urban patterns? What opportunities will such a facility present for economic growth and development within underdeveloped regions through which it passes? What will be the impact of diverting county allocations of highway construction funds to Interstate 5 to make up the state's share of the construction costs for this facility? One can only speculate on the answers to these questions, since evaluations of the implications of these actions were never built into the planning process.

I will conclude this discussion of the impact of transportation policies by pointing out that the state has for some years shown a proposed interregional freeway along the east side of the San Joaquin Valley on the adopted Freeway and Expressway System Plan. I wonder what implications for statewide development are presented by such an interregional facility if it is to be planned and constructed in the same manner as Interstate 5. It would be well if the Transportation Agency examined the impact of the same

hypothetical set of population distribution alternatives for
transportation as were used by the Department of Water Resources
in its Bulletin 160-70 for water.

Next, some comments about the state's policies on open
space preservation. The California Land Conservation Act was
enacted, and a constitutional amendment approved, to provide some
means of assuring that privately owned open space in forest and
agricultural use could be preserved in and around our metropolitan
and urban areas by permitting favorable tax policies on the land
relating to its current use rather than to its speculative potential for urbanization. Experience in many counties of the state,
however, indicates that such purposes have been subverted by a
wholesale inclusion of hundreds of thousands of acres of land in
the program far removed from urban and metropolitan areas, where
pressures for non-urban use do not exist. This is but another
example of how state policies can shape future patterns of development without any conscious debate of what those patterns ought
to be and why.

Another impact of consequence is that posed by problems
in finding suitable sites for nuclear power plants. The Resources
Policy Study mentioned previously called for the establishment of
a statewide policy on energy resources, and the relation of that
policy to land use, population distribution, and environmental
factors. We see no evidence of such policy development to date,
and instead nuclear power sites are selected, evaluated, and
rejected on a site-by-site basis. Isn't it time that such site
requirements were placed in the perspective of total statewide
development policy? Isn't it time that future power requirements
were placed in the perspective of alternatives to conventional
sources of energy? Isn't it time that we recognize the full public interest in the development of energy by public utilities and
government rather than bludgeoning the utilities on a site-by-site basis? The critical mass impact of energy policy on the
future of the state and its regions certainly demands a broader
understanding than that afforded by current practices, which are
tied into the local land-use zoning process.

My final example of a state activity exerting an important
impact upon statewide development is in the area of human resources. Three years ago, in response to federal legislation, the
State Health Planning Council was created to oversee the allocation of millions of dollars of federal funds to foster comprehensive health planning and the delivery of health services to the
people of the state. A critical requirement of that program was
the development of a statewide comprehensive health plan which
would define the roles of state, regional, and local governmental
agencies and of the private sector in meeting the health service
requirements for people of the state.

IMPACT OF STATE POLICY ON CALIFORNIA'S DEVELOPMENT

To date no statewide plan has been developed. Instead, we have fostered the collection of health planning and health delivery operations at local and regional levels which appear to be primarily capable of consuming more and more public funds with questionable results. It appears to me that the rush to accept federal funds has now institutionalized the continued consumption of money rather than the delivery of products and services, and that the concept of a statewide plan may never get off the ground in any meaningful way now that there are so many actors in the game and axes to be ground.

The Responsibilities of State Government

The question now must be raised as to what we might expect from continued over-reliance on single-purpose planning--whether it involves water, transportation, higher education, health, welfare, or any of the myriad of other important operations and services--which fails to provide an understanding of their full implications. The state and federal governments now invest enormous amounts of money for public works and services within metropolitan and rural regions. The continuation of such investment along functional lines of emphasis may well bring the state to the point of unresolvable physical, social, and economic issues in an absolute sense. I am suggesting that the complexity of these issues may be reaching the point where resolution may be possible only in theoretical terms because of the brutal economic and social consequences of actions required for resolution in real terms.

Many actions today tend to reinforce much of the misery of metropolitan development and resource exploitation of the past. While empirical evidence in support of this proposition is often difficult to come by, the indicators of actual experience are difficult to deny. The thirty-year trend toward metropolitan sprawl continues unabated; access to housing, education, and employment remains an elusive dream of millions of poor; the deficiencies of a transportation system which depends mostly on streets and highways continue to increase faster than they can be overcome; conditions of air and water pollution threaten the very existence of the environment; recreation areas are being despoiled through over-use by millions of people who can reach them, while at the same time such areas remain inaccessible to other millions because of poverty.

In the absence of any carefully defined set of alternatives, we reinforce what we have become used to. And what we have become used to is a cycle of ever-increasing demands, ever-increasing public investment, and ever-increasing complexity of the entire set of problems which comprise the environmental crisis in which we find ourselves today. To be sure, we will

solve some of the problems because we must. The public clamor
and political commitment to the solution of some problems has now
been elevated to the point where anything short of solution will
be unacceptable. But even if we solve water, air, and solid waste
pollution problems, will our efforts be placed in a perspective
that views the main problem to be that of improving the quality
of life within our entire physical environment?

Given this proposition, the responsibilities of state
government seem to center on the following:

(1) The state needs to provide its direct assistance and
guidance toward breaking the cycle of ever-increasing
deficiencies and strain upon the quality of urban life;

(2) The state needs a more rational guidance system for its
own operations within both a regional and statewide
context;

(3) The state needs to provide a more rational guidance
system for the actions of local government while providing
local government the opportunity to participate on an
intergovernmental basis in the selection of those state
and federal programs and actions which will influence
greatly the manner in which the regions of the state
develop; and

(4) The state needs to provide a more rational guidance
system for the actions of the federal government, so
that federal actions will not be unresponsive to the
needs and aspirations of 10 percent of the nation's
population.

All of these points are covered well by A.B. 2070 enacted
in 1970. It places the state's planning function in the Governor's office so that functional planning within the operating
arms of state government can, in fact, become tools for implementing a set of deliberately determined objectives for statewide
development. All of these points are covered also by the design
for the proposed study of land-use and population policies completed last spring for OPR but not yet underway. The responsibility for formulating land-use policy is an important consideration of A.B. 2070, and the study, if carried out as designed,
would provide the basis for the Governor's Environmental Report
due initially in July 1972 and every four years thereafter.

The Proposed Study of Land Use and Population Study

Recommendations for land-use and population policies at
the state level were to be the final product of Phase II of the
State Development Plan Program. But for a variety of reasons,

IMPACT OF STATE POLICY ON CALIFORNIA'S DEVELOPMENT

the product was not delivered. Six years later the need for such policy was built into the state's planning law, and the proposed study has been approved for federal funding by the Department of Housing and Urban Development (HUD).

The Land Use and Population Policy Study has several objectives and characteristics which are worthy of mention at this time:

(1) The first objective will be to examine the probable consequences of continuing current patterns of environmental change into the future, when the state will have an additional 10-20 million people. Continuing patterns of growth will be depicted graphically and their implications described in both qualitative and quantitative terms. This will require the identification of the amount and location of lands and other resources which have critical value for maintaining and enhancing the quality of the state's environment--resources which are likely to be lost in the short term through conversion to urban use or through over-use or exploitation for non-urban purposes.

(2) The second objective will be to identify alternative approaches to the further development of the state's total environment--to identify those strategies which, singly or in combination, will provide the best means for dealing effectively with continued growth in population and urbanization and rapidly changing conditions of technological and social change.

A key concept in the definition of alternative development strategies is the need to maintain as many "options" for the future as reasonably may be possible, consistent with the need for action in the short term. This premise of maintaining options is critical to development policy formulation. It suggests that despite certain unpredictable conditions of the future, overall agreement on major questions of land allocation can be reached; it implies flexibility over time to meet changing conditions; it holds that overcommitment to a single approach must be avoided; and it insists that public reaction to clearly defined alternatives is essential.

Another key concept is that "plateaus" of recommended policy would emerge for both early and continuing support for executive and legislative action. The term "plateaus" suggests that each phase of the study will provide policy directions and actions required at that time, to the extent that analysis allows. As additional plateaus are reached, greater definition of policy would be permitted.

Emphasis is also given to the proposition that there can
be no delay in providing an understanding of the first
order of policy and program considerations required in the
short-term. There already is so much relevant data and
information available that it would be a tragic waste of
time to delay the process of analysis and recommendation
until many years of additional study have exposed all
relevant factors.

(3) The third objective will be to provide a level and timing
of analysis which can feed directly into the decision-
making process--to produce specific legislation and programs defining the state's land-use and population policy
and the recasting of operational programs required for
its implementation.

In view of my previous comments concerning the current
capability of the Office of Planning and Research, it would appear
that there is little hope for getting the study underway and
producing by July of 1972. The budgetary support of the present
small staff comes primarily from "soft money"--i.e., federal
money. This dependency on federal money has been a great weakness
of the state's planning function since 1959.

Required Commitments by
Executive and Legislative Branches of State Government

The first commitment must be that of budgetary support.
This must involve the increasing of staff positions of OPR at
least to the level of the mid-1960's. But of equal importance
is to commit a sufficient amount of time to the Land Use and
Population Policy Study by functional units within the transportation, resources, and human resources agencies. This will
multiply manpower availability where it will be needed most to
get the kind of study coordination and technical insight required
to get the job done. As custodians of the state's functional
operations, these agencies can make or break issues, impede or
advance progress, and influence either positively or negatively
the efforts of the Governor and the Legislature to get the information they need. Participation by the functional agencies thus
is essential!

The second commitment required is that of both executive
and legislative leadership. Since 1955 when the State Office
of Planning was first created, the office has been the orphan
stepchild of state government. Since the Office of Planning and
Research is now lodged in the Governor's office, there is created
for the first time the opportunity for the full and systematic
use of the planning function by the Governor, to involve the
Governor's Cabinet, and to set in motion those functional agency

IMPACT OF STATE POLICY ON CALIFORNIA'S DEVELOPMENT

operations which should provide supportive actions within the entire Executive Branch.

The role of the Legislature cannot merely be one of response; the Legislature has the responsibility to act creatively to meet a somewhat different test of the political process. It is the legislative process which must hammer out new mandates, revise codes, provide budgetary support, and monitor progress in programs it has authorized. Through what is undoubtedly the best legislative committee system in the country today, the California Legislature has built up an information and policy base and a capacity for action which must now be extended to embrace concern for the state's planning function. I am suggesting that the "constructive abrasion" which has developed between executive and legislative branches over the past decade be extended to monitor the progress of the OPR. The vehicle for such action may be the newly created Land Use or Environmental Quality Committees of the Assembly, or it may be a joint committee of both Houses. The committee given this charge should be a forceful catalyst in its own right to assure that the Legislature is provided full knowledge of what can and should be done in the short term. The possession of such knowledge is a legislative imperative!

The alternatives to constructive action by the Legislature as well as the Executive Branch in analyzing and debating the options for future development in the state is to depend on the consumer-advocacy approach to create the public and political atmosphere which in time will demand such action. Already two reports are underway by private organizations which seek to do this very thing. One organization, California Tomorrow, is preparing its own version of an initial plan for California. A second organization, established by Ralph Nader, is investigating the political and economic power structure which benefits from the manner in which development decisions are being made in California today. These privately sponsored efforts have resulted at least in part from the frustration surrounding the state's planning function since 1959. Many of the important recommendations of that function have had their greatest impact upon governors and legislatures in other states. A number of other states have looked to California for ideas, creative thought, and directions for action which they have adopted and advanced, and they are openly perplexed by California's capacity for inaction.

The executive and legislative actions which I recommend would go far toward achieving constructive solutions to the dilemmas of state development which have been reported by this panel and by other participants at this conference. I strongly urge that the functions of the Office of Planning and Research be made operational as soon as possible. A.B. 2070 already provides the mandates required for the Office of Planning and Research to produce recommendations for land use, population, and environmental policy. The longer the state waits, the more certain is the prospect that the products called for by A.B. 2070 will be lost by division and fragmentation of responsibilities now assigned to OPR among new agencies, boards, or commissions which might be created to handle related pieces of the total job required. Let us not invent partial substitutes to OPR before OPR is given the Executive and Legislative commitments to produce!

STATE POLICIES ON URBAN-METROPOLITAN RENEWAL

William L. Pereira

Perhaps I should preface my remarks with a confession. I am a city lover. In spite of all the problems of urban living, in spite of the traffic and smog and blight and noise, I am irrevocably committed to living within a metropolitan setting. It is a compulsion shared, for better or for worse, by a majority of my countrymen; two-thirds of the U.S. population are citydwellers, and by the end of the century this proportion will have risen to 85 or 90 percent. It goes without saying that if our urban dilemmas increase at the same rate over the next thirty years, we are in for very serious trouble, if not downright disaster. City planning has long ceased to be an academic professional discipline; today it is our only hope of survival in what is quickly becoming our most urgent national emergency--the urban crisis.

But before we can prescribe for the patient, we must know something of its history. And the city has a long one, stretching back six thousand years to the first major settlements on the banks of the Tigris and the Nile. Like man himself, cities have always been living organisms, in a constant state of flux and change. Sometimes, conceived for expedient or artificial purposes, they are still-born. Alexander the Great founded a dozen cities or more named Alexandria, and only one of them survived to become a thriving metropolis of the ancient world. And sometimes cities are destroyed, and are reborn again and again, like many-layered Troy. But whatever their ultimate fate, history teaches us that cities, subject to the influences of nature and of man, are continuously evolving. It is when they cease to evolve, when they resist the implacable forces of change, that they begin to decline and die.

This is the first lesson we must learn when we address ourselves to the plight of our own contemporary cities. Even while we are studying them they are changing, and unless we understand and accept the dynamics of urban growth and decay we will not be able to diagnose the patient's illness, let alone offer any practicable cure.

Let us consider, for example, urban blight. It is a very familiar phrase these days, used almost indiscriminately to describe any number of civic sicknesses. At times it seems we have almost persuaded ourselves that urban blight is a disease like leaf spot or dry rot, against which we have no defense except to treat it as best we can when it inevitably occurs. And by that time, of course, we have no recourse except radical surgery--in the case of our cities, this usually takes the form of urban renewal.

And yet, while we are tearing down the old houses and hotels to make room for the new anonymous apartment houses, we are--only a few blocks away--probably introducing the virulent strains of the same blight by an ill-considered rezoning or misplaced freeway. "We must think in terms of a preventive pathology instead of a curative pathology," Buckminster Fuller once said. He was talking in terms of economics, but his words hold just as true for urban planning.

The real trouble with our urban planning today is, in fact, that there is so little of it. Urban second-guessing, maybe, or urban patching-up. But the essence of planning of any kind is anticipating problems rather than seeking solutions. And our attention is so riveted on the mistakes made by our predecessors, and doing something about correcting them, that we have neglected the principal obligation of avoiding the same mistakes ourselves.

We have talked about cities as living organisms. And just as in the organic world, the existence of these urban beings is delicately poised between many different influences. Trouble occurs when this balance of nature is disturbed. What we call a ghetto, for instance, is no more than a symptom of such imbalance. More often than not, these areas were once the most fashionable districts of the city. As the urban balance was upset, and people began to move out, others--less fortunate (that is, with fewer options)--moved in to take their place; even in cities, nature abhors a vacuum. The scales were tipped still further-- and the ghetto emerged like an angry sore on the body of the city. (We must remember that this process is not an irreversible one. Georgetown in Washington, Beekman Place in New York, are dramatic examples of how a blighted area can be made a viable and attractive neighborhood again. But this is not possible unless first the balance of community amenities is restored.)

How can we protect this balance of urban nature? One way, of course, is by careful planning--by predetermining the destiny of the area that will best serve the needs and interests of the people and then ensuring that this destiny will be fulfilled. If new zoning is required to assure the optimum "mix" of amenities, it must be undertaken when needed and not wait upon political pressures. If legislation is required to realize the basic goals, it must be enacted. We take for granted that an elementary school, for example, will be provided for every so many thousand citizens. But what of the other features that are equally essential to a balanced urban life--the parks, the recreational facilities, the hospitals, and health-care centers? Why should they not also be made available on a per capita basis, across the board?

To many critics, "aesthetic controls" are fighting words--suggesting, at one extreme, frivolous emphasis on external appearances and, at the other, a sinister restraint of personal liberties. Yet what is less frivolous than concern for protecting the natural beauty of our environment, or more democratic than protecting our fellow citizens from constant assaults by the forces of ugliness, pollution, and unnecessary noise? Urban blight can be visual as well as social, audible as well as economic. Is there any reason why we cannot and should not seek legal protection against crimes on our senses and spirits as well as on our persons and property?

We've already mentioned urban renewal as the popular panacea for most urban ills. But like many powerful medicines, it must be carefully administered. Too often the operation is a success but the patient dies, especially--in this case--if the human values in urban renewal are ignored, if the intimacy and essential character of even a blighted neighborhood are lost when it is transformed into an impersonal machine for living. In Hawaii we are presently engaged in an urban renewal project in a neighborhood where these interpersonal relationships are enormously important and intricate--where, for example, "living above the store" has become virtually a way of life. To renew and revivify the area and still not disrupt the life patterns of its inhabitants is one of the keenest professional challenges we have ever faced.

At the same time, in Houston, we have master-planned and are now designing a whole new downtown area that will literally double the size of the present central business district. Houston Center, which covers 33 contiguous blocks of central Houston, is a once-in-a-lifetime chance to create an urban center from scratch without being restricted by what is there already. In this sense, it is the reverse of urban renewal--"urban newal," if you like.

As a consequence, the project is able to incorporate many of the planning concepts that have been devoutly espoused but seldom realized in the past. Such as: complete separation of pedestrian and vehicular traffic by raising the platform of the entire complex several levels above the street system, and devoting those levels largely to parking. Such as: providing plazas, parks, and promenades among the buildings--altogether a third more open space than is possible in a conventional street grid pattern. Such as: establishing in advance what the proper mix of commercial, residential, recreational uses should be. Such as: integrating horizontal and vertical transportation systems into the basic plan of the development. And so on.

None of these is a new idea; planners have been advocating them all for years. Yet it is very seldom that the opportunity exists to practice what we have all been preaching for so long. But why is this so? Granted that Houston Center is a unique example, is there any reason that enlightened private enterprise, without nearly the resources or such powers as the right of condemnation, should be able to accomplish so much more in urban design than presumably enlightened government? Are imagination and daring and determination the exclusive properties of the private sector? I shouldn't like to think so.

There are two additional points I wish to make. One is that "urban-metropolitan renewal" is not a one-time thing. We cannot turn our back on the problems of the city until the only solution is drastic renovation, any more than we can afford to neglect the knocking in our car until we have blown a gasket. Unlike an automobile, unfortunately, we can't trade our city in for a new model when it develops engine trouble. We must keep it in constant repair. That is the real meaning of urban renewal.

The other point I want to make--or rather reiterate--is the relationship of vitality and growth to change. You cannot have one without the other. That is why we must be very careful always to recognize the difference between conservation and constriction, between protecting the environment and embalming it. Let us be wary of the status quo and the man who wants to preserve it at all costs. The referendum that was circulated some time ago in San Francisco, seeking to limit the height limit of all new construction to six stories, seems to me especially symptomatic of this King Canute syndrome. It is a kind of thinking that could be simplistic and retrogressive.

The fact that "state policies on urban-metropolitan renewal" is a topic of moment to the Assembly Science and Technology Advisory Council is indicative, I think, of California's continuing concern in the urban crisis--a concern that seems to be shared, except in political pronouncements, by few other state governments. But concern is not enough. With the population explosion amplified by the continental tilt, urban problems assume even more critical dimensions in California and must be met with action as well as words on the municipal, state, and federal levels alike.

What form should such action take? First, and most important of all, the state can provide enabling legislation directed towards some form of land use overview that would help offset the helplessness that generally characterizes our typical urban political framework. Too often the city, which is usually a series of cities within a city, finds it impossible to muster the political forces necessary to make large-scale changes possible. Even if some sort of coalition is achieved, the venture

STATE POLICIES ON URBAN-METROPOLITAN RENEWAL

can be delayed and eventually defeated by inadequate legal powers and lack of appropriate revenue sources. One method might be for the state to set up a kind of tribunal to hear proposals from city governments concerning urban development of all kinds. In this respect the state could act as a nonregulatory coordinator and advisor, with enough muscle to push new legislation where and when the need emerges. If nothing else, such concern at the state level might very well lift urban problems above the narrow self-seeking processes which characterize much local politics.

The state research and planning department, which administers federal funds, could and should play a more instrumental role in the planning of our metropolitan areas. State-chartered development organizations, similar to New York's Urban Development Corporation, can preempt some city powers in respect to housing, infrastructure, etc. to accomplish planning objectives that would otherwise never be realized. The lack of adequate middle- and moderate-income housing in the central city is one of the most pressing problems in urban centers today. Federal subsidy is not enough. The state must assume its share of this urgent responsibility.

The coordination of transportation modes, and the research and development of new transit systems, is an area in which the state of California has already pioneered. Much more, however, remains to be done. The ease of access of the working population to the employment centers of the city, like the circulatory system of the human body, determines in large measure the health of the metropolis. No city is an island, and the central city is necessarily affected by the regional centers that surround it. The state has the perspective and should assume the leadership in the large-scale planning on which these strategic relationships depend. Incentive taxes, that reward rather than penalize the highest and best use of urban land, must be instituted if private enterprise is to be encouraged to cooperate meaningfully in urban planning programs.

Finally, the state can be effective in the field of urban education. State-sponsored seminars for city politicians and businessmen, with help from experts in various disciplines, could do much--not only in presenting the value of long-range planning, but also perhaps in transcending the boundaries of politics and competition to create unexpected and productive alliances.

In closing, I would like to say that, in spite of all our urban problems, the future of the city can still be bright. With Morris Ketchum, let us work towards enhancing our man-made beauty:

The city is the natural gathering place for our thinkers, our innovators, and our specialists. It is where education flourishes and art is born. It is the generator of our national wealth. There is no reason why it should be dirty, ugly, and generally unliveable. It should be, in fact, our greatest work of art.

URBAN GROWTH IN CALIFORNIA:
NEW TOWNS AND OTHER POLICY ALTERNATIVES

William Alonso

California, which has always been one of the most urbanized and lustiest growing states in the nation, has recently become aware of the need to develop policies to distribute this growth in desirable ways. The idea that territorial development at the level of a state can or should be planned or guided is a relatively new one, although it is an everyday matter at the level of a city or a county. Further, California's interest in guiding the distribution of its population occurs within a context of renewed efforts to guide population distribution for the nation as a whole. Although the United States had vigorous policies in the nineteenth century for the occupation of the frontier, in this century the principal federal regional concerns have been with problem regions, of which Appalachia is the principal instance. Only by degrees has there been acceptance of the idea of an overall strategy of national teritorial development as opposed to a strategy of putting out fires as they arise. The concept of such management, somewhat misleadingly being called a "national growth policy," began to emerge during the years of the Johnson Administration, but did not receive explicit formulation until President Nixon's 1970 State of the Union Message.

Even now it is extremely difficult to put forth a table of contents for this type of policy. What is its agenda? What things should it be concerned with? What matters can safely be left to market mechanisms and to purely local decisions? What instrumentalities are available and how effective are they? These are difficult questions, at least in the sense that no clear answers have emerged. The United States and California are not alone in sensing the need for policies and actions which cannot yet be defined. International agencies such as the World Bank, AID, and the United Nations are raising precisely these questions, and are engaged in a common search for answers. By contrast, some European countries such as Great Britain and France (which are comparable in scale to California) have long had territorial policies and a wide repertory of programs. However,

---

The material in this paper is based on research sponsored by the Economic Development Administration of the U.S. Department of Commerce.

although these offer interesting lessons, they have not been
sufficiently explicit about their purposes and the assumptions
underlying their strategies to provide full guidelines for our
own efforts.

Within the context of a strongly felt need for policy on
these matters and the lack of clear sense of how such a policy
might be formulated or what it might encompass, it is natural
that new towns should often come to mind. They provide brave
visions of starting afresh without the baggage of previous
history and mistakes. They appear Camelots of the future, proving
grounds for aesthetic, social, economic, and technological break-
throughs. Yet though the new towns have a role to play, I shall
argue that this role is a rather small one, and that it would be
misleading to assign to them a central place in the future development of California's urbanization.

I shall not review here all of the grounds and arguments
that are advanced in favor of new towns. Many of these are rather
vague, and seem to belong to the realm of poetry rather than to
that of policy analysis. Further, the discussions of new towns
are often encrusted with code words which make interpretation
extremely difficult. Instances of these are such words as
"planned," "balanced," "exciting," "variety," "human scale."
Sometimes these words have a vague concrete referent. For instance, "balanced" usually means either or both that there is a
more or less proportional representation of different economic
and ethnic population elements, and that there is about an equal
number of workers and of jobs, so that those who live in the town
can also work in it. "Planned" very often means that there is a
long-run financial and engineering plan that will be efficient
for the development, or that plentiful amenities will be provided.
But, on the whole, the argumentation for new towns resembles more
a Rorschach test for men of good will than a rational evaluation
of pros and cons.

Let me turn first to some questions of the economic
efficiency of new towns. There is no evidence that new towns
lower urban costs. They have not shown that they are able to
capture economies of scale in the production of housing or urban
infrastructure. In housing, for instance, the promising economies
of scale appear to be in the area of prefabrication and of building components, and these economies are not restricted to new
towns. The assembly of large numbers of dwellings at the same
time is obviously an advantage, but only one of several, and
this of course is also available in contexts other than those of
new towns. For infrastructure, new towns face the problem of
having to provide all facilities from the beginning. This burdens
them with a front-end load (a result of the lumpiness of investment) which has caused considerable difficulty to the developers.
In existing cities extensions can usually take advantage of some

slack in the usage of existing capacity and proceed by marginal additions, so that they usually avoid large installations which for many years have too few users. The problem of a front-end load is usually aggravated by the cost of land acquisition, and has proved to be one of the most intractable burdens to new-town developers under current practices. While there has been a new wave of corporate enthusiasm for entering the new-towns field, fueled in part by the provisions in Title VII of the 1970 Housing Act, the experience of corporate ventures thus far has been rather disheartening, and many corporations have pulled back, finding the process very slow and the eventual payoff rather small and uncertain by comparison to alternative investment opportunities.

Many other considerations of economic efficiency come up in the discussion of new towns, but I shall mention only a few. It is sometimes said that new towns can take advantage of lower land costs. The difficulty with this is that the cost of land is really payment for value received. Inaccessible land is always cheap, but seldom desirable. The value of urban land is primarily determined by its accessibility to economic activity. Accessibility might not matter for towns which are totally self-contained as far as labor-markets, but then only if their exports were based on a comparative advantage that did not depend on their location.

There has been considerable confusion on this matter of whether new towns are to be self-contained. Some proponents of new towns imply that those who live there will work there, and that this will serve to reduce commuting costs, pollution, and automobile usage in general. The experience on this is not encouraging. Some of the most admired European new towns exhibit indeed a numerical equivalence between the number of workers and the number of jobs. But if one looks more closely, one sees that there is a tremendous amount of cross-hauling, in some cases approaching 100 percent. All of the current generation of American new towns depend on commuting. In such cases the relative isolation of the new town results in longer trips between work and home and increased commuting costs and automobile usage, counter to the original expectation. This is because modern society is fundamentally based on widespread interaction and a complex web of relations, which would place the isolated town and its people at a disadvantage. Hence, if it is at all possible (and the enormous range of the automobile usually makes it so), people will seek these links and relations, and the town will not endure as a closed economy. For these same reasons of connectivity and opportunity, economic productivity per capita increases with the size of urban places, so that per capita income in cities of a hundred thousand is $1,000 lower than in large cities, even taking into account differences in living costs. This reflects a difference in economic efficiency so large that it overwhelms the doubtful considerations of savings in the provision of urban services or in commuting costs.

A different line of argument in favor of new towns stresses issues of life styles. These arguments are not well developed, and therefore they are quite hard to evaluate. However, two may be singled out for discussion. The first is that the large city is an alienating environment, while new towns, being smaller, would permit levels of social and civic participation that would make people feel that they are more in control of their own destinies. The evidence on this is sketchy and contradictory, and owes as much to novelists as to sociologists. It is as easy to build a case for or against big cities as it is to build a case for or against smaller ones. People seem to be able to be alienated or to lead lives of quiet desperation in either. They also seem to be able to lead rich, full lives in either. But if smaller cities are preferable to some, there even now is no lack of them to choose from, without need for new ones. Yet there is a particular irony to this argument in the case of new towns. Since these towns are to be planned, and since financial and land-use problems demand that the plan be adhered to for about twenty years, during this long period the residents of the town have little room to exercise the normal range of choices open to citizens elsewhere. To some extent they are municipally disenfranchised for the first decade or two, and this is commonly manifested in a struggle between residents and developer. To illustrate, a recurrent theme in this struggle arises because, for a number of sound commercial reasons, new towns tend to start their development with the most expensive housing. For obvious reasons of social status and of municipal fiscal self-interest, the initial residents will usually oppose the extension of the development to those of lower incomes (not necessarily the poor). Parenthetically, it should be noted that the residents derive a fair amount of satisfying togetherness from the solidarity engendered in this struggle.

This brings us to another of the social objectives often cited. This is the "social balance" of new towns. A well-meaning liberalism holds that new towns would provide ideal grounds for thorough social mixtures. But new towns present grave problems for social integration. For instance, since their housing must be new, new towns find it very hard to provide housing for the poorer third (or even half) of the population, while older cities provide housing for those of lower incomes, however imperfectly, through the filtering down of depreciated older dwellings. More fundamentally, the unfortunate class realities of our society intrude themselves into newly built communities. Some studies have found that some of the code words that liberals use to praise new towns, such as "planned," are interpreted by most of the customers as assurances that the developers will exclude lower groups. Other studies have found residents of contemporary

new towns to be upper-class whites who mention as one of their
principal satisfactions the quality and congeniality of their
neighbors. Thus there is the very real danger that new towns,
whatever their intentions, would in effect increase the de facto
segregation of our urban areas.

This last point has obvious links with another commonly
cited purpose of new towns: that of intercepting rural migrants
on the way to the larger cities, giving these breathing space to
absorb and acculturate their present underclasses. This argument
also runs into difficulties when one looks at the facts. In the
first place, the size of these flows is by now quite small, and
the migrants tend to be reasonably well-educated and able to make
at least as good an adjustment as the original residents of the
larger cities. Natural increase, not migration, accounts for
most of the increase of the urban population in the larger urban
areas. Even the number of poor people depends overwhelmingly on
natural increase rather than immigration. Further, since the in-
terception argument has a heavy racial flavor, it is interesting to
look at the behavior of the black population in particular. The
majority of this population in this country is already concentrated in the central cities of metropolitan areas, and is on
the whole far more urbanized than the white population. In addition, the black population is moving steadily from smaller to
larger places within the urban hierarchy. Thus, it would not
seem realistic to think that new towns, which would be relatively
small, would intercept black migrants. The population of new
towns would not be made up by capturing rural to urban migrants
but rather by people who are leaving the cities. Obviously,
self-selection by economic status would result in an almost
wholly white population, accelerating the de facto segregation
of our population.

Beyond this there is the question of how big a role new
towns could play in determining the future distribution of our
population. The most daring national proposals from responsible
sources call for the development between now and the end of this
century of 100 new towns of 100,000 people each and of 10 new
cities of 1,000,000 or more people each. Even a proposal of
this scope would place only 7 percent of the national population
in these new settlements by the end of the century. It would
leave 80 percent of the projected growth to take place in the
existing areas, and 90 percent of all new housing would still
have to be built in existing urban areas. Thus, even if the new
towns were extremely attractive and functional, their contribution
to the solution of our serious urban problems would be at best
marginal.

Indeed, there is today a rather large number of developments which are termed new towns, and it is instructive to see
what they are. They are primarily suburban developments (which

use the term out of fashionableness), retirement communities, and
a few assorted oddments such as hippie settlements. But perhaps
the most pervasive form in California, as in some other states,
is new resort communities of second homes. These present a broad
range of serious problems of urgent importance, ranging from
issues of ecological balances to the privatization of what should
be public lands. In these cases, the problem is not the encouragement of new communities, but their control to public purposes.

But most of today's approaches to new towns suffer from
developer's myopia. They concentrate on issues of bricks and
mortar, the costs of land and of providing services, the cash-
flow problems of the developer and his tax situation. These
things miss the point. The physical plant of the city is not
the city: it is merely the container. The city is the people,
the institutions, and their relations. Questions that loom very
large for the developer can be quite trivial for the city, because
he is only a small part of the whole, although he makes many of
the seminal decisions. The relative unimportance of bricks and
mortar is illustrated by the reconstruction of European cities
flattened during World War II and in California by the dramatic
reemergence of San Francisco after its earthquake. Insofar as
they are needed, new-towns policies and new-towns legislation
should address themselves to the real city, and less to its real
estate.

For all of this, California is indeed a state that has
grown by a process of new towns. It is enough to remember that
in 1860 the population of what is now greater San Francisco was
only 85,000, that of greater Los Angeles 11,000, that of San
Diego 4,000, and that of San Jose 12,000. In the coming decade
the population of California will grow by some 4,000,000 people,
and new urban patterns are certain to emerge. Yet these new
patterns will not be totally new but rather evolutions of the
existing ones. As is frequently the case, the California version
of these patterns is similar to that of the rest of the country,
only more so. Many of the small cities and towns are prospering,
but the majority are declining. In spite of all the preoccupa-
tion with growth, the northern third of the state is losing
population (with the exception of Shasta), and so is its southwestern edge. The inland metropolitan areas of Fresno, Stockton,
and Bakersfield are growing only slowly, and they are exporting
people on the whole. The two great megapolitan areas, San
Francisco and Los Angeles, are growing, but they are losing
population in the center while their suburbs expand. Even so,
these two principal metropolitan areas are growing at about the
same rate as the state or a bit slower. The very fast growth is
taking place in the metropolitan areas which are satellites to
these great centers and in nearby areas which are not yet classified by the census as being within metropolitan areas. Thus
the pattern of suburbanization we have known is now transcending

NEW TOWNS AND OTHER POLICY ALTERNATIVES

the traditional metropolitan area and taking root in what might be termed suburban metropolitan areas. We are seeing the continued adaptation to increasing scale of large urban complexes. The nineteenth-century city had a single center. The larger twentieth-century metropolis could not bear the excessive distances to a single center, and developed a pattern of a hierarchy of centers and subcenters, each somewhat specialized, to maintain shorter functional internal distances. As our urban complexes continue to grow, the emerging megapolitan cluster of metropolitan areas is the next adaptation, with the same logic.

These evolving patterns respond to powerful forces in our economy and our society, and it would take tremendous investment and effort to reverse them. Willful or arbitrary restructuring is neither possible nor desirable. A well-rounded urbanization policy must be defined by the problems to which it is addressed and by the purposes it intends to serve.

It was noted earlier that there is considerable interest but also considerable fumbling in trying to define an agenda or table of contents for such a policy. But a beginning can be made. The list of problems, at least as we now perceive them, is not infinite. There are problems of size: congestion, pollution, access to open land, and possible problems of a social and psychological nature, such as the lack of responsiveness of institutions to individuals, which have their institutional counterpart in the fragmentation of jurisdictions. On the other hand, there are the problems of growth as distinct from those of size. These include local government cash-flow crises to pay for schools, roads, and utilities out of proportion to the existing population and tax base; the disruption of traffic and land uses arising from the successive installation of major new elements; the strains of mutual adjustment of old and new social groups to each other, and of all to a bigger urban scale; and the loss of valued features such as particularly attractive agricultural landscapes which are covered with houses. Although they are less often mentioned, there are also the problems of decline, which are found in many of the smaller communities. These include the need for consolidation, the depreciation of existing capital stock, the loss of morale, the welfare problems of a population which is increasingly composed of the old, the uneducated, and the very young. There are, too, those problems which are problems in cities rather than problems of cities. The prime one of this type is the problem of race, which is a problem of our society as a whole, but which becomes more visible and more explosive in urban context. This list may omit some items and some of its elements might be better labelled, but I believe that there would not be great difficulty in arriving at agreement on some comparable list.

The objectives of an urbanization policy have, on the whole, received less attention than the problems, yet it is of paramount importance to be able to define them if we are serious about moving in the direction of planning or managing the distribution of development rather than plugging up problems as they are discovered. The principal objectives at this point would seem to be three. The first is that commonly called efficiency, which has to do with growth or material development. At the national scale this may be simply interpreted as the growth of per capita income. At the level of the state or the locality the definition is more difficult. While at the national scale we know that the clients are essentially ourselves and our children, at the scale of the state or of localities migration becomes extremely important, and it is harder to tell who are the clients. Thus, one sometimes finds proposals to exclude new migrants from California, presumably because while this may improve the well-being of the newcomers, it might lower that of the present population. And indeed we see this argument more sharply drawn at the local level, where the traditional boosterism is increasingly giving way to proposals by communities to limit their own development through zoning, building controls, and so forth on the basis of self-interest. This raises an important question of conflict among areas where one state or locality, in seeking to stimulate or prevent development for its own benefit, does not affect the overall level of development, but takes development from or pushes it onto other areas. The danger is that if areas, rather than people, are the unit of accounting the calculation will be perverted. It would seem that at the level of the state of California, one of the most useful things that could be done would be the provision of state-wide guidance to local communities as to their interests in these issues and the mechanisms for the resolution of conflict in the interest of the statewide public.

The second of these material objectives is commonly called equity. This has to do with the quality of fairness with which access to resources and consumption are available to different elements in the population. The issues here are those having to do with who bears the costs and benefits of alternative distributions. For instance, depressed areas which are suffering from a decline in employment would benefit from a dispersal of jobs, if not that of people. At the metropolitan scale there is the problem of the suburbanization of the types of jobs most suited to low income populations, who remain locked in the central city. Clearly these equity issues (dealing with who gets what) interact with issues of efficiency (dealing with how much there is altogether). These two objectives, equity and efficiency, involve tradeoffs for almost every issue, such as the location of the new generation of international airports, the California water plan, local zoning or housing plans, industrial development, and highway location.

A third principal objective of policy appears to be an ecological, environmental, or conservationist one, according to

NEW TOWNS AND OTHER POLICY ALTERNATIVES

which certain natural areas are to be preserved almost for their own sake as much as for the users', and certain balances of air, water, and land are to be observed and regulated. This issue has achieved such widespread popularity recently that it is often presented as the principal policy objective. This is obviously an excess of a temporary enthusiasm. The real and difficult questions are going to be the rational tradeoffs between this and the other objectives. It is clear that if it makes certain types of production or certain facilities more costly, the environmental objective will conflict with that of efficiency. But what is less often realized is that the environmental objective may often be in conflict with that of equity. For instance, if a shift is made from automobile to mass transit, this will affect different groups of society very differently, and its effect may well be regressive. Similarly, the conservation of open land at the edges of existing urban areas will conflict with the aims of those population groups which are now achieving the economic level at which they would expect to arrive at a suburban life style.

Other objectives of territorial policy exist, but they are, at least at the moment, in the second rank. These include matters of defense, of international commerce (where California plays a special role with respect to Mexico and the Far East), and local economic stability when local economies are based on such industries as aerospace, electronics, research, or tourism.

Given this tentative list of problems and objectives, there are two types of policies that need to be examined for their territorial consequence. There are those policies that directly affect the way people distribute themselves in space and how they use that space, and those policies which are more indirect in their spatial consequences. The difference between these two is a matter of degree, but nonetheless a real one. Among the policies that directly affect urban space are such obvious ones as zoning and building codes, land banks and general land controls, the forms of taxation of land and improvements, metropolitan and other district governments, the ground rules of local government finance, and their fiscal sources and obligations. These are instances of direct policies affecting primarily the urban areas. In the rural areas there are others, such as the laws relating to the use of water, the upper and lower limits on the size of land holdings, the conventions employed in the assessment of real property, the formulas used in the allocation of highway funds. Although the list is long, it is not so long that one cannot conceive of some coordination of these direct policies and programs at the state or regional levels. Such coordination would undoubtedly help to serve our policy objectives and to better cope with our problems.

But it is the policies which affect space only indirectly, but nonetheless powerfully, that seem to present a more difficult

problem. By way of illustration, there appears underway a
realignment of fiscal responsibility for welfare and school costs
among the federal, state, and local levels. A major realignment
would not only have strong consequences for migration into
California, but would also affect the movements of people and
enterprises within metropolitan areas, and the receptivity of
local governments to diverse populations and land-using activities. Similarly, regulation aimed at pollution will have strong
spatial impacts, perhaps changing the means of transportation,
or effectively prohibiting certain activities in certain places.
Other policies that can have subtle but important effects include
national counter-cyclical actions on the supply and the cost of
money. These obviously are of great consequence to fast-growing
areas, which make heavy use of borrowed monies. Similarly, in
the long run our national policy of trade with China and other
countries in the Orient is of profound significance, as are our
national policies with respect to immigration.

The list of state and local policies that have an indirect
territorial effect is potentially endless, since almost every
policy imaginable has this spatial dimension. And this is the
difficulty. While one may imagine that there could be explicit
coordination of the direct spatial policies, it is not reasonable
to expect that the making of all state and federal policies will
be reorganized around territorial issues. But it may be possible
to establish some systematic procedure to report on the expected
territorial consequences of such policies, possibly in the form
of a staff of analysts advisory to the legislature on these
matters.

In this broad context for state policy for urban and
regional development, it is clear that new towns can have only
a small role, although it may be a very glamorous and visible
one. By the same token, some of the features associated with
new-town development may receive more prominence in the extension
and rebuilding of our urban areas. These include large-scale
land assembly, the coordination and careful phasing of various
types of investment above and below the surface of the ground,
new types of legislation for zoning and building, certain features
of physical design. But while it may be useful as a marketing
device to call any new suburban extension a "new town" or "new
community," and even to call certain inner-city redevelopments
"new towns in town," this should not be confused with new towns
which are set apart and, to a large degree, independent. For
these the principal role would seem to be not that of major
instruments for the redistribution of population but that of
showcases for certain experiments, from which we can learn things
that are useful for the solution of more widespread problems.

These experiments should conform to three criteria:
(1) the lessons to be learned should be useful for tackling

the problems of the larger urban areas; (2) the information to be gained should be reliable--that is to say, the results should not depend on the hothouse conditions of a glamorous experiment; (3) the findings should be available soon enough to make a difference. (It takes about ten years from an idea to some significant development on the ground. If to this we add about ten years to find out what we are trying to find out, and another ten years to replication elsewhere, then the benefits of the experiment fade thirty years into the future.) There are at present few proposed experiments that would meet these three criteria.

In summary, then, new towns might have a small, but important, role in urbanization. However, care must be taken not to think that they can do that which is beyond them. The task of guiding the urban growth of California is going to be a complex, continuing, long-range one, involving to some degree all aspects of our private and public lives. Within this general task new towns are particularly alluring but not terribly significant components. Their danger is that their very appeal sometimes tempts those dealing with the issues of urbanization into a form of escapism.

PART VI

DEMOGRAPHIC RESEARCH AND INFORMATION SYSTEMS
IN STATE GOVERNMENT

DEMOGRAPHIC INFORMATION IN PUBLIC HEALTH DATA

Yvonne Bristol, Harry Greenblatt, and Edwin W. Jackson

Introduction

The traditional role of the Department of Public Health with regard to demographic information is the recording of vital events--specifically marriages, births, deaths, and divorces--and the issuing of statistical reports based on these records. The birth and death records are an important source of health information for surveillance, epidemiological studies, and evaluation of preventive medical programs.

The utility of vital records for public health programs has increased substantially in recent years, because population information is needed in order to deal with the growing health problems of air and water pollution, lack of facilities for solid waste disposal, inadequate health services, and shortages of medical manpower. This interest in demography is intensified by the recognition that the traditional means for handling these problems, such as technical innovations, engineering advances, and modifications in health institutions, are no longer adequate. A broader perspective is required, which sees population growth and distribution as the essential elements of these health problems, and therefore as matters of crucial importance for public health policy-makers.

Progress in Recent Years

There have been a number of new developments toward improving demographic information during the last decade. In the early 1960's the general application of computer technology to data processing, storage, and retrieval was completed, which made it possible for information to be produced in various formats to serve a number of program interests. In addition to technical improvements, there are specific areas where new or enriched demographic information has been developed. These include (1) new information from the birth records on illegitimacy, childspacing, and the Spanish surname population; (2) new information systems-- i.e., divorce registration and therapeutic abortion reporting; (3) the publication of a special report series, combining vital data and census information; (4) the development of cohort studies based on data linkage procedures; and (5) cooperative demographic studies with other investigators.

Illegitimacy. In 1966 a new statistical identification method for counting illegitimate births was adopted in California. This method does not require the addition of a legitimacy question on the birth certificate. It is based on a review of birth records for name discrepancies and other evidence of out-of-wedlock status. The details of the methodology have been published in a journal article[1] and a monograph.[2] Illegitimacy trends since 1967 are now being traced with current data.

Illegitimacy figures are important for social welfare, adoption, and family planning programs, and for determining the effects of abortion practices on illegitimacy trends. The lack of factual information about illegitimacy has caused much confusion in the past and discouraged study of the phenomenon. It is likely that illegitimacy has serious implications for understanding fertility, maternal and child health, and child development, and for policies related to them.

Childspacing. In 1968 a revised birth certificate came into use in California. One of the new items on the form is the date of the birth or fetal death immediately prior to the birth being reported. This information, in conjunction with data on the mother's age, race, and socio-economic level, provides an "early warning system" on emerging fertility patterns. It is too early to establish trends in childspacing, because only two years' experience are available at this point, but in the future this new information will be of real value in discerning changes in childbearing practices, and in predicting fertility patterns.

Spanish Surname Population. Over 10 percent of California's population has Spanish surnames, and most members of this group are of Mexican brith or descent. They constitute a large cultural subgroup in the state. Despite their numbers of nearly 2,000,000, it has been difficult to determine their demographic characteristics. The U.S. Census began to provide basic information on the Spanish surname population in 1960; however, vital statistics and other official records do not identify individuals with Spanish surnames.

In an effort to obtain data on this group, a computer program was developed which determines if a surname is Spanish or not. The program is very accurate, identifying more than 95

---

[1] Beth Berkov, "Illegitimate Births in California," Milbank Memorial Fund Quarterly, 4, October 1968, pp. 473-506.

[2] Beth Berkov and Paul W. Shipley, Illegitimate Births in California: 1966 and 1967 (State of California, Department of Public Health, Bureau of Maternal and Child Health, 1971).

percent of Spanish surnames and less than 2 percent of non-Spanish surnames as "Spanish." Also, its application to vital data is economical: no additional data reduction is required because surnames are routinely keypunched for other purposes. Application of this method to California births shows that over 20 percent of the children born in 1968 had Spanish surnames; in some counties over 50 percent of the births were in this category. These statistics, along with census data, indicate that the Spanish surname population is undergoing rapid changes in composition. It also suggests that its fertility, migratory, and family-formation patterns will have increasing influence on population dynamics in California, and thus merit special study.

Divorce Reporting. Since 1966 California has had a divorce registration and reporting system that is probably more comprehensive than that in any other state in the Union. The origin and nature of the reporting system is described in "Divorce in California,"[3] which also gives extensive information on sociodemographic characteristics of persons seeking divorce in 1966. Data from the divorce reporting system make it possible not only to trace trends in divorce in California, but also to study the family dynamics involved in divorce. Youthful marriage, premarital pregnancy, numbers of children affected, and other related subjects can be studied. In addition, the information can be used to gauge the impact of the new California divorce law that went into effect January 1, 1970.

Therapeutic Abortion Reporting. After the Therapeutic Abortion Act was passed in 1967, an Assembly resolution requested that the Department of Public Health report annually to the legislature on the abortions carried out under the new law. In response to this charge, a voluntary reporting system was established in which hospitals provide age, race, marital status, and other characteristics of their abortion patients. (This information can be used to clarify related demographic phenomena, such as illegitimacy and adoption.) In 1966, the year before the abortion act was passed, it is estimated that over 80,000 California women obtained illegal abortions to terminate unwanted pregnancies. Thus even before legal abortions were available, induced abortions probably reduced the potential number of live births by over 20 percent. The question now is whether the new law will result in a net increase in abortions. If it does, fertility patterns will be affected, and the natural population increase and completed family size may decline. In any event, with the increasing availability of legal abortions, it is likely that

---

[3]"Divorce in California: Initial Complaints for Divorce, Annulment and Separate Maintenance, 1966," State of California, Department of Public Health, Bureau of Vital Statistics.

most abortions will be legal and reported. Under these circumstances, there will be better information to measure the effect of abortions on population dynamics.

Special Reports. As part of its mission to facilitate the planning, operation, and evaluation of state health programs by collecting, interpreting, and disseminating health information, the Department of Public Health began publication of the "California Health Trends" series. The purpose of this series is to describe changing trends in population composition, health patterns, and changes in the physical, social, and biological environments affecting personal health and health services. Five volumes have been published to date, combining 1960 U.S. Census data, California vital statistics, and Department of Finance population estimates with selected data from other departmental data systems to provide reference information needed for state and county health planning. An average of 600 copies of each of these have been distributed to state and local health departments, researchers, libraries, and schools.

The first volume of "California Health Trends"--Population--provides basic demographic data on California since 1860, with emphasis on the decade 1950-60. Its use ensures comparability of statistics based on intercensal and postcensal population estimates. Volume II--Trends in Family Patterns--provides selected trend and census year data concerning marital patterns, families and children, women in the labor force, one-person families, and fertility and family size. This is fundamental baseline data needed for health planning and research. Volume III--Income, Education and Employment Data for Health Planning--focuses on three socio-economic characteristics associated with health status and use of health facilities. Volume IV--County Data--presents a statistical characterization of county population. Data are given for the entire population, with emphasis on indicators of lower socio-economic status. Volume V deals with the subject of fertility. Fertility is important to planners because it is a major factor in determing the size and composition of the population. It is also of direct relevance to programs dealing with mothers and children. Data from both the census and vital registration are included in the volume, with census data providing what might be termed "prevalence" fertility information and birth data providing annual or "incidence" information.

There are plans to update and extend these analyses based on data from the 1960 Census by using data from the 1970 Census and current health data systems. In order to quickly take advantage of the great amount of data available from the 1970 Census, the plan is to purchase most of the 1970 data on computer tapes. Computer pre-programming is underway, based on extensive review with administrative and statistical staff of their needs for census data. This will make it possible to run and distribute the California data within days of its availability.

Data Linkage and Cohort Studies. The use of the computer in handling vital statistics offers new potential for enhancing their demographic contribution. One important application is birth cohort analysis of infant deaths. This requires that individual infant death records be matched with a birth record from the appropriate birth cohort, which is accomplished through the development and use of a special computer program. The cohort approach eliminates errors inherent in the previous method used to measure infant mortality. It has revealed that infant mortality rates among American Indians and Orientals are considerably higher than previously observed. (A description of the new method and findings will be found in a forthcoming article.)[4] From a demographic view, the development of data linkage programs for cohort analysis is important in opening the way for more precise studies of factors and patterns affecting California's population growth--e.g., studies of family formation and dissolution and their relationship to fertility.

Cooperative Demographic Studies. There is a wide range of uses and users of vital statistics information. In most instances the user, whether a demographer or a health planner, is provided with reports published annually, or related tabular information based on a calendar year of events. Recent requests for demographic data based on vital records have become more complex. In order to provide the desired information, computer programs have been modified, certain categories of information have required field evaluation, and sampling of old records has been necessary. At present, this work is being accomplished through cooperative studies with the University of California, supported by a contract agreement with the University. Studies currently underway include (a) trends in illegitimacy, (b) long-term trends in adoptions, and (c) family formation, birth, and dissolution of marriage cohorts.

Current and Future Needs

There is a continuing need for reliable vital statistics and summary data to use as baseline information and for sampling parameters. In addition, there is increased need for comparable and reliable data across a span of time in order to make valid cohort and trend analyses. Improvements in handling of masses of data and in identifying problem areas are also required. This

---

[4]F. Norris, "A Closer Look at Race Differentials in California's Infant Mortality."

includes the application of new techniques for gathering vital and population data, as well as the development of supplemental data resources, such as sample surveys.

Demographic estimates are essential to health program planning and evaluation. Knowledge of current and potential areas of population concentration, changes in composition and both short-term mobility and longer-term migration--all contribute to intelligent analysis and planning. A case in point is the incomplete information on family formation in California due to California residents marrying out-of-state. For some time, records of births and deaths have been exchanged between states to determine out-of-state occurrences of these events to residents of a given state. A similar exchange of records is required for marriages and divorces. It is estimated, for example, that for every 100 marriages taking place in California, there are 30 marriages in Nevada involving California residents. An agreement is needed between states to exchange data, and ultimately individual records, on the occurrence of out-of-state marriages and divorces.

In the 1970 legislative session a number of bills were introduced which concerned environmental health problems. One (SB 546) authorized the Department of Public Health to carry out demographic studies in order to assess the health and environmental effects of population growth, and to recommend programs to respond to projected trends. This legislation acknowledged the need for better demographic information and recognized that population dynamics cannot be separated from environmental health. In order to comply with this legislation and to deal with the demographic elements in its health mission, the Department of Public Health plans to develop population studies as an integral part of health planning and programming. This work will have the following objectives: (a) to understand the interrelationships between environmental health problems and population changes, (b) to predict population trends and their health implications, and (c) to formulate plans and programs appropriate to the observed population trends. Senate Bill 546 carried no appropriations for these activities, and federal research and contract funds are being sought to carry out the work.

The Department of Public Health recognizes that it has unique data sources to study the health implications of population trends. These resources are essential to study social processes related to fertility, which must be better understood if effective population policies are to be developed. Present organization for demographic study in state government is fragmented. It is necessary to integrate many factors in order to develop and maintain a coherent and current profile of California's population, which is needed for the development of sound population policies and for monitoring the effects of these policies once they are established. This capability is of special importance because of the recent legislation on dissolution of marriage and therapeutic abortion. Although neither measure was considered a population bill per se, both will affect fertility patterns and ultimately the natural population growth rate in California.

POPULATION RESEARCH IN THE DEPARTMENT OF FINANCE

Walter P. Hollmann, Isabel Hambright,
and W. Nelson Rasmussen

Introduction

The Population Research Unit of the Department of Finance has for two decades held the responsibility of providing the basic population input figures underlying the budget requests of all state agencies. From this basic responsibility have grown a collection of other duties which include estimates for local governments in behalf of tax subventions, census design and supervision, current estimates of population composition, enrollment projecting for all levels of education, and the projection of population for future planning. Population projections of the Department underlie the latest statement of the California Water Plan, and as they are altered, the Plan and other state projects will need to consider new probable future levels. Many of the ideas expressed in this paper are concerned with the need to discern changes in the state's population and its composition as soon as possible.

One of the goals of this conference is to bring about improvements in the quantity, quality, and availability of population information, and other information related to population. Quite independently, a Subcommittee on Census Data Access was established by the State Interdepartmental Research Coordinating Committee in response to the growing need for cooperative exploitation of the summary data tapes and the public use sample from the Census. The subcommittee, though designed to focus interest on the cooperative use of one source of data--the Census--provided an arena for the interchange of ideas on data in general. This was pursued further by visits to research offices of several departments and discussions with people who are not members of the subcommittee.

Answers to four broad questions were sought: (1) What types of data are collected or generated by each agency? (2) What types of data generated or collected by others are essential to the work of each agency? (3) What are some of the relevant data series that are not fully utilized by a maximum number of users? (4) What additional methods should be investigated to improve information for state planning and decision-making by all branches of government? In connection with this last question, some effort was devoted to evaluating the utility of a possible sample survey.

POPULATION RESEARCH IN THE DEPARTMENT OF FINANCE

In general, the answers were less than surprising, and few (if any) respondents were able to provide answers to all the questions. If there is any general conclusion to be drawn from the exercise, it is that in spite of past efforts to coordinate research, there are still areas where increased cooperation would yield rich rewards. That research is a hardy plant is demonstrated by the fact that it survives at all. All too often the research chief is a prophet without honor. He is expected to provide numbers upon which the administrator will base costly decisions, yet his requests for funds for additional data, however modest, are often subjected to a myopic cost-benefit analysis in which their ultimate value for the future question is ignored. The costs of not knowing are difficult to estimate, but the results make entertaining reading, especially for those not involved. At the very worst, one might find examples of an Orwellian disregard for evidence which does not fit the conclusions, but this was not investigated; a fruitful place to begin might be with those no longer working in state research!

The remarks which follow must be regarded as extremely tentative. The staff time we were able to devote to our investigation was almost always in connection with other work, and the research was necessarily somewhat superficial. It was not possible to study all of the suggestions made in the detail that would satisfy those who work more intimately with the data than we do. In short, further investigation is needed.

Visits were made to people in the Departments of Human Resources Development and Industrial Relations (both in the Human Relations Agency) and to the Departments of Social Welfare and Housing and Community Development. Also consulted were the Department of Water Resources in the Resources Agency, the Division of Highways, and the Departments of Savings and Loan, Public Health, Health Care Services, Mental Hygiene, Motor Vehicles, Rehabilitation, Youth Authority, and Finance.

An attempt was made to learn what data the agencies themselves developed and what data they drew from other agencies. Typically a researcher analyzes the incidence of the social pathology responsible for his agency's existence within a population specific for age, sex, color, or place of report. His case information or "numerator" data are collected by his agency from lower echelons of government or generated from its records. The population or "denominator" data are based upon estimates, usually insufficiently specific for his purposes with respect to compositional details, reference date, or location. These estimates may be less accurate than they might be under improved availability of "symptomatic" data from yet other agencies. Criticisms of the denominator data are never difficult to find; in practice the information is often developed from the same data series--used as indicators--as are later used with them in the calculation of rates. For example, the age group 18-44 is calculated from birth rates, tied to a national trend. The Department of Public Health cannot calculate age-specific birth rates for a given area for this age span without, in effect, reversing the calculation which produced the population! An independent data series is urgently needed. More often, data series which exist are not exploited because techniques and measures of relationship have not been developed. The specimen study by the demographic staff which is cited below illustrates this, while at the same time it demonstrates a happy example of inter-agency cooperation.

Improvement of Normal Data Sources

The improvement of data or the attempt to fill some of the information gaps seems to suggest three levels of effort--not as options to be applied alternatively to all situations, but rather as a stepwise series which would help to provide some more or many more answers to the questions facing researchers, and especially legislators and other policy-makers.

(1) One level would involve modest increases in support to those who administer existing series, enabling them to produce details which are essential to others but heretofore of no interest to those responsible for the data. This type of improvement would typically require a minor change in a software package or a simple revision of an existing questionnaire and the data processing related to it. One example is to be found in the United States Immigration and Naturalization Service, which each January collects age, sex, and migration data from aliens but never keypunches them because its budget does not allow for this additional activity. Another is to be found in the marriage records of the State of Nevada, where residences of bride and groom are collected but not tabulated. A substantial number of Nevada marriages involve California residents, but this piece of the family-formation puzzle lies across the state line while our people in Housing and Community Development and, in the private sector, building, banking, utilities, and home furnishings need projections of housing needs.

(2) A second level would involve the innovative exploitation of data series. For years, for example, California driver's license holders have been required to report changes of address to the Department of Motor Vehicles, Division of Driver Licenses. Although California drivers may be laggard conformers to the requirement, the result is a periodic measure of internal and, within limits, interstate migrants who are also drivers. A recent cooperative arrangement between the Departments of Motor Vehicles and Finance exemplifies the development of additional and improved data through a new approach to an existing file. The table which appears on pages 340-341 below

POPULATION RESEARCH IN THE DEPARTMENT OF FINANCE

shows migration behavior in California during a seven-month period, but the migrants are driver licenses, not people. Unanswered are critical questions such as: How many men, women, and children does a driver's license represent? Is the people/license factor constant from county to county throughout the state? How does it vary through time? What distortions are introduced by the well-recognized lag in reporting? What are the characteristics of the non-driver identification cards which are offered by the Department of Motor Vehicles and are/are not included with the licenses? You are urged to examine the specimen graph provided for Los Angeles County (p. 342) with respect to the relationships of in-, out- and net migration, and with respect to who (in terms of age) is coming in or going out of the county, to see what a powerful estimating tool this might become.

Heretofore, studies have dealt with net migration, but there is no such person as a net migrant. In spite of all of the shortcomings we have noted, the driver's license series offers direct access to a substantial sample of individual migrants. Usually the arrangement of data in a form permitting analysis can be very costly; in drivers' licenses this has already been accomplished. A recent report has stated: "In a nation where one fifth of the inhabitants move each year, the study of residential mobility is highly relevant to understanding the structure of society and the processes of social change....Despite long-continuing scientific concern with shifting patterns of population distribution, knowledge of residential mobility remains sketchy."[1] Some major conclusions on the effect of migration on the total population could be drawn from the driver's license study if some money, administrative changes, and possibly legislation were forthcoming to turn these data into a useful tool for the administrator and legislator. Some questions about both out- and in-migrants, their educational level, causes for their migration, and others could be studied for as little as $5,000-10,000 a year.

A comparable problem exists in the study of ethnic composition. Each autumn for the past few years the Office of Compensatory Education of the State Department of Education has collected ethnic identification data for each public school child in California. The data are available by grade by school district, and some very useful reports have appeared which aggregated the school district data by county. What remains is to relate public school children, ethnically and age-specifically identified, to population of all ages, ethnically identified. A composite method might be attempted relating ethnic death data to population older than a specified age, and school enrollment information to

---

[1] *Migration in the United States*, U.S. Department of Health, Education and Welfare, Public Health Monograph No. 77.

REPORTED ADDRESS CHANGES, CALIFORNIA DRIVER LICENSES:
JULY 1, 1970 TO JANUARY 31, 1971

County	Gains from Other California Counties	Losses to Other California Counties	Gains from Other States	Losses to Other States	Net Change
(1)	(2)	(3)	(4)	(5)	(6)
Alameda	17,469	19,192	6,516	6,108	-1,315
Alpine	33	18	2	4	13
Amador	450	153	23	31	289
Butte	3,353	2,575	288	656	410
Calaveras	521	200	25	27	319
Colusa	290	196	39	17	116
Contra Costa	11,737	10,817	2,897	3,052	765
Del Norte	302	157	89	122	112
El Dorado	2,106	1,021	250	324	1,011
Fresno	5,815	6,113	1,018	1,456	-736
Glenn	440	286	44	40	158
Humboldt	2,210	1,672	305	589	254
Imperial	1,090	1,417	315	384	-396
Inyo	576	260	74	60	330
Kern	5,594	5,389	1,343	1,678	-130
Kings	1,129	1,206	337	340	-80
Lake	1,111	312	71	47	823
Lassen	545	223	84	100	306
Los Angeles	42,896	80,763	38,619	36,475	-35,723
Madera	903	872	84	134	-19
Marin	6,018	4,706	1,895	1,327	1,880
Mariposa	295	116	26	24	181
Mendocino	1,425	923	217	203	516
Merced	1,995	1,803	579	520	251
Modoc	178	99	26	41	64
Mono	300	96	16	26	194
Monterey	4,261	4,002	1,736	1,295	700
Napa	2,027	1,652	300	366	309

POPULATION RESEARCH IN THE DEPARTMENT OF FINANCE

(1)	(2)	(3)	(4)	(5)	(6)
Nevada	1,017	612	72	138	339
Orange	35,850	22,883	9,540	9,765	12,742
Placer	2,817	1,823	233	358	869
Plumas	453	210	37	54	226
Riverside	11,712	8,696	2,679	2,927	2,768
Sacramento	11,290	11,548	2,844	3,886	-1,300
San Benito	347	362	33	50	-32
San Bernardino	14,086	12,484	3,561	4,535	628
San Diego	20,359	13,874	11,764	9,409	8,840
San Francisco	11,016	17,648	5,896	3,107	-3,843
San Joaquin	4,097	4,793	833	1,128	-991
San Luis Obispo	3,799	2,158	434	395	1,680
San Mateo	12,853	14,871	3,345	3,117	-1,790
Santa Barbara	6,039	5,829	1,908	2,086	32
Santa Clara	20,460	17,355	7,716	7,044	3,777
Santa Cruz	4,758	2,496	600	576	2,286
Shasta	2,072	1,776	209	595	-90
Sierra	63	40	1	12	12
Siskiyou	874	391	127	198	412
Solano	3,525	3,557	1,380	1,456	-108
Sonoma	5,862	3,328	815	1,041	2,308
Stanislaus	3,708	3,235	645	850	268
Sutter	1,089	1,235	134	234	-246
Tehama	661	618	74	148	-31
Trinity	301	123	32	20	190
Tulare	3,090	2,832	432	619	71
Tuolumne	891	331	38	51	547
Ventura	9,662	6,721	2,214	2,568	2,587
Yolo	3,037	2,742	498	554	239
Yuba	1,117	1,164	357	372	-62
STATE	311,974	311,974	115,669	112,739	2,930

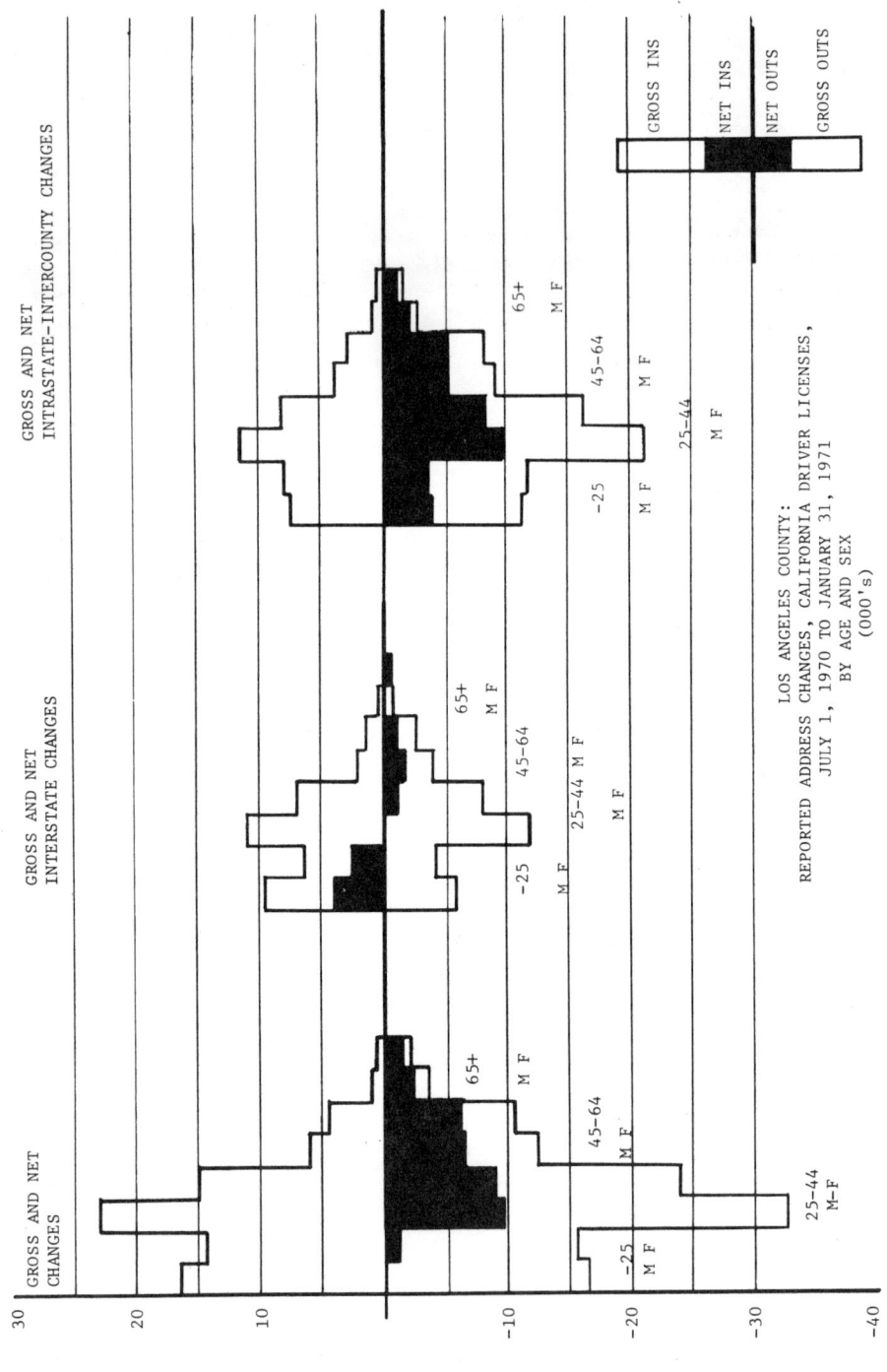

POPULATION RESEARCH IN THE DEPARTMENT OF FINANCE

population of the remaining ages. Unfortunately, the ethnic enrollment data project seems to be enduring a perils-of-Pauline existence, and an attempt to extract death certificates by Spanish surname was dropped in its tracks.

Major Changes and New Sources of Data

The third level of effort would be characterized by new primary data collection. A case might be made, for example, for broadening the applicability of the periodic survey carried out by the Division of Highways (on which $17 million has been spent since 1960) to yield quality-of-housing data required by the Department of Housing and Community Development. Two formidable roadblocks to such an arrangement come to mind--i.e., the very detailed training required of enumerators in a housing quality survey, and the publication schedule and data processing constraints of the Division of Highways; but the potential for payoff surely warrants some study. Doubtless, similar obstacles prevent the ready application of the health survey effort of the Department of Public Health to the data problems of Mental Hygiene or Social Welfare. The enumerations of the Department of Finance, originally designed to provide benchmark data for city population estimates, have seen related service in school districts where they have constituted the first step in a study of construction requirements.

The most ambitious suggestion to emerge from an examination of data needs and extended data sources was that for a periodic survey comparable to the Current Population Survey (CPS) carried on by the U.S. Bureau of the Census. The data for the United States are based upon the responses of 52,000 households; the confidence intervals limit the reliability of results to chiefly nationwide applications. Somewhat broader confidence intervals characterize regional data from the CPS; occasional reports made possible by the sample design deal with an SMSA, but no reliable data for the State of California are regularly available from the CPS. The national CPS has for many years been of invaluable assistance to decision-makers at the federal level, in all three branches of government. A comparable effort at the state level would necessitate a new design.

The idea of a CPS for the state is not a new one. Serious consideration at the staff level in 1964 was followed by a mandate from the legislature in 1967 to investigate such a survey. Further investigations carried out in late 1970 have led to conclusions very similar to those arrived at earlier, with one possible exception. The economies of incorporating the approximately 6,000 responding California households in the federal sample into the state design were further investigated. The tentative conclusion was reached that, although such an attempt would create administrative problems, the complete omission of federal CPS cases, especially in the most densely populated areas, would generate problems of comparability. A suggested design would include about 36,000 households, with an ongoing survey of 3,000 per month. This might be expected to yield satisfactory levels of confidence in any of the variables for which demand has been expressed for counties and county groupings of one million inhabitants. The City of Los Angeles might be divided into two or three areas, with four or five remaining in the County. Satisfactory data would be forthcoming for Alameda, Santa Clara, and San Diego Counties individually and for a group of counties from San Joaquin to the Tehachapis and another north of Sacramento and including the SMSA. Two additional reporting units might be carved from the remaining Bay Area counties. Such a survey, assuming relatively straightforward questions, and basing the estimate on minimal Census Bureau experience, would cost about $720,000 per year, once the design had been completed and the sample drawn. The fact that the state already possesses some potential in its two university survey research organizations at Berkeley and Los Angeles and its limited effort in the Department of Finance suggests a possible cut in the estimated cost, but not below a minimum of $500,000. A less costly and far less useful survey might be designed to yield data of significance only at the state level; this might cost $250,000 annually after the design costs had been met. A much more costly design--one that would yield meaningful results for counties of a half million--might also be investigated.

  A number of state agencies have expressed keen interest in such a survey. Income level and employment status are of more than passing interest to the Departments of Human Resources, Industrial Relations, and Social Welfare. Up-to-date estimates of the age composition (as well as income and employment) would be of interest to Health Care Services and Public Health. An occasional survey of house buying or renting intentions and housing conditions would be helpful to the Departments of Savings and Loan, Real Estate, and Housing and Community Development. A reliable survey of vacancy, as well as of household size, would be useful to all three agencies and to the Department of Finance to aid it in its estimating program. Repeatedly, requirements have been imposed upon state agencies to administer programs or to estimate the effects of policy changes or of legislative actions. In all too many cases, the most fundamental data essential to meet the requirements were lacking. The continuing interest in fair employment practices, in care of the indigent and ill, in poverty programs, in delinquency prevention, in demand for medical or educational or recreational services and facilities sustains the need for population information. It is likely that errors involving far more dollars than the costs of data improvement have been made.

POPULATION RESEARCH IN THE DEPARTMENT OF FINANCE

It is clear that substantial sums of public money devoted to the improvement of demographic data for policy-making, if efficiently administered, could yield savings in excess of the money spent to obtain the data. As a first step, it is recommended that a two-day working conference be sponsored by the Advisory Council. To this conference about eight to twelve persons should be invited, including representatives of the two survey research organizations and the Department of Finance, and one outstanding expert with sample design and/or survey experience from each of the following: Stanford Research Institute, the U.S. Bureau of the Census, UCLA, and UC-Berkeley. The State Department of Public Health and the Division of Highways should also be invited to participate, as should representatives of Assembly and Senate research and the State Office of Planning and Research. It is reasonable to expect that this committee of experts could, in two days time, complete the design of a survey which would contain a synthesis of the experiences of several authorities with the guidance and advice of those with recent local experience.

Finally, it is recommended that if financing for the survey is obtained, the administrative responsibility for its continuation be lodged with a state executive agency competent to evaluate and manipulate the demographic content of the various data series and capable of perceiving the interrelations among the needs of the agencies of state government.

PROPOSAL FOR A CALIFORNIA POPULATION ADVISORY PANEL

Kingsley Davis and Thomas J. Espenshade

We recommend the creation of a California Population Advisory Panel, whose principal purpose would be to lend some direction to overall research and to increase public knowledge concerning California's population. This panel would be a standing committee with regular meetings, and could be appointed by and report to the California Assembly Science and Technology Advisory Council. It would be composed of people both inside and outside of government whose familiarity with population processes and whose professional competence would make them of value to the panel. They could serve on a voluntary basis without remuneration, with the exception of special funds for meetings and travel. In addition to professional demographers and other expert personnel from universities and private research organizations, the panel members might include representatives from the state Departments of Finance, Public Health, Water Resources, Social Welfare, Education, Housing and Community Development, and the Division of Highways.

As conceived, the California Population Advisory Panel would not be a policy-making or legislative body, but would serve primarily in an advisory capacity to specific legislative committees and state agencies. The functions of the panel would be at least fourfold:

1. The panel would act as a sentinel committee to determine the likely demographic consequences (direct and indirect) of specific legislative measures on the size, distribution, and quality of the state's population. It would be the panel's responsibility to recommend additional legislation necessitated by the state's changing demographic conditions.

2. The panel would designate those areas and define those problems where research is most urgently needed for the solution of California's population problems. In addition, the panel could help in the preparation of the proposed Current Population Survey by identifying critical data shortages that must be met before further research can proceed.

3. The panel would have the responsibility of suggesting ways in which research and the increase of public knowledge and awareness concerning population matters could best be carried

PROPOSAL FOR A CALIFORNIA POPULATION ADVISORY PANEL

out. It would advise concerning the organizational structure in terms of which needed research could be conducted. It would investigate sources of funding and the relations between governmental agencies, on the one hand, and universities and private research organizations, on the other. It would facilitate the marshalling of intellectual resources in the state for the purpose of improving the production and distribution of scientific knowledge concerning the state's population problems and their possible solution or amelioration.

4. Since the efficiency of the panel in helping to lay the basis for legislation to deal with population-related matters or in identifying those crucial variables requiring further study would be greatly diminished in the absence of an overall framework within which the decisions on particular matters could be intelligently made, perhaps the most significant function of the panel would be to develop a carefully considered outline and intellectual justification for a statewide population policy. The formulation of such an overall policy or plan would provide a basis for public discussion and for possible legislation.

We are aware of the fact that many of California's population problems originate outside of the state and, as a result, that any state population policy is likely to be frustrated in numerous ways. However, to the extent that each state analyzes its own population problems, and speaks out about them, it will influence the federal government to deal seriously with national and interstate demographic issues.

An important but neglected potential source of demographic knowledge is the state's numerous universities and colleges. With few exceptions, these now offer relatively little instruction on demographic behavior, and such instruction as they do offer tends to be focused on national or international questions rather than on state problems. University research on population is even scarcer than instruction, and it is also usually directed to national or international phenomena, but there are some research facilities on the major campuses--and some training programs--that could be utilized for the state's benefit if such use were encouraged.

Obviously, if they are to do a proper job, the universities and colleges of the state should provide two kinds of training. First, they should give to all students, as part of their general education, a basic understanding of the nature, causes, and consequences of demographic behavior; there is hardly any subject more relevant to any society than this. Second, they should give graduate training in the science of demography to a small group of talented young people, thus providing the state

with professional personnel in this field. In addition, they
should maintain research facilities which would (1) contribute
scientific findings for inclusion in undergraduate instruction,
(2) provide a substantial part of the knowledge required for effective
government policy, and (3) furnish a laboratory in which
graduate students, as part of their training, could gain practical
experience in the activities of professional demography.

To accomplish this, the state's universities and colleges
will require funds. Up to now, the funds they have obtained for
this type of research or training have generally come from federal
or private sources, where the interest was national or international
rather than local. There are exceptions of course, such
as the funding of some demographic research at universities by
the Haynes Foundation in Los Angeles, but to a striking degree the
universities and the non-profit research agencies have dealt with
population without particular reference to California. State
support has gone to more traditional types of subjects, such as
industrial relations, highway engineering, and medieval history.
The proposed panel could explore the possibility of reorganizing
and expanding the facilities for training and research in the
population field in the state's institutions of higher learning,
and could investigate the possibility of using state funds as a
partial support for such changes as may seem desirable.

Of course, more than funds are needed. The universities
have not taken a strong interest in demographic training and research,
particularly with reference to the state itself, because
they have not been encouraged to do so. The role of population
in human affairs has been assumed to be outside public control,
and hence not to be worth the kind of study that goes into public
health, highway planning, public taxation, or city government.
Now that an interest is being taken in population studies, universities
find that they are poorly equipped to offer training
and do research in demography. It takes time to remedy the situation.
An influential state Population Advisory Panel could offer
encouragement to universities and colleges in this field and help
explain the educational and research needs to the state government,
thus strengthening the university contribution to the state's
demographic information system.

In addition to funds and college reorganization, there
is a further requirement for the successful utilization of institutions
of higher education in the population field. This is the
development of a program of cooperation between these institutions
and the agencies of the state that are concerned with the official
collection, use, and publication of basic data. In particular,
it would be helpful if the State Department of Public Health and
the Population Research Unit of the Department of Finance were
involved. Such cooperation would yield many benefits: Graduate
students and faculty members in the universities would develop

PROPOSAL FOR A CALIFORNIA POPULATION ADVISORY PANEL

more interest in California population problems if they had ready access to the basic data being gathered by the state government through its registration and licensing procedures, and had more contact with the people in state agencies who analyze and utilize this information; data collection systems would probably be improved by being more directly exposed to scientific analysis in an academic setting; professional training could be improved through some kind of apprentice program whereby graduate students spent time in a government agency processing basic data on the state's population; analytic studies of the state's population problems could be produced more readily with the help of university personnel and facilities, and in turn these could be used more widely in college and high school education.

One type of information production in which cooperation between universities and the state government would seem to be particularly desirable is survey research. As is well known, the sample survey is one of the most important instruments for finding out about demographic behavior. However, survey research is difficult to organize and expensive to conduct. As a result, a survey research center usually has to be a multi-purpose center-- that is, it has to be able to utilize the survey technique for many different kinds of information. For this reason, most major universities maintain some kind of survey research center as a facility for their faculty, but they find it difficult to support these centers. If there were a regular population survey in California--an instrumentality that seems highly desirable for understanding demographic conduct and public opinion in the state-- then it would be both economic and efficient to make it a cooperative enterprise between the state's governmental agencies, on the one hand, and the universities and private research organizations, on the other. The basic sample-frame design, the corps of interviewers, the necessary office facilities and data processing system--all could be developed within a facility that could make its services available, on a supporting fee basis, to governmental agencies, university researchers, and non-profit professional research organizations. This is only one of the many important ways in which the universities and government agencies could work closely together with respect to population problems and policies in California.

OF DAVIDSON COLLEGE